DELIVEROLOGY 101

MICHAEL BARBER

with Andy Moffit and Paul Kihn

DELIVEROLOGY 101

A Field Guide For Educational Leaders

A Joint Publication

For information:

Corwin
A SAGE Company
2455 Teller Road
Thousand Oaks, California 91320
(800) 233-9936
Fax: (800) 417-2466
www.corwin.com

SAGE India Pvt. Ltd.
B 1/I 1 Mohan Cooperative
Industrial Area
Mathura Road, New Delhi 110 044
India

SAGE Ltd.
1 Oliver's Yard
55 City Road
London EC1Y 1SP
United Kingdom

SAGE Asia-Pacific Pte. Ltd.
33 Pekin Street #02-01
Far East Square
Singapore 048763

Printed in the United States of America

Library of Congress Cataloging-in-Publication Data

Deliverology 101 : a field guide for educational leaders / Michael Barber with Andy Moffit and Paul Kihn.
p. cm.
Includes bibliographical references and index.
ISBN 978-1-4129-8950-3 (pbk.)
1. School improvement programs. 2. Educational leadership. I. Moffit, Andy. II. Kihn, Paul, 1966– III. Ontario Principals' Council. IV. Title.

LB2822.82.B36 2011
371.2′07—dc22 2010036889

This book is printed on acid-free paper.

10 11 12 13 14 10 9 8 7 6 5 4 3 2 1

Acquisitions Editor: Arnis Burvikovs
Associate Editor: Desirée A. Bartlett
Editorial Assistant: Kimberly Greenberg
Production Editor: Cassandra Margaret Seibel
Copy Editor: Adam Dunham
Typesetter: C&M Digitals (P) Ltd.
Proofreader: Christina West
Indexer: Jean Casalegno
Cover Designers: Rose Storey and Anthony Paular
Permissions Editor: Karen Ehrmann

Contents

Preface

> *"There come rare moments, hard to distinguish but fatal to let slip, when all must be set upon a hazard . . ."*
>
> —G. M. Trevelyan, British historian, 1909

The next two years provide a once-in-a-generation opportunity to transform public education in America. If that opportunity is seized, America could lead the world in the quality of its public schools and universities in the 21st century, just as it did for the first two-thirds of the 20th century. Indeed, the United States faces precisely the kind of rare moment that English historian G. M. Trevelyan thought "fatal to let slip."

This moment has been created by an administration that prioritizes education reform; by the $100 billion for education in the federal stimulus package, including almost $5 billion for the "Race to the Top Fund"; by the emergence of an increasingly shared national agenda focused on standards, accountability, data, human capital, and reducing school failure; by the growing interest in international benchmarking in the United States and the emerging understanding around the world of the characteristics of successful system reform. And while the economic crisis is a challenge in so many ways, it is also a spectacular opportunity to recruit more and better people into teaching, if the right kinds of programs can be developed.

In short, we know *what* ought to be done; we know *why* it needs to be done; and the unique opportunity now means that we know *when* we need to do it. The central challenge is that it is not clear at any level in the system *how* to get it done. The presence or absence of the capacity to deliver will make the difference between a once-in-a-generation opportunity seized and a once-in-a-generation opportunity missed.

For more than 25 years, since the (National Commission on Excellence in Education, 1983) publication of *A Nation at Risk* (with its dire warnings of "a rising tide of mediocrity"), a succession of reports and a tidal wave of books have proposed public education reforms of one kind or another. Yet, while some progress has been made, the overall outcomes of a quarter of a century of reform are judged by most people, inside and outside public education, to have been disappointing. And each disappointment fuels further debate, more reports, and more books about what the reform agenda should be.

This is *not* another report or book like that. It is based on a different premise—the premise that much of that disappointment is a result not of failed reform *content* but of failed *implementation*. The American education reform landscape is littered with potentially promising reforms that were not pursued, not sustained, not implemented, and not delivered.

So, if you are looking for another magic formula for reform, don't read this book. Neither should you read further if you are satisfied with current performance. If, however, you are ambitious for reform, determined to bring about dramatic improvements in the outcomes for students, and bold in your belief that both excellence and equity can be delivered across U.S. K–12 and public higher education, then read on.

This book describes a proven set of processes which will ensure your reform is actually delivered in the most profound sense, with the students themselves able to see, feel, and reap the benefits of a much better education. This is a book for people who want to get things done in government; who are as interested in the question *how?* as much as the question *what?*

The term *deliverology* was originally developed in the British civil service as a gentle and light-hearted term of abuse for the process developed by the Prime Minister's Delivery Unit (PMDU), which Tony Blair had me set up; we have chosen to adopt it here and give it a positive definition: It is the emerging science of getting things done in government. The precise definition we have given it is as follows:

> **Deliverology (n.):** a systematic process for driving progress and delivering results in government and the public sector.

Like many of the best ideas for change, deliverology is a simple concept. But, that does not mean it is easy to master. It is not a passing fad, a "flavor of the month," or a piece of jargon to be adopted and discarded when the fashion moves on. Delivery requires persistence, discipline, and rigor: It often requires courageous, difficult decisions in relation to staffing, organization, and relationships with stakeholders, but it will work. The combination of the right mindset with the methods set out in this book will guarantee results.

Guarantee is a strong word. So is *proven,* which appeared a few paragraphs earlier. What evidence do I have to make such claims for deliverology?

In 2001, after winning reelection, Tony Blair, the British prime minister, asked me to set up in No. 10 Downing Street what became known as the Prime Minister's Delivery Unit. His analysis of his first term in office suggested that the British people liked his agenda for education, health, and policing but were disappointed that his ideas had not yet been translated into change on the ground. The British people had given him another chance, but, as he put it the day after the June 2001 election, they had also issued him with an "instruction to deliver." By asking me to set up his Delivery Unit, he was, in effect, passing on that instruction to me.

With a small (and fantastically talented) team, I set about this task. In collaboration with the prime minister and his cabinet, around 20 major goals for the next four or five years were established. They included major reductions in crime, less waiting for public health services, significant increases in the punctuality of trains, and dramatic improvements in school performance.

We then set about developing a set of routines and problem-solving techniques specifically designed to overcome the barriers to delivering results through the vast public bureaucracy that is the British government. Crucially, alongside the routines and techniques, we also thought deeply about how to build constructive working relationships with all the ministers and officials responsible for delivering the prime minister's ambitious agenda. This combination of routines, techniques, and what came to be called "the alchemy of relationships" was quite rapidly seen as a new and radically different approach to delivering results. While at first, we were mocked for inventing deliverology, quite quickly we became seen as persistent, constructive, and helpful.

Within six months or so, the first evidence that our approach could deliver major performance improvements came through when an apparently remorseless rise in street crime was reversed. Less than a year later, further successes were registered in immigration and health. And after three years or so, we realized we had a proven approach that could be applied to any major problem of service delivery and bring results. By the end of Blair's second term (2005), around 80% of the ambitious goals we had set out to achieve had actually been achieved. Of the remaining 20% of targets that had been missed, in almost all cases performance had nevertheless improved. Blair concluded that the Delivery Unit was the best reform of the government machine he ever made. In his memoirs, he comments that the Delivery Unit "as an innovation that was utterly invaluable and proved its worth time and again" (p. 338).

Other governments around the world began to take notice. After all, the challenge of delivery is universal. Every government aspires to deliver improved performance without commensurate increases in taxation. The global economic crisis has made this challenge still more acute. Hence, my account of the four years of striving to deliver for Blair—*Instruction to Deliver* (2008)—has been read by prime ministers, ministers, and top officials in many countries. Since 2005, governments such as those in Australia, Holland, and Canada have looked to this experience in Blair's Britain and, after adapting and refining the approach for their own circumstances, have realized significant benefits. In the United States, Antonio Villaraigosa, the mayor of Los Angeles, created a performance management unit modeled on the British experience; Martin O'Malley, governor of Maryland, is moving in the same direction; and Jeff Zients, chief performance officer in the U.S. Government's Office of Management and Budget, is taking notice too. Meanwhile in U.S. public education, successful reformers such as Joel Klein in New York City; Paul Pastorek in Louisiana; and Charles Reed, chancellor of the California State University system, have also seen the benefits of adopting and adapting the approaches set out in *Instruction to Deliver.*

Deliverology 101 has been written specifically for leaders of American education reform. It draws heavily on *Instruction to Deliver* and freely quotes from it; but instead of telling the story, it describes the routines, techniques, and approaches in the form of a field guide. Moreover, it is based not only on the experience of the Blair administration but also on case studies of successful implementation of reform in the United States and elsewhere. Much of what is described in the book has been piloted in collaboration with state K–12 and major education systems here in the United States and honed and refined as a result.

The American education leaders I know are ambitious for their students, they know that a remarkable opportunity to transform public education is before them, they know what to do, and they know that a major barrier to seizing that opportunity is a severe lack of capacity to deliver. *Deliverology 101* is prepared precisely to address these circumstances.

As I say, there's no need to read it if you want business as usual; but if you want to seize the new day, read on . . . it would be fatal to let it slip.

—Michael Barber
Devon, UK
October 2010

Acknowledgments

A field guide of this kind inevitably depends on a team and not just the listed authors. This field guide is the outcome of a collaborative effort between Achieve, Inc.; Education Trust; and McKinsey & Company. The following people all made vital contributions, which enabled the authors to complete the task.

Editorial oversight and team leadership (McKinsey & Company):
Nick Rodriguez

Research, analysis, and presentation (McKinsey & Company):
Shalini Ananthanarayanan
Ellen Badger
Jacob Bryant
Eileen Chao
Kenneth Cushing
Ali Mir
Jimmy Sarakatsannis
Rebecca Taber

Research, analysis, and critical commentary:
Mike Cohen (Achieve, Inc.)
Matt Gandal (Achieve, Inc.)
Alissa Peltzman (Achieve, Inc.)
Kati Haycock (Education Trust)
Ellyn Artis (Education Trust)
Richard Page-Jones (ISOS)
Simon Rea (ISOS)
Simon Day (ISOS)
Leigh Sandals (ISOS)
Claire O'Connor (Freelance)

Proofreading: In addition to the authors, Alys Barber proofread the text and made possible numerous minor improvements.

All deserve gratitude for the skill, time, and energy invested and for the spirit in which the work was done.

About the Authors

Sir Michael Barber is the founder of the US Education Delivery Institute, which is designed explicitly to help U.S. state education systems strengthen their capacity to deliver results. The US Education Delivery Institute is unique among U.S. nonprofits in that it focuses exclusively on how to get things done, rather than what to do.

Michael Barber is an Expert Partner in McKinsey & Company's Global Public Sector Practice and head of its Global Education Practice. He works on major challenges of performance, organization, and reform in government and the public services, especially education, around the world. He is coauthor of the widely read international benchmarking study *How the World's Best Performing School Systems Come Out on Top* (Barber & Mourshed, 2007).

Prior to joining McKinsey, he was (from 2001) Chief Adviser on Delivery to the British prime minister, Tony Blair. As head of the Prime Minister's Delivery Unit, he was responsible for the oversight of implementation of the prime minister's priority programs in health, education, transport, policing, the criminal justice system, and asylum/immigration.

The approach to delivery he developed is widely seen as constructive and innovative. His book about this experience—*Instruction to Deliver: Fighting to Transform Britain's Public Services*—was described by the *Financial Times* as "one of the best books written on British government for many years" (Bogdanor, 2007, para. 12) and by Tony Blair in his memoirs as a "hallowed text round the world" (p. 503). It has been read by political leaders on five continents.

Between 1997 and 2001, Michael Barber was Chief Adviser to the Secretary of State for Education on School Standards.

His advice on public policy, especially education, has been sought by governments in over 30 countries, including Australia, the United States, Russia, Estonia, Chile, and Hong Kong, and by major international organizations, including the Organization of Economic Co-Operation and Development, The World Bank, and the IMF. He is an Honorary Doctor at the University of Exeter and a Visiting Professor at the Higher School of Economics in Moscow and the Institute of Education, University of London. He is also a Distinguished Visiting Fellow at Harvard.

Andy Moffit is a Senior Practice Expert and a co-founder of McKinsey & Company's Global Education Practice. Andy joined the firm in 2000 and has served clients in the financial services, nonprofit, and public sectors on a wide range of strategic and organizational issues. Since 2005, he has worked exclusively with education clients—large urban districts, state education departments, national foundations and nonprofits, and private sector companies—on large-scale reform and key strategic efforts. He is a frequent commentator at education sector conferences and in publications. Andy was an elementary school teacher in Houston, Texas, from 1991–1993 as a corps member of Teach For America. He is a graduate of the University of Michigan, Oxford University, and Yale Law School, at each of which he studied education law and policy. He is based in McKinsey's Boston office and lives in Providence, RI.

Paul Kihn is an Associate Principal in McKinsey & Company's Global Education Practice, where he specializes in human capital strategy, system transformation, and the delivery of large-scale reform. During his six years at McKinsey, Paul has worked with large urban school districts, local and national nonprofits, and state and federal public sector agencies in K–12 and higher education. Prior to joining McKinsey, Paul worked as a public middle school teacher and administrator and community youth worker in South Africa, Ireland, and New York City. He is a graduate of Yale College and Columbia University's Teachers College and Graduate School of Business. He lives in Washington, DC.

"Don't tell me what. I know what. Tell me how."

—Margaret Thatcher
to her advisers

How to Read This Field Guide

This field guide was written for leaders in American education systems who wish to undertake a *delivery effort,* defined here as the concerted and purposeful application of the deliverology approach to help a system to set and achieve ambitious goals. In particular, this field guide has two intended audiences:

- The *system leader* is the chief state school officer (CSSO) in K–12 education or the CEO, president, or chancellor in higher education. A system leader makes the key decision to start and sponsor the delivery effort.
- The *delivery leader* is the person appointed by the system leader to head the delivery effort on a day-to-day basis, usually with the help of a small staff. The delivery leader is the person who has sleepless nights worrying about whether the system is delivering on the targets it has set.

It will of course also be relevant to education leaders at district and school level and with those in charter chains and nonprofits. The deliverology approach employed in a delivery effort can be broken down into several components, which are summarized in Figure 1.

The proposition of this field guide is as follows: If your system faithfully implements each of these components, it will achieve visible and measurable results in student outcomes.

The field guide is organized as follows: The executive summary gives a brief overview of the complete approach. After that, the field guide's five chapters, containing 15 modules, correspond to the lettered and numbered categories in Figure 1. Each module covers a specific component of the framework in detail, including the following elements (an illustrative example of each is given):

- Narrative text that gives a conceptual explanation of each component, including:
  - The roles to be played by the system leader and delivery leader (see Figure 2)
  - The specific process steps that the component will entail and/or principles for implementation (see Figure 3)

Figure 1

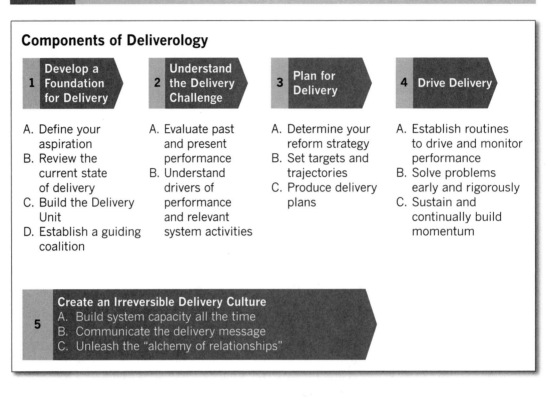

Components of Deliverology

1 Develop a Foundation for Delivery	2 Understand the Delivery Challenge	3 Plan for Delivery	4 Drive Delivery
A. Define your aspiration B. Review the current state of delivery C. Build the Delivery Unit D. Establish a guiding coalition	A. Evaluate past and present performance B. Understand drivers of performance and relevant system activities	A. Determine your reform strategy B. Set targets and trajectories C. Produce delivery plans	A. Establish routines to drive and monitor performance B. Solve problems early and rigorously C. Sustain and continually build momentum

5 **Create an Irreversible Delivery Culture**
A. Build system capacity all the time
B. Communicate the delivery message
C. Unleash the "alchemy of relationships"

Figure 2

ROLES OF SYSTEM LEADER AND DELIVERY LEADER

Delivery capacity will often be reviewed before the Delivery Unit is completely set up; in some cases, you may find yourself alone as delivery leader when the review occurs.

Figure 3

PROCESS STEPS

Step 1: Understand the landscape of your system
Step 2: Conduct a delivery capacity review
Step 3: Organize your delivery effort to improve capacity

- Elements that help to illustrate and bring each component to life, including:
    - Exhibits which give tools, templates, illustrative examples, and real-life examples of the concepts in action (see Figure 4)
- Asides and quotations, including references to *Instruction to Deliver*
- Case examples from both the PMDU and other sources that give a more extensive example of the concepts in action (see Figure 5)

Figure 4

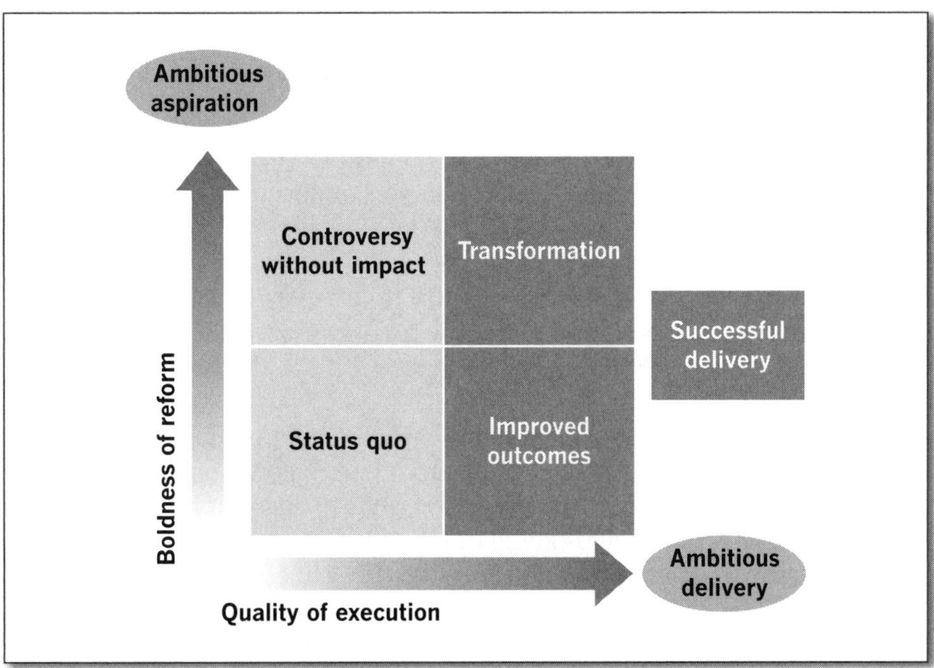

Figure 5

CASE EXAMPLE

Setting up a Delivery Unit in a K–12 SEA

In one K–12 SEA, the CSSO set out to build a Delivery Unit that would drive toward an ambitious goal: having an 85% cohort graduation rate by the year 2016.

For full-time Delivery Unit staff, the delivery leader knew that she needed to have team members who could act as internal consultants, asking system staff to do things that were sometimes uncomfortable (and asking the same of herself). Moreover, the Delivery Unit staff needed to be comfortable under ambiguity, convinced of the need to improve, and receptive to feedback that would allow this improvement within themselves.

While the field guide draws case examples from many sources, a few feature most prominently:

- The PMDU itself (for more, see *Instruction to Deliver*)[1]
- Recent work with state K–12 SEAs and higher education systems (note that in many cases, these examples have been disguised in order to protect sensitive information)

1. For more on the PMDU, please see Barber, *Instruction to Deliver: Fighting to Transform Britain's Public Services*. London: Methuen Publishing, 2008. It will be cited in this field guide simply as *Instruction to Deliver*.

- Montgomery County Public Schools (MCPS) in Montgomery County, Maryland, under the superintendency of Jerry Weast[2]

HOW SHOULD YOU READ THIS GUIDE?

If you are a system leader, then the executive summary is addressed to you and should give you a sense of the overall approach. If you decide to undertake a delivery effort, Chapter 1 will help you to develop the right foundation. In particular, read Module 1C, Build the Delivery Unit, for tips on what to look for as you appoint a delivery leader and find other staff for the effort. You might also read Module 3A, Determine your reform strategy, as it gets to the heart of your direction-setting role as a system leader. Beyond this, your delivery leader will help you to engage with the delivery effort where necessary.

If you are a delivery leader, then the 15 detailed modules of the field guide are addressed to you. They are a comprehensive manual that can serve as the "how-to" guide for the delivery effort that you lead. While you will benefit from a complete reading of the guide, its real value for you will be as a reference manual to guide you through whatever stage of delivery you happen to be in. To get your bearings, Module 1B, Review the current state of delivery, will help you understand what parts of the field guide are most relevant for your system and sequence the activities in your delivery effort accordingly. For example, some system leaders will already have defined an aspiration (Module 1A) and a strategy to go with it (Module 3A) prior to the start of a delivery effort. In cases in which you already have an aspiration and a strategy, your role will be to understand what is in place, push to improve it if necessary, and then build upon it through the activities in other modules. Other system leaders will be starting from scratch, in which case your role will be to work with them to undertake each component in a way that makes sense for your system.

While this field guide has a definite point of view about the ideal practices a system should undertake in its delivery effort, it is not finally dogmatic about these practices. Every system faces a unique set of circumstances and challenges, and what worked in the U.K. (or, indeed, in the state next door) may not necessarily be appropriate for your system. As you will see, the case studies and examples in the field guide demonstrate that it is possible to deviate from "ideal practice" while still upholding the principles espoused in each module. Over time, your experiences will serve to update this field guide and to add to the library of case studies that inform its approach.

2. For more on MCPS, please see Childress, Doyle, and Thomas, *Leading for Equity: The Pursuit of Excellence in the Montgomery County Public Schools.* Cambridge: Harvard Education Press, 2009. It will be cited in this field guide simply as *Leading for Equity.*

Executive Summary

As a system leader, you have decided that the status quo is insufficient and that a delivery effort will be needed to achieve a transformational change in your system's performance. What does adopting an end-to-end deliverology approach in your system entail?

1. Develop a foundation for delivery. Every strong delivery effort has a few prerequisites that must be put in place before you begin: a clear idea of what the system should deliver, an understanding of *where* and *how* delivery must improve, a *talented team* to run the delivery effort on your behalf, and sufficient *alignment* at the top to get things done. As system leader, you will start the delivery effort by putting these in place.

A. *Define your aspiration. "If there were no constraints or if there were a national emergency, what would you do?"* (Tony Blair, quoted in *Instruction to Deliver,* 218). You will begin by developing your system's vision of what you care most about, what you want to do about it, and how you will measure success. If your system has existing aspirations, you will identify, clarify, and redefine them if necessary. If not, you will lead your system to define its aspirations for the first time.

B. *Review the current state of delivery. "At the most basic level, there was no Delivery Unit to inherit, so the people would have to be found, the methodologies invented, the processes designed and the relationships established"* (*Instruction to Deliver,* 48). Each module in this field guide describes various *delivery activities* that will help you to achieve your aspiration. In order to build on the activities that are already in place—and to shore up areas where you are weak—you will map out the landscape of your system and conduct a *delivery capacity review* to evaluate the existence and quality of its delivery activities.

C. *Build the Delivery Unit. "Who is the person . . . who spends most of his/her time on the priority and has sleepless nights, worrying about hitting the targets?"* (*Instruction to Deliver,* 106). Armed with the information from your delivery capacity review, you will appoint your delivery leader (if you have not already done so) and work with him to design, organize, and build a high-performing *Delivery Unit* to oversee your delivery effort. This unit will be the primary source of a new delivery culture that is characterized by five words: *ambition, focus, clarity, urgency,* and *irreversibility* (see Module 1C).

D. *Establish a guiding coalition. "One or two people, even in powerful positions, will always struggle to achieve dramatic change, but seven people in key positions who agree profoundly about what they want to do and how they want to do it, can change the world"* (*Instruction to Deliver,* 237). As the final part of your foundation for delivery, you will identify the right people and work informally to align each of them with the aims of your delivery effort. This group will be your *guiding coalition.*

2. Understand the delivery challenge. Knowing the nature of the problem you face will be crucial to success. With your foundation in place, your Delivery Unit will begin its work with a diagnosis of both the size and nature of the barriers that your system faces to the delivery of your aspiration.

A. *Evaluate past and present performance. "Gathering data, it turns out, is not only powerful; it's fascinating too"* (*Instruction to Deliver,* 89). To understand where you are going, you need to understand where you have been and where you are now. Your Delivery Unit will begin its diagnosis by identifying the data most indicative of performance—especially your *target metrics,* which measure achievement of your aspiration—and analyzing that data for patterns of strong and weak performance. This analysis will rely on *benchmarks* of your system against history, against its own top performers, and against other systems, both domestically and around the world.

B. *Understand drivers of performance and related system activities. "Good data, while essential, is only a start—you then have to use it!"* (*Instruction to Deliver,* 88). After its initial analysis, your Delivery Unit will focus on patterns of weak performance, digging deeper to identify (1) the underlying *drivers* of weak performance and (2) existing *system activities,* if any, that are intended to address these challenges. Your Delivery Unit will evaluate the efficacy of each activity and use *delivery chain analysis* to identify potential improvements.

3. Plan for delivery. You have defined where you want to be, and you have learned where you are. The next logical question is, How are we going to get there? With the facts about performance in hand, your Delivery Unit will support you to define your system's approach to addressing the delivery challenge, to set a concrete and measurable definition of success, and to produce plans that will help your system to get there.

A. *Determine your reform strategy. "The solutions lie not in one simple remedy, but in the sustained implementation of a combination of actions"* (*Instruction to Deliver,* 90). Your Delivery Unit's analysis of the delivery challenge will help you to set the strategic direction for your system. This strategy consists of a theory of change, which gives it internal coherence, and a series of interventions selected according to this theory of change and benchmarked against practices around the world that alter existing system activities or introduce new ones. These interventions are selected, combined, and sequenced to have the maximum possible impact on your target metrics.

B. *Set targets and trajectories. Targets "translated airy aspirations into specific measurable commitments"* (*Instruction to Deliver,* 50). With a clear idea of system performance and a strategy to improve it, your Delivery Unit has the evidence that it needs to set *targets* for your target metrics that are specific, measurable, ambitious, realistic, and time-limited (SMART). The ambition and realism of each target will be balanced by its underlying *trajectory,* a set of interim targets that are based on evidence from performance benchmarking and the projected efficacy of your reform strategy. Where necessary, your Delivery Unit will also support you in negotiating *subtargets* with local units, such as campuses and school districts.

C. *Produce delivery plans. "We wanted real, messy, practical plans, with folds and creases, scribbled notes in the margins and coffee stains"* (*Instruction to Deliver,* 84). Once a strategy, targets, and trajectories have been agreed upon, your Delivery Unit will organize your system to deliver, identifying *delivery plan owners* who will be accountable and helping them write *delivery plans,* clearly spelling out how each element of the strategy will be executed.

4. Drive delivery. Your system's strategy, targets, trajectories, and plans all represent commitments made by your system, which, if honored, should generate real results. Your Delivery Unit's role will be to track progress against these commitments, to identify challenges and change course where required, and above all to push your system to keep its promises.

A. *Establish routines to drive and monitor performance. "Without the routines, events cannot be fully understood and, more importantly, results will never be delivered"* (*Instruction to Deliver,* 112). Once your system has started delivery, you will need to know—as frequently as possible—how well your system is doing at executing your strategy and what kinds of results are being achieved. To this end, your Delivery Unit will establish a set of *delivery routines* allowing you and other leaders to review performance, discuss major issues, and make decisions to drive delivery forward. The schedule of routines, and the deadlines imposed by them, will create a consistent sense of urgency for the delivery plan owners in your system.

B. *Solve problems early and rigorously. "The Delivery Unit provided the Prime Minister with a means of responding systematically when there was a major delivery failure, rather than relying on . . . 'government by spasm'"* (*Instruction to Deliver,* 160). In addition to regular routines, your Delivery Unit will also develop *conditional routines* to deal with arising problems. Your Delivery Unit will identify these problems early and develop a system of criteria for classifying them according to severity. It will work with your system to allocate resources and energy to these problems according to their classification, ranging from increased scrutiny to full-blown crisis management.

C. *Sustain and continually build momentum. "The wire is high and the roar of the crowd may be less positive than before, but this is no time to wobble"* (*Guardian* editorial, quoted in *Instruction to Deliver,* 196). When the first reports of positive results come in, your system may be tempted to declare victory and take the pressure off itself. Your Delivery Unit will help you fight this temptation and persist through distractions and monotony, managing those who resist change, continuously challenging the status quo, and celebrating success only when there is truly something to celebrate.

5. Create an irreversible delivery culture. The tools and tactics of delivery are necessary elements for success, but they cannot ensure it will be achieved. Change will be irreversible only when you have succeeded in changing your system's culture, widening the circle of your delivery effort's leadership to include senior leaders, middle managers, the front line, and even the public. Therefore, you and your Delivery Unit will underpin every activity in your effort, as described in Chapters 1 through 4, with efforts to build the skills and mindsets, send the messages, and develop the relationships that are instrumental to creating a culture of delivery.

A. *Build system capacity all the time. "The quality of leadership at every level is decisive"* (*Instruction to Deliver,* 194). In order to set your system up for success, your Delivery Unit will constantly evaluate and improve your system's *capacity.* Capacity refers to the structure, resources, competencies, and motivation that will allow everyone—from the Delivery Unit itself to the front line—to carry out the activities that are necessary for delivery. To build capacity, your Delivery Unit will as necessary drive reorganizations, provide formal training, establish feedback loops, codify learnings, act as the role model for delivery culture, and push responsibility for delivery out into your system.

B. *Communicate the delivery message. "How will key messages about the change programme be communicated . . . ?"* (*Instruction to Deliver,* 77). One of John Kotter's (1996) "eight most common errors in change programs" is "undercommunicating by a factor of 10 (or 100 or even 1000)" (p. 4). Your Delivery Unit will help you plan communications about your delivery effort as a whole and about itself and its own work as necessary. It will do this by identifying and understanding the relevant stakeholders and developing a communication plan that articulates the right messages, modes, timing, and messengers of communication for each stakeholder.

C. *Unleash the "alchemy of relationships." "Unless we had worked out early on how we would make each of our key relationships a 'win-win' . . . we would never have been given the chance to develop the techniques [of delivery] at all"* (*Instruction to Deliver,* 51). Your Delivery Unit's success will stand or fall on the strength of the relationships it builds with everyone in your system. For this reason, your Delivery Unit will focus on building high-quality relationships through its interactions with all stakeholders, keeping people in touch and informed, declaring and living by the values of its *brand,* seeking the "win-win" in every relationship, and managing conflict actively and ethically.

1

Develop a Foundation for Delivery

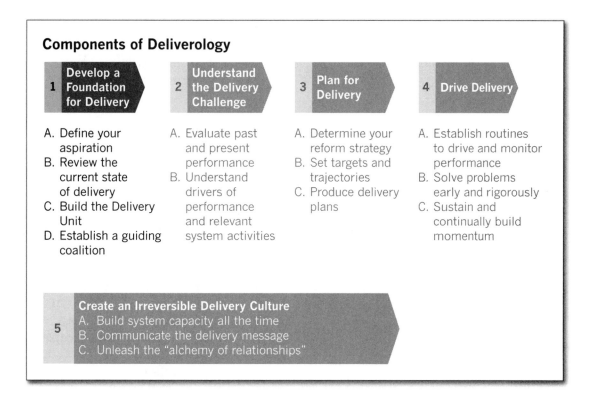

Components of Deliverology

1 Develop a Foundation for Delivery	2 Understand the Delivery Challenge	3 Plan for Delivery	4 Drive Delivery
A. Define your aspiration B. Review the current state of delivery C. Build the Delivery Unit D. Establish a guiding coalition	A. Evaluate past and present performance B. Understand drivers of performance and relevant system activities	A. Determine your reform strategy B. Set targets and trajectories C. Produce delivery plans	A. Establish routines to drive and monitor performance B. Solve problems early and rigorously C. Sustain and continually build momentum

5 **Create an Irreversible Delivery Culture**
A. Build system capacity all the time
B. Communicate the delivery message
C. Unleash the "alchemy of relationships"

Every strong delivery effort has a few prerequisites that must be put in place before you begin: a clear idea of what the system should deliver, an understanding of where and how delivery must improve, a talented team that will run the delivery effort on your behalf, and sufficient alignment at the top to get things done.

Not all delivery efforts are created equal. The efficacy of your effort will depend on what has already been done, your system's specific strengths and weaknesses, and the resources that are available to you. In order to launch your delivery effort, you must build an accurate understanding of the system you will be working with. You must understand the context of your system's history, mission, and ambition. You must understand the nuances of the challenge at hand. And you must build the necessary support system to help you confront this challenge.

This chapter will help you develop the foundation for your delivery effort. It consists of four modules:

A. Define your aspiration

B. Review the current state of delivery

C. Build the Delivery Unit

D. Establish a guiding coalition

With this foundation in place, your delivery effort will be well positioned to achieve real results for your system.

1A. DEFINE YOUR ASPIRATION

"Only those who dare to fail greatly can ever achieve greatly."

—Robert F. Kennedy

Note to delivery leaders: *Aspiration-setting is primarily the responsibility of the system leader. This module is a guide for how a system leader should set the system's aspirations. Your role as delivery leader is highlighted where appropriate.*

"What do you want?" is a basic but often unasked question. System leaders must understand what their system wants, or what kind of change it needs. Many attempts at delivery have been derailed because those in charge assumed that a system's leaders all shared the same aspirations, when in fact they did not. Other efforts have failed because leaders agreed on the wrong things, were insufficiently ambitious, or simply had ill-defined goals. Aspirations set the direction of a system's change and motivate people toward that direction.

DIRECTION AND MOTIVATION

"Where direction was clarified—as in Education under Blunkett or the Treasury under Gordon Brown—the civil servants were highly motivated. Where [it] was lacking—as in Social Security—motivation was, of course, less evident." (*Instruction to Deliver,* 45)

This module will explore what an aspiration is and define some criteria and approaches for clarifying and/or setting a system's aspirations. An aspiration is your system's answer to three questions:

- What do we care about?
- What are we going to do about it?
- How will we measure success?

To have an impact, a system's aspirations must be clear, sharp, and understandable to everyone. Common aspirations form the basis for all efforts at delivery because they signify a shared understanding of what success would look like. Shared aspirations become a powerful tool that your Delivery Unit can invoke during its work with the front line. How much more difficult would it have been for NASA leaders to motivate their agency to put a man on the moon if they were without President Kennedy's famously expressed aspiration to back them up? An aspiration acts as a system's backbone, the goal to be insisted upon when others are thinking of giving up, or giving in to the mistaken belief that outcomes are not in our power to control or influence.

As defined here, an aspiration is not necessarily a specific and time-bound target (for more on target setting, see Chapter 3, Plan for Delivery). However, as the three defining questions above suggest, an aspiration should lend itself to measurement by one or more target metrics: metrics that the system uses to represent the actual outcomes desired by a system.

An aspiration is, at a minimum, a verbal expression of the specific outcome (or outcomes) that a system strives to influence or attain, and the direction of that desired influence or attainment. It is often derived from a system's overall mission but is more specific. The American Cancer Society's mission, for example, is to "eliminate cancer as a major health problem" (ACS, n.d.). That mission may embrace many aspirations: providing universal access to cancer screening, increasing awareness about cancer risk factors, ensuring the provision of life-saving treatment, and so on. Likewise, in his first speech to Congress in 2009, President Barack Obama set an aspiration that the United States would have the highest proportion of college graduates in the world by the year 2020. Though this was a measurable aspiration, much remained to be done to clarify exactly what measures to use. Exhibit 1A.1 indicates examples of aspiration setting in public policy, education, and the nonprofit sector.

Aspirations set the foundation for delivery because they set the bar for what the system will be asked to achieve. The relationship between aspiration and delivery can be summarized in Exhibit 1A.2. The nature of your aspiration determines how bold the reform will be, while the quality of your delivery effort determines how well executed the reform will be.

The ideal is to have both a bold aspiration and excellent execution, but this will be challenging for obvious reasons. However, watering down the aspiration too much results in a defense of the status quo, which, in an era of rising public expectations, is a recipe for managed decline. The equation changes when the horizontal axis becomes the focus. A not very radical but plausible idea, implemented well, will make a difference and deliver improved outcomes. This can buy you the right to increase the boldness of your aspirations and deliver transformation.

This map will be a useful guide as you identify, evaluate, and help create your system's aspirations. By plotting your aspirations onto this map, you will have an idea of the balance of your ambitions, with clear implications for you. If most of your current aspirations are on the left-hand side, you will need to shift them to the right. Incidentally, a controversy without

Exhibit 1A.1 Aspirations in education, public policy, and the nonprofit sector—examples

	Aspiration	**Target metric**
San Jose Unified School District	We seek to prepare every high school student to be ready for college upon graduation.	• Graduation success rates against rigorous requirements aligned with the A–G requirements of the University of California system
City of Los Angeles	We want to improve public services in six key areas: education, economic development, transportation, energy and environment, public safety and security, and fiscal responsibility.	• Education—graduation and drop-out rates • Economic—residential and commercial construction • Transportation—synchronization of traffic signals • Energy and environment—percent of city trucks meeting diesel emissions standards • Safety/security—gang-related murders per capita per time period • Fiscal—level of deficit (holding taxes constant)
One Campaign	We want the commitment of world leaders to fight extreme poverty and preventable disease.	• Track progress on specific initiatives of Global Call to Action Against Poverty (GCAP) for each country • Analyze and track each country's budget for GCAP campaigns • Track countries that do and do not honor their commitments • Track countries that do not participate in any initiatives related to fighting poverty

Exhibit 1A.2 A map of delivery: Aspirations push the boldness of reform while delivery pushes the quality of execution

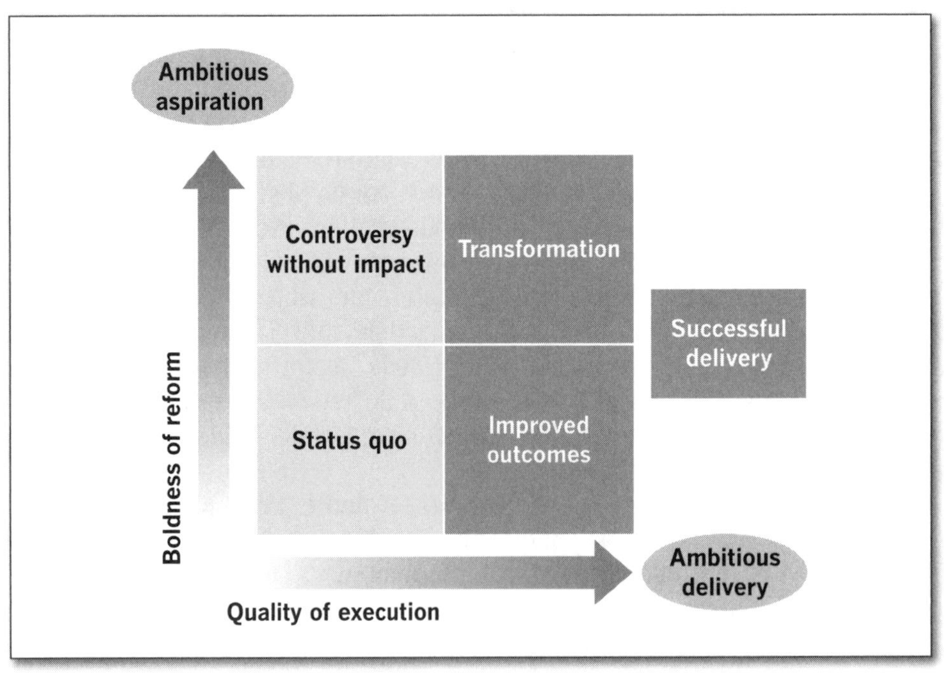

impact might be worthwhile as a step on the way to transformation, but it should be avoided as an end state. If the whole portfolio is destined to end up in the "Transformation" box, then the program is probably too risky. If it is all headed for the "Improved outcomes" box, then it probably lacks ambition. The more ambitious your aspiration is, the more rigorous you must be with delivery to ensure that it can lead to transformation.

ROLES OF SYSTEM LEADER AND DELIVERY LEADER

Setting a system's aspirations is primarily the responsibility of the system leader. If it already exists, your Delivery Unit (the person or group responsible for driving the achievement of system aspirations—see Module 1C for more information) may be called upon to assist the system leader in doing this. Over time, your role as delivery leader will be to ensure that this aspiration remains sufficiently focused, clear, and shared by system leaders—and to push for clarification or redefinition where necessary. Systems lacking ambitious aspirations are sometimes set right by their Delivery Units, which can point out this need and bring the right people together to meet it.

PROCESS STEPS

Step 1: Identify existing aspirations
Step 2: Clarify existing aspirations
Step 3: Refine or define new aspirations if necessary

Step 1: Identify existing aspirations

The aspirations for most systems will not be set from a blank slate. For many, aspirations usually exist in some form, and usually systems are not completely free to define their own aspirations: mission statements, laws and regulations governing the system, and existing commitments made by other leaders all have an influence.

As a first step, system leaders must identify their system's existing aspirations and any external influences on those aspirations. Some examples of external influences are included in Exhibit 1A.3, and key questions for doing this are given in Exhibit 1A.4.

As prime minister, Tony Blair wanted to target several areas of concern for which well-defined aspirations were lacking. The Prime Minister's Delivery Unit (PMDU) leader worked with the prime minister, ministers, and half a dozen members of Blair's policy team to establish priority areas for which aspirations were set. The key was to focus aspirations on a narrow set of themes in order to have a clear message of delivery and increase chances of success.

Step 2: Clarify existing aspirations

Once existing aspirations have been identified by the system leader, she must examine them to determine whether they are fit for anchoring delivery

Exhibit 1A.3 External influence on system aspirations—examples

No Child Left Behind Act	Requires that all students in the United States perform at grade level according to state standards by 2014. This effectively means that no state K–12 system can avoid including performance on state assessments as part of its aspiration.
Presidential goal for college attainment	In his first speech to a joint session of Congress, President Barack Obama made the pledge that "by 2020, America will once again have the highest proportion of college graduates in the world." Though not backed up by legislation, this pledge will influence the aspirations of state university systems throughout the United States.

Exhibit 1A.4 Identifying a system's existing aspirations—questions for consideration

Alignment on aspirations	• What are the system leader's aspirations? Are they well known? • What are the views of the top 7–10 people in the system's leadership on the system leader's aspirations? Are they aligned? • What are the views of the middle managers and the front line about these aspirations? Are they aware of them? • Does the system itself have aspirations, articulated either publicly or internally? What are the strategy documents (strategic plans, goals, etc.) that set out the system aspirations?
External influences	• Does the system have a mission statement? How does it affect aspirations? • Does the system define its aspirations with governing laws and regulations? Do those laws and regulations set out specific measures to which the system is held accountable? • Have previous system leaders or leaders with some kind of oversight responsibility, effectively set aspirations? • If the system leader is an elected official or an appointee of an elected official, is she accountable to an electoral mandate that must be considered when setting aspirations? • What do the users of the system's services want? What do other stakeholders who are affected by the system's work want?

efforts. Questions to consider when shaping existing aspirations are presented in the following paragraphs:

- **What moral purpose do the aspirations serve? Should they be achieved, why will that matter?** Without an aspiration connected to the college- and career-readiness agenda, a K–12 state education agency (SEA) may be neglecting one of the most important elements of its organizational mission. Likewise with a hospital and the reduction of mortality rates.
- **Are the aspirations sufficiently ambitious? If achieved, will they make a substantial impact on the things the system cares about?**

Is the conception of "ambitious" embodied in the aspirations truly supported by the data? (For more on this, see Module 3B, Set targets and trajectories.) Aspirations should guard against complacency and take account of how the world is changing; for example, it would do no good for an antipoverty campaign to set an aspiration to ensure that all incomes are at least $1 per day if trends show that this income will be insufficient to pull a household out of poverty five years from now.

- **Can the aspirations be summarized in one or more metrics that can be calculated using data that are readily available? If not, what would be required to collect the necessary data?** Is there an alternative metric or metrics that can be calculated using available data? While there should theoretically be few limitations on aspirations based on availability of data, some criteria may be difficult to measure.
- **Are the aspirations sufficiently focused?** Are there two or three big aspirations, or dozens of small ones? Are the aspirations so large, or so numerous, as to be incoherent?
- **Are the aspirations shared?** That is, is the leadership team aligned on these aspirations? Are there exceptions to this alignment? How serious are they? How well do people throughout the system, from middle managers, such as principals, to front line actors, such as teachers, understand these aspirations? How well do users and the public understand them? Could they name them if asked?

Depending on how these clarifying questions are answered, the appropriateness of endorsing, altering, or redefining a system's aspirations can be decided.

FOCUSED ASPIRATION

"We were already agreed that the departments to focus on were Health, Education, Transport and the Home Office, and no others. What [Tony] Blair made clear in this meeting, however, was that he also wanted to narrow the focus within each departmental area. 'I want the Delivery Unit focused on issues of real salience . . . for example, in transport, I only want [the PMDU] to sort out the railways.' In fact, at that stage the Prime Minister's determination to narrow the focus . . . was such that I was worried our scope would be too limited, but over time this rigorous prioritization was completely vindicated." (*Instruction to Deliver,* 49)

Step 3: Refine or define new aspirations if necessary

If existing aspirations are insufficiently clear, insufficiently focused, or insufficiently shared, then their redefinition, narrowing, and/or dissemination will be necessary.

There are two ways of setting aspirations. The first is consultative, and the second is to lead from the front. In a consultative method, the leader brings together a group of key stakeholders and holds an open discussion. Depending on what was discovered in Step 1, the makeup of this group will vary. If the system's internal control over its aspirations is substantial, the group may simply be the system's leadership team. If, on the other hand, the desired change requires a change in an external constraint such as a law or regulation, the group may combine lawmakers, internal leadership, and even interested third parties who have influence.

Agreement among stakeholders can be achieved in a number of ways. For small changes, a series of individual consultations might be all that is needed, followed by broad communication of the new aspirations. For larger changes, it might be advisable to convene a workshop—a meeting of all stakeholders to discuss and agree collectively on a new aspiration—or to conduct a wider consultative exercise that involves substantial public input from a variety of sources.

The consultative model is not always appropriate; sometimes, to aspire means to lead from the front. Leaders often mistakenly believe that they must trade off ambition for efficacy in government, while the reverse is sometimes true. We have already referred to President Kennedy's aspiration to land a man on the moon. It is generally agreed that his expressed goal of achieving this by 1970 spurred the NASA engineers toward success. Would Kennedy's goal have had the same effect if it had not been so ambitious—if, say, the deadline had been 2020 instead of 1970? If he had consulted widely, would it have been set at all? Expressed ambition creates urgency that can be a real asset in getting things done. It can be crucial in generating the early wins that a system needs in order to have the right to continue its work. System leaders should therefore develop reasonable, ambitious, and non-negotiable aspirations and demonstrate to stakeholders their willingness to "go it alone" if that is what success demands.

Exhibit 1A.5 summarizes these two models of aspiration setting and some guidelines for when each is appropriate.

Exhibit 1A.5 Models of aspiration setting

Model	"Lead from the front"	Consultative
Description	• Leader asserts an aspiration and invests his or her own political capital to support the aspiration.	• Leader convenes a series of workshops or meetings to develop new aspirations collaboratively. • Stakeholders may include system leaders, local leaders, frontline staff, and/or community groups.
When to use	• Leader needs to create a sense of urgency in the organization. • Leader wants to communicate that certain aspirations are important enough to be non-negotiable. • Leader fears that consultative method would produce watered-down aspirations.	• Leader needs to secure buy-in from key stakeholders by involving them early. • System needs to demonstrate that it listens and responds to stakeholders (e.g., teachers feel they have no voice in reform decisions).

Tips from delivery practitioners

• Involving system actors in the process of creating aspirations increases the likelihood they will embrace and support them. However, a consultative approach can make it more challenging to set highly ambitious aspirations.

Conclusion

In this module, you have learned the following aspiration-setting processes:

- How to identify a system's existing aspirations and the context surrounding them.
- How to clarify these aspirations to see if they are fit to anchor delivery efforts.
- How to identify and bring stakeholders together to refine, redefine, and/or narrow system aspirations.

When aspiration setting is complete, the system will have an agreed-upon, well-articulated set of aspirations along with one or more metrics to measure progress according to available or collectable data. This data will become the basis for understanding current performance and for setting system goals.

1B. REVIEW THE CURRENT STATE OF DELIVERY

> *"You try getting change in the public sector and the public services. I bear the scars on my back after two years in government and heaven knows what it will be like after a bit longer."*
>
> —Former U.K. Prime Minister Tony Blair

In his 1999 "scars on my back" speech, Tony Blair underscored a real challenge that he faced. Blair's Labour Party had won a resounding victory in elections just two years earlier, and Blair himself had near complete mastery of the political scene. In trying to effect change, however, the prime minister discovered nonetheless that the levers he controlled were weak, the leaders of the public service workforce were prepared to defend a manifestly inadequate status quo, and there were no systems in place to drive and monitor delivery.

Tony Blair learned a hard lesson in his first term: Those who seek to make change ignore the inner workings of the bureaucracy—and the use of delivery tools to make change happen—at their peril. Leaders must always work through those that they lead. Making change happen requires a clear understanding of an entire ecosystem of people and organizations that will play a part in implementing your reforms as well as a set of defined activities that will push delivery forward.

In this module, you will learn to examine your system's capacity to deliver your aspiration. A system's capacity to deliver, or *delivery capacity,* can be measured according to the kinds of *delivery activities* a system is undertaking and how effective they are in improving the impact of the *system's activities.* In order to fully understand these activities, you must first also get a general sense of the landscape of the *system actors,* the people or organizations that drive the *system's activities.*

Here, a distinction is being made between delivery activities and system activities.

- **Delivery activities** are the specific activities described in this field guide, usually undertaken by your Delivery Unit and system leadership team, that help make delivery happen. Examples include analyzing system performance against the aspiration or running routines to monitor progress.

- **System activities** are those undertaken by system actors to achieve the system's aspiration. This is the "real work" of any system. It can consist of day-to-day work, such as classroom teaching, or specific programs, such as outreach for low-income students to help improve freshman year retention rates in college.

As indicated above, the capacity to deliver is a strict measurement of the presence and quality of your system's delivery activities but not its system activities. You will gain a better understanding of system activities in Module 2B when you develop delivery chains to assess the types of changes you want to make in your reform strategy. Then in Module 5A, you will learn the tools to help build both delivery capacity and system capacity based on the gaps you have identified in this module and Module 2B. This module focuses on simply understanding the current state of delivery in the system, which is important at this early stage in the delivery process because it can inform the way that your delivery effort is organized.

ROLES OF SYSTEM LEADER AND DELIVERY LEADER

Delivery capacity will often be reviewed before the Delivery Unit is completely set up; in some cases, you may find yourself alone as delivery leader when the review occurs. Your role is to work with the system leader to conduct the review, and use its results to inform the way you design and set up your Delivery Unit (see Module 1C). Sometimes, the system leader may conduct the review prior to your arrival as delivery leader, in which case your role will be to use the results of the review to inform your management of the Delivery Unit.

PROCESS STEPS

Step 1: Understand the landscape of your system
Step 2: Conduct a delivery capacity review
Step 3: Organize your delivery effort to improve capacity

Step 1: Understand the landscape of your system

In order to better understand your delivery capacity, you need to develop a general understanding of your system: Who are the main players, and what are their roles and relative influence in the system? To do this, it is helpful to make a list of the major system actors, their roles, and their relationships with one another. This is similar to creating an organization chart for your system. Later, you will learn in Module 2B about creating delivery chains—the set of system actors that contribute to a specific system activity. The system map is a broader overview that provides you with baseline knowledge about your system.

Most system leaders and their teams should be able to draw such a map easily, but it may take a few interviews to develop an understanding of influences and relationships. Exhibits 1B.1 and 1B.2 are examples of system maps for both a higher education system and a K–12 SEA.

Once you understand the landscape of your system, you can better understand the state of delivery of this system through a proper delivery capacity review.

Step 2: Conduct a baseline delivery capacity review

A *delivery capacity review* is a tool that you can use to assess the ability of your system to perform the delivery activities associated with each of five stages of delivery. These stages are embodied in five sets of questions.

1. Has your system *developed a foundation for delivery?* Do system leaders and their top teams share an ambitious aspiration? Do they understand the current state of delivery? Have they set up a Delivery Unit and assembled a guiding coalition to drive and lead the achievement of that aspiration?
2. Does your system *understand the delivery challenge?* Does your system understand the opportunity to improve performance and the barriers to exploiting that opportunity? Does your system have the ability to collect and analyze performance data related to your aspiration, including leading indicators? Do system leaders use this data to understand the most important patterns of performance? Do they understand, and regularly assess, the drivers of their biggest performance challenges and the efficacy of current system activities in addressing those challenges? Do they constantly search for ideas and lessons from analogous situations, states, and systems that have overcome these challenges?
3. Does your system *plan for delivery?* Do system leaders have an integrated reform strategy grounded in a theory of change? Have they done a rigorous and evidence-based analysis of that strategy to set an ambitious but realistic target and trajectory for delivery of the aspiration? Have they broken this strategy down into delivery plans that establish the tangible **action steps** that will make it happen?
4. Does your system *drive delivery?* What regular routines have system leaders established to ensure that they are getting the information they need, on a regular enough basis, to know whether the delivery effort is on track? When problems arise, do they have an approach for solving them quickly, systematically, and rigorously? Beyond monitoring, what mechanisms have they put in place to push those who are successful to the next level?
5. Does your system *create a culture of delivery?* What measures do system leaders and their top teams undertake to ensure that people and organizations throughout the system are able to execute on their delivery plans? What is the story that they tell stakeholders about the delivery effort? Is the quality of relationships throughout the delivery system—and, particularly, the delivery chains—sufficient to enable successful delivery?

Exhibit 1B.1 System map for the California State University System

Governmental

Non-governmental

Federal Government

Department of Finance

California Legislature

The Governor

Appoint

California Student Aid Commission

Appoint

Education Code/ State Budget

Appoint Trustees

Request State General Fund Support

Trustees of the California State University

Appoint

Title 5/Trustee Resolutions

Report

The Chancellor

Executive Order/ Coded Memo

Report

Appoint

Campus Presidents

Campus Academic Senate

President's Directives

Financial aid administration

Campus Community

University Policy Statement

Lobbying/ advocacy

Advisory

Campus advocacy

California State Student Association

California Faculty Association

Academic Senate CSU

CSU Associated Students (on each campus)

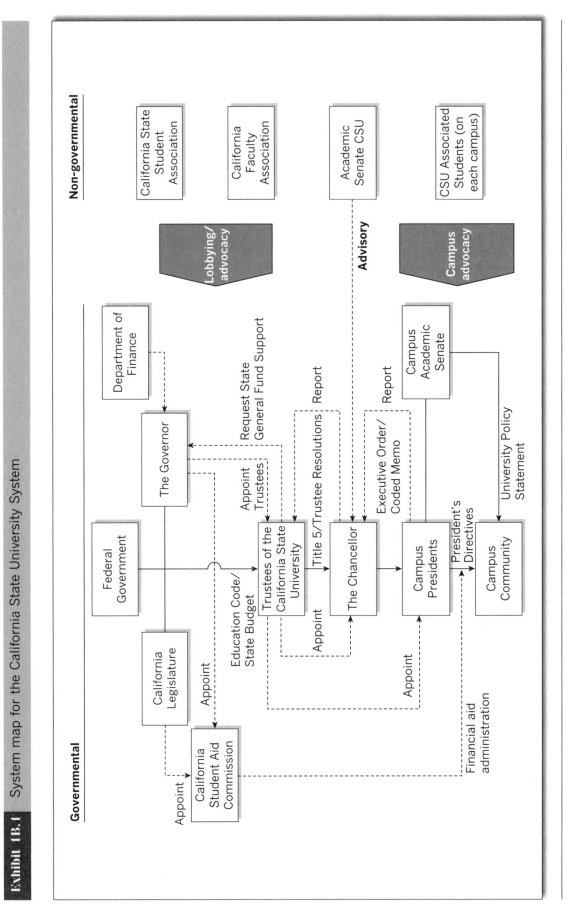

SOURCE: "University Governance and Administration," California State University, Cal-State Chico (http://www.csuchico.edu/catalog/cat09/01Front/05CSU_UnivAdministration.pdf); interviews.

Exhibit 1B.2 System map for California's K–12 system

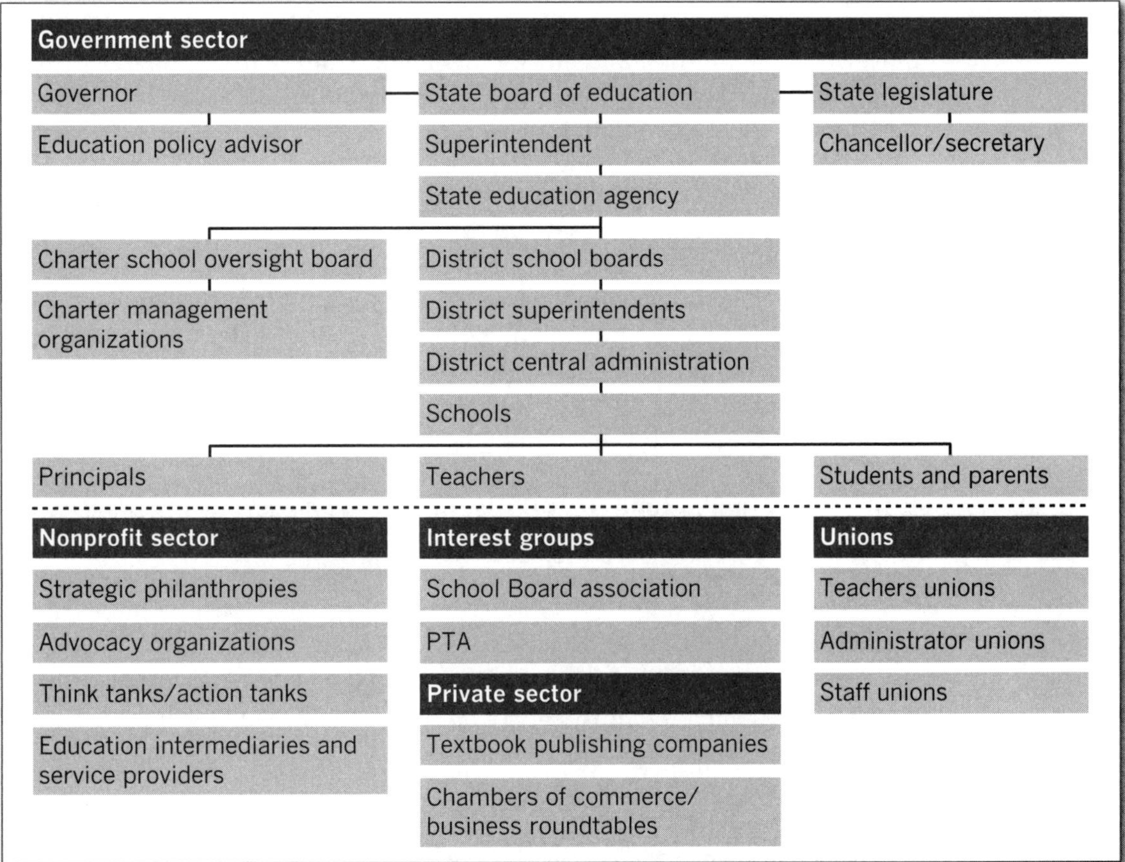

STARTING FROM SCRATCH

The PMDU had to start from the ground up, as the British government at that time had not established a systematic approach to delivery:

"At the most basic level, there was no Delivery Unit to inherit, so the people would have to be found, the methodologies invented, the processes designed and the relationships established. We had to develop techniques or methods that would result in convincing, reliable, evidence-based answers to our five questions." (*Instruction to Deliver,* 48)

In order to ensure that the results are both objective and grounded in a thorough understanding of your system, your delivery capacity review is best conducted by a joint team consisting of

- You and/or Delivery Unit staff (if there are any);
- A handful of crucial people on your system leadership team; and
- Staff from an independent entity, which has delivery expertise.

This combination of participants ensures both insider and outsider perspectives, which are necessary to ensure productive dialogue about the state of delivery in your system and lay the foundations for progress.

A delivery capacity review should not take a long time to conduct—maybe a week at the most, depending on available time, organizational complexity, and the condition of the organization's capacity. Sometimes, you will only have time to ask a few leaders and stakeholders some key questions that will allow you to make quick judgments about delivery capacity. Other times, you may have more time in which to conduct a thorough review and reach a deeper understanding.

A delivery capacity review will help you in several ways:

- It will establish a baseline against which you can measure your progress in building your capacity to deliver;
- It will provide you with the context and insight necessary to be effective in coaching and advising others in your Unit or delivery organization;
- It will facilitate the engagement of a wide group of stakeholders involved in the delivery effort; and
- It will deepen your own understanding of excellent delivery.

While the nature and form of the delivery capacity review process will vary depending on system context, all delivery capacity reviews should be conducted according to a certain set of principles. These principles, and the tools that can help you to put them into action, are summarized in Exhibit 1B.3.

The most important of these tools is the delivery *capacity review rubric,* a detailed questionnaire that explores multiple dimensions of each aspect of the

Exhibit 1B.3 Principles and tools for conducting a delivery capacity review

Principles		Tools for conducting a review
Understanding, not evaluation	The purpose of the review is to build a collective understanding of the current delivery activities and how to improve them, not to evaluate performance for accountability purposes.	• Delivery capacity review "rubric"with detailed questions about each delivery activity, and descriptions of what "good" and "bad" look like, to be used for self-scoring and external judgment • Interviews with system actors at all levels based on the rubric • Focus groups with system actors at all levels based on the rubric • Surveys based on the rubric
An external perspective	To ensure objectivity, it is strongly recommended that you conduct it in collaboration with an external stakeholder or some other independent entity with expertise in delivery. If your review is only internal, your system will risk myopia about what "good" truly looks like.	
Transparency	Within your system, this is a transparent process, with open and honest dialogue between you, your Delivery Unit, the independent entity, and, potentially, others in the system. You should inform all participants of the purpose of the process.	
Collaboration	This process is conducted by a joint team composed of staff, you, an independent entity, and members of your delivery team.	

delivery framework (see Exhibit 1B.4). For each of the components in this field guide, the rubric describes model "good" and "bad" states of delivery, and potential sources for evidence to support the reviewer's judgment. The rubric uses a four-point scale, which helps prevent a convergence to the middle and forces a real judgment about how good or bad delivery is. The rubric is a tool for scoring the system's delivery approach on all of these dimensions, but it is also the basis of all other questioning and probing tools that the team will use in the delivery capacity review process (interview protocols, focus group plans, surveys, etc.).

Exhibit 1B.4 The delivery capacity review rubric

This tool defines characteristics of strong delivery and asks critical questions for each part of the delivery framework

Example questions	Best case (Green)	Worst case (Red)	Rating
• Does your system have a theory of change that articulates how it believes it will achieve its aspiration? • Does your system have a reform strategy with a coherent set of interventions that are consistent with the theory of change? • Are the interventions powerful on their own, with proven or promising efficacy to improve performance against the aspiration? • Are the interventions integrated, having a combined effect that is more powerful than their individual effects would otherwise have been? • Are the interventions sequenced to balance resources required, impact, and interdependencies over time?	• System has a well-defined theory of change that tells a coherent and compelling story about how the system achieve its aspiration. • Different possible interventions are analyzed in terms of expected impact, cost, feasibility, scale, rigor, and requirements for skill and participation along the delivery chain; this analysis informs the choice and sequencing of interventions. • Chosen combination of interventions represents a coherent strategy, is aligned with the theory of change, and is complementary and mutually reinforcing.	• System lacks a well-defined theory of change. • Combination of interventions lacks coherence. Little or no benefit arises from implementing all the interventions as part of a single strategy. • Little analysis of different combinations of interventions or interdependencies between them. • Interventions themselves have little evidence that they have large impact on performance against the aspiration.	

For the complete delivery capacity review rubric, please see the Appendix A1.

Depending on whether your system has begun to act on the aspiration defined in Module 1A, you may need to anchor your delivery capacity review questions on some other, prior aspiration of the system leader in order to understand current delivery activities.

What process should you use to get the information that will allow you to make these judgments? Depending on your situation, your delivery capacity review process may be more or less involved. Some systems simply conduct a focused interview (based on the rubric) with a few members of the system leadership team then convene these leaders in a single meeting to compare results. For others with more time, the process may look something more like what is shown in Exhibit 1B.5.

Exhibit 1B.5 Delivery capacity review process—example

	Process introduction	Self-review	Focus group	Interviews	Conclusions, recommendations, follow-up	Ongoing review
Description	• Staff orient system leaders to purpose, structure, and outcomes of delivery capacity review process • May be delivered as meeting or workshop • Agree on potential focus group members and interviewees	• Prior to focus groups and interviews, participants review and complete selfscore version of rubric, describing model delivery approach and consideration of how their system measures up	• Joint team discussion with system head and top team members on system's delivery history, current delivery approach, and barriers to delivery	• Confidential one-on-one interviews by joint team and/or outside experts with key actors in and outside the system • Interviewees are cross-section of leadership, mid-management, front line, particularly those responsible for system aspiration	• Joint team draws conclusions about system's strengths and weaknesses; briefly summarizes key issues and general recommendations for improvement • Joint team, system top team meet to discuss	• Staff revisit initial conclusions with the system delivery leader • Together, they revise understanding of the state of delivery and agree on baseline for future comparison
Maximum Duration	• 1 hour	• 1–2 days	• Half to full day	• 2–3 days	• 2 days	• 2–3 days, every 18–24 months, as needed

The process begins with an introductory session, during which joint team members are oriented to the delivery capacity review process. Reviews then begin with a period of self-review, during which you, your delivery team, and all identified focus group and interview participants use the delivery capacity review rubric to consider your system's current delivery approach.

Once reflections are complete, the joint team convenes a focus group and conducts a series of interviews, both with a cross section of participants from system leadership, middle management, and the front line, as well as stakeholders external to the system. From these activities, the joint team develops conclusions and recommendations about the system's strengths and weaknesses with respect to delivery.

A delivery capacity review will establish a baseline that must be updated periodically. As your system's delivery approach grows and matures, and as a stronger and more collaborative relationship develops between you and joint team members, you will want to form a new joint team every 18 to 24 months to revisit and improve your understanding of your system's delivery capacity.

The following are examples of how a K–12 SEA and higher education system conducted their delivery capacity reviews. The higher education example includes a sample of a completed delivery review rubric.

CASE EXAMPLE

Reviewing delivery capacity in K–12 and higher education systems

In one K–12 SEA, time was short, so the team assisting the staff in setting up the Delivery Unit conducted a quick series of interviews with key personnel in the SEA. Rather than score their system against the formal rubric, they instead collapsed their results into a series of key findings and implications for the delivery effort (see Exhibit 1B.6).

Exhibit 1B.6 Findings and implications for K–12 capacity review

Finding	Implication
• Mid-level personnel want more top-down engagement and feedback on plans and goals.	• Practical direction provided through delivery may quickly build support.
• There is no single owner of any of the ambitious goals.	• Complexity will require SEA to find ways to foster collective responsibility for goals and collaboration.
• Accountability is tied to running programs rather than achieving student outcomes.	• Shifting to outcomes-based accountability will require investment to change mind sets and to build problem solving capabilities.
• Failure to meet targets results in change in target as opposed to change in plans.	• True trajectory construction will be an entirely new exercise for the SEA—relentless focus and urgency may meet resistance.

(Continued)

(Continued)

Finding	Implication
• Delivery is being executed reasonably well in isolated pockets of SEA.[1]	• How can we build on this as we develop SEA's capacity (e.g., what should be the role of the program leader X)?
• Many units' plans prioritize initiatives based on attached funding rather than proven efficacy.	• Is this a problem to solve or work around?
• Goal setting, planning, and bimonthly reports required by CSSO's Office, but there is little feedback provided.	• Staff may be skeptical about these aspects of delivery; countering this skepticism will require highlighting what differentiates delivery from past efforts and identifying quick wins.
• Availability of real-time data for specific metrics is limited (organization is rich in annual data only).	• Capacity will have to be built to problem solve methods of estimating progress via indicators.
• People feel consumed with ad hoc requests that could be predicted (e.g., frequent requests during legislative session).	• How do we begin building the mindset that developments should not take staff by surprise?

SOURCE: Interviews with SEA officials.

1. Program X is constructing strong delivery systems, independently overcoming barriers, and driving excellent progress against SMART targets.

By contrast, the new Delivery Unit for a higher education system undertook a more formal review process. Over the course of one week, they set up interviews (based on the rubric) with several key officials in the system office. They then collated those results and produced a formal traffic-light judgment for each component of the delivery framework. The Delivery Unit shared these results with the system CEO privately before debriefing with the senior staff as a whole. The debrief was designed to explore the findings and improve mutual understanding of the rationale behind each judgment. For each of the categories, the Delivery Unit provided some preliminary thoughts on what kinds of concrete actions the system could undertake to improve performance. The meeting concluded with an agreement that the system leadership would decide where it wanted to focus improvement efforts so that the Delivery Unit could develop a more robust work plan for these areas. Some partial results from this process are shown in the Exhibit 1B.7.

These results were illuminating for several staff members. In particular, the results brought on the realization that the system had taken on a firefighting culture, tending to the crises of the moment and therefore not focusing on a consistent set of priorities. Because delivery would require focus, they agreed that this would mean letting some fires burn out while others would require less leadership attention.

The team followed up with a list of short-term and long-term actions that the system should take to "move toward green." This list (Exhibit 1B.8) would ultimately shape and inform their entire delivery effort.

Exhibit 1B.7 Partial delivery capacity review results: Higher education system

R	Red
YR	Yellow-Red
YG	Yellow-Green
G	Green

Aspect of delivery	Characteristics	Strength	Rationale
3) Plan for Delivery	**3A) Determine reform strategy:** Does system take cohesive approach to initiatives, maximizing and understanding interdependencies?	R	Significant opportunity for greater holistic approach to activities and identification of interdependencies
	3B) Set goals and establish trajectories: Has aspiration been translated to concrete targets and cascaded down to relevant level? Have realistic trajectories been created for tracking performance?	R	Significant data tracking to monitor progress but great opportunity to increase use of targets and trajectories
	3C) Produce delivery plans: Does system use meaningful plans against which to track performance?	R	Implementation plans not widely used for system's efforts. Request-for-proposal driven processes do require plans of bidders
4) Drive Delivery	**4A) Ensure start of delivery and establish routines:** Is there a regular, fact-based, results-driven cycle of routines to monitor progress and correct course where required?	R	Data available for fact-based decision making, but routines focus on fire fighting over ongoing performance assessment and reaction; open culture of discussion
	4B) Solve problems early and rigorously: Are there mechanisms to ensure problems are identified and raised early and solved in order of priority?	YG	Problems addressed quickly when surfaced; learnings shared with other affected stakeholders but not always within system leadership
	4C) Build and sustain momentum: How does the system maintain dedication to the approach through adversity and celebrate success?	YR	Reliant on individual commitment and monthly board meetings

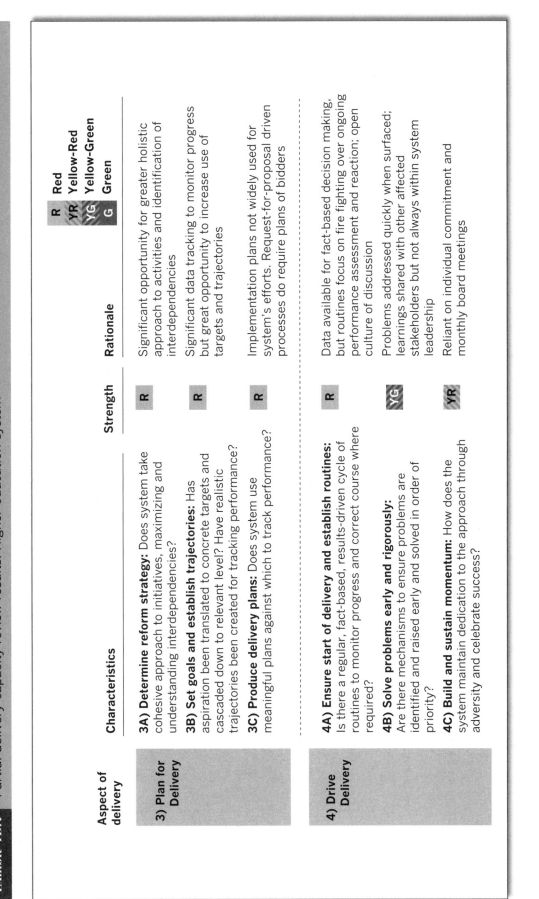

Exhibit 1B.8 Moving toward green—partial list of possible actions based on delivery capacity review results

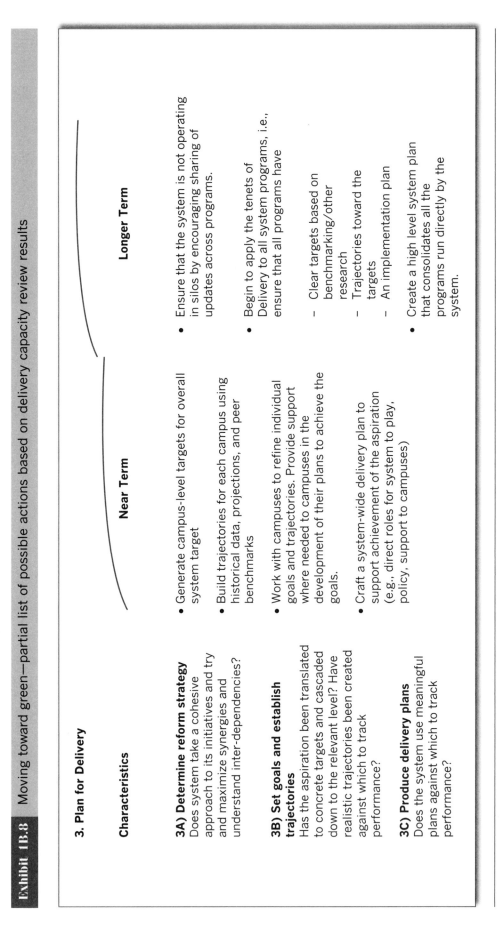

3. Plan for Delivery

Characteristics	Near Term	Longer Term
3A) Determine reform strategy Does system take a cohesive approach to its initiatives and try and maximize synergies and understand inter-dependencies?	• Generate campus-level targets for overall system target • Build trajectories for each campus using historical data, projections, and peer benchmarks	• Ensure that the system is not operating in silos by encouraging sharing of updates across programs.
3B) Set goals and establish trajectories Has the aspiration been translated to concrete targets and cascaded down to the relevant level? Have realistic trajectories been created against which to track performance?	• Work with campuses to refine individual goals and trajectories. Provide support where needed to campuses in the development of their plans to achieve the goals.	• Begin to apply the tenets of Delivery to all system programs, i.e., ensure that all programs have – Clear targets based on benchmarking/other research – Trajectories toward the targets – An implementation plan
3C) Produce delivery plans Does the system use meaningful plans against which to track performance?	• Craft a system-wide delivery plan to support achievement of the aspiration (e.g., direct roles for system to play, policy, support to campuses)	• Create a high level system plan that consolidates all the programs run directly by the system.

SOURCE: Higher education system.

Step 3: Organize your delivery effort to improve capacity

Your delivery capacity review will yield insights for improving your capacity to deliver throughout the lifetime of your delivery effort. The review may have implications for the design choices that you make in setting up your Delivery Unit (for more, see Module 1C).

- **Staff selection.** You may choose to recruit Delivery Unit staff from the departments or local units where delivery activities are strongest. For example, if a strong system of performance routines is already in place, you may want to recruit some of the people responsible for these routines to work in your Delivery Unit.
- **Functional capability.** Your delivery capacity review will help you understand where you can take advantage of existing capabilities to support your Unit's work. It will also tell you which capabilities your Delivery Unit will need to develop on its own. The most obvious example of this is data: Some Delivery Units will need to build in-house data capability, while others with sufficient infrastructure will merely need to share resources from that infrastructure.

Second, your delivery capacity review will have implications for where your Delivery Unit should focus its energy. Depending on the existence and strength of your system's existing delivery activities, your Unit may be called upon to emphasize some activities in this field guide over others. For example, your Delivery Unit may discover that your system does a poor job of understanding its own performance and the underlying causes of performance, in which case it will need to focus on modules 2A and 2B in this field guide. On the other hand, your Unit may find that your system's reform strategy is coherent, balanced, and fit for purpose. In such cases, the delivery capacity review group may choose to work with your leadership team to ensure that your strategy is aligned with their analysis of performance and with the goals and trajectories that they help you set (Module 3B), but they will not focus heavily on the substance of the strategy itself (Module 3A). Because time is of the essence and resources are limited, the delivery activity triage that the delivery capacity review provides will help you deploy your Delivery Unit for maximum effectiveness.

Conclusion

By now, you have learned

- What delivery capacity is and why it is important;
- How to map the landscape of your system; and
- How to conduct a delivery capacity review, and how to use its results to strengthen your delivery effort.

With a thorough understanding of your system's delivery capacity, you and your Delivery Unit will have gained vital insight for the work to come. You will know which delivery activities are strong and should be built upon, and where the Delivery Unit will need to focus its energy to ensure that progress is made. With this knowledge in hand, you are ready to build your Delivery Unit.

1C. BUILD THE DELIVERY UNIT

> *"Who is the person . . . who spends most of his/her time on the priority and has sleepless nights, worrying about hitting the targets?"*
>
> —*Instruction to Deliver* (106)

Most systems espouse "accountability" or "performance management," and create chief performance officers and other similarly titled positions for the purpose of getting things done. On a deeper level, however, the commitment to action can be wanting. This is often because delivery has not been understood in all its complexity. As defined in this field guide, delivery is an integrated set of tools and activities that work together to improve performance such that the whole is greater than the sum of the parts. Many systems have adopted the parts, but few have created the whole. Moreover, the parts are often implemented with poor fidelity to the guiding principles of delivery. The Delivery Unit is created to ensure that delivery is achieved in accordance to the guiding principles and is the driving force of delivery. Simply defined, a Delivery Unit is the person or group responsible for driving the achievement of system aspirations, no matter what.

During his tenure as U.K. prime minister, Tony Blair established the Prime Minister's Delivery Unit (PMDU) on a simple theory of change: A small, flexible, highly capable team, with the system leader's backing and the latitude to operate outside the line management chain, can exercise meaningful influence over the activities of that system, no matter how vast its bureaucracy. The PMDU demonstrated its adherence to this principle with the *leverage ratio,* which compared the money spent on the Delivery Unit with the money spent on the public services that the unit influenced. The ratio the PMDU achieved turned out to be about 1:50,000.

While there may be other effective paradigms for driving delivery, this field guide proceeds from the same theory of change that motivated the PMDU. The key to efficient delivery of aspirations lies in the design, organization, and development of a Delivery Unit whose influence and leverage is maximized. A Delivery Unit has an internal mandate for urgent and visible action. Delivery Unit staff monitor and challenge progress, attending both to information and people to make sure that results are on track.

A Delivery Unit should not be confused with *system actors,* the people and organizations in your system who hold direct responsibility for implementation of system activities. One of the most important principles of Delivery Unit design is that the unit should be outside the line management structure of the system and report directly to the system leader. Rather than exerting its own authority, the Delivery Unit acts as an amplifier of the system leader's authority over the actors in the system, providing a careful balance of support and challenge to those who are responsible for implementation.

To do this credibly, a Delivery Unit must be a highly capable organization with a strong culture. The system leader must understand the benefits of investing small but significant resources to build a Delivery Unit that is up to this standard and be well aware of the risks of failing to do so.

This module contains instructions for setting up, organizing, and developing a Delivery Unit to the highest standards. In addition to outlining design principles and ways to organize a unit's activities, the module also introduces the equally important principles for developing the unit's *culture of delivery.* As we will see in Chapter 5, the presence of this culture in the Delivery Unit is the key to the leverage it exerts over the system and so ultimately to its success.

ROLES OF SYSTEM LEADER AND DELIVERY LEADER

The system leader's role is to recruit and hire the most talented delivery leader he can find and work with him or her to build the Delivery Unit. The system leader must also make crucial design choices about the Delivery Unit—in particular, its location in the system as a whole and the resources (both human and financial) that are devoted to it. As the delivery leader, your role will be to advise the system leader on some of these choices, to organize the Delivery Unit's work, and to build its culture.

PROCESS STEPS

Step 1: Design the Delivery Unit
Step 2: Organize the Delivery Unit
Step 3: Build the Delivery Unit's capacity and culture

Step 1: Design the Delivery Unit

Delivery Units will take different forms in different system contexts. In small or resource-constrained systems, there may not even be an official "Delivery Unit," and only one full-time staff person might be designated. In some systems, the unit may have a different name. In Los Angeles, the Delivery Unit was called the Performance Management Unit. While the name and size of Delivery Units may vary, roles and functions need to be clear.

A few principles are always relevant to Delivery Unit design.

WHAT'S IN A NAME? WHY THE LOS ANGELES PERFORMANCE MANAGEMENT UNIT IS NOT A DELIVERY UNIT

"The Mayor was so taken with the whole notion of performance management as a Tony Blair–tested tool and approach . . . the PMU [Performance Management Unit] grew out of this . . . I am not sure we discussed its naming thoroughly but . . . to an American ear, "delivery unit" sounds like an obstetrics ward!"

—Robin Kramer, Chief of Staff, Office of Mayor Villaraigosa, March 2005–September 2009

- **The unit should designate a full-time (or nearly full-time) delivery leader who reports directly to the system leader.** This person must have the trust of the system leader and the system leader's top team.
- **The unit should be small.** The PMDU worked with a bureaucracy that provided multiple services to over 60 million Britons, but it was never larger than around 40 people. Most systems will provide services to a smaller population and will have a much smaller Delivery Unit. Smallness has several advantages: flexibility; the ability to be selective; and, perhaps most importantly, the ability to build and maintain a cohesive culture.
- **The unit leader and staff should reside outside the system's line management hierarchy.** They should not be managed by any of the people or organizations they are trying to influence, nor should they directly manage any of these people or organizations. This will allow the unit to balance its mandate to support and to challenge, to be a "critical friend" delivering difficult messages, but to sustain trust and credibility with actors in the system.
- **The time of the delivery leader and Delivery Unit staff should be mainly—exclusively, if possible—dedicated to delivery.** This facilitates the development of a delivery culture and ensures that learning about delivery will occur at the maximum possible speed.
- **Delivery Unit staff should be drawn from among the most talented and qualified people that can be found—inside or outside the system.** There simply is no substitute for staffing a Delivery Unit with the right people: As the PMDU leader noted, "A small number of excellent people is infinitely better than a large number of ordinary people" (*Instruction to Deliver,* 64). Potential staff should be screened for five core competencies:

  - **Problem solving.** The ability to break down complex and ambiguous problems into manageable pieces and to constantly seek solutions.
  - **Relationship management.** Sensitivity, empathy, fairness, and humility.
  - **Data analysis.** Basic "numeracy," the ability to understand, interpret, and draw implications from large quantities of data. For some in the Delivery Unit, deeper proficiency may be required (e.g., use of data analysis software and tools), depending on whether this capacity exists elsewhere in the system.
  - **Feedback and coaching.** A mindset of continuous reflection on and learning from one's own experiences and those of others, and the ability to communicate these lessons in a thoughtful and specific way.
  - **A delivery mindset.** A key competency in adding value to a delivery effort. The individual must have a very strong, positive, can-do attitude to push through the many instances when delivery can be frustrating and challenging.

The decision to keep the PMDU staff small yielded a number of benefits, both in terms of internal interactions within the unit and its ability to be effective externally.

A SMALL, POTENT UNIT

"I was committed to a maximum of 49 [people], but in fact kept it at around 35 to 40. This was a happy number. We could all fit in one room so everyone could easily keep well-informed; I could personally involve myself in the appointment of every single member of staff so I could build a consistent, can-do culture and maintain quality; our budget was limited and flexibility relatively easy to achieve . . . The quality of our people became renowned across Whitehall. Once the reputation was established, good people wanted to work for us so we could constantly build and enhance the quality. This was, in turn, crucial to the relationship with Permanent Secretaries. They quickly realized that meetings with the Delivery Unit, while they might be challenging, were nearly always worthwhile." (*Instruction to Deliver,* 63)

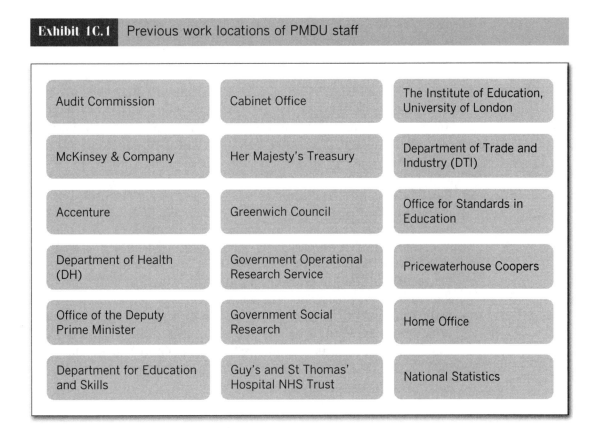

Exhibit 1C.1 below shows the experience of some of the PMDU staff prior to their employment with the PMDU. The strength of the PMDU staff came from its mix of experiences and skills, as demonstrated by the variety of both public and private employers represented. The combination of expertise made the PMDU a powerful collection of highly capable and highly knowledgeable people. Your ambition in building your Delivery Unit should be correspondingly high. Following the principles above will help ensure that your Delivery Unit is created to the highest possible standard.

Exhibit 1C.1 Previous work locations of PMDU staff

Audit Commission	Cabinet Office	The Institute of Education, University of London
McKinsey & Company	Her Majesty's Treasury	Department of Trade and Industry (DTI)
Accenture	Greenwich Council	Office for Standards in Education
Department of Health (DH)	Government Operational Research Service	Pricewaterhouse Coopers
Office of the Deputy Prime Minister	Government Social Research	Home Office
Department for Education and Skills	Guy's and St Thomas' Hospital NHS Trust	National Statistics

CASE EXAMPLE

Delivery Units and finance functions: A critical relationship

There is often confusion when it comes to the relationship between the Delivery Unit and the finance function (treasury, department of finance, or other such agency) in a system. Finance functions often play the role of demanding results for the money they allocate; if you are not careful, the finance function could see your Delivery Unit as an agency competing for turf, as an additional lobbying force for money for favored programs, or—worse—as irrelevant.

The PMDU solved this problem by building its system of targets on the Public Service Agreement (PSA) system that the U.K. Treasury Department had established. In essence, the Delivery Unit adopted a subset of the PSA targets, which represented agreements between the Treasury and relevant departments that they would reach a certain level of performance based on the money spent. This allowed the PMDU to focus on helping the departments to achieve these targets, knowing that they were already subject to this agreement and should (at least in theory) have sufficient funds to be successful. The Treasury came to see the PMDU as a helpful ally, even giving the PMDU much sought-after office space in its building in the later years of Tony Blair's second term.

Step 2: Organize the Delivery Unit

Once your Delivery Unit has been created with the right responsibilities and the right people, you can begin the task of organizing it. The key consideration in Delivery Unit organization is how will Delivery Unit staff interact with your system? In particular, how will your Delivery Unit staff organize themselves regularly to serve and oversee the various departments (or other similar organizations) responsible for implementing system activities? In general, Delivery Unit staff should organize to interact with these departments in a way that ensures the following:

- **Continuity in the relationship between the Delivery Unit and the departments being overseen.** This might take the form of a single point of contact or "account manager," perhaps even to the point where a Delivery Unit staff member is embedded in, drawn from, or shared with the unit being overseen. Continuity is important both for the quality of the relationship and for the expertise of the Delivery Unit with respect to the departments it serves.
- **Objectivity of the Delivery Unit staff with respect to the departments they oversee.** This principle is in tension with the first, as discontinuity (e.g., rotation to different departments) helps to mitigate the risk that Delivery Unit staff "go native" with respect to the departments they oversee.

- **Sufficient skill and scope—both in data analytics and problem solving—to meet the needs of the departments being overseen.** If capacity needs change rapidly over time, this might imply a need for ongoing flexibility in the allocation of capacity.
- **Multiple perspectives in every decision.** Because so many of the Delivery Unit's judgments are qualitative, they are of higher quality when pressure tested by multiple people from different backgrounds. This implies that the Delivery Unit should work in teams—or at least temporary groups—to solve any given problem.

Exhibits 1C.2 and 1C.3 illustrate two different types of Delivery Unit organization in the PMDU, one from the earlier years and one from the later years of Tony Blair's second term as prime minister. The first is a flat, functional structure, in which a group of "account managers" are dedicated to the various departments while all other resources are essentially free floating, allocated according to need at a weekly staff meeting. This structure trades off some continuity, but delivers well on the other three principles (objectivity, skill scope, and multiple perspectives), and allows for maximum flexibility. It is particularly appropriate for the early years of a Delivery Unit, when so little is known about how capacity should ideally be arranged.

Exhibit 1C.2 Prime Minister's Delivery Unit—functional organization

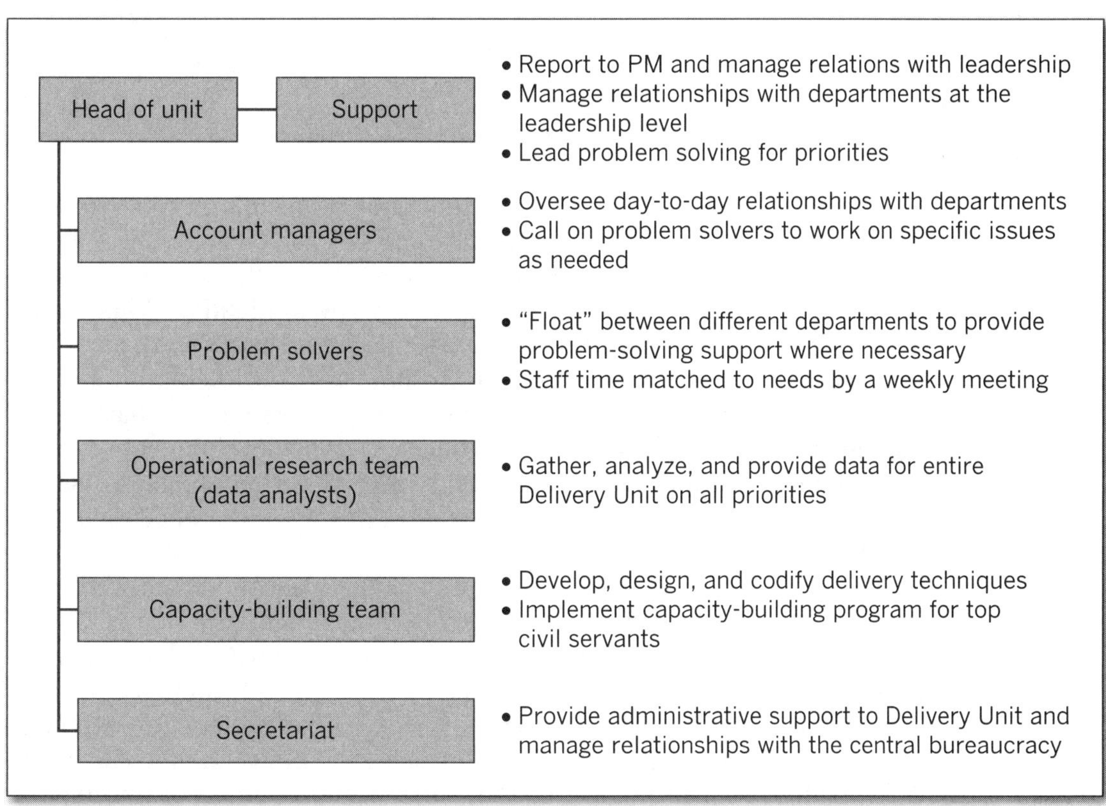

Head of unit
Support
• Report to PM and manage relations with leadership
• Manage relationships with departments at the leadership level
• Lead problem solving for priorities
Account managers
• Oversee day-to-day relationships with departments
• Call on problem solvers to work on specific issues as needed
Problem solvers
• "Float" between different departments to provide problem-solving support where necessary
• Staff time matched to needs by a weekly meeting
Operational research team (data analysts)
• Gather, analyze, and provide data for entire Delivery Unit on all priorities
Capacity-building team
• Develop, design, and codify delivery techniques
• Implement capacity-building program for top civil servants
Secretariat
• Provide administrative support to Delivery Unit and manage relationships with the central bureaucracy

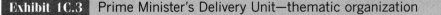

Exhibit 1C.3 Prime Minister's Delivery Unit—thematic organization

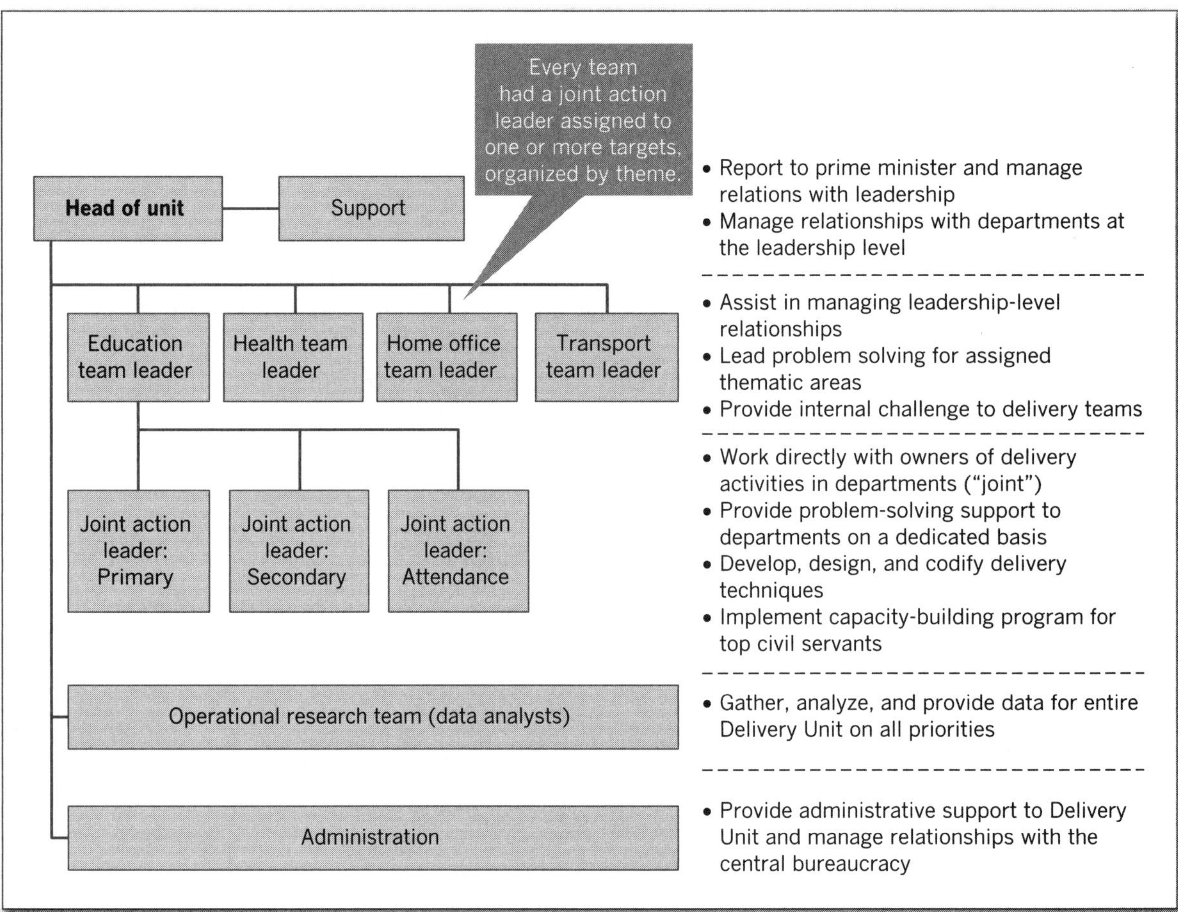
Every team had a joint action leader assigned to one or more targets, organized by theme.
Head of unit
Support
Education team leader
Health team leader
Home office team leader
Transport team leader
Joint action leader: Primary
Joint action leader: Secondary
Joint action leader: Attendance
Operational research team (data analysts)
Administration
• Report to prime minister and manage relations with leadership
• Manage relationships with departments at the leadership level
• Assist in managing leadership-level relationships
• Lead problem solving for assigned thematic areas
• Provide internal challenge to delivery teams
• Work directly with owners of delivery activities in departments ("joint")
• Provide problem-solving support to departments on a dedicated basis
• Develop, design, and codify delivery techniques
• Implement capacity-building program for top civil servants
• Gather, analyze, and provide data for entire Delivery Unit on all priorities
• Provide administrative support to Delivery Unit and manage relationships with the central bureaucracy

The second structure uses teams that are organized according to broad themes. The senior managers handle interactions and provide internal problem solving to the team as a whole. Each thematic team is then broken into subthemed teams, headed by a "joint action leader." This person works with counterparts within the system—often the delivery plan owners (see Module 3C) whose targets are linked to the thematic area—to ensure progress. Crossteam units handle administration and data analysis. This arrangement prioritizes continuity and the development of expertise and may be appropriate if credibility with departments is an issue or when a unit has a mature staff with wide exposure and a good depth and breadth of skills.

It is sometimes useful to articulate the interaction model between your Delivery Unit and your system in more detail. Exhibits 1C.4 and 1C.5 were created by the PMDU to explain its interaction model with relevant departments as well as the role of joint action leaders. The interaction model not only details how interaction would occur (e.g., via challenge meetings or delivery reviews) but also the level at which each interaction would occur. This painted a clear picture of the relative importance of each type of interaction and also set expectations for interaction on both sides.

The Delivery Unit they built was organized in the following way:

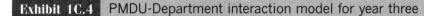

Exhibit 1C.4 PMDU-Department interaction model for year three

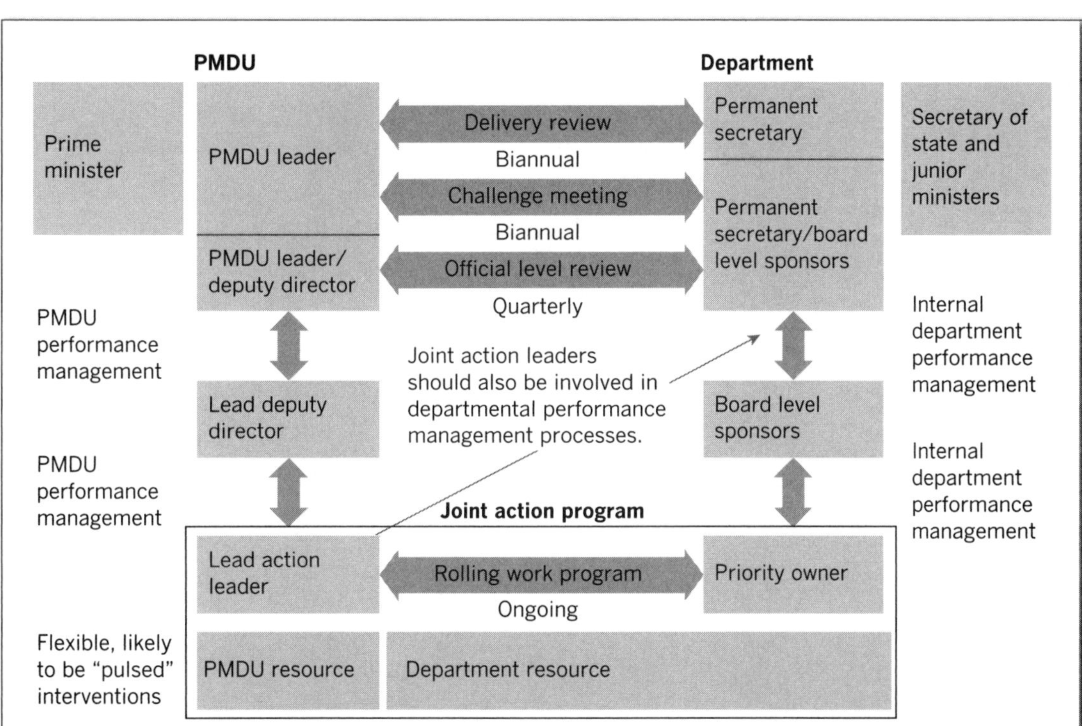

CASE EXAMPLE

Setting up a Delivery Unit in a higher education system

The Louisiana Board of Regents (LBR) Commissioner formed a Delivery Unit as part of her system's participation in the Access to Success initiative of the Education Trust and the National Association of System Heads. She set a target with multiple dimensions: to produce 10,000 more graduates per year by 2015 and to do so while cutting in half the gaps in college access and graduation rates that separate under-represented minorities and low-income students from their peers.

The LBR's role—a coordinating board with oversight of four different state university systems—posed a unique challenge in the construction of a Delivery Unit. For a time, the team constructing the Delivery Unit deliberated over whether a system-level Delivery Unit was appropriate at all. However, in the end, they decided to construct a Delivery Unit at the LBR level. This decision was driven by an underlying and simple tenet of deliverology: *You should not set an ambitious target if you do not intend to build the capacity to deliver that target.*

Due to the LBR's small size, its Delivery Unit consists of two people, including a delivery leader who dedicates 50% of his time to the effort. Because of the importance of the four constituent systems as drivers of delivery, the LBR Delivery Unit is setting itself up to train each separate system office to implement delivery efforts of their own.

Exhibit 1C.5 How the Joint Action program fits in to the PMDU model

Joint action program

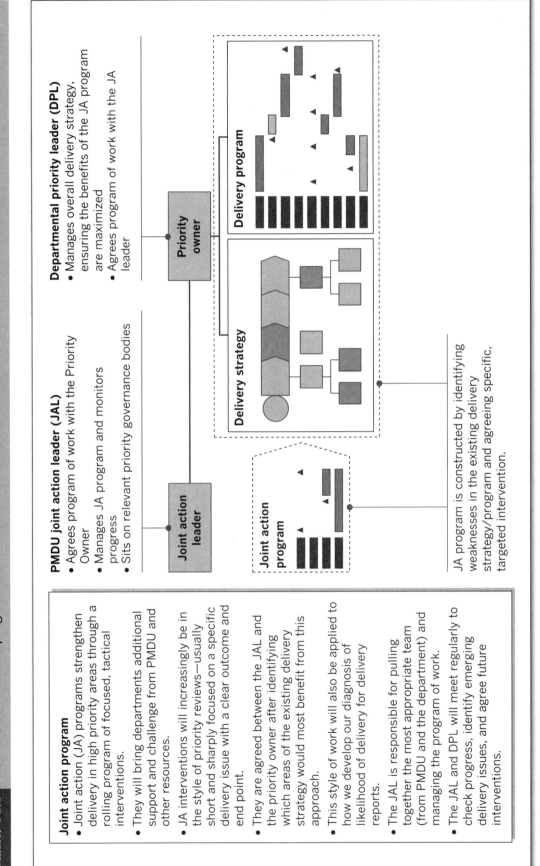

- Joint action (JA) programs strengthen delivery in high priority areas through a rolling program of focused, tactical interventions.
- They will bring departments additional support and challenge from PMDU and other resources.
- JA interventions will increasingly be in the style of priority reviews—usually short and sharply focused on a specific delivery issue with a clear outcome and end point.
- They are agreed between the JAL and the priority owner after identifying which areas of the existing delivery strategy would most benefit from this approach.
- This style of work will also be applied to how we develop our diagnosis of likelihood of delivery for delivery reports.
- The JAL is responsible for pulling together the most appropriate team (from PMDU and the department) and managing the program of work.
- The JAL and DPL will meet regularly to check progress, identify emerging delivery issues, and agree future interventions.

PMDU joint action leader (JAL)

- Agrees program of work with the Priority Owner
- Manages JA program and monitors progress
- Sits on relevant priority governance bodies

Departmental priority leader (DPL)

- Manages overall delivery strategy, ensuring the benefits of the JA program are maximized
- Agrees program of work with the JA leader

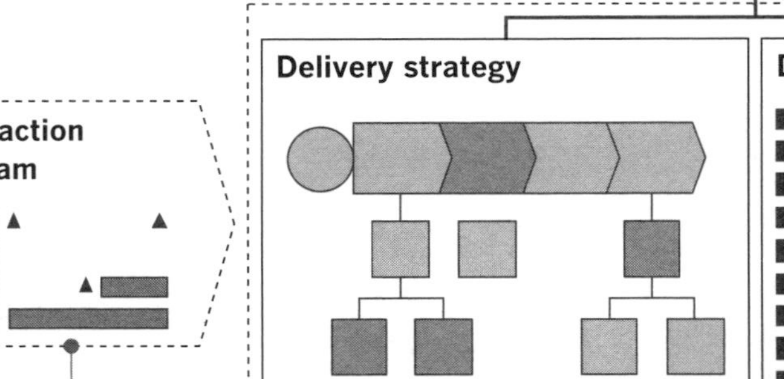

JA program is constructed by identifying weaknesses in the existing delivery strategy/program and agreeing specific, targeted intervention.

Exhibit 1C.6 K-12 Delivery Unit structure—single target, four programs overseen

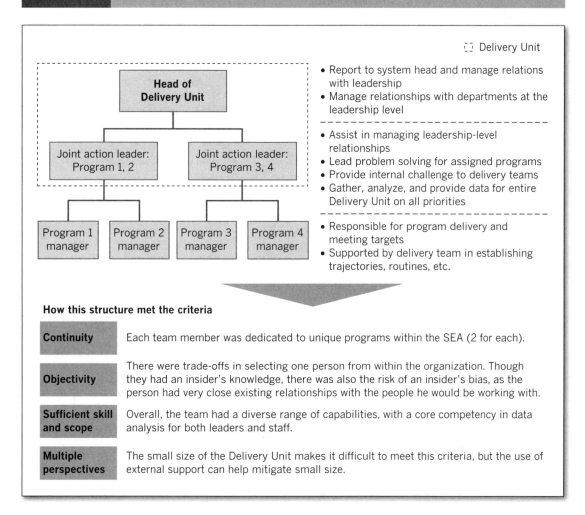

How this structure met the criteria

Criterion	
Continuity	Each team member was dedicated to unique programs within the SEA (2 for each).
Objectivity	There were trade-offs in selecting one person from within the organization. Though they had an insider's knowledge, there was also the risk of an insider's bias, as the person had very close existing relationships with the people he would be working with.
Sufficient skill and scope	Overall, the team had a diverse range of capabilities, with a core competency in data analysis for both leaders and staff.
Multiple perspectives	The small size of the Delivery Unit makes it difficult to meet this criteria, but the use of external support can help mitigate small size.

Step 3: Build the Delivery Unit's capacity and culture

Delivery Unit staff will learn a great deal from their day-to-day work. However, a Delivery Unit will only be credible with others in the system if it is able to learn faster about delivery than anybody else, and a Delivery Unit will only be able to spread a delivery culture if it embodies that culture so thoroughly that it serves as the white-hot source for everyone else (for more on how your Unit will spread delivery culture, see Chapter 5).

What exactly is a culture of delivery? As explained in *Instruction to Deliver,* a culture of delivery can be summarized in five words: ambition, focus, clarity, urgency, and irreversibility.

Ambition. Often, the best delivery comes about when people work back from a seemingly impossible outcome. A Delivery Unit's job is to amplify your aspiration as system leader, to make it something that is insisted on in every communication and every contact, and to stick to it no matter what the circumstances. Moreover, the Delivery Unit should constantly challenge performance and ask difficult questions, laboring to take excuses off the table when they are offered.

Exhibit 1C.7 Higher education Delivery Unit structure—coordinating board, multiple systems overseen

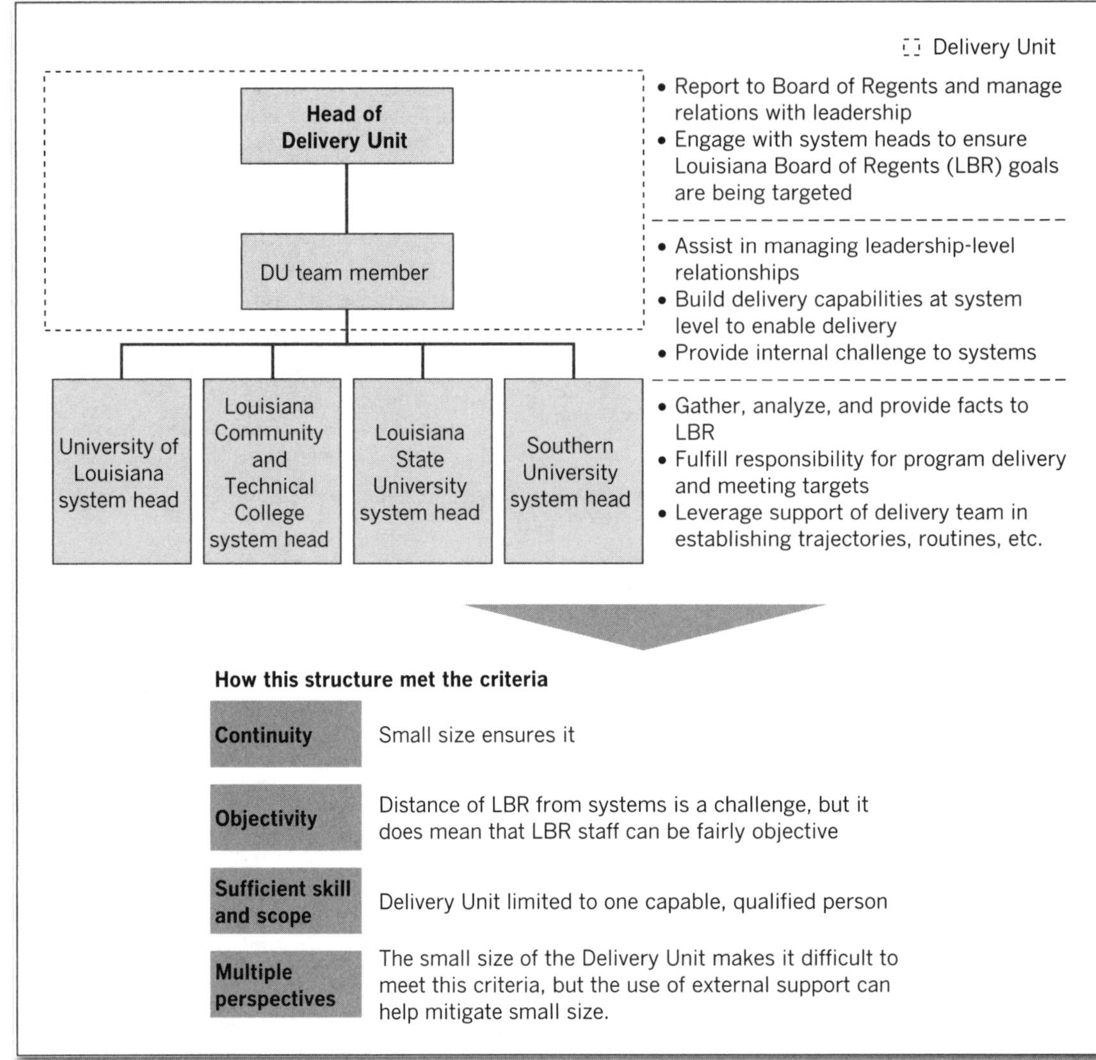
Delivery Unit
Head of Delivery Unit
DU team member
University of Louisiana system head
Louisiana Community and Technical College system head
Louisiana State University system head
Southern University system head
• Report to Board of Regents and manage relations with leadership
• Engage with system heads to ensure Louisiana Board of Regents (LBR) goals are being targeted
• Assist in managing leadership-level relationships
• Build delivery capabilities at system level to enable delivery
• Provide internal challenge to systems
• Gather, analyze, and provide facts to LBR
• Fulfill responsibility for program delivery and meeting targets
• Leverage support of delivery team in establishing trajectories, routines, etc.
How this structure met the criteria
Continuity
Small size ensures it
Objectivity
Distance of LBR from systems is a challenge, but it does mean that LBR staff can be fairly objective
Sufficient skill and scope
Delivery Unit limited to one capable, qualified person
Multiple perspectives
The small size of the Delivery Unit makes it difficult to meet this criteria, but the use of external support can help mitigate small size.

THE CONSTANT PERFORMANCE CHALLENGE

"In a change programme as dramatic as the one needed here, 'Someone,' as I put it to my staff in my farewell note, 'has to be the unreasonable one.' If you once start accepting the excuses, however plausible, it is a slippery slope. As I look back on four years in the Delivery Unit, I regret a number of cases of giving a department the benefit of the doubt; I can't remember a single case of regretting being too tough." (*Instruction to Deliver,* 154).

"I spent hours trying to understand why health waiting times and the waiting list were not falling as fast as they should have been. I debated with the Home Office their complacency over the burglary figures—yes, they were falling, but they had not fallen far enough to make people feel that crime was low, as had happened in New York City. And with my team, we challenged the Department for Education to strengthen its plan for education in London." (*Instruction to Deliver,* 177)

Focus. Delivery requires sustained prioritization. It demands consistent focus on a narrow set of targets and the data that show what progress is being made. But the targets, however good, and the data, however clear, are only imperfect representations of something even more important—that is, the real-world outcomes that matter to citizens. The central focus should therefore be on the consistent application of solutions that work. "So much of human progress is based on the systematic application of simple truths." (*Instruction to Deliver,* 286).

Clarity. Above all, clarity about the diagnosis is needed. What is the problem? Why have attempts to solve it failed? What do we know about the causal relationships? How secure is our knowledge of the problem? The Delivery Unit must be supremely committed to acting based on facts and evidence, and communicating judgments objectively, transparently, and clearly. The Delivery Unit staff seeks out facts from every source—from the front line, performance data, or a global search for internal and external best practices around the country and the world.

Urgency. Delivery can be described as "gentle pressure, relentlessly applied" (*Instruction to Deliver,* 119). Though a Delivery Unit should wield its authority with humility and acknowledge competing priorities and unexpected situations (especially as relates to the time of the system leader and actors in the system), it should also consistently push for faster progress, knowing full well that the bias of any system is in the other direction. In addition, the Delivery Unit should be thoroughly grounded in the moral purpose of the delivery effort, acting, in a very real sense, as the conscience of the bureaucracy.

URGENCY WITH A MORAL PURPOSE

"When I told a senior official in the Department that I had been shocked to discover so many people died every year of infections caught in hospital, he shrugged and said, 'hospitals are dangerous places; 5000 people have died in this way every year for many years.' It was one of many examples I came across of passive (and immoral) acceptance of the unacceptable. How many lives might have been saved if top officials had demanded the problem be tackled without waiting to be asked? How much better might our public services have become if a restless search for improvement was a firmly established part of civil service culture?" (*Instruction to Deliver,* 231)

Irreversibility. This most challenging concept gets at the idea that success must be sustained and seen through. How can the changes be made to stick? Irreversibility means not being satisfied merely with an improvement in outcomes but asking whether the structures and culture are in place that will guarantee the right trajectory of results for the foreseeable future. Irreversibility means not yielding to the temptation of complacency or celebrating success too early. It is structure and incentives changed, leadership transformed, culture shifted, visible results achieved, and credibility established.

As these five words make clear, delivery is much more than a series of activities; it is fundamentally a state of mind, one that must be inculcated deeply in you and your Delivery Unit staff if the system is to succeed.

THE PMDU'S FIVE QUESTIONS

"There are thousands of people in government bureaucracies whose job it is to complicate matters . . . To get anything done, a countervailing force is required; people who will simplify, keep bringing people back to the fundamentals:

- What are you trying to do?
- How are you trying to do it?
- How do you know you are succeeding?
- If you're not succeeding, how will you change things?
- How can we help you?

These five simple questions became the essence of the Delivery Unit. The secret lay in asking them calmly and persistently." (*Instruction to Deliver,* 73)

A concrete example of how this culture might play out is given in the sample "contract" in Exhibit 1C.8, which describes, to a department that will be working with the Delivery Unit, what they can expect the Delivery Unit to do, and what they can expect it not to do. Module 5C explains more about how the PMDU used this contract to build positive relationships within the system.

Exhibit 1C.8 The Delivery Unit "contract" with the actors in the system it serves

Ambition	Focus	Clarity	Urgency	Irreversibility

The unit will	**The unit will not**
• Keep the system leader well informed • Consistently pursue key priorities • Use data and evidence • Be plain speaking • Identify problems early • Use imaginative problem solving • Learn from and spread best practices • Recognize differences and similarities between departments • Build capacity • Simplify things • Focus on action and urgency • Ask the important questions • Make heroes of people who deliver • Champion the belief that it can be done	• Be just another committee or task force • Be burdensome and bureaucratic • Distract people from their key tasks • Take the credit for delivery that belongs to others • Get in the way of delivery • Micromanage • Offer opinion without evidence • Have a short-term outlook • Change the goalposts

How should you go about building this kind of culture in your Delivery Unit? Your Delivery Unit's culture, along with the structures, resources and competencies described above, are all components of your Delivery Unit's *capacity* (not to be confused with your system's delivery capacity, as defined in Module 1B, Review the current state of delivery). Throughout delivery efforts, your Unit should be concerned with building this kind of capacity and spreading it to the actors in the system. This topic is explored in more detail in Module 5A, Build capacity all the time.

Delivery culture will not come easily. Even with the best people organized in the most optimal way, you should still recognize the time, energy, and resources required to build this culture in your Unit. The quality of your system's culture will be largely determined by the quality of your Delivery Unit's culture.

Conclusion

By now, you have learned the following aspects of Delivery Unit construction:

- How to build and design a high-performing Delivery Unit;
- How to organize a Delivery Unit to suit a system's needs; and
- The five key words of delivery, and their centrality to delivery culture

With the right design, the right people, the right organization, and the right culture, a Delivery Unit can be a system's greatest asset. A high-quality Delivery Unit will manage the delivery effort both by managing the delivery activities (outlined in the next three chapters) and by disseminating the delivery culture that will ultimately make change irreversible. With your Delivery Unit in place, you can now turn to building the coalition for the delivery effort.

1D. ESTABLISH A GUIDING COALITION ■

"Never doubt that a small group of thoughtful, committed people can change the world. Indeed, it is the only thing that ever has."

—Margaret Mead

Your Delivery Unit can be a powerful catalyst for change. Its success in driving this change will depend in part on the quality of its work, the strength of its culture, and the quality of its relationships. However, success will also depend on leadership—specifically, the alignment of crucial leaders behind your delivery effort and the aspirations it supports.

One or two people, even in powerful positions, will always struggle to achieve dramatic change. But seven people in key positions who agree profoundly about what they want to do and how they want to do it can change the world. This is what John Kotter calls a *guiding coalition.*

A guiding coalition is not a steering committee or a formal decision-making body, nor is it a leadership team. Fundamentally, a guiding coalition is the group of people that enables the pursuit of your system's aspirations by (1) removing bureaucratic barriers to change, (2) using their influence to support your Unit's work at crucial moments, and (3) giving you counsel and guidance in your efforts. They are a subset of influential people in the system who are capable of making a big difference if they act in concert. They are a sounding board for your system leader and for you, and their opinions will likely guide and shape many of the decisions that you make.

The coalition itself may not be formal, and their structure depends on how you and the system leader would like to structure it, as well as the preferences of the guiding coalition members. Exhibit 1D.1 is an example of different levels of formality in guiding coalitions.

Lastly, as demonstrated in Exhibit 1D.2, guiding coalition members are the first core supporters in what will become a much larger effort to align people and organizations around the aspirations that your delivery effort supports, widening the "circles of leadership" of your delivery effort all the way to users and the public. For more on your Unit's role in this broader effort, see Chapter 5.

Guiding coalitions are helpful in ensuring the success of any delivery effort. This module will describe the characteristics of an effective guiding coalition, as well as some simple tools and tactics for identifying and building one.

Exhibit 1D.1 Guiding coalitions can succeed either as informal networks or formally coordinated teams

Degree of formality

Informal network → Coordinated team

	San Jose Unified School District	Ontario Ministry of Education
Case example	• System chief Linda Murray made special effort to bring leader of teachers' union into guiding coalition. – Weekly one-on-one meetings built a strong relationship and earned union head's support for aspirations. • She made parallel investments with other stakeholders.	• Minister of Education Gerard Kennedy planned a sustained series of formal and informal meetings with a range of stakeholders. • Guiding coalition members developed, assessed, and refined execution and communication plans and met regularly with Premier Dalton McGuinty.
Benefits	• Win critics' support for aspirations by listening and responding to concerns	• Present a unified front • Use coordinated team to generate momentum
Drawbacks	• Ensure that delivery effort does not become too fragmented or uncoordinated	• Ensure that coalition does not create cumbersome new processes or slow down delivery

SOURCE: Interviews.

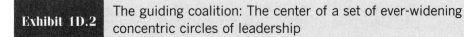

Exhibit 1D.2 The guiding coalition: The center of a set of ever-widening concentric circles of leadership

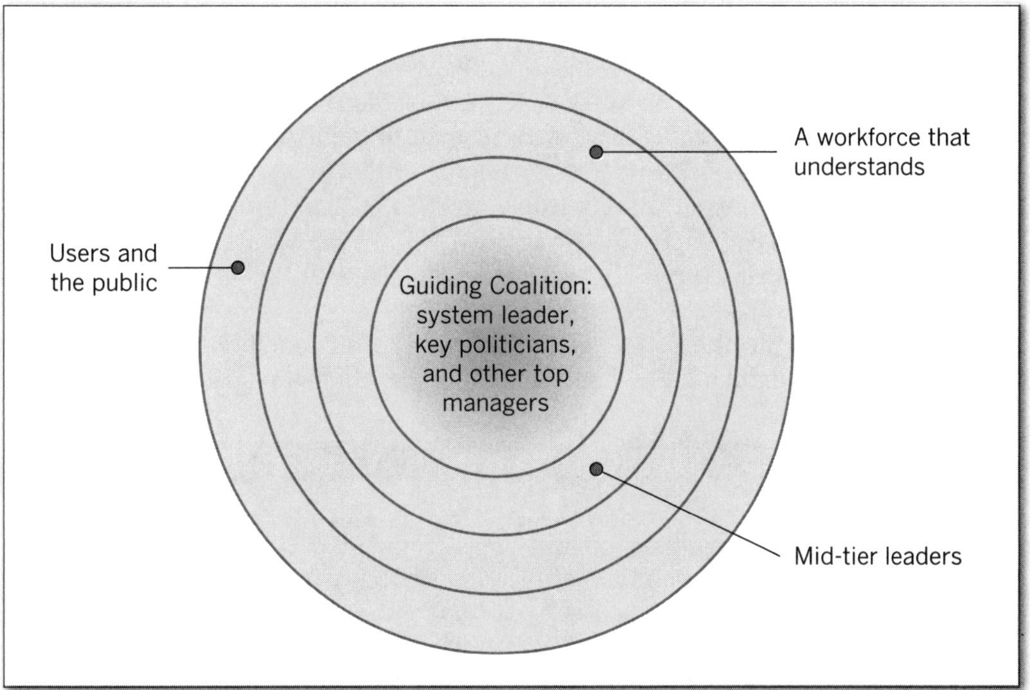

ROLES OF SYSTEM LEADER AND DELIVERY LEADER

The system leader must play a very large role in building and aligning a guiding coalition around the aspirations that your Delivery Unit supports. As delivery leader, your role will be to identify the guiding coalition members that are needed and to support the system leader in building the necessary alignment among them. You will need to cultivate relationships with these members and help the system leader do the same.

PROCESS STEPS

Step 1: Identify a potential guiding coalition for each aspiration

Step 2: Build trust and alignment among guiding coalition members

Step 1: Identify a potential guiding coalition for each aspiration

While choosing a guiding coalition is not a formal (or even a publicly known) process, it still requires careful and deliberate thought on your part and on the part of the system leader. For each aspiration, start by identifying potential members: Who are the 20 people with the most power to affect your system's work with respect to that aspiration? This power can take any of the following forms:

- **Leadership.** Responsibility for strategy and/or policy relevant to the aspiration
- **Management.** Overseeing the planning and/or implementation of system activities relevant to the aspiration
- **Position power.** Other constitutional, statutory, or regulatory authority over affairs relevant to the aspiration
- **Expertise.** Deep knowledge of the major issues involved and/or your system's existing work with respect to the aspiration
- **Credibility.** Respect from and/or authority over a critical mass of people in your system whose work is critical to the aspiration

In identifying these 20 individuals, look back at the list of system actors that you developed as part of Module 1B.

In the U.K., the PMDU leader thoughtfully made note of the leaders who were most influential and sought to build relationships with them.

GUIDING COALITIONS IN THE PMDU

"In government [building a guiding coalition] is not so much a question of management teams as of securing committed (and of course talented) people in the seven to ten key positions that influence policy and implementation—for example, the Secretary of State, the relevant Minister of State, the Permanent Secretary, key civil servants, the Political Adviser, the No. 10 Policy Directorate staff member, the head of the relevant inspectorate . . . or the equivalent." (*Instruction to Deliver,* 237)

Some typical sources for guiding coalition members in K–12 and higher education are listed in Exhibit 1D.3.

Exhibit 1D.3 Typical sources of guiding coalition members

K–12	Higher education
• Governor's office (particularly K–12 education advisers) • Legislature (particularly crucial committee chairs or their advisers) • Office of the Secretary of Education • State Board of Education • Department of Education (specific staff may depend on specific aspiration) • Unions, including teachers and administrators • School boards association • Superintendents of largest 10 districts	• Governor's office (particularly higher education advisers) • Legislature (particularly crucial committee chairs or their advisers) • Higher education governing board • System office (specific staff may depend on specific aspiration) • Unions and/or faculty senates • Campus presidents or chancellors

Once you have identified these potential members, you can whittle the list down by excluding those who would be unlikely ever to support the system aspiration. This is not to say that there should be no disagreement among the members of your guiding coalition; in fact, often guiding coalition members will not start out in full agreement with you, and part of the purpose of the coalition is to build that agreement (see Step 2). However, nearly every system will feature powerful people who are so recalcitrant in their opposition to your aspiration that you will have no choice but to work around them. If you include them in your guiding coalition, you run the risk of poisoning your delivery effort.

In one K–12 SEA, for example, the appropriations committee chair in one house of the legislature was a strong proponent of a bill that would create a "career diploma" as an alternative to the college and career-ready diploma the state had in place—effectively lowering standards by offering students a way out of the tougher requirements. Though this person clearly had position power, he would have been an unsuitable member of a guiding coalition to improve college and career-ready graduation rates.

From those potential members who remain on your list, you can now select the group of roughly 7 to 10 people in whom you will invest. To do this, you will want to go beyond the individual characteristics of each person and ask about the characteristics of potential groups. Use the following criteria.

- **Diversity.** Is the group influential in relevant but varying circles? If your guiding coalition only has a limited influence sphere, you risk not reaching all parties you need in order to be successful.
- **Balance.** Does the group balance the different types of power? A combination of leadership, management, position power, expertise, and credibility is essential.
- **Potential to work together.** To the extent they are called upon to act in concert, is there a potential in this group to build collective agreement and commitment to the aspiration and (eventually) the strategy behind it? Are there any relationships between potential group members that could cause trouble?

Finally, once you have identified a potential guiding coalition for each aspiration, you will want to check for overlap. For multiple aspirations that are very similar (e.g., aspirations all within the field of education), you may find that the guiding coalition is more or less the same group.

Exhibit 1D.4 K–12 example: Potential guiding coalition members

Aspiration: Ensure that students graduate from the system college and career-ready						
		Criteria to maximize		Criteria to balance and diversify		Other considerations
Person	**Alignment with aspiration**	**Potential for alignment with aspiration**	**Relative power**	**Type of power**	**Sphere of influence**	**Potential for difficulty with others**
Governor's education adviser	Low (lack of awareness)	High	High	Position	Governor's office	None

(Continued)

Exhibit 1D.4 (Continued)

Person	Alignment with aspiration	Potential for alignment with aspiration	Relative power	Type of power	Sphere of influence	Potential for difficulty with others
Senate education committee chair	Very low (staunch opposition)	Very low	Very high	Position	Legislature	Bad relationship with Chief State School Officer
Teachers' union leader	Low	High	Very high	Credibility	Teacher workforce	Somewhat suspicious of governor
Deputy Superintendent	Low (lack of trust)	High	High	Leadership	Department of Education	None

CASE EXAMPLE

A guiding coalition in higher education: Power, diversity, or both?

One higher education system identified potential members for its guiding coalition following the process laid out in Exhibit 1D.5.

Exhibit 1D.5 Process used by leadership team of a higher education system to develop a guiding coalition

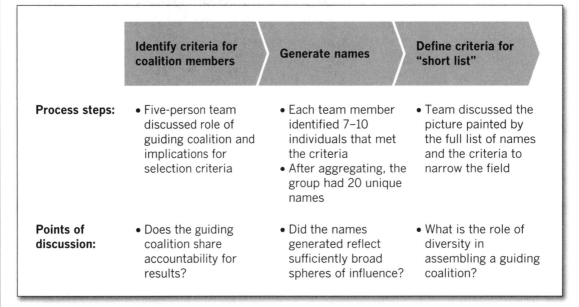

	Identify criteria for coalition members	Generate names	Define criteria for "short list"
Process steps:	• Five-person team discussed role of guiding coalition and implications for selection criteria	• Each team member identified 7–10 individuals that met the criteria • After aggregating, the group had 20 unique names	• Team discussed the picture painted by the full list of names and the criteria to narrow the field
Points of discussion:	• Does the guiding coalition share accountability for results?	• Did the names generated reflect sufficiently broad spheres of influence?	• What is the role of diversity in assembling a guiding coalition?

This higher education system relied on a group of leaders to identify its guiding coalition rather than just the system leader. The points of discussion reflect some of the difficult issues that they discussed as they narrowed down their options.

Diversity was particular concern. After the group had agreed on about 20 unique names for potential members, someone remarked that the list consisted almost entirely of White men—and this in a system whose targets explicitly focused on the achievement of minority and low-income students. This sparked a challenging discussion about when the power in a system lies with a group that is not diverse. Do you opt to increase diversity in your guiding coalition at the expense of influence? Some clearly thought that this was the right thing to do while others gravitated toward a focus on influential people—whoever they were. Still others thought that it was a false choice—that there was an influence associated with diversity that simply was not reflected in the group's exercise.

When you construct your guiding coalition, you may face similar issues. The right answer for you will depend on your objectives for the coalition as well as the extent to which its work is public.

While your responsibility as delivery leader is to ensure that these guiding coalitions exist, the coalition building must be led (even if under your heavy advisement) by the system leader even if he or she relies on a group of leaders to come to the final coalition.

Step 2: Build trust and alignment among guiding coalition members

Once you have identified the right group of people, the next step is to build this group into a true guiding coalition. This will rarely warrant a formal invitation or announcement; rather, you must develop a specific strategy for reaching out to and aligning people who may have disparate backgrounds and views (again, the template you filled out in Step 1 will be a helpful starting point as you build this strategy). You will be successful if the members of your guiding coalition:

- Share your system's aspirations;
- Share your values; and
- Share your strategy for achieving the aspiration (see Module 3A, Determine your reform strategy) and approach to delivery.

For the most part, this will require that guiding coalition members not only agree with you on each of these things but also that they play an active role in helping to shape them. To the extent that they can be involved in aspiration setting, they should be. As the time comes to craft a strategy, their input will be crucial.

The techniques for facilitating this alignment are fairly basic: interactions with guiding coalition members that include one-on-one conversations, meetings that include some or all of the members of the coalition, and one-way communications to coalition members. In some cases, a more formal gathering—such as a retreat to set aspirations or develop a strategy—may be appropriate.

As you establish meaningful connections with members of the guiding coalition, a few general relationship-building principles will be useful:

NEVER FORGETTING THE MORAL PURPOSE

"[I] made a mental note to keep asking myself the moral questions at the heart of the delivery agenda. To what extent was our work making Britain more prosperous, more equitable and more socially cohesive? I made a point of raising these issues all the time with staff, individually and collectively. I wanted to be sure we never lost sight of what our real mission was." (*Instruction to Deliver,* 146)

- **Find common ground.** Depending on the situation, you and your guiding coalition members may have a lot in common and just need to iron out the details, or you may encounter more disagreement than you expect. One thing that you may start with is the shared commitment to improve the organization and/or its core mission even if you do not yet agree on the best way to do this. As obvious as it may seem, verbalizing these commonalities will start to build relationships between people, especially if members of your coalition initially feel that their desires are in opposition to those of the majority. (For more on finding common ground, please see Module 5C.)
- **Confront opposing beliefs.** There will almost always be opposing viewpoints within your coalition, especially at first. Ignoring these issues will not resolve them. Remember that the people you have gathered have expertise in many areas and may offer perspectives that others have not considered. Be willing to name conflicts between these perspectives, walk toward them, and discuss them in the open (for more on conflict resolution, please see Module 5C). On the one hand, your system leader will play an important facilitative role here, legitimizing dissent and creating a safe space where, in internal discussions, people feel free to speak their minds. On the other hand, your system leader should also set the expectation that, once a decision is taken, members of a guiding coalition must support it publicly. Endless public debate will create problems that could potentially derail your delivery effort.
- **Build internal trust.** While alignment and commitment to the vision are important, internal trust is what will cement your coalition's success as a working team. Trust-building activities should revolve around people rather than topics. This is where creating opportunities for coalition members to get to know each other outside the work context (e.g., through a retreat) will be crucial. For more information on building trust and relationships, please see Module 5C, Unleash the "alchemy of relationships." The following examples show how different LEAs built trust amongst their key stakeholders, many of whom could be considered part of their guiding coalition.
- **Continuously return to the moral purpose.** Members will have competing priorities, differing opinions, and strong beliefs, but there will always be one common thread: their staunch belief in the moral purpose of your change. It is important to remind them of this at every opportunity, as it will continually inspire them and drive them to further help your efforts.

Building a solid relationship with members of the guiding coalition will be crucial in aiding the success of the effort. After all, the guiding coalition will only be as helpful as the strength of the relationships you have with its members. In addition, a strong guiding coalition increases the speed at which you can operate as well, because they will be able to remove barriers within the bureaucracy. Below are two case examples of successful relationships with members of the guiding coalition and the benefits that resulted.

CASE EXAMPLE

Building alignment in San Jose Unified School District

In the mid-1990s, San Jose Unified School District superintendent Linda Murray set a bold goal that every student would graduate from high school college ready. With these higher expectations came higher levels of support from the district for students and an increased emphasis on professional development for teachers.

Murray made a special effort to bring the leader of the teachers' union into her guiding coalition. Every Monday morning, Murray met with the union leader for three hours, building a close relationship that both secured her support and led to solutions benefiting teachers and students. An important outcome of this relationship was a union-created early retirement program giving some of the district's most resistant teachers an attractive way to exit. The program retired 300 teachers and created savings that were used to increase salaries for new hires, making it easier to bring reform-minded teachers into the district.

The result was higher standards, higher achievement, and higher graduation rates of college and career-ready students.

CASE EXAMPLE

In Chicago, the school system CEO worked to build a wide base of support for his controversial reforms

Arne Duncan, CEO of the Chicago Public School system from 2001 to 2008, led a controversial program to close failing schools and open new schools in their place. He faced strong opposition but managed to maintain sufficient support from the mayor and political community to legitimize his efforts.

Renaissance 2010	The opposition	Building a guiding coalition
• The plan, launched by Duncan in 2004 and signed into law by Mayor Daley, called for 100 new schools in Chicago by 2010. • As each school opened, a failing school would close. Schools were opened in a competitive process with charter, contract, and/or the public school system competing. • Schools would receive more freedom than traditional public schools in return for greater accountability.	• Opposition was loud and fierce, led by the Chicago Teachers Union (new schools were not unionized), neighborhood groups (some of whom feared gentrification), and parents (some of whom were unhappy about their children being forced to attend a new school).	• The most critical factor was the alliance between Duncan and Mayor Daley; without the other, neither could have had the legitimacy to close dozens of schools • Duncan had close ties to the Chicago Business Roundtable and cultivated the support of local leaders for political help, fundraising aid, and fostering links between education and jobs.

(Continued)

(Continued)

While a June 2009 report indicates that there is not yet sufficient outcome data to fully understand how well Renaissance 2010 schools are serving students, they have managed to achieve higher attendance rates than most other Chicago Public Schools high schools and have put in place a number of promising practices that bode well for future student achievement outcomes.

SOURCE: Humphrey, et al. (2010). *High School Reform in Chicago Public Schools: Renaissance 2010.* SRI International and The Consortium on Chicago School Research.

Finally, another means to build a guiding coalition is to work in reverse, by influencing the selection of people for key positions within the system—the types of key positions that would qualify their holders to be a part of your guiding coalition. At times, you or the system leader may have influence over who is selected to fill key positions in the system. You may, for example, have the governor's ear as she selects her top education adviser. To the extent you can, it makes sense to use this influence to push for the selection of people who are likely to be aligned with your system aspiration and eager to do something about it.

Conclusion

In this module, you have learned

- What a guiding coalition is and why it is important;
- Criteria for selecting guiding coalition members; and
- Basic principles and techniques for building alignment and trust in your guiding coalition.

An up-front investment of the system leader's time in building a guiding coalition will pay dividends down the road as your Delivery Unit embarks on its work. Your guiding coalition members will act reflexively to make things easier for you, whether in small details, such as when something comes across their desk for them to sign, or in larger matters such as statements to the press. At other times, when you have specific things you need from them, their alignment will help you to ask for what you need and obtain it easily. However, once you establish a guiding coalition, you must continue to work at maintaining it. It is very easy for members to lose touch as people get caught up in their day-to-day responsibilities, and all evidence suggests that a coalition will be temporary unless worked at constantly.

With an aspiration set, an understanding of the current state of delivery, a Delivery Unit in place, and a guiding coalition to support your aspiration, you are ready to embark on the core activities of delivery—starting by getting a better understanding of the challenges your system faces.

2

Understand the Delivery Challenge

Components of Deliverology

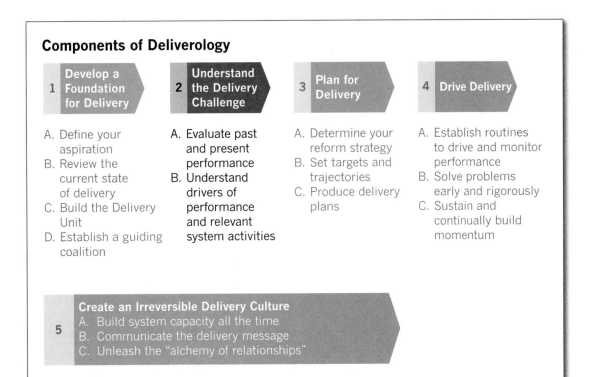

1 Develop a Foundation for Delivery
A. Define your aspiration
B. Review the current state of delivery
C. Build the Delivery Unit
D. Establish a guiding coalition

2 Understand the Delivery Challenge
A. Evaluate past and present performance
B. Understand drivers of performance and relevant system activities

3 Plan for Delivery
A. Determine your reform strategy
B. Set targets and trajectories
C. Produce delivery plans

4 Drive Delivery
A. Establish routines to drive and monitor performance
B. Solve problems early and rigorously
C. Sustain and continually build momentum

5 Create an Irreversible Delivery Culture
A. Build system capacity all the time
B. Communicate the delivery message
C. Unleash the "alchemy of relationships"

Once you have built the foundation for delivery, you will be able to drive forward the delivery effort. How will you deliver your system's aspiration? Chapters 2 and 3 will take you through the processes of translating your aspiration into a diagnosis of the barriers to achieving it, a strategy to overcome those barriers, targets to measure progress, and a plan for implementation.

Exhibit 2 gives an overview of this process and summarizes the most important relationships between the concepts that we will introduce. We will return to this "delivery pyramid" from time to time in order to clarify where we are in the process.

Chapter 2 focuses specifically on the top half of the pyramid shown in Exhibit 2. This part is about understanding *the delivery challenge:* the nature and size of the barriers that your system faces to delivery of your aspiration, and what your system is currently doing about them. Modules 2A and 2B lay out a diagnostic process that will help you understand your system's performance and its current activities, providing you with crucial information for the development of your strategy, targets, and delivery plans (discussed in Chapter 3). The two modules of Chapter 2 are

A. Evaluate past and present performance

B. Identify drivers of performance and related system activities

In some systems, particularly those with good data analysis capability, and where the patterns of underperformance are clearly understood, the process can begin at the *driver* level, which aims to understand the causes of these patterns. In other systems, the process may start at the *system activities* level, in which current system activities are identified to determine improvement measures.

2A. EVALUATE PAST AND PRESENT PERFORMANCE

"The farther backward you can look, the farther forward you can see."

—Winston Churchill

Before you can understand where you are going, you have to know where you are. Knowledge of past and present performance is critically important for understanding what your system needs in order to move toward its aspiration. In this module, you will learn to locate the data that is most indicative of performance against your aspiration and to organize and analyze this data to identify patterns in performance. It is important to remember that the data and analysis you choose to do will be driven by the system's aspiration. The patterns revealed will then help you identify the most significant barriers that the system faces with respect to achieving this aspiration. Then, you can pinpoint where change is needed.

Exhibit 2 Moving from aspiration to implementation: The delivery pyramid

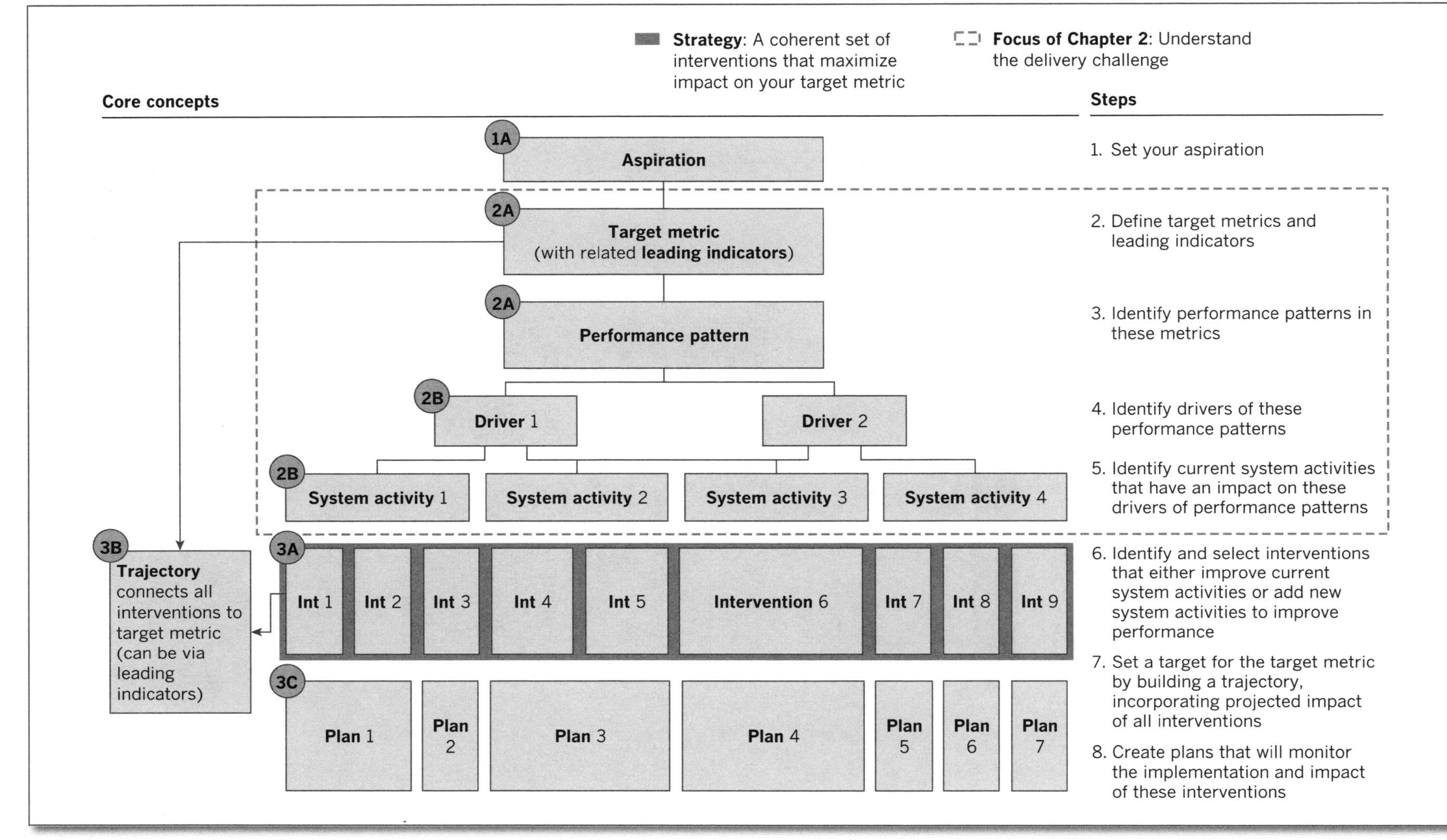

Strategy: A coherent set of interventions that maximize impact on your target metric
Focus of Chapter 2: Understand the delivery challenge
Core concepts
Steps
1A
Aspiration
2A
Target metric
(with related leading indicators)
2A
Performance pattern
2B
Driver 1
Driver 2
2B
System activity 1
System activity 2
System activity 3
System activity 4
3B
Trajectory connects all interventions to target metric (can be via leading indicators)
3A
Int 1
Int 2
Int 3
Int 4
Int 5
Intervention 6
Int 7
Int 8
Int 9
3C
Plan 1
Plan 2
Plan 3
Plan 4
Plan 5
Plan 6
Plan 7
1. Set your aspiration
2. Define target metrics and leading indicators
3. Identify performance patterns in these metrics
4. Identify drivers of these performance patterns
5. Identify current system activities that have an impact on these drivers of performance patterns
6. Identify and select interventions that either improve current system activities or add new system activities to improve performance
7. Set a target for the target metric by building a trajectory, incorporating projected impact of all interventions
8. Create plans that will monitor the implementation and impact of these interventions

ROLES OF SYSTEM LEADER AND DELIVERY LEADER

Many systems already analyze performance data extensively, and some already have a clear idea of what performance patterns exist. If your system falls into one of these categories, your Unit's role is to work with those who analyze the data to ensure that their analyses yield usable insights for system leaders. If your system exhibits weaker data capability, then your Unit will need to play a more active role in obtaining, analyzing, and interpreting relevant data, using the steps that follow. System leaders do not have a major role in this process, but because they are responsible for setting the system's overall strategic direction, they will benefit from understanding your findings and discussing implications with you on a regular basis.

PROCESS STEPS

Step 1: Determine the data most indicative of performance
Step 2: Organize available data for analysis
Step 3: Analyze the data to identify performance patterns

Step 1: Determine the data most indicative of performance

To understand your system's past and present performance, you will first need to determine what data is most indicative of performance against your aspiration. Three types of data will help you understand a system's performance against its aspiration:

- Target metrics
- Leading indicators
- Indicators of unintended consequences

Target metrics, as introduced in Module 1A, are used to measure the achievement of your system's aspiration. Target metrics exactly measure actual outcomes in the area of aspiration: In K–12 education, for example, if your aspiration is to increase the number of students graduating from high school who are ready for college and career, the associated target metric might be the college- and career-ready graduation rate (though further and more specific definition of this measurement may be required).

Leading indicators are metrics that help you predict the future performance of the target metric, either because (1) they are mathematical components of the target metric, which are reported earlier or more frequently than the target metric; or (2) when reported, they are correlated in some way to the future performance of the target metric. Most of the time, a leading indicator is so called because it "leads" the target metric and can therefore be used as an early warning for potential performance issues with respect to the target metric. Some examples:

- To graduate from college, students must complete a great number of tasks, from selecting a curriculum, to enrolling each semester, to passing their classes. Their success in these tasks can be measured and seen as a leading indicator of the graduation rate—"leading" because they can be calculated earlier.
- In K–12 education, outcomes at one grade level can predict outcomes at another. In the U.K., research (Sammons, Nuttall, Cuttance, & Thomas, 1995; Sammons, Thomas, Mortimore, 1997) found that the single most important predictor of a student's success in any high school subject was the literacy test score taken by that same student at age 11.

Exhibit 2A.1, from The Education Trust, gives an example of some of the most current thinking on leading indicators for higher education systems that are focused on access and success.

Indicators of unintended consequences measure the possible negative consequences of pursuing your aspiration, particularly when that pursuit is centered on a specific target metric. These indicators are necessary because, when a system focuses its activities on achieving a particular target, areas outside the scope of that target could be perversely affected. In

Exhibit 2A.1 Access and success: Leading indicators in higher education

Leading indicator category	Potential leading indicators
1. Early momentum: credit accumulation	• Students completing 20 or more nonremedial credits in the first year • Students achieving a 30 unit threshold in the first year • Credit accumulation in first two years of community college (leads to increased likelihood of transfer) • Withdrawal from/repetition of 20% or fewer courses
2. Summer session and continuous enrollment	• Number of summer sessions enrolled • Summer school credits earned by community college students • Number of summer credits earned by African American students
3. Successful completion of developmental/remedial education requirements	• Enrollment in and completion of first remedial course in sequence • Enrollment in subsequent courses in remedial sequence • Enrollment in college-level courses by developmental completers
4. Success in key entry level mathematics and English courses	• Completion of college-level math course in the first two years
5. Financial aid in support of full-time attendance	• Lack of sufficient funds cited by student as reason for part time attendance • Amount of grant aid • Hours worked by student
6. Dropout recovery: helping those with substantial credits return and complete a degree	• Number of students who return after dropping out

SOURCE: Based on information from Identifying Action Plan Priorities: Leading Indicators and Sample Interventions, The Education Trust, June 2009.

K–12 education, for example, a perverse indicator for an aspiration to increase graduation rates could be the dropout rate of students of higher income, a potential unintended consequence of a focus on preventing dropouts among students of lower income.

It is important to track these indicators, even if you do not believe that your effort will result in negative consequences. Tracking them can help you to ensure that your reforms are not causing any negative consequences, and they can also help you quiet the naysayers of your delivery effort who want to use the threat of unintended consequences as an excuse for inaction.

TAKING EXCUSES OFF THE TABLE

"I found that whenever a new target or goal is set, those who defend the status quo instantly explain all the unintended consequences that will ensue. With the focus on literacy and numeracy, such people predicted that the science results would go down. (They didn't—they went up because children who can read, write and do mathematics better also do better in science.) When we focused on reducing street crime in 2002, senior police predicted that, as street crime fell, burglary and car crime would inevitably rise (they didn't—they continued to fall, because good policing is good policing). So in the Delivery Unit, our reaction to all these dire predications was not to accept them at face value since they so often proved to be urban myths, but always to agree we would check. Then, if the fear proved unfounded, the urban myth would be exploded; and if it proved justified, a political choice could be made about whether it was a price worth paying." (*Instruction to Deliver,* 81)

The specific metrics that your Unit uses will depend on the nature of your system and its aspiration. Exhibit 2A.2 gives an example of how a K–12 system might select its metrics, based on an aspiration to increase students' access to institutes of higher education.

Exhibit 2A.2 Sample performance metrics for a K-12 system

Aspiration: Increase students' access to institutions of higher education		
	Questions to consider	**Example**
Target metrics	• How will you measure success? • What is the best metric for your desired outcome or outcomes?	• Graduation rate • Student enrollment rate in higher education institutions
Leading indicators	• What needs to happen in order for the target metric to move? • What factors are mathematically related to the target metric? • What factors do we know to affect performance on the target metric, according to fact-based evidence?	• SAT/ACT test-taking rate • Enrollment rates for all college and career-ready core courses • Completion of Algebra I by end of sophomore year • Percent of seniors who apply to at least one higher education institution
Indicators of unintended consequences	• In what areas could the delivery effort unintentionally have a negative impact? • What metrics can we use to identify if this is happening?	• High school drop-out rate due to increased standards • Achievement and attainment of students who do not graduate college and career ready

Step 2: Organize available data for analysis

Once you have identified the target metrics and other indicators relevant to your aspiration, several factors should determine the actual set of data you will use to understand past and present performance:

- Focus only on target metrics and leading indicators; indicators of unintended consequences will become important later, when you are monitoring progress.
- If your system has no data on the target metrics or leading indicators identified for your delivery effort, do not let this prevent you from analyzing and acting on what is available. Go ahead and conduct whatever level of performance analysis, as described below, that can be supported by the performance data you do have. The lack of data itself will then become an issue that your reform strategy must address (for more on this, see Module 3A).
- If your system has abundant data for all metrics, be economical about what you analyze, remembering that a rougher, quicker understanding of your performance is usually preferable to a more time-consuming, thorough endeavor. The best available data will have these characteristics:
    - **Relevance.** Is the data strongly related to your aspiration, either because it is a target metric, leading indicator, or closely related to one of these? Ideally, you would analyze the target metric and most relevant leading indicators.
    - **Clarity.** Is the data easy to understand?
    - **Detail.** Does the data provide enough detail for a variety of analyses?
    - **Robustness.** Has the data been measured long enough and consistently enough to allow you to identify past trends? Will it continue to be measured in the future?
    - **Acceptance.** Is the data noncontroversial and accepted by those who will need to understand and agree with your assessment of current performance?
    - **Accuracy.** Do you have confidence in the accuracy of the source, collection mechanism, and reporting mechanism for the data?

After your Unit has determined the subset of data that you will use to understand performance, you will need to organize the data for analysis. For each target metric and leading indicator you will use, you will need to make two determinations: How you will *group* the data and how you will *compare* it.

First, what *level of analysis* will you look at in the data? At the most granular level, you can look at the performance of individual people (e.g., students or teachers). Beyond that, you can look at performance units: entities such as classrooms, schools, districts, campuses, and even whole systems for which data on individual performance can be averaged and/or aggregated in some way. For example, for an indicator like "success in freshman year," performance can be measured at the level of the student, class, graduation year cohort, campus, set of campuses, and so on.

Second, how will you group this data better to understand and compare performance? You will need to group the data along the *dimensions* of comparison that will help you better understand where patterns exist. For example, suppose that you are analyzing "freshman year success rate" at the student level. You would ask, "Among which groupings of students could success in freshman year potentially be different? Ethnographic and demographic categories? Graduation year cohorts? Students in different quintiles of performance?"

Broadly speaking, you can use three types of dimensions to group this data.

- **Cases.** This is a comparison of each individual "record" of performance data at whatever level of analysis you have chosen (e.g., school by school, campus by campus, teacher by teacher). This will provide tremendous insight, but will only be possible where the number of cases is small (e.g., less than 300). For example, this dimension of analysis might be appropriate if you are trying to determine the graduation rate for each of 10 campuses in a higher education system. However, it will be inappropriate if you are trying to individually analyze the records of over 1 million students.
- **Characteristics.** Where too many cases exist for individual analysis, you may want to group your data by characteristic (e.g., locality, student demographics, urbanity, size). Several K–12 districts group their schools according to the relative concentration of economic disadvantage present in each, for example. In both K–12 and higher education, more complex typologies that combine many of these factors are used to create peer groups of similar schools, campuses, or districts. If your level of analysis is the student, you might take the average performance of different subgroups of students, such as students of lower income, students in special education, or students of underrepresented minority groups. What is the historical performance of each of these?
- **Performance bands.** When dealing with multiple cases with varying characteristics (that make it difficult to group them), it may be helpful to break down the data by performance band. Grouping cases into high and low performers, quartiles, or even deciles, can reveal a number of subtrends, especially as regards the nature and extent of inequality in a system.

Exhibit 2A.3 shows a sample K–12 map of potential analyses that could be conducted by selecting the levels of analysis and the dimensions of comparison by which the units are grouped.

Step 3: Analyze the data to identify performance patterns

A *performance pattern* is a theme or trend in a system's performance on a particular metric with respect to a particular benchmark that is consistent and recurring across levels of analysis and dimensions of comparison. A performance pattern helps identify where (and to what extent) your system performs well or poorly with respect to its aspiration. In the K–12 context, a performance pattern might be a statement such as, "Fourth-grade achievement is on average 15% lower in rural schools than in urban schools." Identifying performance patterns is essential to understanding the delivery challenge, as it allows you to see patterns of underperformance that get to heart of the challenges you will need to confront.

Exhibit 2A.3 Organize the selected metrics for analysis by determining what performance units and dimensions of comparison you will look at

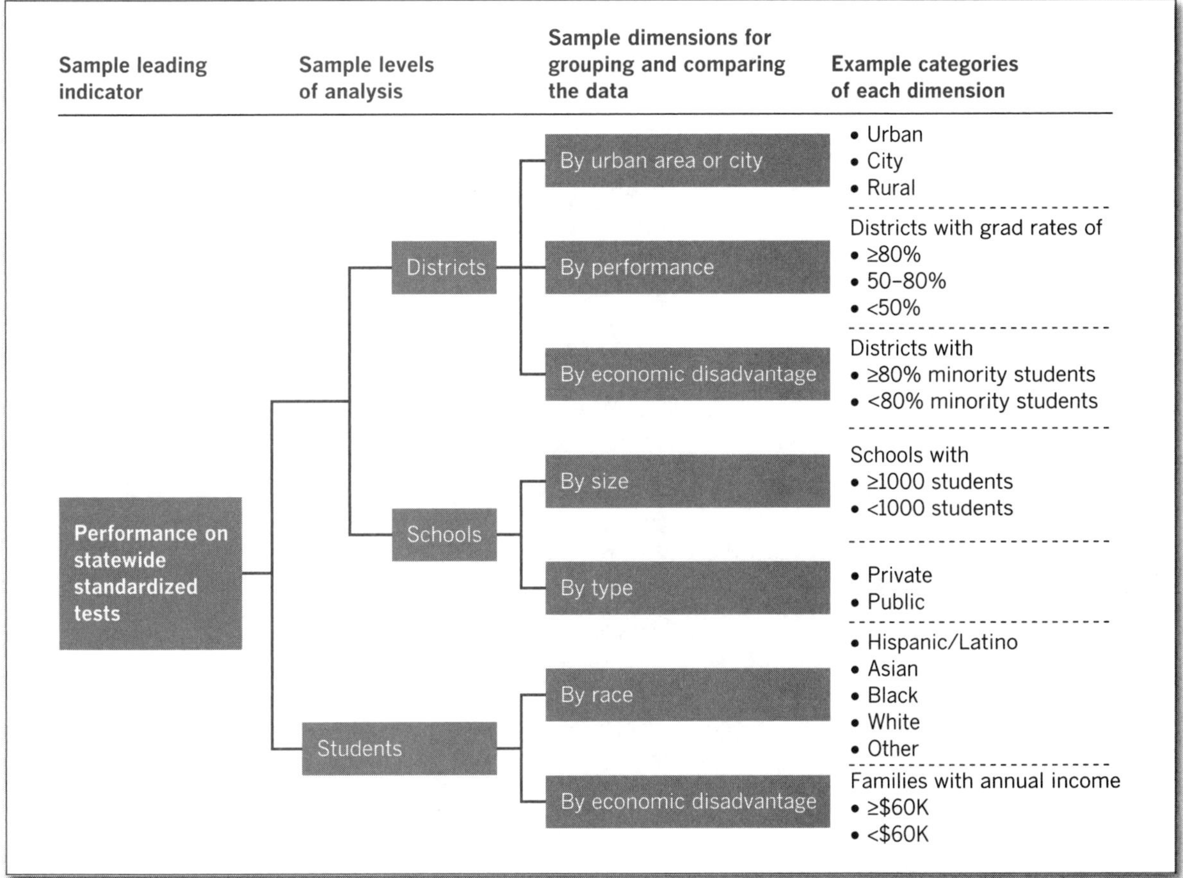

The most straightforward way to analyze your system's data and identify performance patterns is through the use of comparative benchmarking. Exhibit 2A.4 shows the five types of comparative benchmarking that are possible. Of these five types of benchmarking, four can be used to compare performance data:

- **Historical comparisons.** How does performance today compare with performance in the past? This comparison can be made at any level of analysis and for any dimension of comparison.
- **Internal peer comparisons.** Within your system, how does performance differ between groups with similar characteristics? If you group by performance level, how well do top performers do against low performers? How large is the gap between these different groups?
- **External peer comparisons.** How does your system performance compare, both now and historically, to different systems across the country? How do individuals or performance units in your system perform compared to similar units or subgroups in a peer system?
- **International comparisons.** How does the system's performance compare with the performance of systems in other countries, both now and historically?

Exhibit 2A.4 Five types of benchmarking

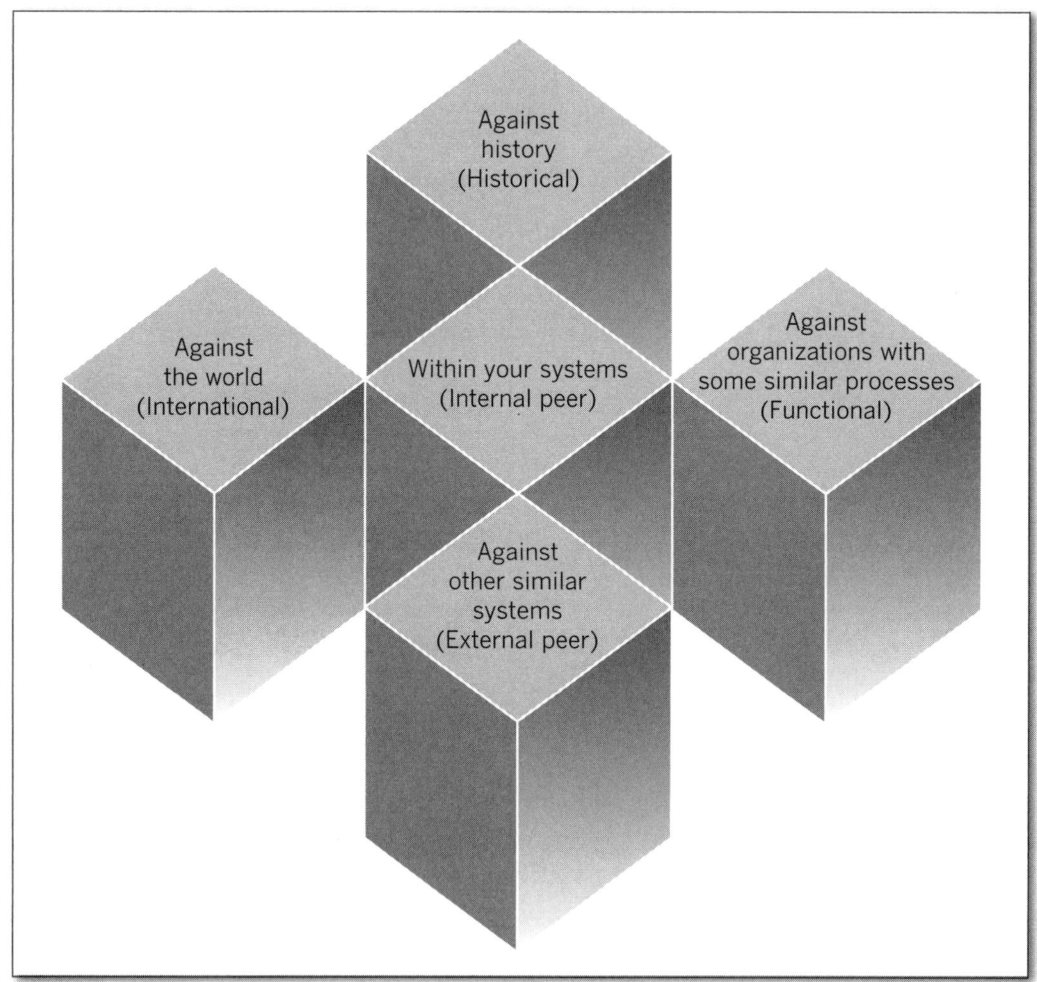

Functional comparisons, which typically investigate organizations in other sectors that perform similar functions (e.g., human resource management), may not contribute to your understanding of current performance. However, they will come into play when you are generating ideas for how to improve your system's performance (see Module 3A).

To take an example from the field of higher education, suppose that the target metric is the graduation rate of students in underrepresented minorities (URM). Accordingly, different types of benchmarking would be possible. A historical comparison could be made of a university system's URM student graduation rate over the last 20 years. An internal comparison might set the average URM graduation rate against those of campuses with similar characteristics. Alternatively, it may group the campuses in the system based on the high and low minority graduation rates and determine the gap between the two groups. An external peer comparison might look at several other states' university systems as well as the range of performance in those systems. An international comparison might compare performance to that of a specific university system within a different country or to the performance of an entire country on similar metrics.

Exhibits 2A.5, 2A.6, 2A.7, and 2A.8 display examples in K–12 education of each type of relevant benchmarking comparison.

Exhibit 2A.5 Historical comparison: Historical data allows comparison of achievement levels across time

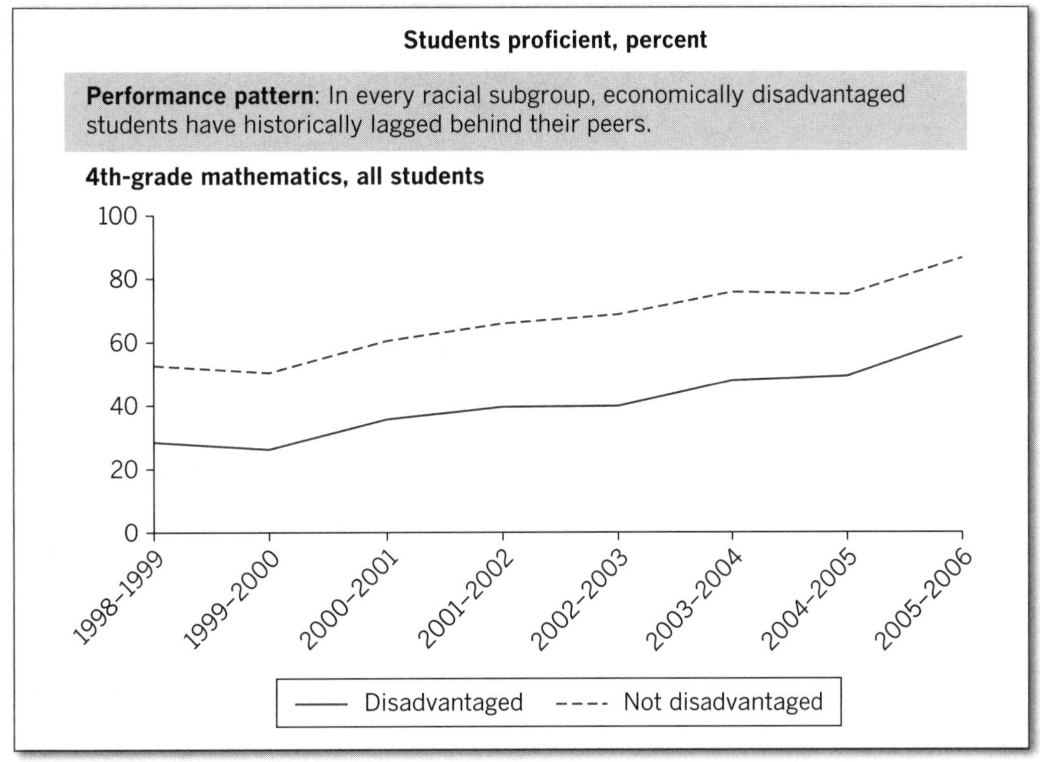

SOURCE: Ohio Department of Education (n.d.).

Exhibit 2A.6 Internal comparison: A certain SEA grouped its schools based on a "disadvantage" index for comparison

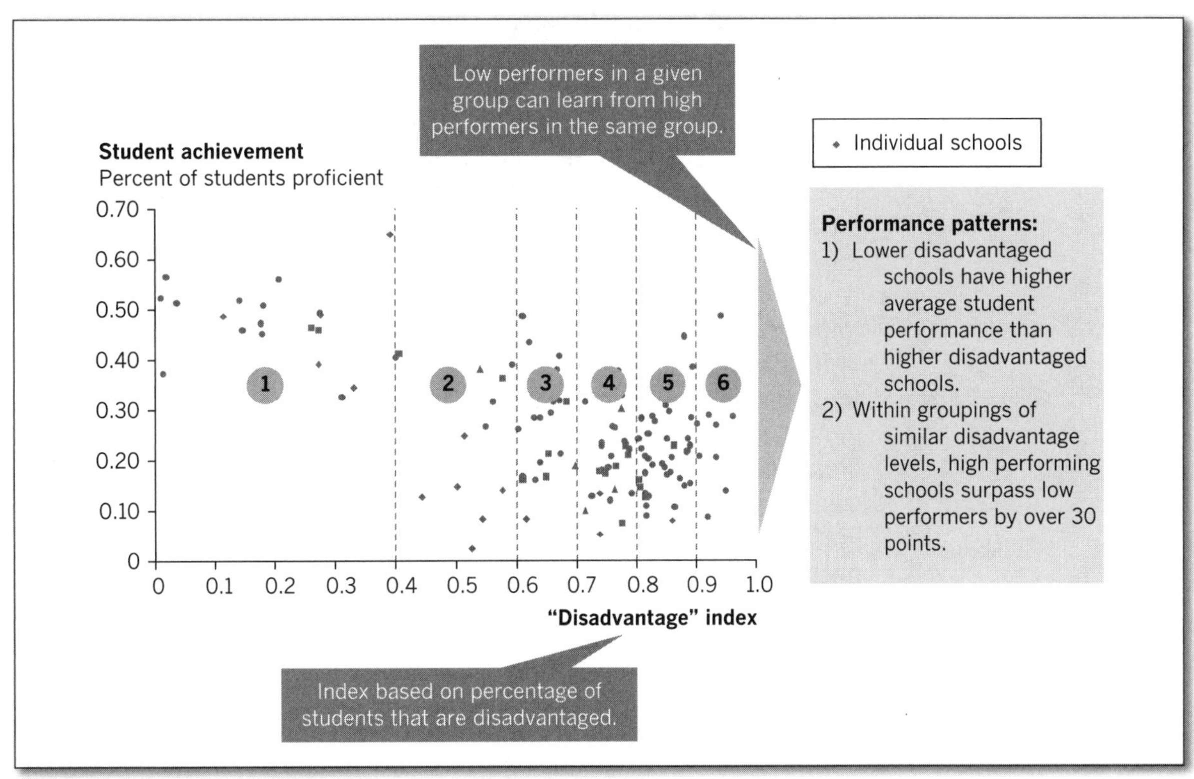

Exhibit 2A.7 External comparison: College Results Online allows peer comparisons in higher education institutions across state systems

Performance pattern: A state university from State A has a 10% lower graduation rate than a state university from State D, despite having a similar percentage of students receiving Pell grants and similar student revenue.

	Graduation rate %	Pell recipients %	Under-represented minority %	2-year/ 4-year	Revenue/ student FTE $	Admissions %
State A university	40	70	92	4	6,500	23
State B university	35	82	40	4	4,000	48
State C university	80	50	36	4	4,100	70
State D university	50	70	91	4	6,250	42
State E university	43	52	78	4	7,200	63
State F university	78	32	25	2	4,000	74
State G university	76	45	75	4	6,900	82
State H university	49	76	86	4	8,100	31
State I university	62	48	62	4	5,700	25
State J university	51	54	33	4	6,200	68
State K university	68	70	84	2	7,100	51
State L university	75	81	53	2	5,700	72

Given all the possible combinations between levels of analysis, dimensions of comparison for grouping them, and benchmarks available, many different analyses can be performed. How then should you decide which analyses will yield the most insight about performance patterns? The following principles should guide you.

- **Begin with a hypothesis.** From your knowledge of your system, do you suspect that certain areas are more likely to have performance problems than others? Can you test that hypothesis by looking at the data in a certain way? To generate a solid hypothesis, be sure to ask good, tough questions of those who know the system well.
- **Avoid too much complexity.** Remember, this is an exercise to achieve improved outcomes, not a detailed research study. For this reason, it is best to use analyses that are simple enough to yield clear, consistent conclusions. For example, if a K–12 system compared the performance of its minority students from rural neighborhoods against that of another system's White students from suburban neighborhoods, that system might find it difficult to draw meaningful conclusions about performance because the number of dimensions in use create an overly specific comparison. The system will not be able to tell if the performance difference is due to the difference in ethnicity, the urban or suburban neighborhoods, system characteristics, or a combination of all three. Therefore, choose simple analyses that handle one level of

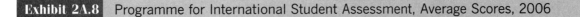

Exhibit 2A.8 Programme for International Student Assessment, Average Scores, 2006

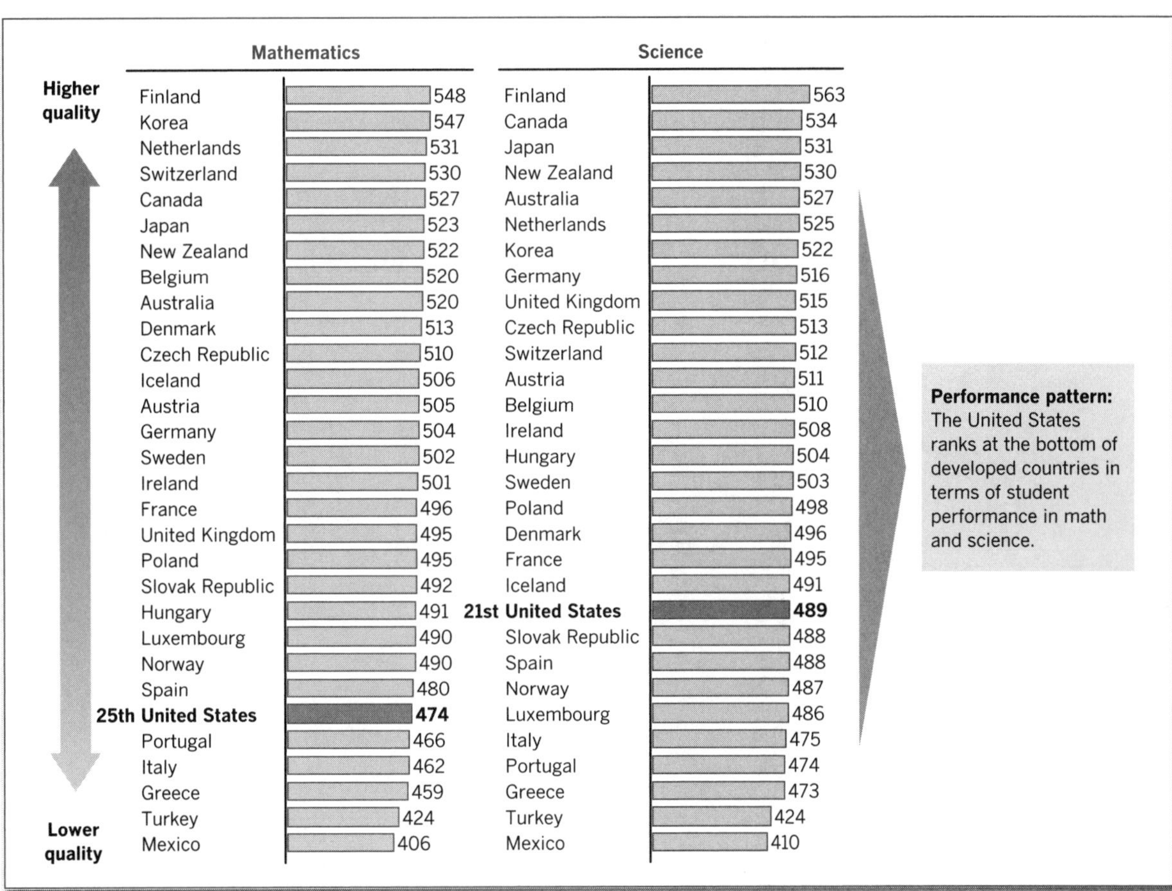

SOURCE: The Organisation for Economic Co-operation and Development (OECD), Programme for International Student Assessment (PISA).

NOTE: Results for OECD countries; OECD partner countries not included; differences may not be statistically significant. The United States scores relatively better on international tests in the early years (Trends in International Mathematics and Science Study) for fourth and eighth graders.

analysis at a time and limit the number of dimensions of comparison. As Einstein is reported to have put it, "Make everything as simple as possible, but not simpler."

- **Recognize persistent patterns.** In order to determine whether a certain dimension of comparison (e.g., racial discrimination) is really driving differences in performance, test this particular dimension against several others and see if the pattern holds. For example, if you find that underrepresented minorities underperform their peers in general, does this pattern remain even when you only consider students who are economically disadvantaged? If not, then economic disadvantage may be a more powerful explanatory variable. Sometimes, both race and class may matter, as shown in Exhibit 2A.9.
- **Understand the magnitude of performance gaps.** To know whether underperformance in a certain area is a significant issue, you need to know how many performance units are affected relative to the total system, and how substantial that impact is. A trend in

Exhibit 2A.9 In Ohio, two dimensions of comparison—economic disadvantage and race—were found to influence performance separately

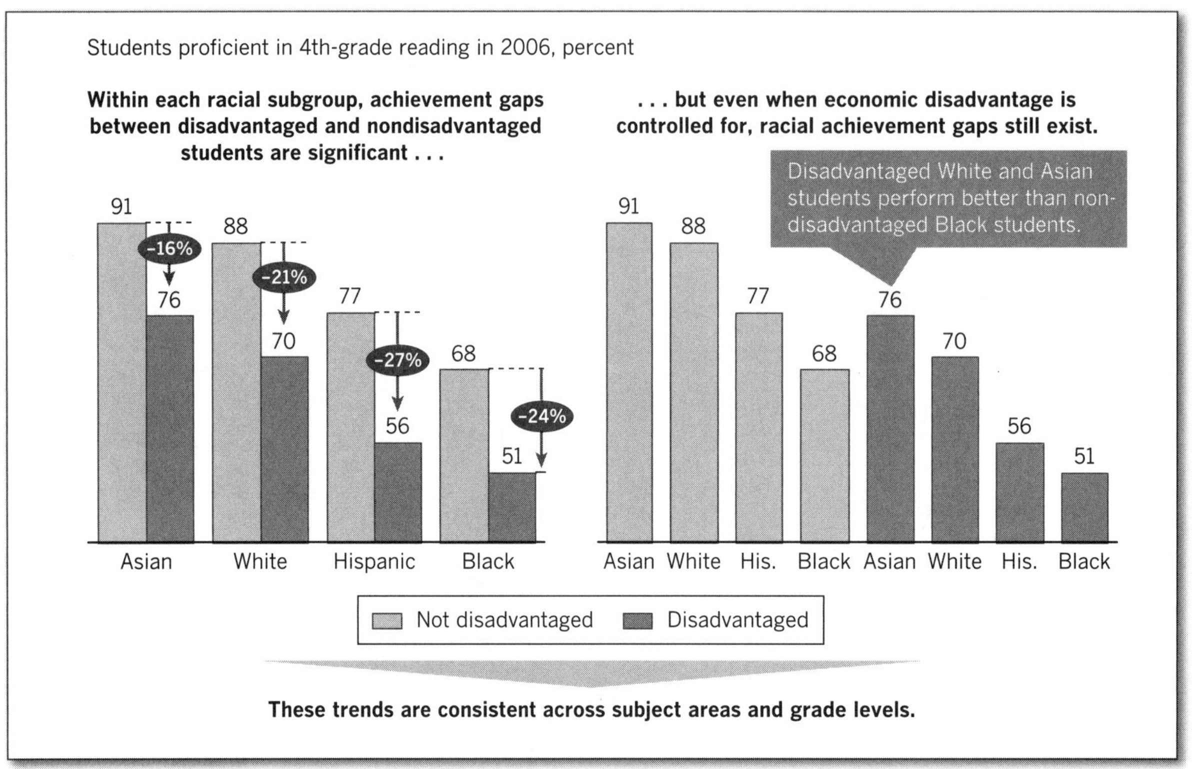

SOURCE: Ohio Department of Education. (n.d.).

performance should not be considered a true performance pattern if its occurrence and impact are relatively minor (no matter how interesting that trend may be).

Your analyses should produce a set of performance patterns that answer the following questions:

- On which aspects of the aspiration does your system perform well (if any)? How well?
- On which aspects of the aspiration does your system perform poorly? How poorly?

Exhibits 2A.10 and 2A.11 present examples of different kinds of performance patterns.

The example shown in Exhibit 2A.12, from Ohio's K–12 system, reveals how multiple analyses can be synthesized into a handful of broad performance patterns. In this case, the analysis compared the performance of all students who are economically disadvantaged versus that of all students who are nondisadvantaged over time across several ethnographic categories. Across the board, it was discovered that students who are economically disadvantaged performed more poorly than students who are nondisadvantaged.

Searching through data is not the only way to identify performance patterns, as the case example, A tale of two districts, on page 60 demonstrates.

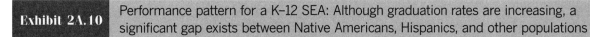

Exhibit 2A.10 Performance pattern for a K–12 SEA: Although graduation rates are increasing, a significant gap exists between Native Americans, Hispanics, and other populations

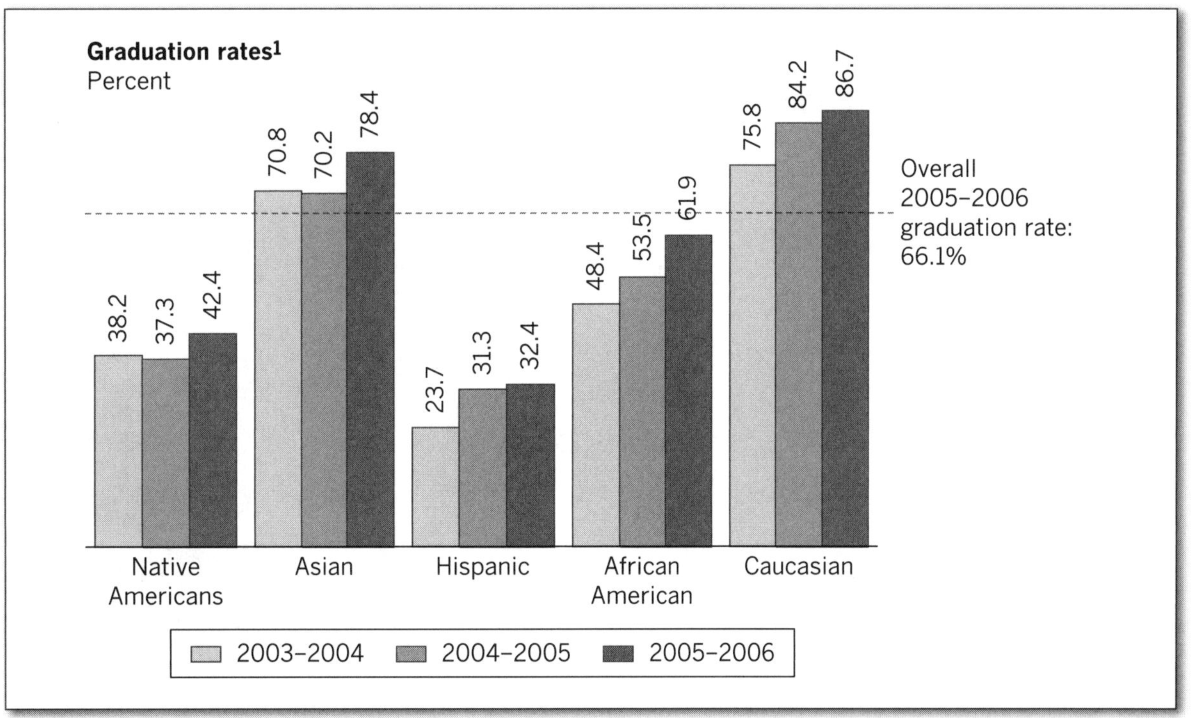

SOURCE: State Department of Education.

1. Data comes from State Dept of Education posting as of April 2007.

Exhibit 2A.11 Performance pattern for a national system: A substantial gender gap in student performance exists, starting as early as third grade

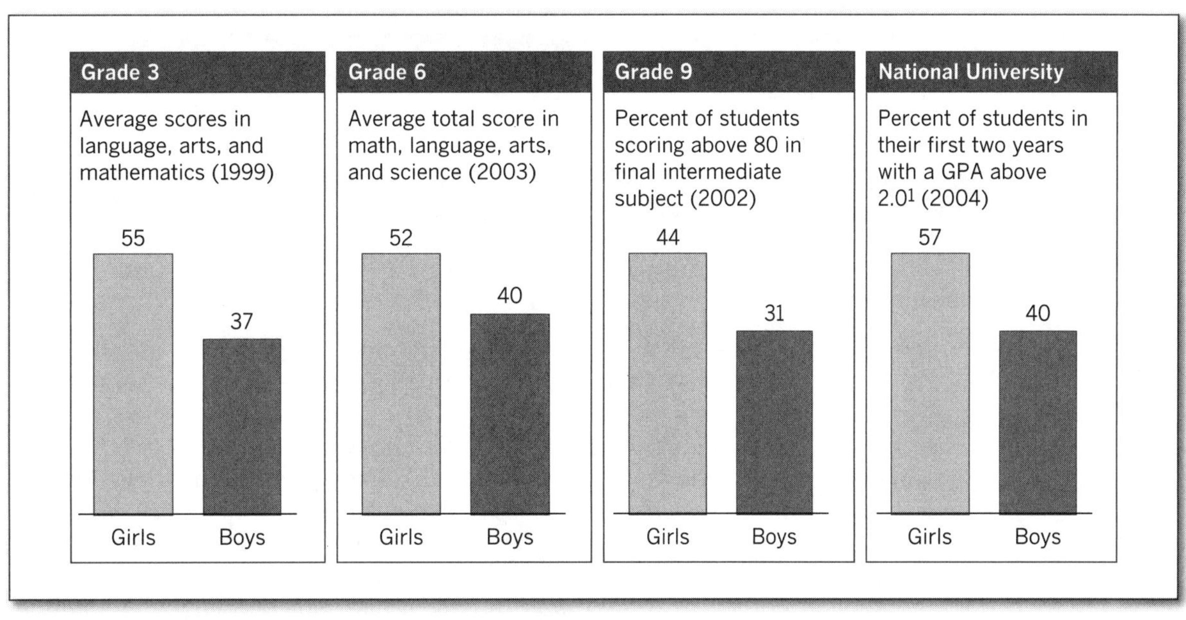

SOURCE: Illustrative examples.

1. Students need a GPA above 2.0 to continue their studies.

Exhibit 2A.12 Achievement relied on multiple analyses of student data to surface overarching performance patterns in Ohio

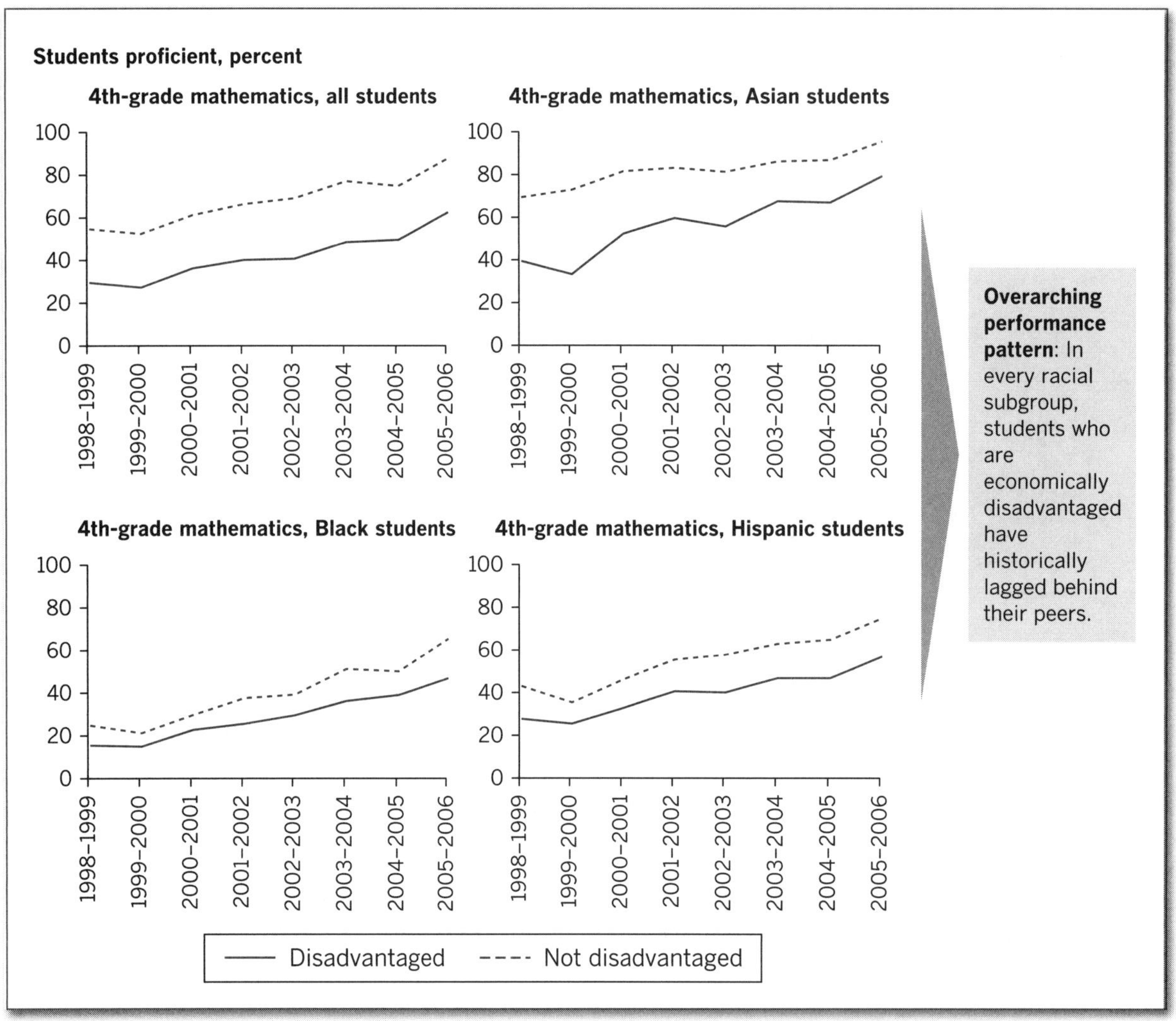

SOURCE: Ohio Department of Education (n.d.).

CASE EXAMPLE

A tale of two districts: Performance patterns in Montgomery County, Maryland

Montgomery County Public Schools Superintendent Jerry Weast identified the most important performance pattern in his district through personal observation:

"In order to get to know the district, Weast literally 'rode the bus,' hitchhiking with the early-morning mail run as it left headquarters for the districts' two-hundred plus mail stops. Up close and personal, in late summer 1999, Weast 'discovered' a district within a district. Weast's reading of [socioeconomic] data, combined with his school-visiting blitz, convinced him that there were two Montgomery Counties. One area was largely urban, surrounding municipal centers and major transportation arteries . . . Weast called it the Red Zone.

Everything outside of it he called the Green Zone. The Red Zone was made up primarily of immigrant families, Hispanics and African Americans, many of whom were living in poverty. The performance of students in this area was far below the academic performance of the students in the Green Zone. It was only a matter of time before the weight of the Red Zone's inequalities engulfed the Green Zone, which would have a profound effect on the county's traditionally high average test scores." (*Leading for Equity*, 18)

Careful and thoughtful analysis of your performance data can help you to uncover performance patterns that will yield insights about the most difficult challenges facing your system that create barriers to achieving your aspiration. These insights should then suggest areas to explore for corrective action. We will investigate these areas in the next module.

Conclusion

By now, you have learned

- How to identify the data that shows your system's past and present performance in relation to the aspiration;
- The various options for analyzing and comparing that data;
- The five ways to benchmark your system's performance; and
- What performance patterns are, why they are important, and how to identify them.

All of these analyses should be performed with an eye toward the aspiration your system has set. The set of performance patterns generated in this module will tell you how well your system is performing against its aspiration and in what particular areas. They will not, however, help you get beneath the surface to identify the drivers of performance. Revealing a pattern of underperformance is just the beginning; only understanding the cause of that pattern will allow you to successfully address it and improve your system's performance. We turn to this in the next module.

2B. UNDERSTAND DRIVERS OF PERFORMANCE AND RELATED SYSTEM ACTIVITIES

"Good data, while essential, is only a start—you then have to use it!"

—*Instruction to Deliver* (88)

Identifying performance patterns is crucial to understanding the delivery challenge, but knowledge of those patterns alone will not help your system improve performance. You also need to understand the drivers of these performance patterns as well as the activities that your system is currently undertaking to address these drivers. With this information, you will then be able to begin to determine the potential changes (interventions) that you can make as part of your delivery effort to achieve your system's aspiration.

While your system's patterns of strong performance may be useful as examples of "best practice," your delivery effort will likely need to address the patterns (and drivers) of underperformance first and foremost. This module will therefore focus on identifying the drivers of (and activities related to) underperformance, although the same processes can be used to identify the drivers of strong performance patterns.

ROLES OF SYSTEM LEADER AND DELIVERY LEADER

Most of the steps in this module will be undertaken by your Delivery Unit. Your role is to conduct the problem solving necessary to identify the drivers of underperformance or to verify any drivers that have been previously identified by your system. Your Unit will also be responsible for identifying and evaluating existing system activities that relate to performance against your aspiration, in order to further understand the delivery challenge and begin identifying the range of options for improving delivery. The system leader's role is to serve as a source of system knowledge as you progress through the diagnosis, reacting to and pressure testing your findings as they emerge. Ultimately, your system leader may use your findings as the basis for setting the direction of strategy and creating her story (see Modules 3A and 5B).

PROCESS STEPS

Step 1: Identify the drivers of your performance patterns

Step 2: Identify and evaluate system activities related to drivers of performance patterns

Step 1: Identify the drivers of your performance patterns

Once your system has identified patterns of underperformance in its data on both your target metric and leading indicators, the next logical step is to try to understand the root causes, or *drivers* of these patterns.

Depending on your system's context, you may have a better or worse idea of what these drivers are. Some challenges are so common, or have been so well researched, that there is often a list of "usual suspects" to which you can turn. In other cases, the answer might not be immediately apparent, but some basic brainstorming and common sense might be all you need. However, more formal problem-solving tools may be warranted if

- Your drivers of underperformance are unclear;
- The answers depend on specific facts on the ground that you will need to investigate; or
- You wish to ensure that you are being more comprehensive in your approach to the problem.

One of the most common tools for uncovering the driver of an observed performance pattern is the *hypothesis tree.* Hypothesis trees allow for a comprehensive identification of potential drivers of a given pattern, which can then be narrowed down and tested to determine the most important drivers. To build and "prune" a hypothesis tree for a given performance pattern, follow these steps:

- **Ask why.** Start with the performance pattern itself. What are the potential reasons why your system may be exhibiting this pattern? By continually asking why, you will be able to dig deeper toward the drivers of underperformance.
- **Brainstorm a list of hypotheses** to answer the why question. Apply two principles as you build this list:
  - It should be *collectively exhaustive:* Your list of hypotheses, taken together, should cover all possibilities for answering the why question.
  - It should be *mutually exclusive:* Each hypothesis should not overlap with any of the other hypotheses.
- Eliminate some hypotheses with simple criteria:
  - **Evidence.** Is there a substantial body of evidence (e.g., data or analyses) that disproves your hypothesis?
  - **Scope.** Is addressing this potential driver of performance within the scope of your system's authority or capacity?
  - **Values.** Would addressing this potential driver of performance be consistent with your system's values? (For example, you would not want to close achievement gaps by lowering the overall achievement of students of greater privilege).
- **Repeat** to the appropriate level of depth. For the hypotheses that remain, you may need to ask why again. For each of these why questions, you will generate a further series of sub-hypotheses—some of which you will quickly eliminate and some of which might further beg the why question, and so forth. The point is to build your tree out to a series of hypotheses that you believe are potential drivers of the patterns of underperformance. If, at each step, your list of hypotheses is collectively exhaustive and mutually exclusive for their respective why question, then the list of hypotheses that emerges at the end of your tree will become your comprehensive and clear set of potential drivers of underperformance.

The example in Exhibit 2B.1 shows how these steps can be used to identify potential drivers of a pattern of underperformance in higher education.

Exhibit 2B.2 is an example of how one school district followed a single branch of the hypothesis tree, trying to identify the root causes of underperformance by asking a series of why questions.

In developing your hypothesis, it is often helpful to engage as many stakeholders as possible, as different groups will have different perspectives on the problem. For the district in Exhibit 2B.2, Superintendent Jerry Weast arrived at these conclusions by seeking feedback from a diverse group of individuals. Via a series of town hall-style meetings across the district, Weast engaged the community in an interactive process of problem identification that ultimately informed the district's reform strategy (*Leading for Equity,* 153).

Exhibit 2B.1 Hypothesis tree example: Identifying potential drivers for a graduation rate gap

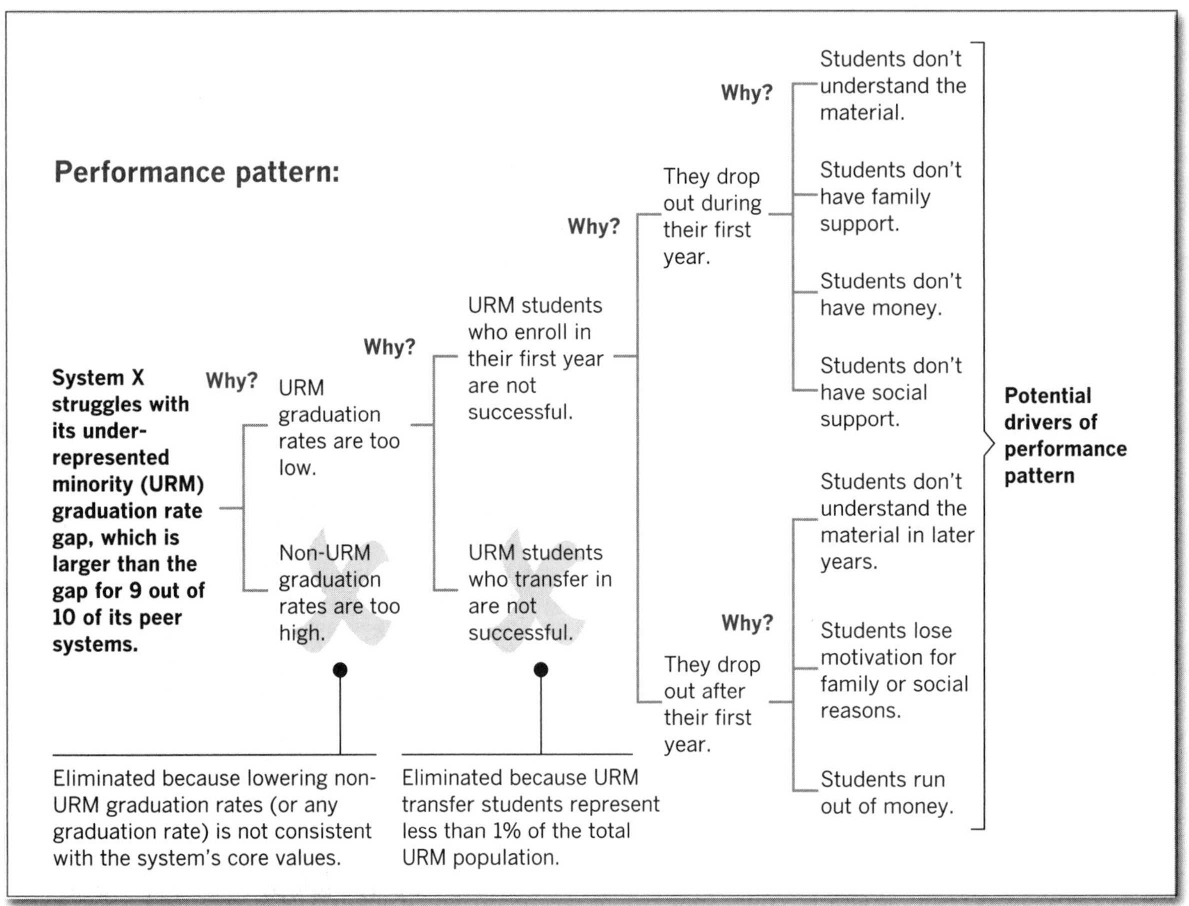

Once you have developed this list of hypotheses, you should test them to determine which ones are your true drivers of performance. The key to hypothesis testing is to understand "what you would have to believe" for each hypothesis to be true: What evidence would you need to see—qualitative or quantitative—in order to believe the hypothesis? For each hypothesis and "what you would have to believe" statement, use the following tools to find and examine evidence that will allow you to prove or disprove the hypothesis:

- **Data analysis.** Do your analyses of existing data—or of other data that you will need to collect—support the hypothesis?
- **Existing work.** Has somebody else already done research and/or analysis that tests and proves your hypothesis in other, similar contexts?
- **Interviews.** Are there system personnel, stakeholders, or end users you could speak with who are particularly close to this hypothesis and could provide a valuable perspective? Are there external people who can provide an objective perspective?
- **Frontline visits.** Could you benefit from seeing the potential hypothesis "in action" on the frontline?

- **Surveys.** Can the opinions of a large sample of people in your system suffice to prove or disprove the hypothesis?
- **Workshops.** Is the knowledge you need concentrated in a relatively small group of people? Can you bring them together to discuss and agree on the most likely drivers of performance patterns? Can workshops generate new understanding altogether?
- **Benchmarks.** Recall the five types of benchmarking from the previous module. Do historical, internal, external, international, or functional comparisons support your hypothesis?

In conducting these hypothesis tests, you should test not only for whether the hypothesis is true but also for magnitude: If a hypothesis is true, what does the evidence suggest about the size of its contribution to the pattern of underperformance in question? In the end, those hypotheses that are the largest contributors will emerge as your primary drivers of underperformance.

Exhibit 2B.2 Root cause analysis

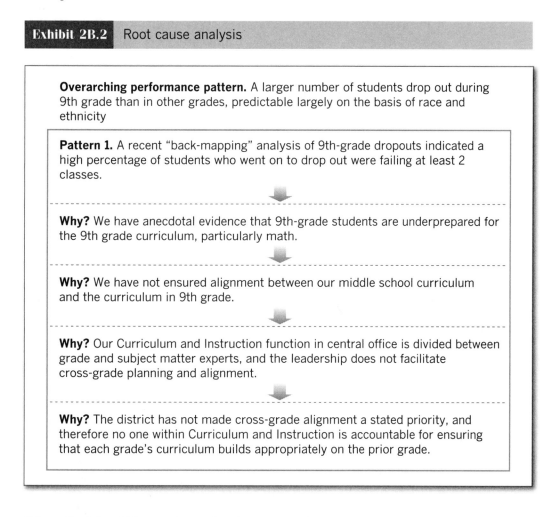

Overarching performance pattern. A larger number of students drop out during 9th grade than in other grades, predictable largely on the basis of race and ethnicity

Pattern 1. A recent "back-mapping" analysis of 9th-grade dropouts indicated a high percentage of students who went on to drop out were failing at least 2 classes.

Why? We have anecdotal evidence that 9th-grade students are underprepared for the 9th grade curriculum, particularly math.

Why? We have not ensured alignment between our middle school curriculum and the curriculum in 9th grade.

Why? Our Curriculum and Instruction function in central office is divided between grade and subject matter experts, and the leadership does not facilitate cross-grade planning and alignment.

Why? The district has not made cross-grade alignment a stated priority, and therefore no one within Curriculum and Instruction is accountable for ensuring that each grade's curriculum builds appropriately on the prior grade.

Step 2: Identify and evaluate system activities related to drivers of performance patterns

Understanding the delivery challenge is not limited only to patterns of underperformance and their primary drivers. You will need to know what your system is currently doing to try to address these drivers of underperformance, so you can evaluate whether current efforts are sufficient and recommend changes where necessary.

Recall that *system activities* are activities undertaken by **actors** in your system that will help it to achieve its aspiration. System activities include both programs (e.g., an after-school program to improve literacy) and day-to-day activities (e.g., classroom teaching and evaluation of student work). For the purposes of this module, we will be concerned with current system activities that are likely to have an impact on the drivers of underperformance identified in the previous step.

To identify these activities, ask a series of simple questions for each driver of underperformance.

- What programs are likely to have an impact on the driver of performance? Are specific efforts being undertaken at the system level that are intended to affect this driver? For example, if college graduation rates are being adversely affected by a lack of student comprehension of the material in freshman courses, then efforts to redesign these courses (if they exist) should be included on your list of program priorities. Note that these programs could be implemented at the system level or at levels closer to the frontline, such as a local education agency (LEA), school, or campus.
- What day-to-day work is likely to have an impact on the cause of underperformance? Pursuing the example from the previous point, the basic design and teaching of those same freshmen courses might be considered a relevant system activity.

Your list of system activities may be more or less comprehensive, depending on the time available to you, the familiarity of the driver of underperformance, and your existing knowledge of your system. Again, you may need only to include an easy list of "usual suspects." If, on the other hand, knowledge about the kinds of activities that affect your specific drivers of underperformance is scarce—or if most of the relevant activities take place at a level other than the system level—further investigation might be necessary. In general, a combination of interviews with system actors (system leaders and staff or a selection of campus, LEA, or school leaders) and a review of relevant documents (strategic plans and/or budgets) should be sufficient to generate the list.

Once you have generated the list of system activities that you want to focus on, the next step is to build a profile for each activity that will help you to understand and evaluate its effectiveness and implementation. The first part of an activity profile should answer the following questions:

- **Description.** What is the activity? How and why is it supposed to work? Who are its beneficiaries? How many are affected?
- **Impact.** What is the intended impact? What does the evidence say, if anything, about actual impact?
- **Resources.** What human and financial resources does the activity require?

Exhibit 2B.3 gives an example of how these questions can be answered for an after-school literacy program in K–12 education.

Exhibit 2B.3 Activity profile for an after-school literacy program

	Description	Example
Description	• What is the activity? • How and why is it supposed to work? • Who are the activity's beneficiaries? • How many beneficiaries are impacted?	• State provides funding for an after-school "literacy hour" for students in need of extra help. • Literacy hour curriculum to follow a specific and evidence-based model articulated at the state level. • Program is intended to benefit elementary school students who are one or more grade levels behind in reading. • Out of 24,000 eligible students, 2,000 students participate in 100 elementary schools.
Impact	• What is the intended impact? • What does the evidence say, if anything, about actual impact?	• Program is intended to raise the reading scores of students so that they are at grade level. • No attempt has been made to track impact quantitatively, though anecdotal evidence suggests that students who stick with the program can move up to two grade levels in a single year.
Resources	• What human/financial resources are used for this activity?	• $1.1 million per year. • One hundred teachers accept stipends to coordinate and teach the program at participating elementary schools.

The second part of the activity profile is an understanding and evaluation of implementation: Who are the actors that are involved in implementing the activity? What is the role of each and the relationship between them? How does implementation play out, and where could it be improved?

The most robust tool for answering these questions is the delivery chain analysis. A delivery chain is the set of **system actors** (people or organizations), and the relationships between them, through which a given system activity will be implemented. A delivery chain has one question at its core: Starting from the policy intent of a leader in your system and ending with the frontline behaviors and practices that this policy is designed to influence, how—and through whom—does a system activity actually happen?

DELIVERY CHAINS DEFINED

"The best way to think about it is to imagine what is implicit when a Minister makes a promise. Supposing that a Minister promises, as David Blunkett did, to improve standards of reading and writing among 11-year-olds. Implicit in this commitment is that, in one way or another, the Minister can influence what happens inside the head of an 11-year-old in, for example, Widnes. The delivery chain makes that connection explicit; so in this case, what is the connection between the child in Widnes and the Minister in Westminster? What happens inside that 11-year-old's head is influenced chiefly by her teacher—the first link in the chain; the teacher is influenced by the school's Literacy Coordinator who, in turn, is influenced by the headteacher—the second and third links in the chain.

(Continued)

(Continued)

The headteacher is influenced by the governors [of the school] and the local authority, who are influenced by the Regional Director of the National Literacy Strategy, who answers to the National Director of the strategy. He in turn answers to the Head of the Standards and Effectiveness Unit . . . who answers to the Minister. And thus we have established the delivery chain . . . Note that it does not depend on a line management relationship, this being only one of the many possible means of exerting influence along the chain." (*Instruction to Deliver,* 85–86)

To conduct a delivery chain analysis, ask the following questions:

- Who are all the system actors (people or organizations) that could conceivably be involved, directly or indirectly, in implementing or influencing the implementation of this activity? Remember that this does not just include line authority in your system, which in any case may be unclear; it also includes actors who may have informal but significant influence.
- For each system actor, what role does that individual play in influencing or contributing to the implementation of the activity? How large is his or her influence relative to other system actors?
- What are all the relationships of influence between these system actors? For each relationship:
  - In which direction does influence flow (from whom to whom)?
  - Is it formal (line authority) or informal influence?
  - How strong or weak is the influence?

Your answers to these questions should help you to draw a map of the delivery chain for each activity. Depending on the needs of your system, a delivery chain map may vary in its level of detail. The following is a list of elements that the most detailed delivery chain maps should include.

- A visual differentiation of the location of each system actor (for example, grouping all state-level actors in one space, with campus, LEA, or school level actors in another).
- A visual indication of the level of each actor's influence on the implementation of the activity (for example, by varying the size of the "boxes" that represent each actor, or by thickening the lines from a particular actor with higher influence).
- A visual indication of the nature of each relationship between actors (for example, an arrow indicating the direction of influence, varying patterns of arrows to indicate formal or informal relationships, and varying sizes of arrows to indicate the strength of relationships).
- A summary of the role played by each actor in implementing or influencing the implementation of the activity.

An example of a detailed delivery chain, again for the above-profiled after-school literacy program, is given in Exhibit 2B.4.

Exhibit 2B.4 Delivery chain for an after-school literacy program—example

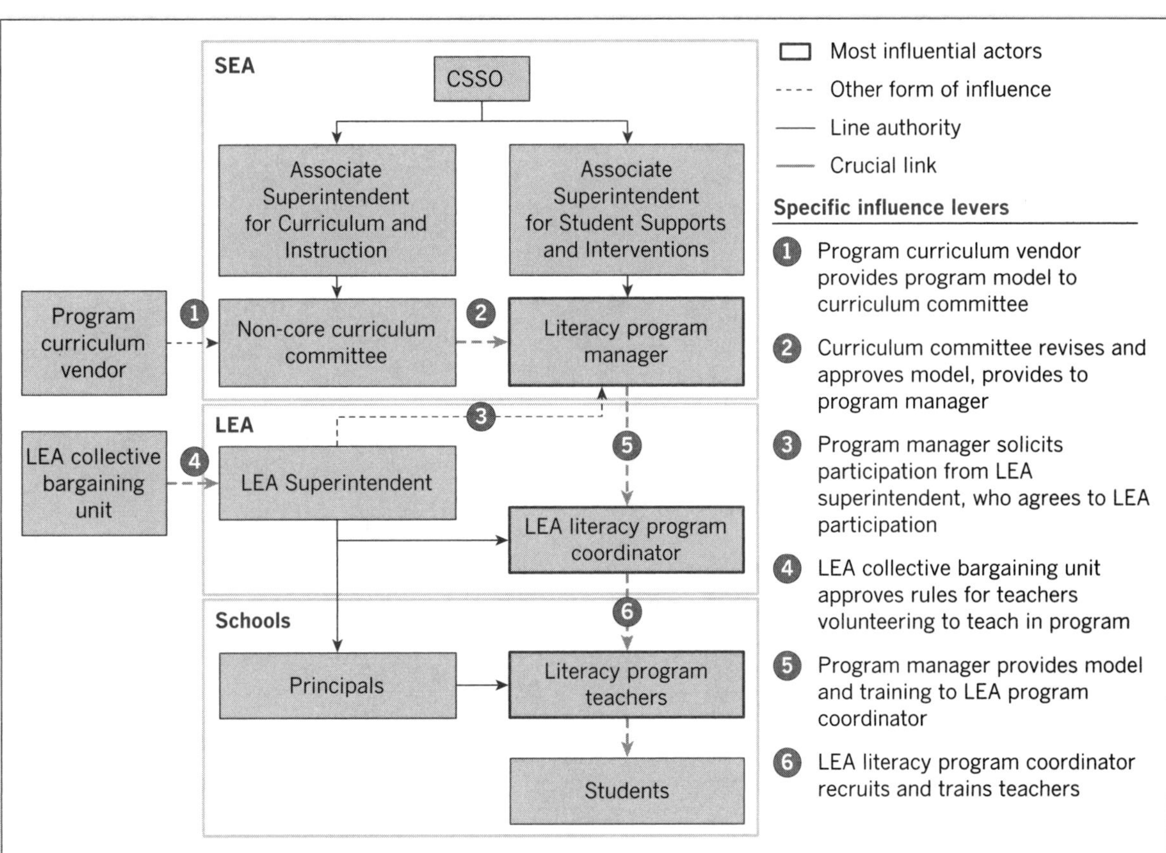

A few real (but less detailed) delivery chains from other systems are given in Exhibits 2B.5 and 2B.6. The first illustrates a delivery chain for the U.K.'s national literacy strategy, implemented to improve standards of reading and writing among 11 year olds. This chain is rather strong as it shows a simple and linear structure, with both formal and informal influence relationships. The second demonstrates a weaker chain for a system activity for a K–12 SEA, where formal lines of command are more complicated and there is more influence from several external actors.

Delivery chains paint a picture of how easily (or not) intent at the system level will translate to impact at the student level. As such, they are useful tools for helping you to evaluate and improve the effectiveness of implementation. In particular, delivery chain analysis will help you to overcome the oft-repeated excuse that system leaders have no meaningful influence over what happens on the frontline. This is an especially acute problem in K–12 and higher education, where loosely coupled systems of governance lead to unclear, weak, and even hostile relationships between system-level actors (K–12 SEAs and higher education system offices) and more local actors (LEAs, schools, and campuses).

Delivery chain analysis will help you evaluate what kinds of influence levers your system already uses for each activity. Then, rather than starting from the presumption that a system can do nothing to influence local implementation, the ensuing evaluation of each activity should instead ask the

Exhibit 2B.5 Delivery chain for the U.K. national literacy strategy

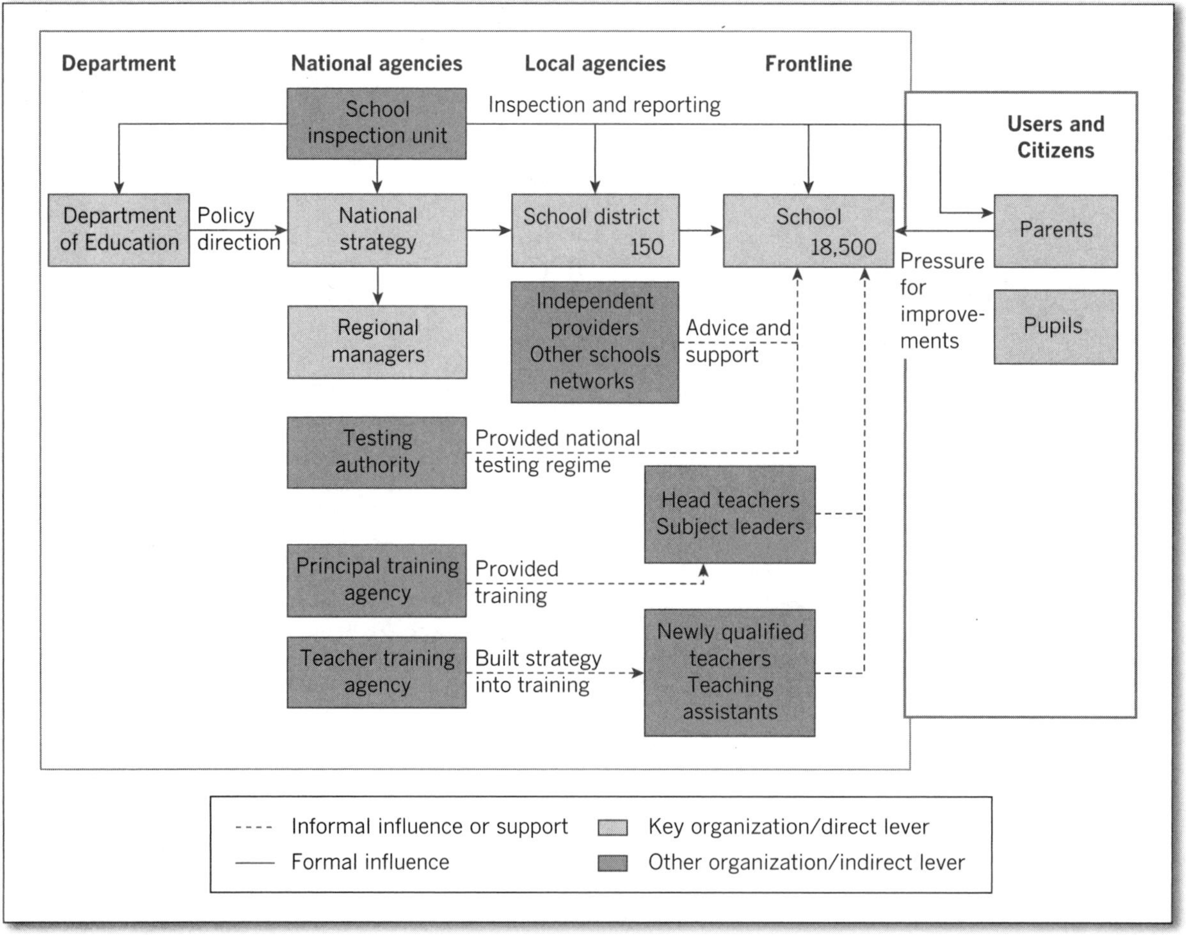

SOURCE: Prime Minister's Delivery Unit.

question, Where are there weak links, and what can be done to strengthen the delivery chain?

To evaluate each delivery chain for areas to improve, ask the following questions:

- What are the problem areas—areas in which implementation goes wrong? For example, you might discover that the after-school literacy program is not being carried out with fidelity at each school, such that some schools are achieving results and others are not.
- For each problem area, can you trace it back to a design weakness in the delivery chain? There are two types of design weaknesses:
  - A *weak link* has its source in actors who are not playing their intended roles or in a relationship that is flawed. Are the right signals being sent to that actor, and is there sufficient leverage to allow other actors to influence that actor appropriately? You may find it helpful to benchmark various parts of the chain with similar chains in other systems, or even other parts of the chain in the same system, to assess the true quality of the chain. Consider some potential weak links that could be causing the problem:

Exhibit 2B.6 Delivery chain for a program to improve ninth-grade achievement—example

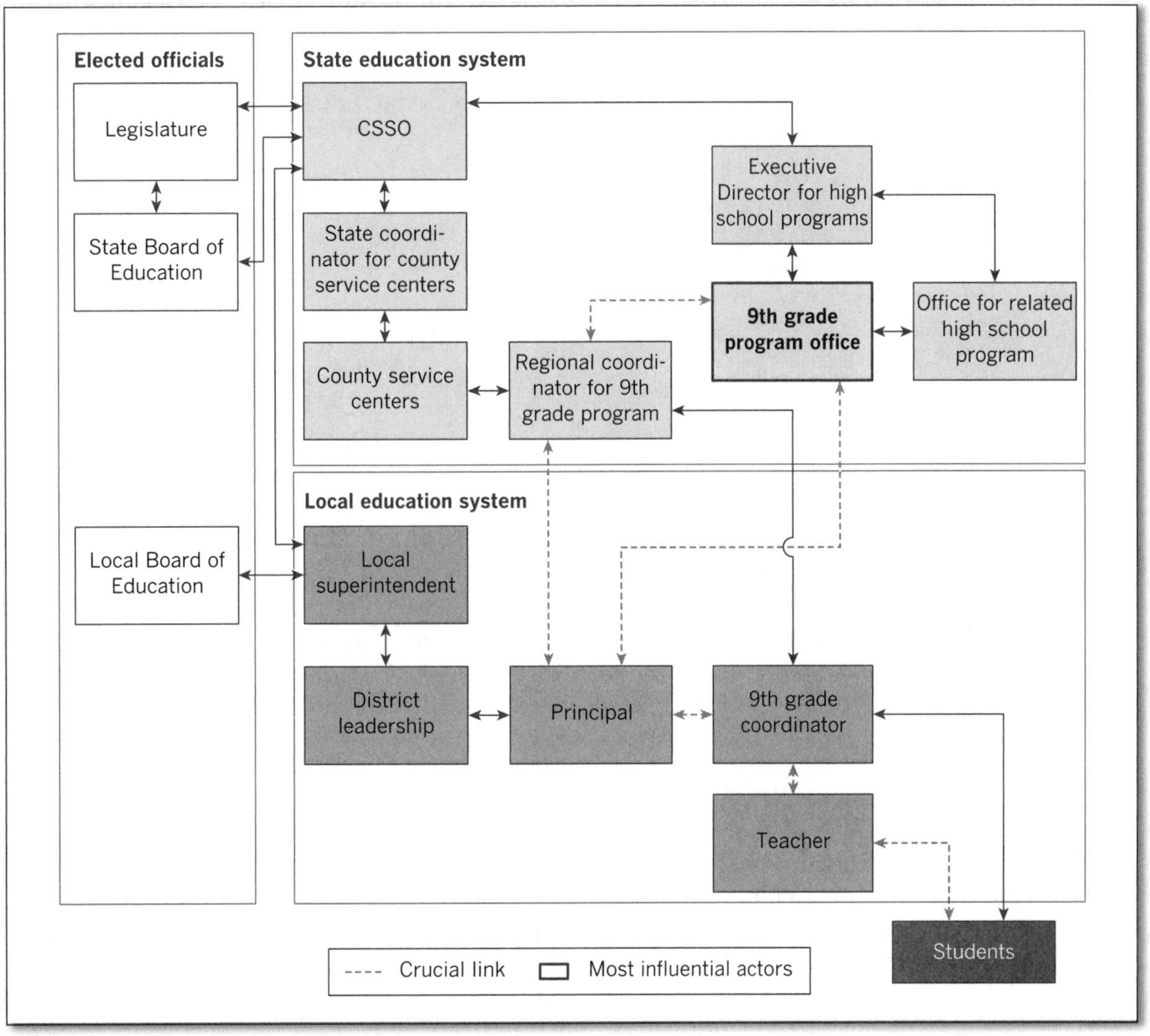

Elected officials
Legislature
State Board of Education
Local Board of Education

State education system
CSSO
State coordinator for county service centers
County service centers
Regional coordinator for 9th grade program
Executive Director for high school programs
9th grade program office
Office for related high school program

Local education system
Local superintendent
District leadership
Principal
9th grade coordinator
Teacher
Students

---- Crucial link ▭ Most influential actors

SOURCE: Illustrative example for K–12 SEA.

- The official at the SEA responsible for the literacy program is not accurately and promulgating the model for the program, in which case the weak link is the relationship between the official and their immediate superior at the SEA;
- Some individual LEAs are ignoring the promulgated model, in which case the weak link is the relationship between LEAs and the official; or
- Local collective bargaining contracts prevent some LEAs from selecting the most effective teachers for the program, in which case the weak link is between LEAs and their local teacher unions (note that this potential weak link is not within the line authority, but it may play a large role nonetheless).

- **Unnecessary complexity** applies not just to a single link in the chain but to a whole area of it (or possibly the entire chain). For the most part, complexity is correlated to the number of actors that have a role in implementation. Does an activity require approval, permission and/or input from too many people or organizations?

THE NECESSITY OF DELIVERY CHAINS

"There must be some kind of delivery chain if there is to be delivery. If it cannot be specified, nothing will happen . . . We found that, in a number of cases, the responsible officials had decided in their own minds that because they did not have direct line management responsibility, they had no influence at all. In a phrase I came to hate, they would say: 'we only have rubber levers.' Some officials wallowed in this powerlessness because it enabled them to abdicate responsibility—if results were not delivered, at least it was not their fault . . . Instead of setting out to decide what they could do and how they might do it, they decided what they couldn't do and how they might explain away the inevitable failure which would result." (*Instruction to Deliver,* 86)

Are there ways that you can streamline the chain in accordance with the principle known as Occam's razor, "plurality should not be posited without necessity"?

- What are your recommendations to strengthen the delivery chain, either by strengthening weak links or by simplifying the chain to eliminate them? For example, an SEA may improve its influence over LEAs by making some discretionary funding conditional on the behavior it seeks, by building trust-based relationships with LEA leadership, or by demonstrating competence in its support for LEAs to implement the activity in question. Alternatively, it may find a way to bypass the LEA and go directly to schools, teachers, or students if that is appropriate for the activity. Again, benchmarking in this context could be another way to determine improvements you could make to strengthen the chain.

Exhibits 2B.7 and 2B.8 give a template for systematic evaluation of each of your delivery chains according to the above questions, along with an example drawn from the after-school literacy program above.

This step has demonstrated how delivery chains will help you to understand your system's delivery challenge in the first instance. This understanding will feed directly into your reform strategy in the next module. However, delivery chains will resurface as a core problem-solving tool throughout your delivery effort. In particular,

- **Delivery chains will help you to produce delivery plans for the various elements of your reform strategy (see Module 3C).** One of the most important aspects of planning is a grounding in facts. Plans must be credible in every aspect, including the story they tell about which delivery actors will be responsible for implementation. A delivery chain analysis ensures that delivery plans will rely on solid relationships with influential delivery actors. It will also take excuses off the table, especially with middle managers who claim that they have no influence over system performance.
- **Delivery chains will help you to diagnose and solve problems during delivery (see Module 4B).** Delivery chain analysis provides a comprehensive framework for troubleshooting when problems arise. By definition, delivery problems for a given activity will have their source somewhere in that activity's delivery chain, so the identified delivery actors and the relationships between them comprise the complete set of potential places to look for the causes of these problems. The delivery chain analysis thus allows for problem solving that is rigorous and comprehensive.

Exhibit 2B.7 Evaluation of delivery chain for after-school literacy program—K–12 example

Problem area	Sources of problem area		Recommendations to improve
	Description	**Type**	
• Program model not implemented with fidelity at all sites	• The number of people at the SEA who are responsible for deciding and approving the program model is inefficiently large; in particular, the literacy program manager never feels full ownership of a program model "imposed" by the curriculum and instruction division	• Unnecessary complexity at SEA level	• Allow literacy program coordinator to have direct interface with vendor to design and create curriculum, with only notification to curriculum and instruction division
	• Literacy program manager at SEA does not have capacity to train all LEA coordinators to properly promulgate model	• Weak link: literacy program manager to LEA literacy program coordinator	• Create an opportunity for training to happen "all at once" by sponsoring a conference for all LEA literacy program coordinators
• Even where program model is promulgated correctly, it can be ineffectively delivered	• Senior teachers have first right of refusal to teach for this program due to collective bargaining rules, so some teachers in program are ineffective	• Weak link: collective bargaining unit to superintendent	• Negotiate agreement with collective bargaining units to allow principals or the LEA program coordinator to select teachers

Conclusion

By now, you have learned

- How to use hypothesis trees to identify the drivers of performance patterns; and
- How to identify and profile system activities that are likely to have an impact on these drivers.

At this stage, you have completed the "top half" of the delivery pyramid that we introduced at the beginning of this chapter: You have identified target metrics and leading indicators for each aspiration, you have found patterns of underperformance for these metrics, you have identified the most important drivers of these patterns, and you have identified and evaluated the current system activities that are most likely to have an impact on these drivers. Exhibit 2B.8 summarizes how a K–12 SEA might undertake this process, using the first five steps in our delivery pyramid (the remaining steps, shown here but not highlighted, will be covered in Chapter 3). For simplicity's sake, we follow the thread of only one aspiration, target metric, leading indicator, pattern, driver, and system activity. In a real analysis, the base of this pyramid would, of course, be much wider.

With this knowledge in hand, you are ready to plan for delivery.

Exhibit 2B.8 K–12 system going from aspiration to implementation: The delivery pyramid in practice

	Step	Aspect to determine	Example
Chapter 2	1	**Aspiration**	• State leads the nation in college and career-readiness
	2	**Target metric** and related leading indicators	• Target metric: College and career-ready (CCR) graduation rate • Leading indicator example: Algebra II course enrollment and passage rates
	3	**Performance pattern**	• CCR graduation rate in low-SES population is lower than the national average for low-SES students, and has been declining for each year that it has been measured
	4	**Drivers** of performance pattern	• Students are inadequately prepared to succeed in core CCR courses
	5	**System activities** that address driver	• Peer tutoring program that provides targeted help to students for core CCR courses
Chapter 3	6	**Interventions that improve or add system activities**	**Identified changes to existing system activity** ① Improve quality of program • Select more effective teachers • Improve curriculum ② Improve reach of program (offer at more schools) **Added additional system activities** ③ Add double periods for students who are struggling in CCR courses
	7	**Trajectory** of target metric, with accompanying **target**	① Created baseline (CCR Grad rate; Today; Time) ② Added impact of interventions (CCR Grad rate; Today; Time) ③ Set target It is projected that the 3 interventions will raise CCR graduation rates by 15% over 5 years. After checking with stakeholders and schools to make sure it was realistic and ambitious enough, target is set: Raise graduation rates by 20% by 2017
	8	**Plans** by intervention	Plan developed for ① Improve quality of program. Tracks: • Target: CCR graduation rate • Leading indicator: number of students enrolled in and passing core CCR courses • Other milestone: number of schools using new curriculum

3

Plan for Delivery

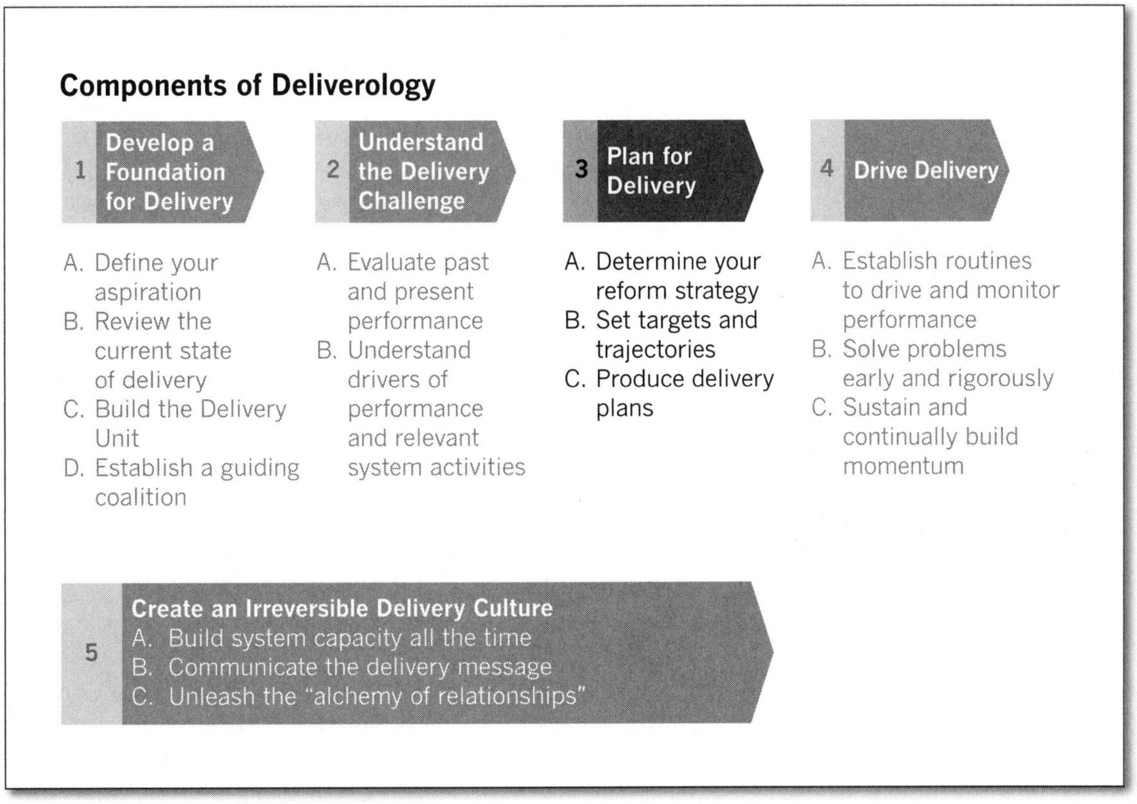

Components of Deliverology

1 Develop a Foundation for Delivery

A. Define your aspiration
B. Review the current state of delivery
C. Build the Delivery Unit
D. Establish a guiding coalition

2 Understand the Delivery Challenge

A. Evaluate past and present performance
B. Understand drivers of performance and relevant system activities

3 Plan for Delivery

A. Determine your reform strategy
B. Set targets and trajectories
C. Produce delivery plans

4 Drive Delivery

A. Establish routines to drive and monitor performance
B. Solve problems early and rigorously
C. Sustain and continually build momentum

5 Create an Irreversible Delivery Culture

A. Build system capacity all the time
B. Communicate the delivery message
C. Unleash the "alchemy of relationships"

You have defined where you want to be, and you have learned where you are. The next logical question is, "How are we going to get there?" With the facts about performance in hand, it is time to help your **system leader** define your **system's** approach to addressing the **delivery challenge**, to set a concrete and measurable definition of success, and to produce plans that will help your system to get there.

The diagnosis that you conducted in Chapter 2 was the first part of moving from **aspiration** to implementation. In this chapter, you will use the information you have gathered to complete the process. Returning to our **delivery pyramid**, we will now focus on the last three steps: determining the **interventions** of your **reform strategy**, setting the **targets**, and developing the plans around those targets (Exhibit 3).

These last three steps are described in the following modules:

A. Determine your reform strategy

B. Set targets and trajectories

C. Produce delivery plans

3A. DETERMINE YOUR REFORM STRATEGY

"It is undesirable to traverse a chasm in two leaps."

—Attributed to David Lloyd George,
Former Prime Minister of the U.K.

Note to delivery leaders*: Strategy is primarily the responsibility of the system leader. This module is primarily a guide for system leaders on public sector strategy. Your role as* ***delivery leader*** *is highlighted where appropriate.*

With a thorough understanding of the challenge you face, as well as what your system is (and is not) doing to overcome that challenge, your system now has the information it needs to inform its overall **strategy.** The building blocks of that strategy are interventions: changes to system activities that are designed to help your system achieve its aspiration.

Interventions can take two forms:

- Changes to current system activities (including improvements to activities, expansions of effective activities, and removal/replacement of ineffective activities); and
- Creation of new system activities to address unmet needs.

It is critically important for your Delivery Unit to recognize that there are no "silver bullets" in a delivery effort—no quick substitutes for a careful, well-prepared and executed strategy. No matter how compelling an individual intervention may seem, only a careful selection and combination of interventions can yield the transformation in performance that you require to achieve your system's aspiration. The thoughtfulness of this combination will make the difference between true strategy and a mere grab bag of initiatives.

Exhibit 3 Moving from aspiration to implementation: The "delivery pyramid"

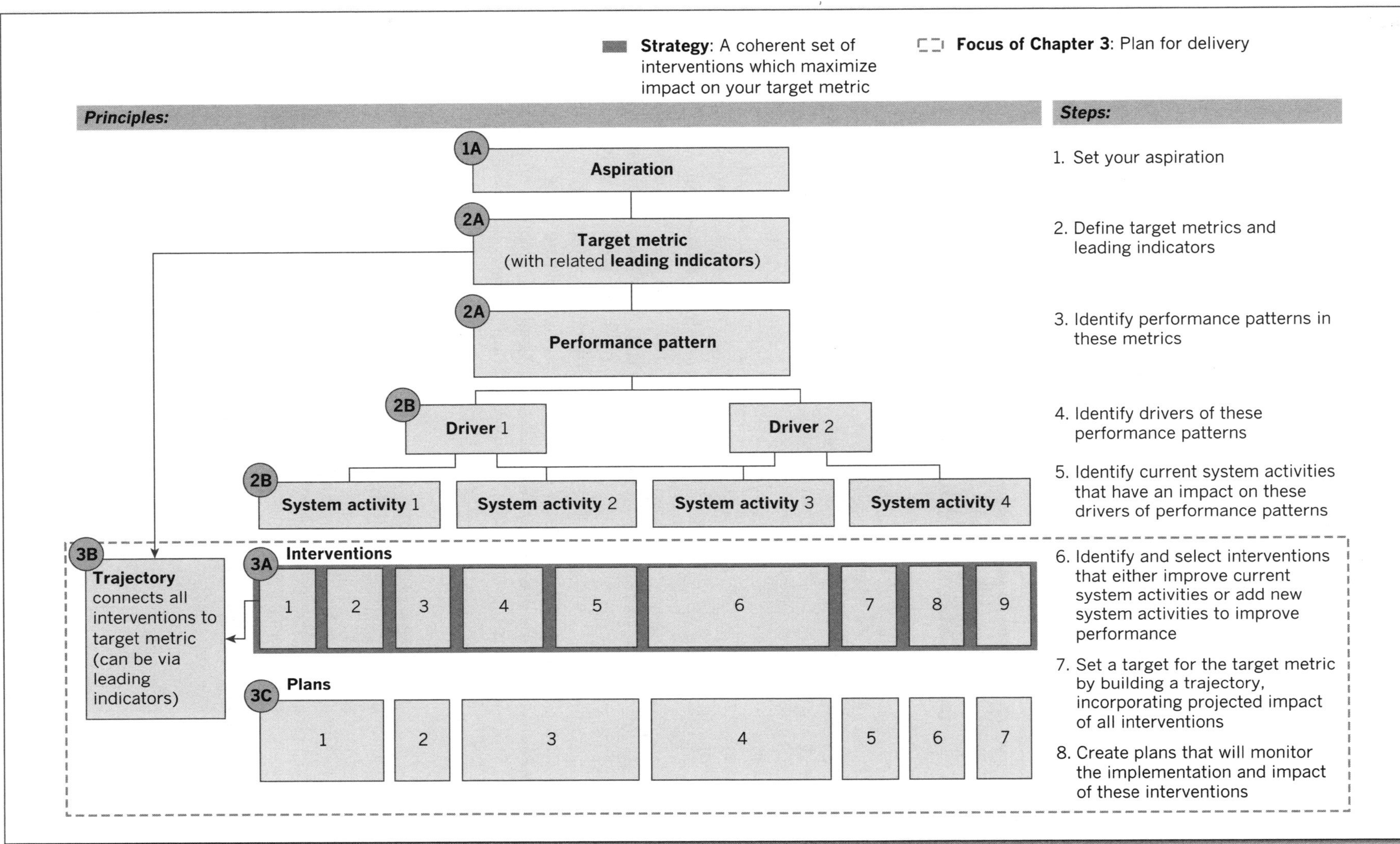
Strategy: A coherent set of interventions which maximize impact on your target metric
Focus of Chapter 3: Plan for delivery
Principles:
1A
Aspiration
2A
Target metric
(with related leading indicators)
2A
Performance pattern
2B
Driver 1
Driver 2
2B
System activity 1
System activity 2
System activity 3
System activity 4
3B
Trajectory
connects all interventions to target metric (can be via leading indicators)
3A
Interventions
1
2
3
4
5
6
7
8
9
3C
Plans
1
2
3
4
5
6
7
Steps:
1. Set your aspiration
2. Define target metrics and leading indicators
3. Identify performance patterns in these metrics
4. Identify drivers of these performance patterns
5. Identify current system activities that have an impact on these drivers of performance patterns
6. Identify and select interventions that either improve current system activities or add new system activities to improve performance
7. Set a target for the target metric by building a trajectory, incorporating projected impact of all interventions
8. Create plans that will monitor the implementation and impact of these interventions

For this reason, the definition of *strategy* is as follows: A strategy is a coherent set of interventions that combine to maximize impact on your target metrics. The interventions in a strategy are chosen and arranged according to four principles:

- Each intervention is consistent with your **theory of change** (defined on page 79), which lends your strategy its internal coherence.
- Each intervention is *powerful on its own,* proven or promising in its potential impact (per dollar spent) on your target metrics.
- The interventions in a strategy are *integrated,* building on each other such that the effect of the whole is greater than the sum of the parts.
- The interventions in a strategy are *sequenced,* taking into account their interdependencies with each other, your resources over time, and the constant need to build momentum and sustain energy.

MORE THAN THE SUM OF THE PARTS

"To judge from the press commentary on government, it would be easy to think that, for each of the vast array of problems facing modern societies, there are obvious right and wrong solutions—and, the argument goes, if only those obtuse politicians would select the right ones, all would be well. In fact, major public service and/or social problems are usually much more complex than that. The solutions lie not in one simple remedy, but in the sustained implementation of a combination of actions." (*Instruction to Deliver,* 90)

Strategy is important for several reasons. First, without it, your system may struggle to deliver anything beyond incremental improvement. Second, strategy clarifies a system's efforts. By articulating the core work of your system, a strategy serves as a true compass for your Delivery Unit and the system actors responsible for delivery. Lastly, a well-crafted strategy will be an important tool for communication, as it allows people to see the realistic connection between the work that is being done and the final aspiration, further driving motivation and inspiration.

This module will teach you how to create your strategy by articulating or identifying your system's theory of change, selecting a combination of aligned interventions, and then integrating and sequencing those interventions in a way that maximizes their effect.

ROLES OF SYSTEM LEADER AND DELIVERY LEADER

Your system leader and her team are responsible for setting the strategy, particularly the theory of change. The scope of your Delivery Unit's work will vary depending on the quality of any existing strategy that your system has developed. On one hand, if your system has a well-developed strategy, your Unit may need to only identify the theory of change in place, understand the existing strategy and interventions, and then test them to ensure that they are consistent and sufficient to achieve the aspiration. On the other hand, if strategy is poorly defined, your Delivery Unit has the responsibility to point this out and to catalyze strategy development by those responsible.

As delivery leader, your influence over strategy will occur mostly through your delivery activities, and it will be substantial but indirect. In the course of setting trajectories (Module 3B), producing delivery plans (Module 3C), and monitoring progress (Chapter 4), your Unit will surface feedback that will reflect back on the strategy. You will thus provide the system leader with a unique and influential perspective on the top team, as you will be the only person who understands delivery at the system, middle management, and frontline levels.

PROCESS STEPS

Step 1: Determine the theory of change
Step 2: Identify the interventions that could improve delivery
Step 3: Select and sequence interventions to develop your strategy

Step 1: Determine the theory of change

A *theory of change* succinctly articulates your system's belief about the best way to achieve its aspiration. Your theory of change will be an organizing force for your strategy. As Professor Michael Fullan (2008) writes, "Good theories are critical because they give you a handle on the underlying reason (really the underlying thinking) behind actions and their consequences. Without a good theory, all you can do is acquire techniques" (p. 16). A theory of change is expressed as a set of interrelated themes that focus your system's efforts on those things that are most likely to affect your target metric. These themes can be content areas that the system will focus on, models of implementation, or a combination of the two. For example, high standards, quality teachers, and a focus on struggling schools are examples of content-area themes, while command and control, devolution and transparency, and "quasi markets" are examples of models of implementation.

CASE EXAMPLE

An approach to a theory of change

The article "Three Paradigms of Public-Sector Reform" (Barber, 2007) describes a general theory of change framework. This framework, which includes both models of implementation and content areas, can be applied broadly to public sector reform.

This framework shows three models of implementation that a government can choose: command and control, devolution and transparency, and quasi markets. These models can only be effective if they are combined with a focus on two others: (1) capability, **capacity,** and culture and (2) performance management. The entire theory of change is guided by the strategic direction: the content-area themes that are specific to the situation the government faces. These components are explained in more detail below.

(Continued)

(Continued)

Exhibit 3A.1 A theory of change

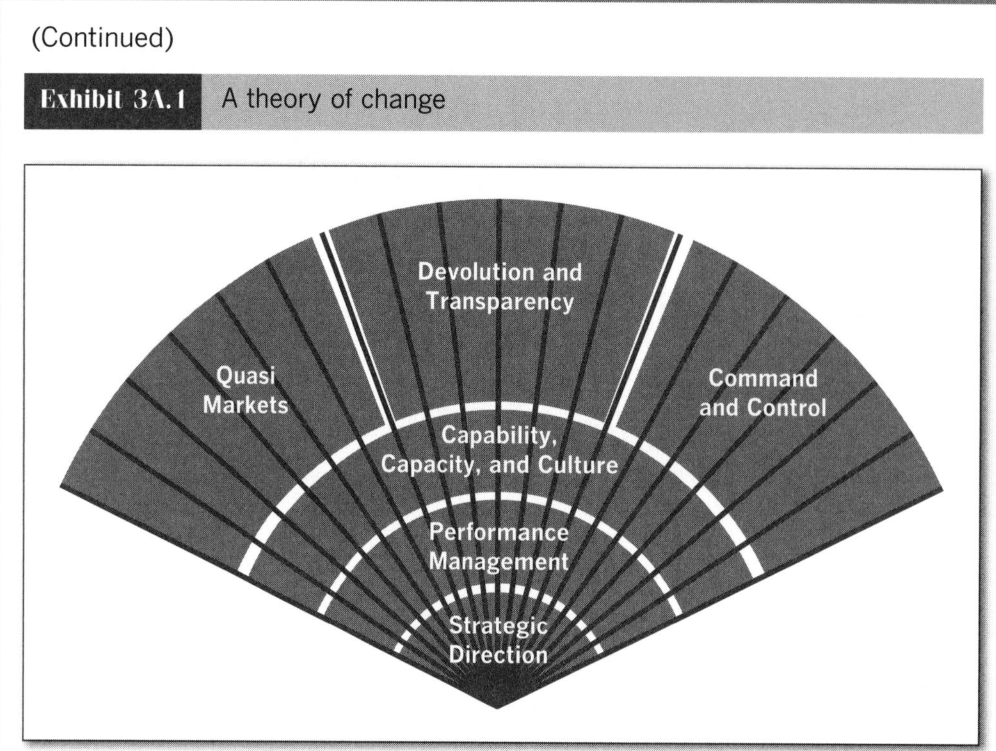

Command and control is a top-down approach to delivering change. For example, a state education department may create a curriculum for a particular course and mandate that all struggling schools use this curriculum (usually through a lever such as funding). Direct command and control requires a strong set of delivery chains for the activities being implemented. This approach can be useful during the start of a delivery effort, when you know little about system actors and their relative capacity. In a command and control model, it is important to be unapologetic for the changes undertaken, but it is also crucial that the system leader's ability to enforce decisions down the delivery chain not be overestimated. Command and control is only as effective as the direction from the top, and therefore excellent execution is key in this implementation principle. When the center controls the details of reform, it is paramount that the center is making the right decisions. There is nothing worse than command and control incompetently implemented.

Devolution and transparency involves pushing responsibility for specific decisions away from the center and toward the frontline and relying on transparency of results and incentive systems to drive performance. In the example of the state education system, this principle could involve providing the desired curriculum as a model but allowing schools to choose their own approach, checking only that they deliver the required results. For devolution and transparency, operational flexibility and accurate reporting are key.

The quasi markets approach involves defining a "customer" or "user," giving that person or organization some choice between providers of services, and allowing competition for users to drive performance of those providers. The most obvious (and perhaps controversial) example of this in K–12 education is a school voucher program (or, to a lesser extent, charter schools), in which the customers are students, and the providers are schools. In the case of the state education system example, a state could set certain standards for what students must know and be able to do in order to pass the course but leave it up to the individual districts to purchase curricular services to meet those standards. The "customer" in this case is the district, and their choice of providers will spur a competition to develop the curriculum that is most likely to help students reach the required standard. For quasi markets to be successful, there must be a clearly defined user, user choice and flexibility, multiple options, and funding that follows the choices made by the user.

Each **model of implementation** is appropriate in different circumstances, and a single system can employ all three for different types of interventions and at different points in time. One crude but useful guide for choosing a model is to ask about the current performance of the government service in question. In the U.K. under Prime Minister Tony Blair, the PMDU used a four-point scale designed to encompass the full range of performance for the various public services whose improvement was sought (Exhibit 3A.2).

Command and control may be necessary for moving your system from "awful" to "adequate," as the system may demand strong, effective intervention. To move from "good" to "great," devolution and transparency or quasi markets would likely be necessary to harness sufficient initiative and innovation to make the leap. Circumstances appropriate to each of the models of implementation are summarized in Exhibit 3A.3.

Actual and political conditions mean the three models will often be applied in combination. For example, New York City's school reform has explicitly combined elements of all three approaches (Exhibit 3A.4). This exhibit also draws attention to some of the issues the different models raise. For example, as quasi market pressures are introduced, the threat to equity must be managed. This is evident in Sweden, where the government has welcomed independent providers of new schools. To prevent cherry-picking, however, these schools are not permitted to select students on the basis of academic performance.

Exhibit 3A.2 A four-point scale for public services

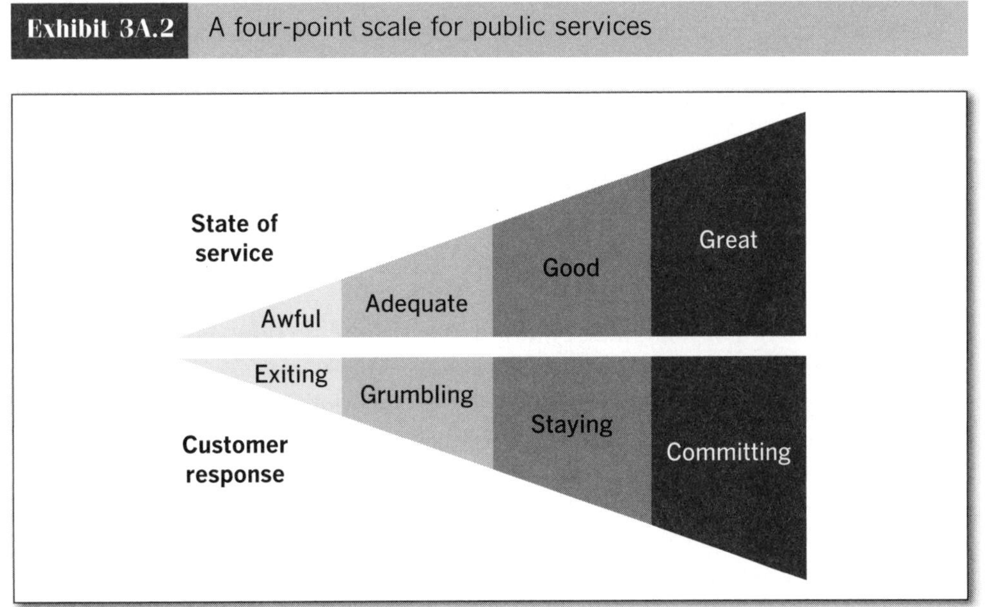

(Continued)

(Continued)

Exhibit 3A.3 Choosing among the options

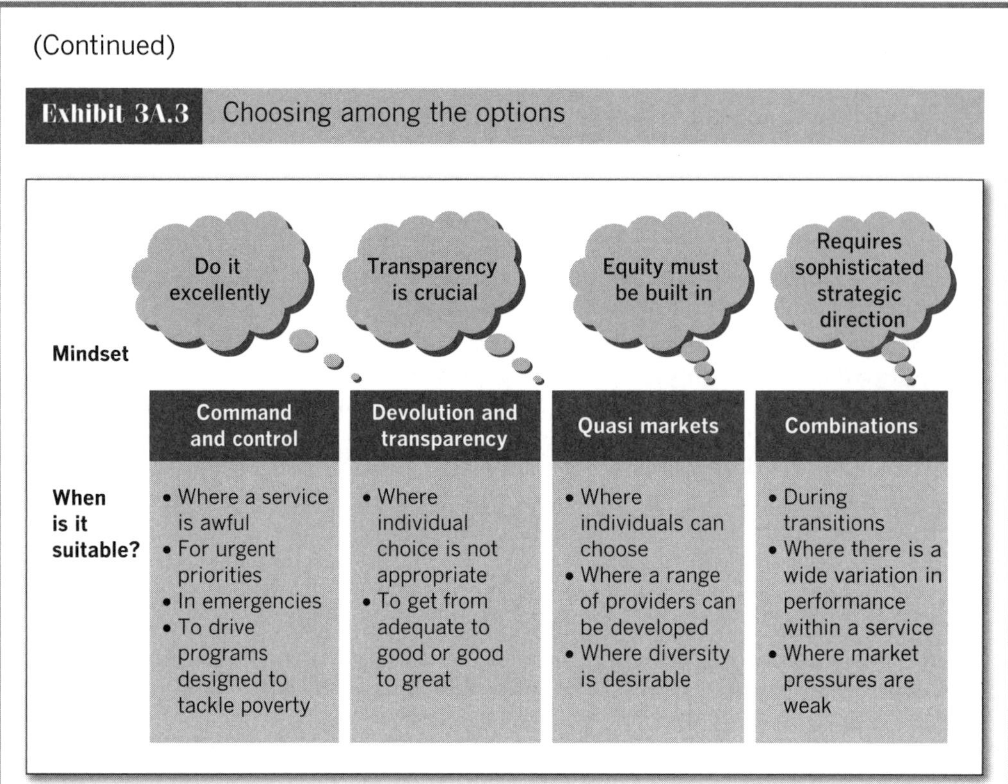

Do it excellently
Transparency is crucial
Equity must be built in
Requires sophisticated strategic direction
Mindset
Command and control
Devolution and transparency
Quasi markets
Combinations
When is it suitable?
• Where a service is awful
• For urgent priorities
• In emergencies
• To drive programs designed to tackle poverty
• Where individual choice is not appropriate
• To get from adequate to good or good to great
• Where individuals can choose
• Where a range of providers can be developed
• Where diversity is desirable
• During transitions
• Where there is a wide variation in performance within a service
• Where market pressures are weak

In this generalized theory of change, any model of implementation you choose will only be effective if three underlying requirements are in place. First, you need to ensure that the system delivering the service has the capability, capacity, and culture to be effective. This means they need to have the right skills and attitude to get the job done (see Module 5A for more on how to build capacity). Second, you need to have a performance management system: Data on performance must be transparent so that people can understand their progress, the government can intervene if there are problems, and the system can make more informed choices about the reform it wants to create. Finally, you must have strategic direction—specific content areas on which your system focuses—in order to gain and maintain public confidence.

A good theory of change should also articulate how its themes are interrelated and why they have been chosen.

If your system leader has not clearly defined a theory of change for the system, your Delivery Unit can use the following guiding questions to arrive at a working definition.

- Looking back on the **performance patterns** and causes identified in Chapter 2, in which content areas could the impact on your aspiration be greatest? Which performance patterns or causes leave the most room for your system to grow? For example, *teacher effectiveness* may be chosen as a theme in K–12 education, both because it is an

Exhibit 3A.4 NYCDOE has used a combination of implementation models to advance its theory of change

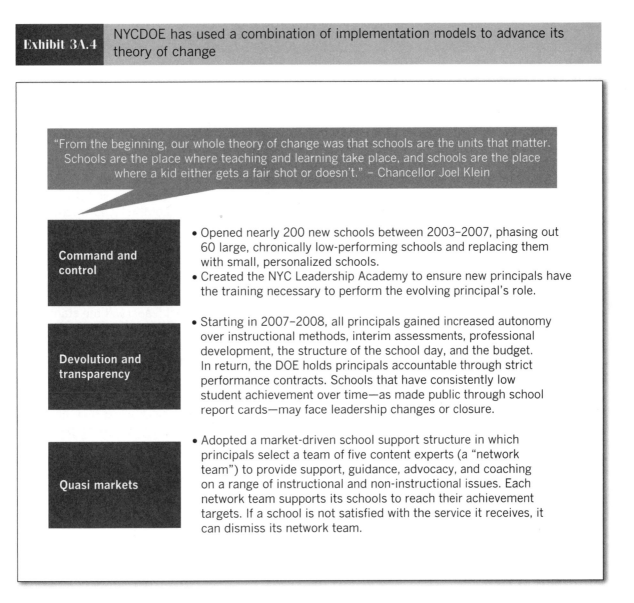

"From the beginning, our whole theory of change was that schools are the units that matter. Schools are the place where teaching and learning take place, and schools are the place where a kid either gets a fair shot or doesn't." - Chancellor Joel Klein

Command and control

- Opened nearly 200 new schools between 2003–2007, phasing out 60 large, chronically low-performing schools and replacing them with small, personalized schools.
- Created the NYC Leadership Academy to ensure new principals have the training necessary to perform the evolving principal's role.

Devolution and transparency

- Starting in 2007–2008, all principals gained increased autonomy over instructional methods, interim assessments, professional development, the structure of the school day, and the budget. In return, the DOE holds principals accountable through strict performance contracts. Schools that have consistently low student achievement over time—as made public through school report cards—may face leadership changes or closure.

- Adopted a market-driven school support structure in which principals select a team of five content experts (a "network team") to provide support, guidance, advocacy, and coaching on a range of instructional and non-instructional issues. Each network team supports its schools to reach their achievement targets. If a school is not satisfied with the service it receives, it can dismiss its network team.

important **driver** of almost any important outcome and because benchmarks suggest that your system has a substantial gap to close with others that are best in class.

- What are your system's strengths? Which of these can be best exploited to achieve your system's aspiration? For example, if your system is very good at *innovation,* a model of implementation that maximizes innovative potential, such as quasi markets, might be considered for adoption.
- Are crucial enablers of your broader strategy not yet in place? For example, if your *data infrastructure* is lacking, and you know that you cannot focus on another theme (e.g., devolution and transparency) without it, then the development of world-class data systems may become a theme in your system's strategy.

CASE EXAMPLE

Theory of change for federal education policy: The Race to the Top Fund

The 2009 American Reinvestment and Recovery Act (ARRA) included a potentially revolutionary provision for education: the authorization of nearly $5 billion in funds that the Department of Education could award, at its discretion, to states that seek to create the conditions for education innovation and reform.

A fund such as this is only as good as its theory of change: How would the Department of Education distribute the money? What policies and practices (or promises of them) would it reward? The theory of change for the Race to the Top Fund is summarized in the themes in Exhibit 3A.5.

In a 2009 speech to Achieve's annual leadership meeting, Joanne Weiss of the Department for Education explained how the pieces fit together:

> "Standards and assessments are the core of our agenda—common, career and college ready standards, and the assessments that measure them—these are the bedrock on which the rest of the reforms are built.
>
> Sitting on top of that foundation, we need great teachers and great school leaders. If the standards tell us what matters, the teachers and principals are the ones who translate that into instruction and who guide our students' learning. Our entire human capital agenda is built around these two facts: (1) great teaching matters, and (2) great teaching happens more consistently in schools led by great principals . . .
>
> The next element of our agenda concerns data. To guide their students' learning, educators need good information about what students know and can do, and they need it available at their fingertips so that they can adjust and differentiate their instruction appropriately. When coupled with strong professional development and a school-wide culture of continuous improvement, data is a powerful lever for change.
>
> Fourth and finally, we have a moral obligation to turn around our persistently lower-performing schools. No system is stronger than its weakest link, and we have to focus special and particular attention on the neediest of the children we serve.
>
> We have to make sure that they have the best of the best, because when you're far behind, you need support the most—these students need access to the best teachers and the best principals running the best, most effective schools. And they need it urgently."

Exhibit 3A.5 Race to the Top priority areas

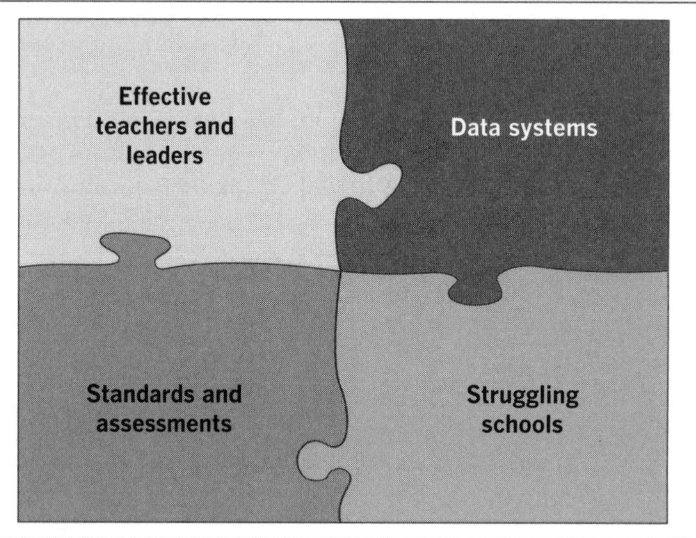

Step 2: Identify the interventions that could improve delivery

Once you have identified or determined your theory of change, you can begin the process of identifying the interventions that will comprise your strategy. Recall that interventions can take either of two forms:

- Changes to current system activities (including improvements to activities, expansions of effective activities, and removal/replacement of ineffective activities); and
- Creation of new system activities to address unmet needs.

CASE EXAMPLE

Removing distractors

While removing or decreasing the scope of current system activities may not seem like significant interventions, they are actually very powerful means to drive effective delivery. By deprioritizing less effective activities, you are removing distractors from the main mission of your reform. Sometimes, to be able to achieve success in the most important areas, you may need to be less demanding in other areas.

For example, in the United Kingdom, the Department of Education made it clear that it was focusing on achievement in math and English, and some teachers reacted by arguing that the degree of prescription in the rest of the national curriculum should be reduced. In response, the government relaxed the national curriculum requirements outside of math and English. This allowed improvement in these priority areas that otherwise would not have been possible.

Some distractors can be so explosive that it is worth paying for their removal. In 2004, Ontario's government agreed to a four-year pay deal with teacher unions so that contract negotiations over that period would not distract from the government's focus on math, English, and graduation rates.

As noted above, interventions are the building blocks of your strategy; your Delivery Unit can play a pivotal role in understanding potential interventions and advising your system leader on their fit with your system's emerging strategy.

In order to determine the range of interventions available, you will begin by examining current system activities. For this, you can use both the activity profiles and drivers of underperformance that you created in Chapter 2. The activity profiles will allow you to identify potential interventions that involve changes to current system activities. After this step, you can return to your identified drivers of underperformance, ask if there are any drivers that are not being addressed by current system activities, and identify additional interventions that involve the introduction of new system activities if necessary. Exhibit 3A.6 summarizes this process.

First, you will examine each activity's profile to judge whether the activity has added significantly to the attainment of your aspiration (as measured by your target metric). Making this judgment is not an exact science; understanding a specific activity's contribution to an overall target metric can be difficult, and the definition of *significant* can be a matter of judgment. Your system leader and other critical **stakeholders** can help to establish an

Exhibit 3A.6 Activity evaluation process to determine potential interventions

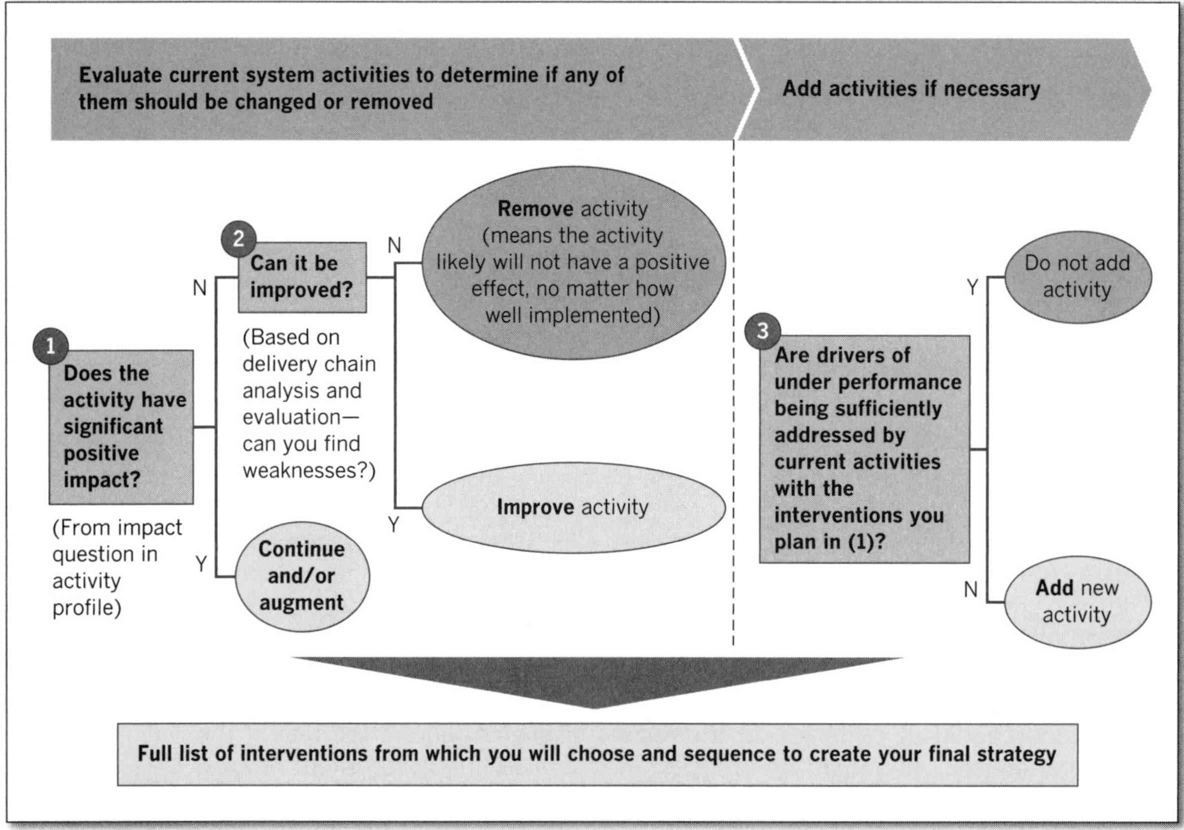

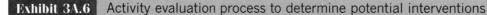

agreed standard here. Your Delivery Unit can contribute by going beyond the data to report how activities play out at the frontline.

Sometimes, the data may be insufficient to allow an accurate understanding of an activity's impact on the target metric. If you nonetheless believe that the activity can make an impact on student outcomes, then the intervention should be to improve the tracking of data to verify this.

For those activities that appear to have a significant impact on your target metric, you can either decide to leave them as they are or to expand their reach (e.g., to have more schools adopt a successful program or to allow for increased student enrollment). However, if an activity is not having an impact, you need to determine whether there is room for improvement. Are there particular ways to improve implementation for the activity in question? Could you improve impact by increasing funding or using funding more efficiently? These options will become your first set of potential interventions.

CASE EXAMPLE

Sometimes, the need to change the delivery chain structure is so pressing that it becomes an intervention in and of itself. In Montgomery County, Superintendent Jerry Weast recognized this need and pushed to reorganize the school district accordingly.

> "The reorganization was designed to support student achievement by focusing system assets and resources directly on schools. According to the new plan, clusters of schools would be supported by a matrix of teams, each reporting to one of six community superintendents. This new system was in marked contrast to the old structure in which principals had run their schools for several years with very little oversight or support and without a clear districtwide strategy." (*Leading for Equity,* 94)

If the delivery chain seems to be sound but the activity still fails to advance the aspiration, then the activity itself may be the problem. In such cases, you should consider removing the activity and replacing it with one that will use your system's resources better.

Finally, once you have identified all potential interventions that are focused on changing current system activities, the next question is aimed at a deeper level: Do these current activities adequately address the most critical drivers of system underperformance? If not, you should consider the last type of intervention: adding new activities. As there will likely be many possible new activities, you should prioritize those that are consistent with your theory of change, likely to achieve impact with respect to your system's aspiration, and appropriate to the strengths of your system. You can turn to several sources to find ideas for new activities.

- **Research.** Are there activities that are proven to help achieve your aspiration, or address one or more of the drivers of underperformance you identified?
- **Benchmarks.**
  - *Historic and internal.* What are the best practices within your system, or what activities have contributed to themes of strong performance, in the past or present? Can those activities be replicated or expanded across your system?
  - *External and international.* Has any system in the world achieved what you want your system to achieve? If so, what activities did they use? What are the implications for your system?
  - *Functional.* Do systems in different sectors excel at a function critical to your system's successful delivery? (e.g., Who are the best managers of talent? They may not be school systems.)
- **Organizations with expertise.** There are several organizations with deep knowledge in K–12 and higher education best practices, such as The Education Trust or Achieve. Organizations like these can recommend activities appropriate to your situation.

The result of this process should be a complete list of potential interventions that your system could undertake in order to achieve your aspiration. The next step is to craft a coherent strategy from this list.

Step 3: Select and sequence interventions to develop your strategy

How can you develop a list of potential interventions into a full strategy? Remember, each intervention in your strategy must be

- Consistent with your *theory of change;*
- *Powerful on its own,* generating the most impact per dollar;
- *Integrated,* building on each other such that the effect of the whole is greater than the sum of the parts; and
- *Sequenced,* taking into account their interdependence with other interventions, your resources over time, and the constant need to build momentum and sustain energy.

In Step 2, you identified interventions consistent with your theory of change (the first principle in the list above). In Step 3, you will test these interventions for their fit with the other three principles. In order to do this, you will need to evaluate potential interventions according to a list of criteria. To evaluate interventions that involve changing current activities, you may need to draw again upon information collected in their activity profiles. To evaluate interventions that propose new activities, you may need to profile these potential activities using the same process described in Module 2B.

The criteria by which you will evaluate potential interventions, both individually and as a group, are summarized in Exhibit 3A.7.

Exhibit 3A.7 Principles for selecting and sequencing interventions to create a cohesive strategy

Principles	Description	Example
Choose interventions that are **powerful** on their own	• Maximize impact on aspiration based on research (with strong track records of impact in other programs) • Minimize resources spent for impact achieved	• Choose to focus on teacher effectiveness rather than an additional lunch support program as it is shown to have a stronger impact on graduation rates for the money spent
Maximize **integration** effect	• Choose interventions that strengthen each other	• Improve both teacher effectiveness and curriculum as the former increases efficacy of the latter • Choose not to invest in a proven peer counseling program because it will not build on the momentum of other planned interventions
Sequence to balance resources, impact, and interdependencies over time	• Ensure that given human and financial resources are sufficient and adequately spaced through the effort over time • Minimize the number and length of periods where there is no impact or evidence of progress • Take into account interdependent interventions, if one may have to come before another. Allow them to build off each other in a logical, efficient manner	• Launch student counseling program in lowest-performing campuses first before expanding to all campuses because it will have greater impact • Equip teachers to use new curriculum before evaluating the quality of instruction

In a difficult economic environment, the first category will be especially important. This is why it is so important to document the financial resources required for every activity as part of its profile. Benchmarking is a key tool to use to estimate the efficient cost of your interventions.

The process of selecting and sequencing interventions will be iterative. For example, you may choose many strong and integrated interventions and find that, even if they all begin implementation immediately, noticeable impact will not come until Year 3. In this case, you may decide to add an intervention that delivers some quick wins in Years 1 and 2, which may require you to eliminate or scale back some of your other interventions.

Through this iterative process, you should eventually arrive at a coherent strategy that tells a clear and compelling story about how the interventions you selected will drive significant and balanced progress toward your aspiration.

Exhibit 3A.8 gives a few examples how systems selected, integrated, and sequenced interventions.

Exhibit 3A.8 Selecting and sequencing interventions in two LEAs

Principles	Mid-sized urban school district	Montgomery County Public Schools
Choose interventions that are **powerful** on their own	• Identified teacher effectiveness as a critical lever in improving student achievement and selected several promising strategies to build district's teacher effectiveness levels, including – Improving evaluation process – Improving hiring processes – Creating teacher residency program – Creating high-impact teacher roles	• Created a new strategic planning process based on the well-respected Baldrige quality system • Modeled its accountability and organizational learning system on the New York City Police Department's successful CompStat model
Maximize **integration** effect	• Strengthened its evaluation process, allowing the district to identify those teachers who are qualified to fill new high-impact (and more highly compensated) roles before launching the new roles • Improved hiring practices, making system better equipped to replace those teachers found unsatisfactory in more rigorous evaluation process	• Reorganized top leadership structure in MCPS, creating community superintendents who oversaw clusters of schools and reported to the chief performance officer. • Relied on this new configuration to implement a new strategic planning process and an accountability organization learning system
Sequence to balance resources, impact, and interdependencies over time	• *Interdependencies*: District was able to focus on teacher effectiveness because it had previously developed strong school leadership and curriculum • *Impact*: The district created an intensive on-boarding process for new teachers, but understood that program's impact would not be seen for several years. In the short term, district raised its hiring standards.	• *Resources*: Unable to do everything at once, the district first made significant investments in building the instructional capacity of teachers in the lowest-performing schools, rolling it out to the remaining schools later.

SOURCE: Interviews, *Leading for Equity*, pp. 7–8.

Note that this process may generate many interventions for your system to implement; be sure that your Delivery Unit focuses on monitoring only those with the highest impact in terms of the target metric, as the efficacy of the unit will be diluted if the unit's resources are spread too thin.

Conclusion

By now, you have learned

- What a strategy is, what a theory of change is, and why they are important;
- How to identify potential interventions to achieve your system's aspiration; and
- How to combine and sequence interventions to form a coherent strategy.

The strategy resulting from this process is the blueprint that will guide your system toward its aspiration. It is the first piece of your overall plan for delivery. The next module will teach you how to quantify and project the impact of the interventions you have chosen, setting specific targets in light of both your aspiration and your strategy for achieving it.

3B. SET TARGETS AND TRAJECTORIES

"You have to draw the line somewhere."

—Anonymous

Any credible government must have clear objectives and a way to know at a given moment whether it is on track to achieving them. With aspirations, a strategy, and target metrics measuring success, your system is ready to set targets: commitments by your system to achieve specific levels of performance on its target metrics by a defined point in time.

While few would disagree in the abstract with the idea of having a target, some might find setting specific time-bound targets risky, especially in the public sector, where positive public perception is crucial but control over outcomes can be challenging. For system leaders, specific targets create the real possibility of "failure."

This module lays out an approach that will help your system set targets that are connected with realities on the ground. At its heart is a simple concept: A properly defined, well-thought-out target should actually increase the probability of accomplishment, by explicitly connecting system aspirations to the facts on the ground.

CASE EXAMPLE

The power of a number

A well-understood target can also help incite your system staff to action, as the chief officer of one K–12 state school found, "We needed to reach an 85 percent graduation rate target. In one of the staff's cubicles, there was a piece of paper with a single number circled: 8,700. This was the number of students we had said we needed to achieve our target. Our people are being mobilized around this number and it is very powerful."

Good targets are defined by five characteristics that comprise the SMART framework:

- ***S*pecific.** A target must leave nobody guessing as to its meaning and implications for the expected change.
- ***M*easurable.** A concrete and agreed-upon standard should be established for measuring progress.
- ***A*mbitious.** A good target should feel like a stretch from the current level of performance and inspire your system to rise to a new challenge.
- ***R*ealistic.** A target should be grounded concretely in the internal and external affecting factors—otherwise a target is little more than a guess.
- ***T*ime limited.** Your target should have a defined deadline, both to create a sense of urgency and to allow for accountability.

The most difficult characteristics to combine are ambition and realism. To start with, there appears to be an inherent tension between them. An ambitious target can drive improvement, but an unrealistic one will discourage those responsible for achieving it. On the other hand, aiming too low—underpromising and overdelivering—risks generalizing an acceptance of incremental rather than transformational change.

Perhaps more importantly, the relative ambition or realism of a target is difficult to understand on its face. To many, ambition and realism are matters of opinion owing to the lack of evidence connecting proposed actions to planned outcomes. This is precisely why every target should be accompanied by a *trajectory*.

A *trajectory* is an evidence-based projection of a metric's path over time from its current level to the level suggested by the target. It is your best estimate of the levels of performance your system will achieve en route to achieving its overall target.

Trajectories are crucial pieces of the delivery effort for two reasons. First, because they are based on evidence from both your planned strategy and benchmarks of what is possible, trajectories allow for a meaningful debate over whether a target is ambitious and realistic. More importantly, trajectories serve as a tool to understand your system's progress toward its target on a frequent basis. They allow you to monitor and manage performance, identifying problems early in order to solve them before they endanger the success of your delivery effort. Presented well, trajectories have a powerful visual impact that can clearly communicate the gap between performance and expectation at any point in time. While routines are the core drivers of delivery (see Module 4A), the most important analyses in these routines are the analyses of performance against trajectory. Trajectories (and the targets at the end of each one) underpin your delivery effort and are the anchor on which much of your monitoring in Chapter 4 will be based.

For obvious reasons, trajectory setting is not a perfect science: The evidence will not always be clear, and sometimes it will

THE TRAJECTORY AS LEARNING TOOL

"The combination of the trajectory and the actual data enables constant learning. Thus, for example, [emergency room] waiting times data can be analyzed against trajectory. Supposing aggregate performance is off track, there may still be some hospitals where it is on track. Then the question arises, what are they doing that the others are not? Or it may be on track with, say, ear, nose and throat operations and severely off track in orthopedics. Again, the question arises, what explains the variation?" (*Instruction to Deliver,* 90)

be difficult to find. However, this should not be an excuse to make no estimate at all; rather, it is better to make the best informed guess you can, and then compare it to what in fact happens. You can then review the assumptions behind the guess in the light of the real data as they come in and refine the analysis. The combination of a defined trajectory and constant comparisons to actual data will allow for the kind of timely course correction and problem solving that your system needs to achieve its aspiration. In short, a trajectory enables the system to learn more rapidly and effectively than otherwise would be the case.

ROLES OF SYSTEM LEADER AND DELIVERY LEADER

Your role and the system leader's role will vary depending on whether your system already has set targets; but in every case, you will work with the system leader to facilitate the trajectory-setting process at the system level. Throughout the process, your advice will help the system leader weigh the evidence against the imperative for ambition. The system leader's role is to use this information to set appropriate targets and trajectories. Depending on the system, others may be involved in this decision making as well.

In cases where it is necessary to agree on individual **performance unit** targets, your Delivery Unit can play a role in brokering the negotiations between system leadership and the relevant performance units.

CASE EXAMPLE

Which comes first, the target or the trajectory?

In an ideal world, the evidence base from your trajectory would help you set a target that is both realistic and ambitious. However, circumstances do not always allow for the trajectory to come before the target. Sometimes the target is not entirely in your system's control and may be imposed on you. At other times, your system leader may wish to set the target before the trajectory for other reasons.

- Set minimum standards. When a moral purpose is the most relevant benchmark, targets are set based on the idea that everyone deserves a minimum standard; for example, the idea that all students should graduate high school with the ability to read at a certain grade level.
- Galvanize the system with a **calculated bounce.** Sometimes the evidence is too constrictive of our idea of what is possible. Would JFK have set a goal of putting a man on the moon by the end of the 1960s if he had taken only the evidence into account? Setting an ambitious target first can inspire a system to action. A "calculated bounce" is a projected leap from today's level of performance to a level that is inspirationally ambitious. It signals a transformation in performance and a substantial change from business as usual and usually is in the form of a public commitment. Despite their value in driving motivation and action, however, these bounces are risky. Some examples of calculated bounces:
    - British Prime Minister Tony Blair's promise in January 2003 to halve the number of asylum applications in less than 9 months.
    - President Obama's (2009a) promise that "by 2020, America will once again have the highest proportion of college graduates in the world" (para. 66).

Process steps

The process steps discussed below assume that, beginning with the evidence and analysis, you build a trajectory that will inform the target that your system sets. In cases where the trajectory cannot come first (such as those mentioned above), you may still use the steps below, but with one modification: You start with the overall target as given, and your objective is to build a trajectory that will achieve that target.

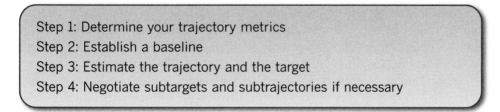

> Step 1: Determine your trajectory metrics
> Step 2: Establish a baseline
> Step 3: Estimate the trajectory and the target
> Step 4: Negotiate subtargets and subtrajectories if necessary

These process steps are adapted from the trajectory methodology developed by Tony O'Connor, the Chief Analyst in the Prime Minister's Delivery Unit, which is summarized in Exhibit 3B.1. Each of the first three steps covers one or more of these critical questions.

Step 1: Determine your trajectory metrics

In Chapter 2, you identified key metrics that could be used for trajectories and analyzed existing patterns in these metrics. From among these metrics, you should choose the ones for which you want to establish targets and trajectories. At a minimum, you should build a trajectory

Exhibit 3B.1 Questions to consider when constructing a trajectory

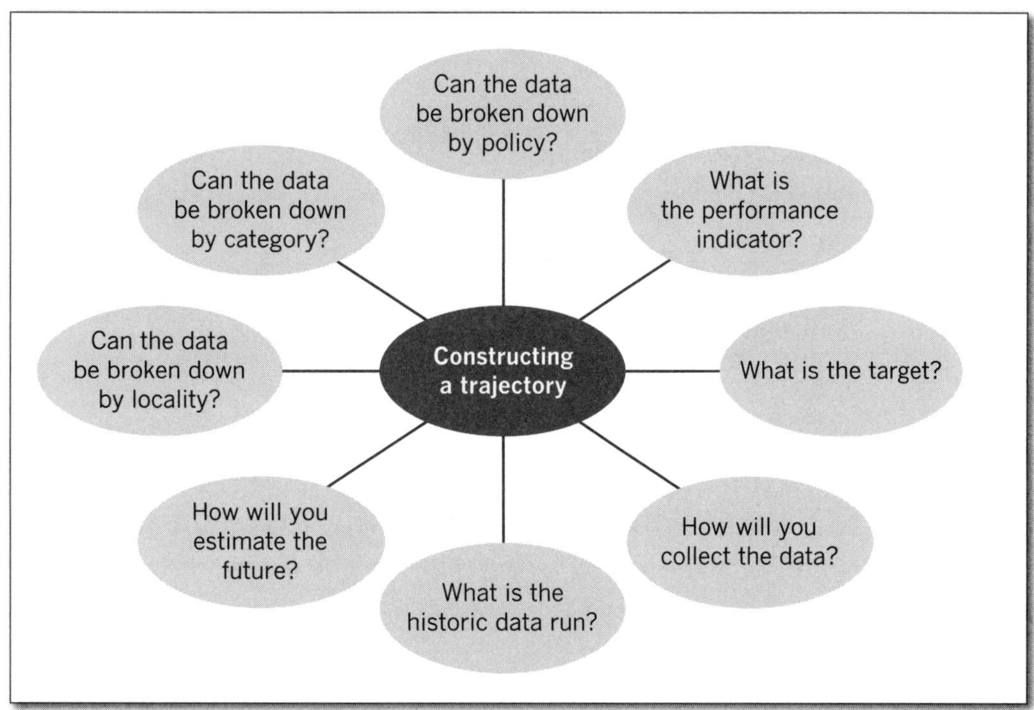

and set a target for your target metric, as it is the most direct representation of your system's aspiration. You may also decide to establish trajectories for other indicators (like **leading indicators**) in order to track progress on a more frequent basis. For example, if your target metric is a K–12 system's college- and career-ready graduation rate, and you know that college and career readiness depends heavily on teacher effectiveness, you may choose to set trajectories for both college- and career-ready graduation rates and for teacher-effectiveness levels (see Exhibit 3B.2).

Your metric should be clear and precise, with a definition that leaves no one in doubt as to its meaning. This precision can sometimes require that metric formulas be relatively complex, as a sampling of the metrics for the "Access to Success Initiative" shows (see Exhibit 3B.3).

Sometimes, a proposed target metric that is vital to your delivery effort will not have been collected or reported properly. In such cases, your role will be to draw attention to the need for new data infrastructure and/or processes to track this metric as soon as possible. Even the PMDU did not begin in a data-rich environment in all of the priority areas it covered. Its refusal to accept the situation it inherited, however, was a key factor in its success.

Exhibit 3B.2 Step 1: Determine your trajectory metrics

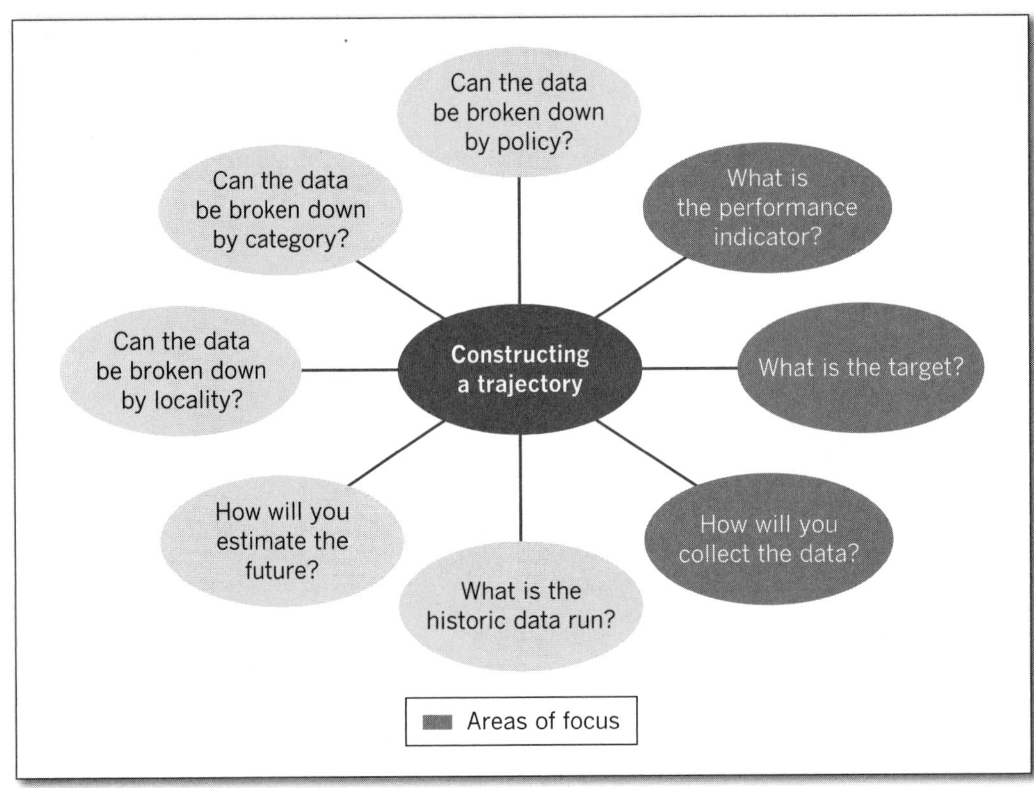

Exhibit 3B.3 Target metrics for the Education Trust's Access to Success program

Aspiration: Enhance student **access** and **success** in higher education, especially for low-income students and students of color

Sample target metrics	Calculation	Important features
• Low-income freshman **access** to bachelor and associate degree programs	% freshman receiving Pell Grants % of state's high school graduates from low-income families	• Readily available data source • Specific proxy for measuring broad concept of "access"
• Low-income freshman **success** in bachelor and associate degree programs	Pell recipient graduation rate Non-Pell recipient graduation rate	• Provides a comparison point against other student groups
• Student progress to degrees	• Year-to-year retention rate of - Low-income students (as defined by Pell status) - Under-represented minorities	• Supporting measure to primary success metric, graduation rate • Offer early indicators of progress to aspiration

SOURCE: The Education Trust.

Exhibit 3B.4 shows how California's K–12 system planned for the creation of a data system that addressed its needs.

Step 2: Establish a baseline

Before you decide where you want your target metric to be in the future, you must understand where it would be if no changes were to occur. This process is called establishing the baseline (see Exhibit 3B.5).

Using the information you have already gathered in Module 2A on performance patterns, you will focus in this step only on the **historical comparison** to determine the trends:

INSISTING ON GETTING THE RIGHT DATA

"In some cases, it took two or even three years to overcome resistance to improving data systems and for the data to begin to flow, but without fail, once the change had occurred, everyone agreed it was vastly for the better. In fact, I would argue that—unsung though it is—this was one of the Delivery Unit's most significant achievements." (*Instruction to Deliver*, 89)

- Has past progress been linear?
- If there were peaks and troughs, what caused them?
- Can you identify "seasonality" in the data that must be accounted for?

Exhibit 3B.4 California recognized the need for better data to drive improvement and created a phased plan for addressing this need

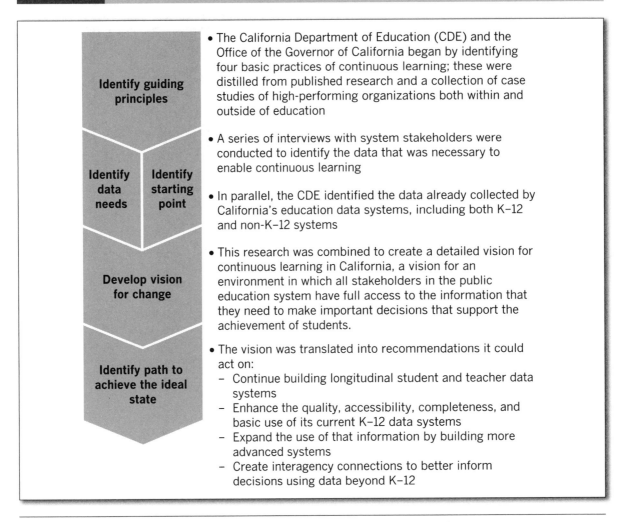

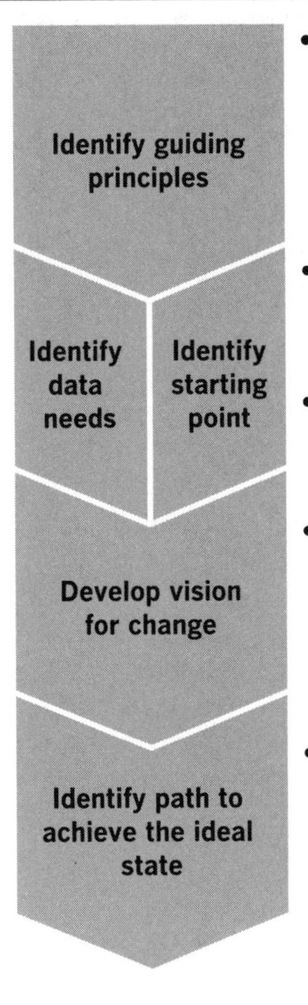

- The California Department of Education (CDE) and the Office of the Governor of California began by identifying four basic practices of continuous learning; these were distilled from published research and a collection of case studies of high-performing organizations both within and outside of education
- A series of interviews with system stakeholders were conducted to identify the data that was necessary to enable continuous learning
- In parallel, the CDE identified the data already collected by California's education data systems, including both K–12 and non-K–12 systems
- This research was combined to create a detailed vision for continuous learning in California, a vision for an environment in which all stakeholders in the public education system have full access to the information that they need to make important decisions that support the achievement of students.
- The vision was translated into recommendations it could act on:
  - Continue building longitudinal student and teacher data systems
  - Enhance the quality, accessibility, completeness, and basic use of its current K–12 data systems
  - Expand the use of that information by building more advanced systems
  - Create interagency connections to better inform decisions using data beyond K–12

SOURCE: Framework for a Comprehensive Education Data System in California (December 2008).

Using those trends, you should project the baseline future for that data, assuming no interventions. This projection must take into account the predicted movement of any other major external factors that would affect the target metric. For example, if the historical data show that a K–12 district has graduated 1,000 students every year for the past 20 years, a reasonable extrapolation would hold that 1,000 will also graduate annually over the next 5 years. But, what if a "baby boom" of students currently in middle school will add 100 more students per graduating class? You must take this into account and estimate the number of additional expected graduates from this enrollment growth in the next 5 years. This is critical to ensuring that a target is sufficiently ambitious; after all, it would make little sense to give the system credit for 100 additional graduates that it did nothing to earn.

Establishing a baseline is not a trivial task: Even if nothing changes, the estimate of future performance relies on several projections about your core data and external factors that are out of your control. For example, when the Access to Success (A2S) initiative set out to establish a baseline

Exhibit 3B.5 Step 2: Establish a baseline

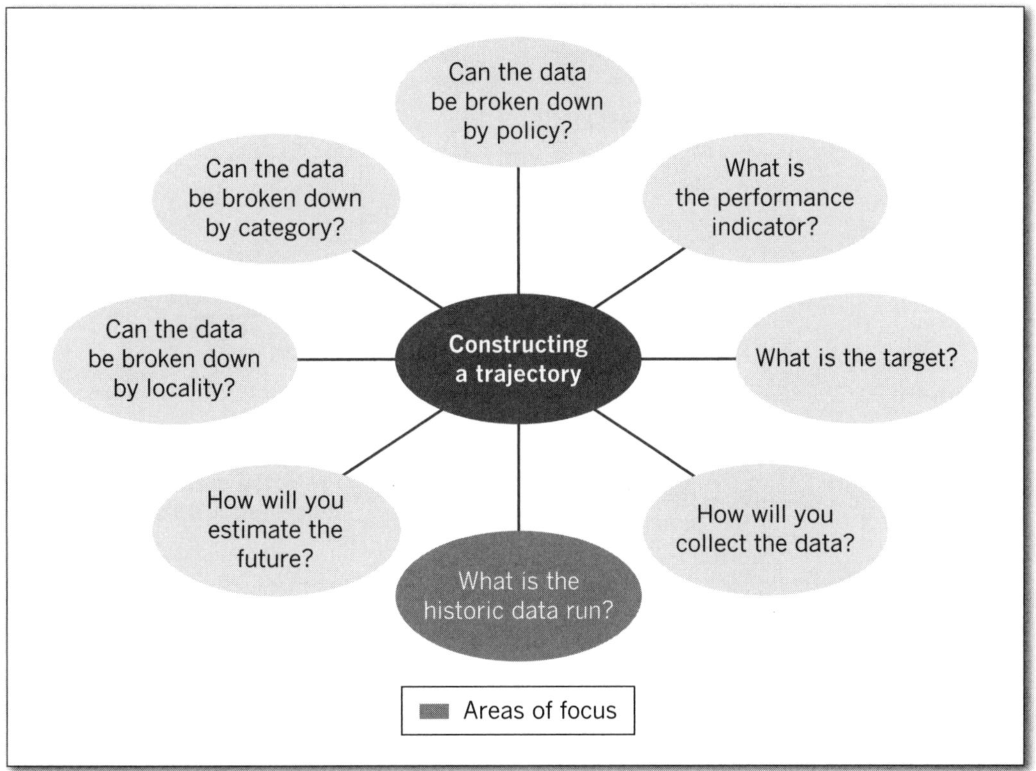

of projected college degree production for state systems, it incorporated into its model estimates of future high school graduation rates and population growth rates—two independent variables that would have an impact on absolute degree production.

A baseline is important because it will help you to understand your starting point. In the example on page 98, a K–12 system has set a target of graduating 80% of its student's college and career ready by 2017. This translates to 81,700 graduates. The baseline establishes the gap that the system must close in order to reach this target (Exhibit 3B.6).

In addition to building a baseline for the overall system (e.g., "the system will have 1,200 graduates in five years"), segmenting the baseline into performance units may help in understanding the projected differences in performance between them (e.g., "District A will have 400 graduates, District B will have 800 graduates"). This segmenting will help you to identify the future impact of reforms that may affect different segments differently. The segmenting will also ultimately define an achievable trajectory, as reaching the overall system target may mean very different targets for different groups. To do this, you will use information you already have from your analysis of performance patterns.

In your performance pattern analysis in Module 2A, you may have analyzed the data at various levels of analysis (students, teachers, and performance units such as schools, campuses, and LEAs). For any of these levels of analysis, you may also have grouped the data for comparison along any of three *dimensions:* individuals, characteristics, and

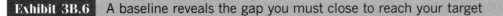

Exhibit 3B.6 A baseline reveals the gap you must close to reach your target

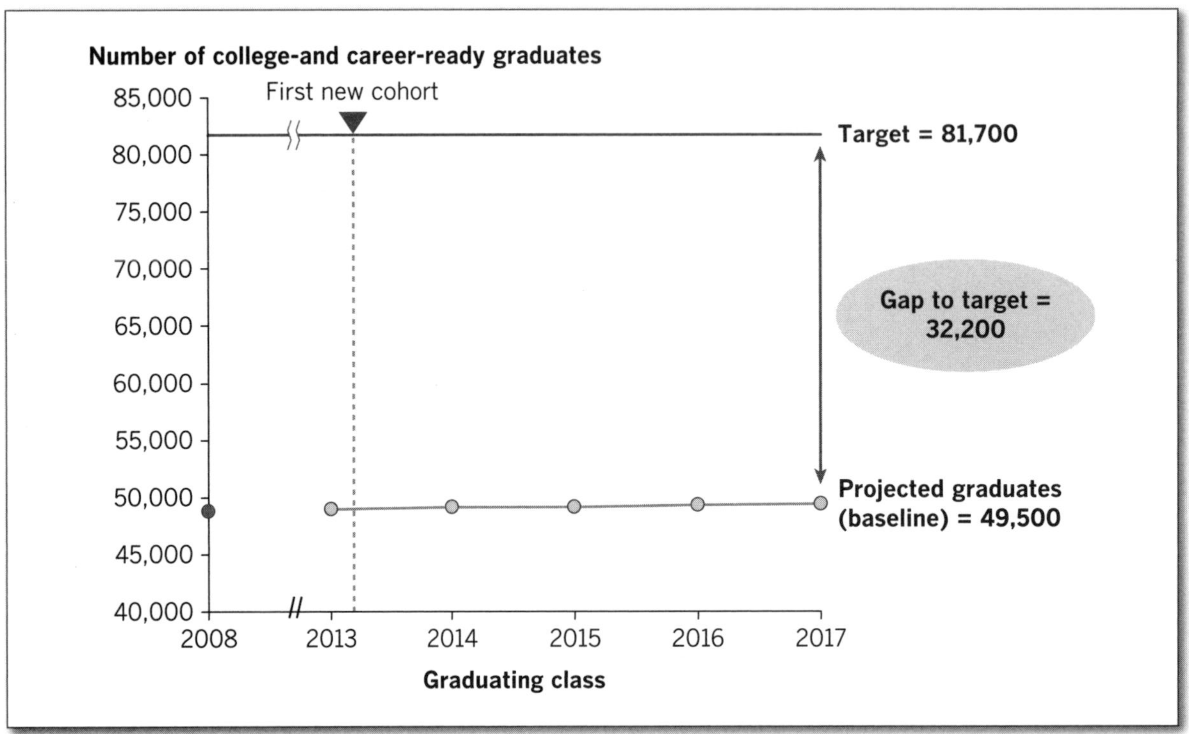

performance units. These same groupings will help you to build your baseline.

- **Individuals.** As noted in Module 2A, an individual comparison of students, teachers, or performance units is possible where the number of performance units is small. For a higher education system with fewer than two dozen campuses, this may be an especially powerful approach, as it will help you to take individual campus histories into account in building your baseline. For a K–12 system with hundreds of districts and thousands of schools, it may be necessary to group performance units in some meaningful way.
- **Characteristics.** Grouping your students, teachers, or performance units by characteristic will help you to make baseline predictions based on the historical performance of groups of similar performance units (or gaps in performance between these groups). If you are comparing students, you might take the average performance of different subgroups of students, such as students of low-income, students in special education, or students of under-represented minority. What is the historical performance of each of these, both in absolute terms and relative to each other? If you compare schools, campuses, or LEAs, you can group according to statistical averages of student characteristics in those performance units (e.g., schools with high proportions of economically disadvantaged students) or characteristics that are specific to the units themselves (e.g., student demographics).

- **Performance bands.** Finally, it may also make sense to separate students, teachers, or performance units by performance level. For example, what is the average performance of the top decile of students compared to the bottom decile? The top and bottom quartile of schools, campuses, or districts? How can this information help you to project future performance?

To build a baseline for these groups, you go through the same process you did for the system average: Take the historical data for these subgroups, and use the trends evident to extrapolate a future trend.

The baselines you have built show you where your target metric will be in a defined period of time without any change for both the entire system on average and by subgroups of students, teachers, or performance units. Based on this information, you can now begin Step 3, to create the ambitious and realistic target you plan to achieve with the delivery effort (Exhibit 3B.7).

Step 3: Estimate the trajectory and the target

There are two approaches that will help you to ground both your target and your trajectory in the available evidence. To the extent possible, you should use both approaches, using one to test the results produced by the other in an iterative manner. The first approach, the use of benchmarks, allows you to calibrate ambition and realism based on what other systems or groups of students, teachers, and performance units within those systems have

Exhibit 3B.7 Step 3: Estimate the trajectory and the target

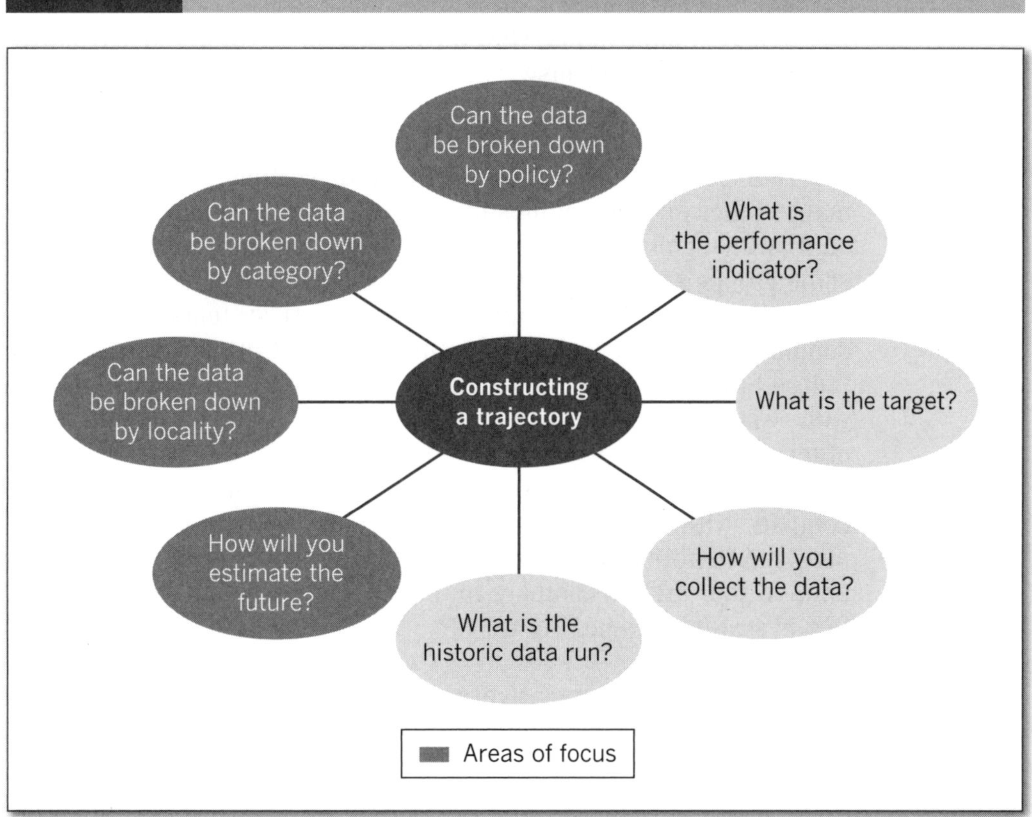

accomplished. The second, the use of interventions, draws the explicit connection between your system's planned strategy and its projected impact on the target metric. It is a way of checking whether the changes you implement can actually get you to where you want to be. By adjusting your trajectory and target via these two methods, you should be able to arrive at a final result that is both realistic and ambitious (or, as described above, to build a trajectory that can plausibly get you to a predefined target). The approach you choose to take first will depend on the availability of the data.

Using benchmarks. The benchmarking approach is driven by one basic question: "Given others' performance, what can or should I expect my performance to be?" This question should be asked not only for the system as a whole but also for two out of the three groupings of students, teachers, and performance units identified in the previous step: groupings by characteristic and groupings by performance band.

In each of these cases, the point is to ask "what if" questions. What would be the impact on my target metric if the bottom quartile of students performed at the level of the third quartile? If my system improved to the level of the top-performing system in the United States? If my students of low income closed the achievement gap with their peers by 50%?

Running these scenarios will predict certain effects on your target metric. The key is to construct a series of "what ifs" that together tell a plausible story about the future evolution of performance in your system and yield an overall estimate of your trajectory. The use of benchmarks will help you to understand whether this story is plausible.

To review from Module 2A, a system can conduct five types of benchmarking. Of these, you can use four to compare performance:

- **Historical comparisons.** How have levels of the target metric moved in the past? (Example answer: Graduation rates have been increasing an average of 0.5% per year in the past five years.) To what extent should you expect the system or its subgroups to outperform history?
- **Internal peer comparisons.** Within your system, how does performance differ between groups of students, teachers, and performance units with similar characteristics? What does the performance of some groups suggest about what others should be able to attain?
- **External peer comparisons.** How does your system's performance compare, both now and historically, to that of other systems in the United States? How do students, teachers, and performance units in your system compare to their peers with similar characteristics in other systems?
- **International comparisons.** How does the system's performance compare with the performance of systems in other countries, both now and historically? How do students, teachers, and performance units in your system compare to their peers with similar characteristics in systems around the world?

Exhibit 3B.8 is an illustrative example of a map of the potential what ifs of a benchmarking analysis, using a K–12 system target and

Exhibit 3B.8 Different ways of determining a target via benchmarking: K–12 example

Target metric: college- and career-ready graduation rates			
Level of analysis	**System**	**Schools**	
Dimension of comparison	**Whole system**	**Groups of schools with similar characteristics**	**Performance bands of schools**
Benchmark type: Historical comparisons	• What if graduation rates for my system grew by 50% above the five-year historic average?	• What if graduation rates in my urban schools grew by 50% above the five-year historic average?	• What if graduation rates for the bottom quartile of schools grew by 50% above the five-year historic average?
Benchmark type: Internal peer comparisons	• N/A	• What if all my urban schools achieved graduation rates of the system's top-performing ones?	• What if the bottom quartile of schools raised their graduation rates to the average of the third quartile?
Benchmark type: External peer comparisons	• What if my system's graduation rates reached the level of the top-performing U.S. state?	• What if all my urban schools achieved graduation rates of the nation's top-performing urban schools?	• What if the bottom quartile of schools raised their graduation rates to the U.S. average?
Benchmark type: International comparisons	• What if my system's graduation rates reached the level of the 90th percentile of school systems worldwide?	• What if my urban schools all achieved graduation rates of the top-performing urban schools worldwide?	• What if the bottom quartile of schools raised their graduation rates to the international average?

anchoring on the entire system and its schools as the two levels of analysis. As you can see, there are many possible combinations even for this one example. Depending on the availability of data, you should select a manageable subset of potential analyses that make the most sense for your system.

Three examples of benchmarking analysis are provided. Exhibit 3B.9 shows an analysis by the Education Trust of degree attainment across the 50 states, indicating how states could set their trajectories by aspiring to the degree attainment of the top 10 states.

The next example, Exhibit 3B.10, shows the attempt of leaders of a K–12 SEA to estimate a trajectory for dropout reduction. The exhibit explores the possibility of reducing the dropout rate in each school so that no school has a dropout rate greater than the current 75th percentile school.

The third example, Exhibit 3B.11, shows how the Delta Cost Project modeled the potential impact of higher graduation rates on overall degree attainment in the United States. The dashed line represents the number of degrees

Exhibit 3B.9 External benchmarking, system level: What if a state system increased its degree attainment rate to that of the top 10 states?

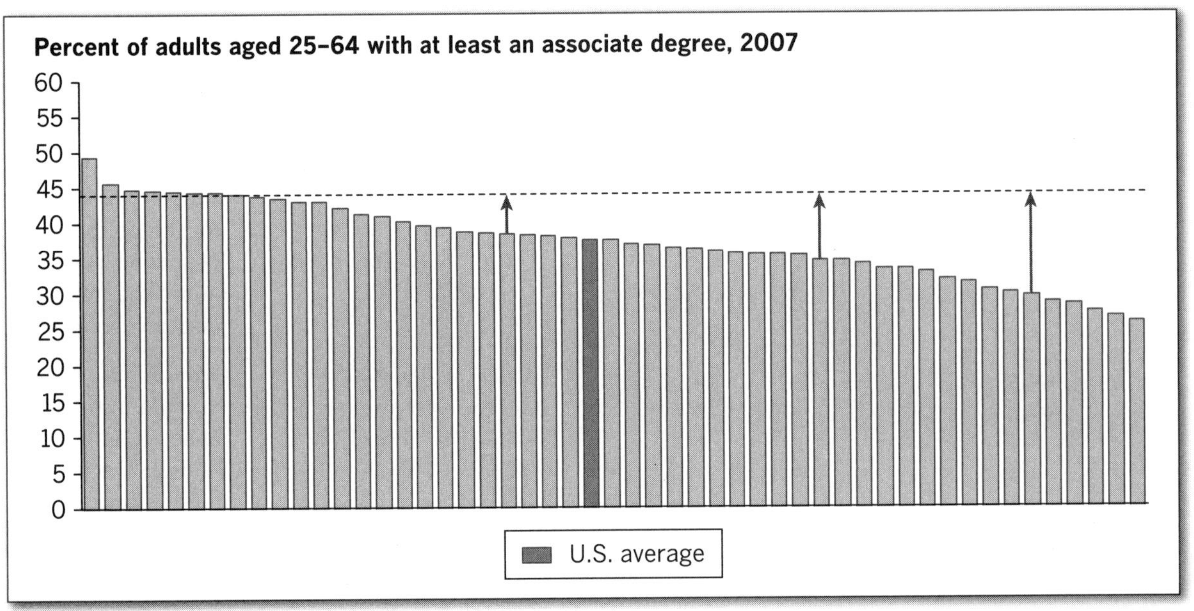

SOURCE: NCHEMS.

Exhibit 3B.10 Internal benchmarking, school level: What if the high schools with the highest number of dropouts improved to the level of the 75th percentile school?

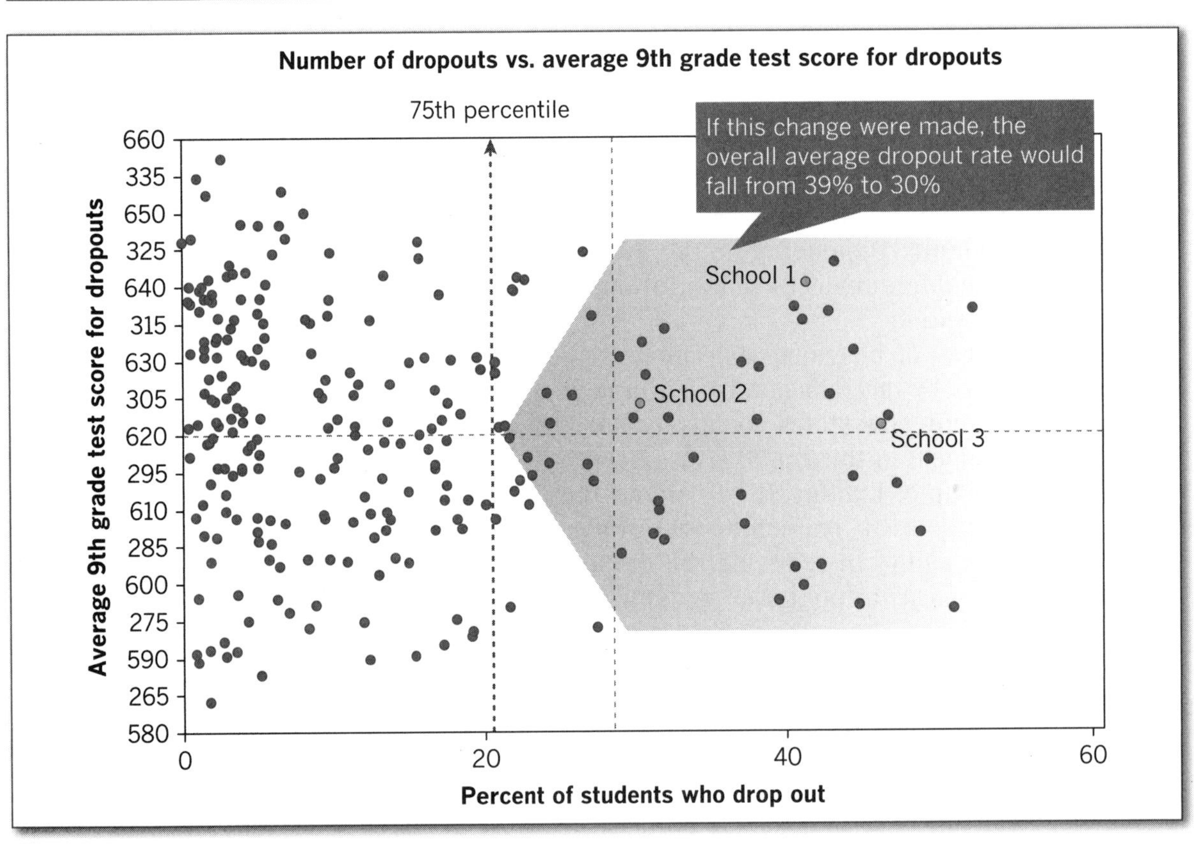

needed to reach 51% attainment, the number represented by President Obama's aspiration. The dark and light shaded areas represent the contribution to degree attainment that would result from raising graduation rates to those of the best-performing systems for all four types of colleges. As you can see, the impact is significant, but not sufficient. This is a good example of the use of trajectory setting to try to reach a predefined target.

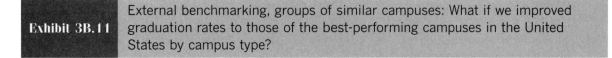

Exhibit 3B.11 External benchmarking, groups of similar campuses: What if we improved graduation rates to those of the best-performing campuses in the United States by campus type?

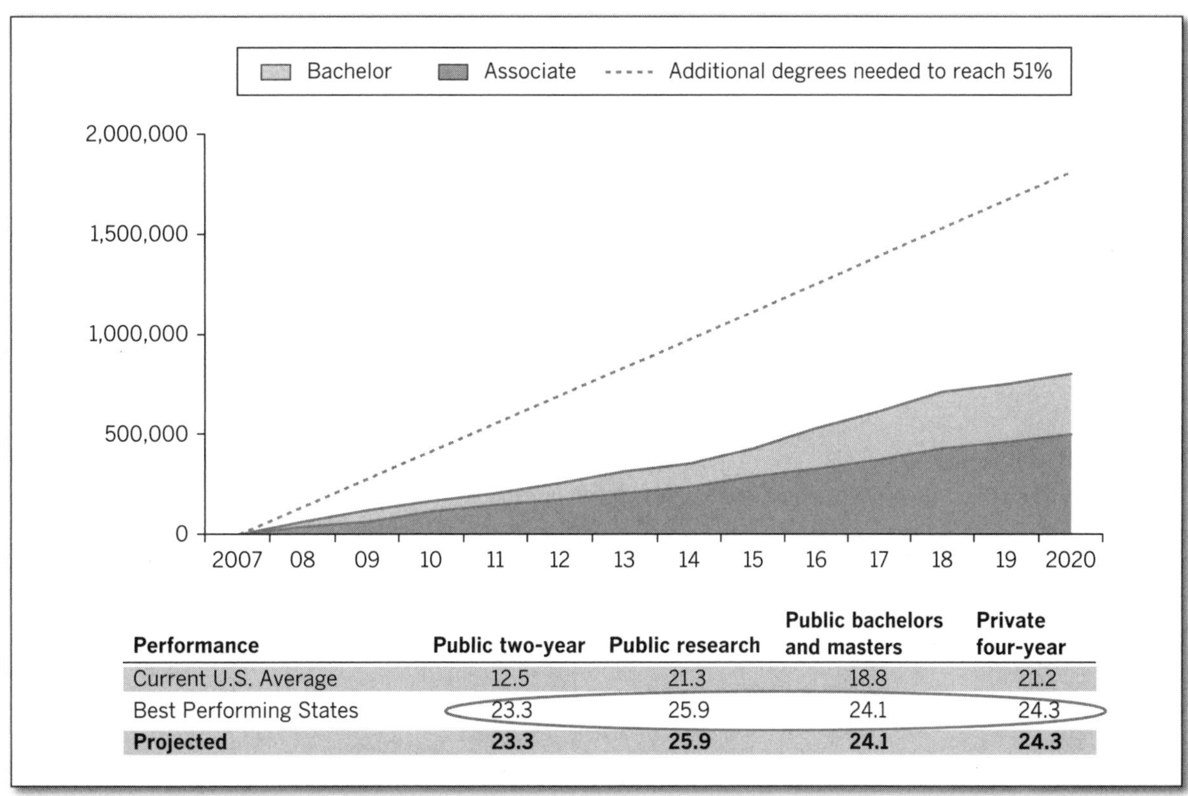

Performance	Public two-year	Public research	Public bachelors and masters	Private four-year
Current U.S. Average	12.5	21.3	18.8	21.2
Best Performing States	23.3	25.9	24.1	24.3
Projected	**23.3**	**25.9**	**24.1**	**24.3**

CASE EXAMPLE

Using benchmarks to assess a target's feasibility in a higher education system

Sometimes, a trajectory can simply help people to believe that a target can be hit. One higher education system CEO recently committed to producing a total of 42,000 graduates by the year 2015. In order to assess this target's feasibility, the Delivery Unit constructed a baseline trajectory from some conservative assumptions about the "productivity" of the system—the number of graduates (awards conferred) per student enrolled—over the period from now until 2015. This estimate, given in Exhibit 3B.12, revealed that the system had a gap of about 3,000 graduates to close.

(Continued)

(Continued)

On closer inspection, the target did not seem as daunting as it originally sounded. Using benchmarks of productivity from peer universities around the country, the Delivery Unit determined that the target could be nearly hit by a modest increase in productivity—the equivalent of increasing the productivity of less than half of their campuses to the average level of their peers.

Exhibit 3B.12 Baseline trajectory

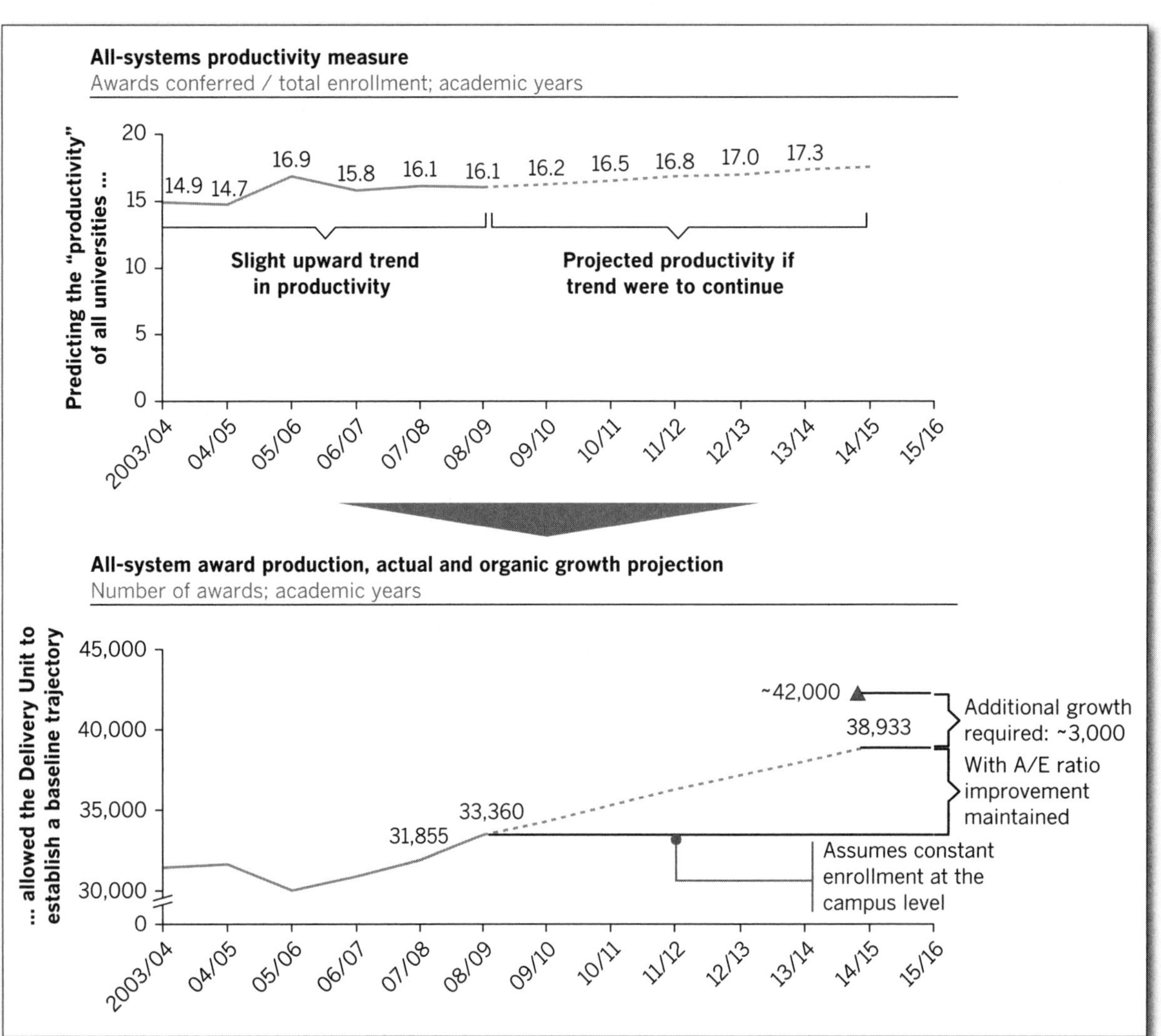

SOURCE: Higher education system (disguised).

This information not only reassured system officials that the target was feasible—it sparked a new conversation about whether the target should be higher.

Exhibit 3B.13 Benchmarking analysis of target, annual degrees conferred

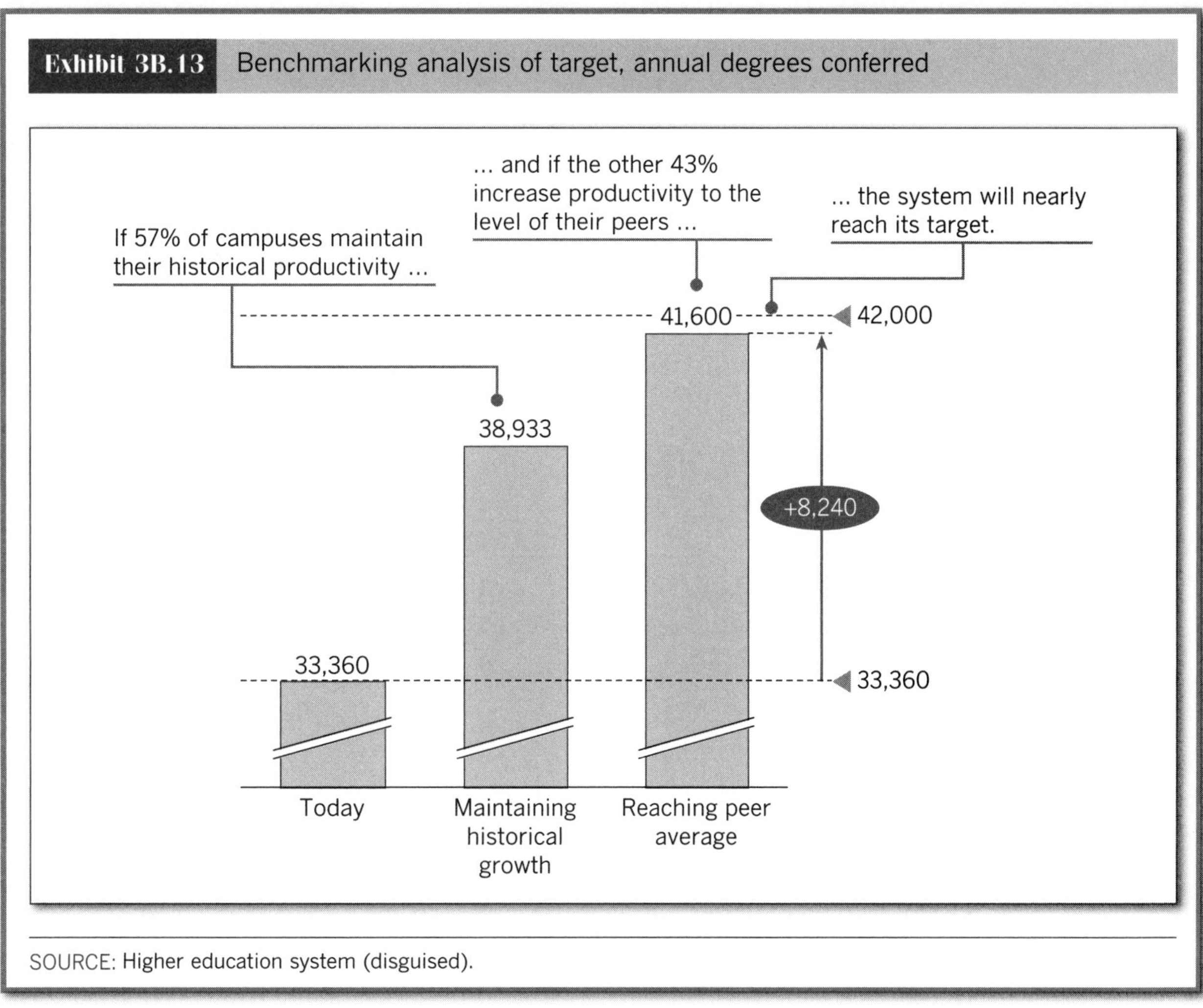

SOURCE: Higher education system (disguised).

Using Interventions. In Module 3A, your system chose a set of integrated interventions to improve performance that were based on changing current system activities or introducing new activities. As part of that process, you used research, benchmarks, and pragmatism to estimate each intervention's potential impact over time. By refining and aggregating this information, as well as your planned sequencing of changes, you should be able to establish a projected timetable for the future impact of your strategy.

Begin by ensuring that you have a reasonable estimate of the impact of each planned intervention on the target metric over time. In some cases, this estimate will be complete from your work in the previous module. In others, you will have to do some additional analysis to arrive at an estimate.

Remember, estimating impact over time is not an exact science, and some estimates will be cruder than others for want of robust data or solid research. Tricky questions will abound. For example, if research shows that improving an after-school curriculum increased graduates by 20% in one year, how can that 20% be extrapolated and applied to your system, year over year? Would this impact be larger for poorer performing schools? Would there be a discount in impact for schools that do not take up the new curriculum or resist switching?

Ultimately, it is up to your Delivery Unit and those responsible for implementing the intervention to make the best judgment they can—informed by as many facts as possible and backed by sound logic—of how specific interventions will work together to affect your target metric.

The following two examples show how K–12 systems can estimate potential impact of state-level programs. Exhibit 3B.14 gives an estimate that combines projected scale (the number of students the program will serve) with projected efficacy (the link between the number of students served and the number of new graduates) to estimate the impact on the target metric (number of graduates).

In Exhibit 3B.15, a different approach is taken, wherein an intervention's potential impact is estimated according to leading indicators: the individual

Exhibit 3B.14 Methodology for estimating the impact of a K–12 dropout prevention program on graduation rates

	2009/2010	2010/2011	2011/2012	2012/2013	2013/2014	2014/2015	2015/2016
Scale: How many students will the program serve?	400	800	1,200	1,600	2,000	2,400	2,800
Efficacy: How will the program impact graduation rates?	← 25 new graduates per 100 students served →						
Additional graduates for trajectory	100	200	300	400	500	600	700

Exhibit 3B.15 Estimated impact of an extended learning time program on math course passage rates for disadvantaged students*

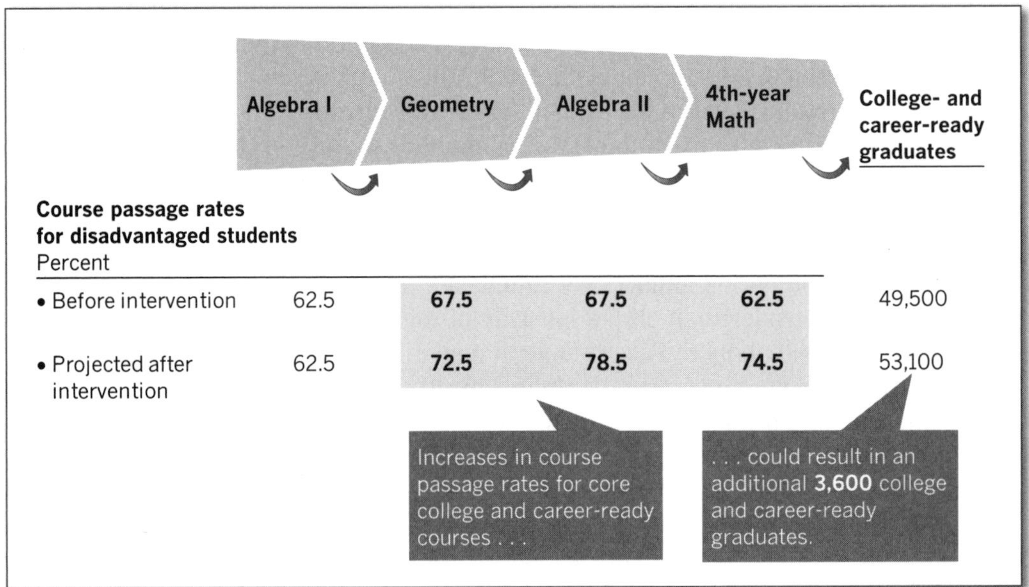

*Overall impact on system; rates based on 50% improvement in select Math, 15% in English, 33% of failing students

course passage rates for college and career-ready diploma requirements. This estimate acts through the leading indicators to affect the target metric, the number of college- and career-ready graduates.

As you refine your estimates based on available research and evidence, you should keep in mind the following considerations:

- What characteristics of your system differ from those of the system in the research or evidence that might influence the results of the intervention in your system? For example, your system may have a lower graduation rate to start with, so the impact could be higher in your system as compared to the research.
- What are the effects of combining interventions? Could there be diminishing returns? For example, if one study shows that improving an after-school tutoring program increased graduates by X% and another study showed introducing a private tutor program increased graduation by Y%, do you believe that the combined effect on graduation should be X% + Y%? Would the impact of private tutoring be less on a student who is already taking the after-school program?
- What does the trajectory look like over time? Research may only give an impact at a certain point in time, and you will need to apply judgment to understand if that impact comes at the beginning of the intervention, toward the tail end, or evenly throughout. For example, if you are implementing teacher effectiveness training to improve graduation rates, then you may assume that most of the impact will come at the later years because it will take a few years for the effects to kick in. On the other hand, a remedial tutoring program for seniors that are on the margin of failure may deliver results within the first year.

Once you have estimated potential effects over time for all of your interventions, aggregate this information to plot the trajectory of your target metric. Example trajectories are laid out in Exhibits 3B.16 and 3B.17. Exhibit 3B.16 gives a simple and straightforward example. Here, a state has set a goal for improving college and career readiness among its high school graduates. In this situation, every intervention is assumed to have the same level of increase every year. This could be because it is assumed that the impact per school is the same, and the intervention expands to a similar number of new schools every year, thereby adding the same number of graduates every year.

However, this evenness does not always hold true, as Exhibit 3B.17 demonstrates. Depending on the start times of each intervention and the differential impact over time within each intervention, trajectories may take on any number of shapes. Exhibit 3B.17 gives an example of a trajectory with both staggered start times and differential impact of each intervention over time. The different increases in graduates for each program each year can be due to different rates of expansion to new schools over time or expected changes in the efficacy of a program.

This last exhibit also illustrates what happens when one tries to build a trajectory to a predefined target. In this case, it turned out that the interventions planned were not nearly enough to get the system to its goal. If this happens, the system must find other interventions that will allow it to achieve its target (and therefore return to the strategy to add interventions).

Exhibit 3B.16 Series of plans for achieving a state's 2017 college- and career-ready goal

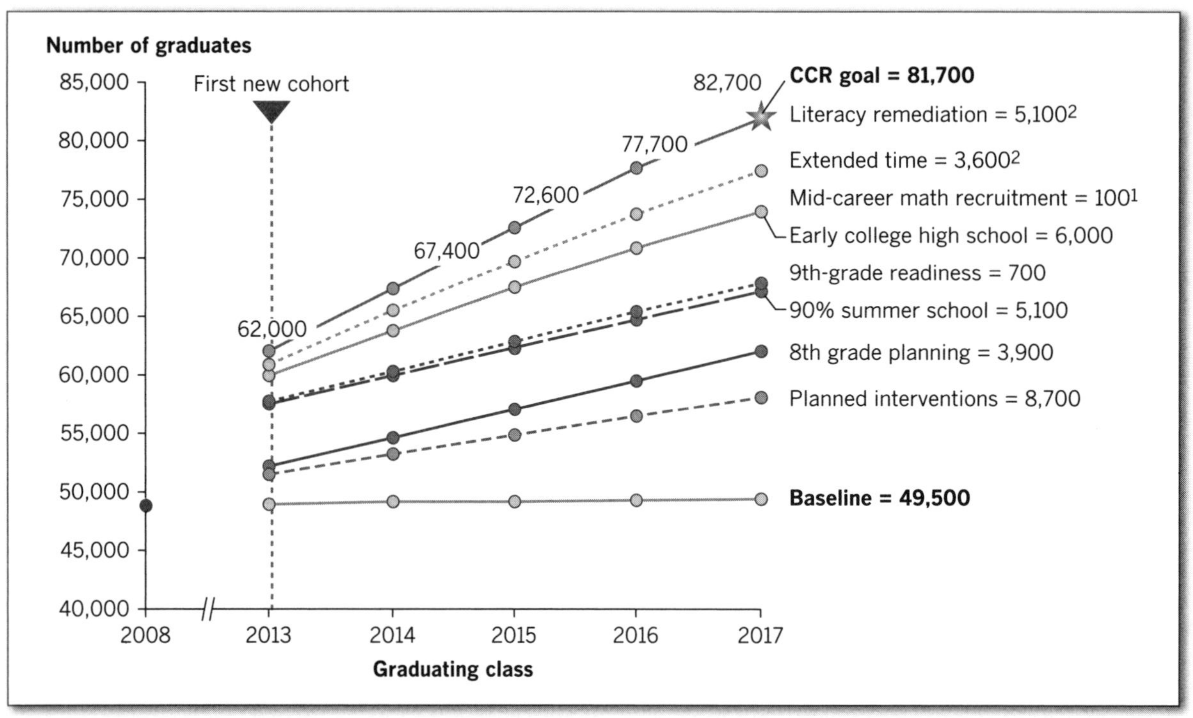

SOURCE: Team analysis.

1. Impact masked by students' failing English sequence.

2. Includes impact of other initiatives.

Exhibit 3B.17 A trajectory with staggered start times and differential impact of each intervention over time

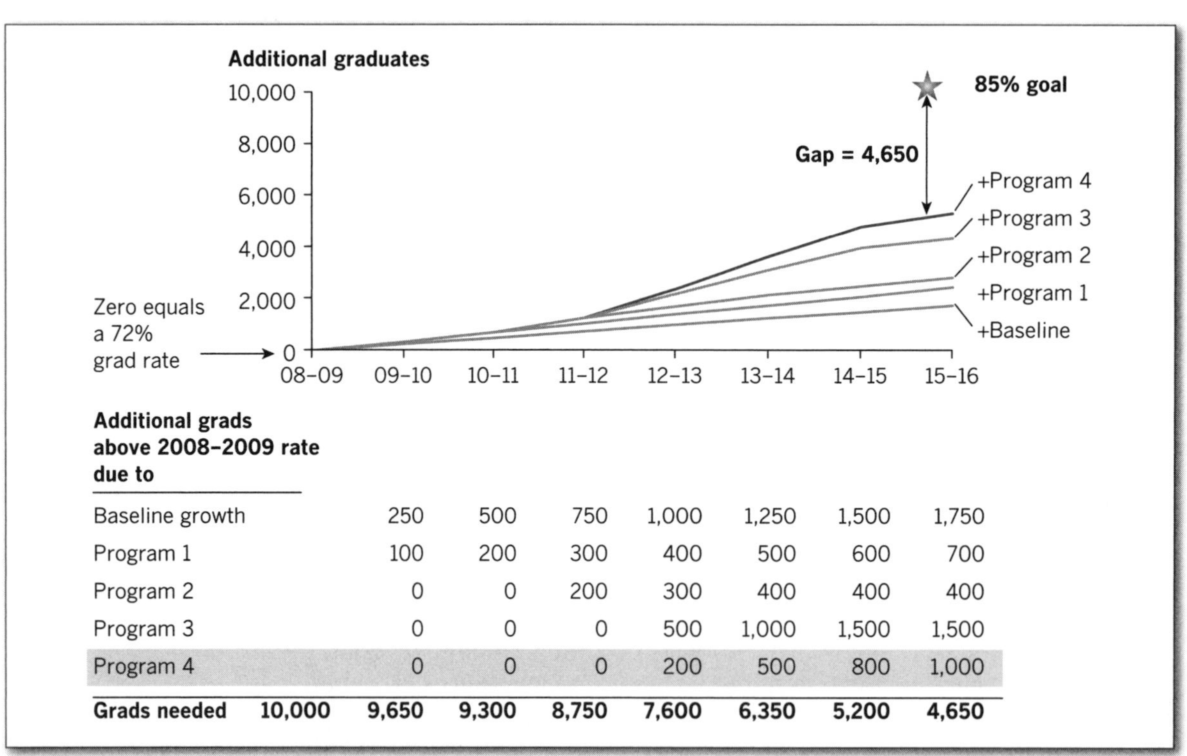

Additional grads above 2008–2009 rate due to								
Baseline growth		250	500	750	1,000	1,250	1,500	1,750
Program 1		100	200	300	400	500	600	700
Program 2		0	0	200	300	400	400	400
Program 3		0	0	0	500	1,000	1,500	1,500
Program 4		0	0	0	200	500	800	1,000
Grads needed	**10,000**	**9,650**	**9,300**	**8,750**	**7,600**	**6,350**	**5,200**	**4,650**

This highlights another important use of trajectories: By making explicit the connection between planned action and desired outcomes, they help system actors to understand the scale of the challenge confronting them and instill a sense of urgency. When the trajectory in Exhibit 3B.15 was presented to system staff, the shift in mindset was palpable.

There is no right order in which to employ the benchmarking and intervention-based approaches to building trajectories. Some systems begin with benchmarks and then see if they can build a plausible set of interventions to achieve them. Others begin with interventions and then use the benchmarks as a reality check. You will likely need to take a pragmatic view, using a combination of approaches that makes the best use of the data available to you. In any case, be prepared for the trajectory-setting process to feed back into your overall strategy; as with the example in the last exhibit, if the interventions you chose in Module 3A are not sufficient to deliver an ambitious target, you may need to revisit them.

From this process, a trajectory should emerge that has been validated by multiple perspectives and thoroughly tested for ambition and realism. The process will also give you powerful insight into the potential efficacy of your interventions and the realism and ambition of the trajectory being set. Perhaps most importantly, this process will give you your target (if one has not been predefined for you already): the endpoint of your trajectory.

Step 4: Negotiate subtargets and subtrajectories if necessary

Through this process, you have set targets not only for your overall system but have also developed a general understanding of what this target implies for the subgroups described above (e.g., groups of students, teachers, and performance units with similar characteristics). Sometimes, it may be necessary to develop subtargets (and, possibly, subtrajectories) that allocate a share of your overall target to the various performance units and can be used to manage each unit's performance. Subtargets and subtrajectories will be particularly important when performance units are powerful and/or few in number (as in most university systems).

Subtargets and subtrajectories will help you increase the reliability of your overall system target and trajectory, both by establishing an accountability mechanism for others in your system and by encouraging those others to buy into and "own" specific pieces of your overall target and trajectory.

There are several options for negotiating a subtarget or subtrajectory between a system and its performance units. Regardless of your approach, however, one principle should guide your work: You should enter any negotiation armed with as full an understanding as possible of a performance unit's data and a perspective on what ambition and realism should look like for that performance unit.

As already noted, the process of trajectory setting above could leave you with a fairly good estimate of the expected contributions of the various performance units in your system, especially if you relied heavily on benchmarking to draw the trajectory. If you decide to set subtargets or subtrajectories, you should, however, revisit this analysis to make sure that your subtargets or subtrajectories are defensible (as, after all, it may have been a more or less important part of your overall trajectory-setting process).

Depending on the availability of data, structure of influence in your system, and capacity of your performance units, there are three broad options for negotiating subtargets or subtrajectories with your performance units:

- **Top down.** Your Delivery Unit and/or system leadership suggest subtargets and subtrajectories for performance units; performance units challenge them if necessary. This method of negotiation is best if
  - You are adopting a command and control theory of change;
  - Performance units lack the individual capacity to analyze data and develop reasonable trajectories; and
  - The central Delivery Unit has sufficiently detailed data at the performance unit level such that suggested subtargets or subtrajectories are evidenced based and appropriately tailored to different types of units.
- **Bottom up.** Subtargets or subtrajectories are solicited from performance units and are then verified or challenged by the Delivery Unit if necessary. This method of negotiation is best if
  - You are adopting a devolution and transparency or quasi market theory of change;
  - Too many performance units require individual trajectories for the Delivery Unit to initially develop them all; and
  - The Delivery Unit lacks sufficiently detailed performance data (on relevant indicators and metrics) to determine ambitious, realistic trajectories for performance units.
- **Hybrid.** Representatives from the Delivery Unit and the relevant performance units hold a series of collaborative discussions regarding the data and the overall target and trajectory, leading to a back-and-forth negotiation. This method of negotiation is best if
  - You think that the dialogue itself will have intrinsic merit and strengthen the system's capacity to deliver;
  - Performance units do not yet buy into the delivery effort, making it unlikely that a bottom-up approach would result in well-crafted trajectories and it is risky to use a top-down approach (as it could give the appearance of a Delivery Unit "ivory tower"); and
  - There is enough time to merit the lengthier process that a hybrid model entails.

Exhibit 3B.18 shows how targets can be set top down, bottom up, or as a hybrid.

Exhibit 3B.19 illustrates the different processes used by university systems in Louisiana and North Carolina for negotiating targets and trajectories with individual campuses.

In negotiations that you will have in both the bottom up and hybrid models, you should make sure to push for the adoption of ambitious targets, as performance units often tend to be more conservative. How will you challenge the "laggards" who do not wish to be ambitious at all? Again, having the facts is essential: If your negotiator has sufficient data to show that a performance unit's target is significantly lower than that of all similar performance units, this information may be sufficient to change the result of the negotiation. In any case, it may sometimes be impractical to

Exhibit 3B.18 Targets can be set top down, bottom up, or through a hybrid approach

Top-down	Bottom-up
• **Targets may be imposed on the system for multiple reasons:** • *Set minimum standards.* These standards often reflect a belief that everyone deserves a minimum standard (e.g., no one should wait more than four hours to see a doctor in an emergency room) or that a certain standard is necessary to compete (e.g., students must perform at a certain level relative to peers in other countries) • *Create "calculated bounce."* At other times, the system leader may try to inspire the system to act by setting an ambitious target. A "calculated bounce" is a projected leap from current level of performance to a level that is inspirationally ambitious. It signals a transformation in performance and is usually in the form of a public commitment • It is **not necessary to understand how the system will deliver on the target in advance** – the target will prompt the system to figure that out!	• At other times, the system may be able to set its own target. In this instance, it should **build its trajectory** – the improvement above its baseline it can expect from the interventions that comprise its reform strategy – and **then** assess **whether that achieves an overall target that is ambitious enough:** • If it is, the system can begin building plans to deliver on that target • If it is not, the system must identify additional interventions that will positively affect the target metric until it is satisfied that it has set an aspirational target

Hybrid

- Representatives from the Delivery Unit and the relevant performance units hold a series of collaborative discussions regarding the overall target where an understanding of "what it would take" to achieve the target is contrasted against a judgment of whether the overall target is aspirational enough
- While this process takes longer, it is often useful in creating a realistic yet aspirational target

gain agreement from every performance unit. You will need to balance the need for agreement with the need for urgency; after all, a few laggards should not be allowed to hold up implementation.

There are some additional variations on this approach. You might choose only to negotiate a target with performance units, train them to build their own trajectories, and manage only to the target. This alternative may have the benefit of empowering your performance units to self-discover the power of trajectories and to use them as true learning tools.

Once your system and the relevant performance units have agreed on a subtarget or subtrajectory, you may need to revisit your overall trajectory and adjust it in light of new information. As subtargets or trajectories represent agreements between your system and its performance units on their planned outcomes, it would be unfair to retain an overall trajectory that is out of step with these agreements.

Exhibit 3B.19 Two university systems chose different approaches to setting targets with their performance units (campuses)

	Louisiana Board of Regents: "Top-down"	**University of North Carolina system: "Bottom-up"**
Process used	• An overall goal of additional degrees to be achieved was selected for the state as a whole • In order to determine it was feasible, the Board calculated reasonable – Shares for the four state systems – Shares for each public campus in state	• New president refocused system on access, retention, graduation • System level accountability measures set • System prepared and shared data with campuses • Campuses submitted plans with proposed retention and graduation rates • Independent review of plans by external consultant • System and campus met to discuss and agree on a goal
Questions to consider	• Will the systems align around and embrace this goal? • Will the campuses align around and embrace this goal?	• Do the campus goals add together to meet state needs?

Conclusion

By now, you have learned

- Why trajectories are crucial to helping you gauge the ambition and realism of the targets that your system sets;
- A step-by-step methodology for developing a trajectory, using both benchmarks and planned interventions; and
- Some principles and methods for negotiating subtargets and subtrajectories with your campuses, districts, and/or schools.

Setting trajectories and targets can be a challenging exercise, but the process is crucial to your ability to monitor performance as delivery begins. With targets and trajectories in place and an agreed strategy to achieve them, it is time to help your system to produce the more detailed plans that will serve as the blueprint for execution.

3C. PRODUCE DELIVERY PLANS

"A goal without a plan is just a wish."

—Anonymous

With a target and trajectory established, your system has reached agreement on the various interventions that will constitute its strategy. The next step is to organize your system to implement these interventions. The primary tool for this is the delivery plan: the guiding tool that system actors responsible for interventions will use to carry them out.

Delivery plans are important as operational tools: For the system actor who is ultimately responsible for an intervention, as well as the layer (or layers) of others who report to that person, delivery plans provide a specific road map for how interventions should proceed.

As important as the plan itself (if not more so) is the process of its creation. The exercise of delivery planning forces a series of problem-solving conversations that help system actors to understand what they will need to do. As Dwight Eisenhower is reported to have said, "The plan is nothing. The planning is everything."

Finally, along with targets and trajectories, delivery plans provide one more anchor for your Delivery Unit's efforts to monitor progress; they will provide additional metrics and milestones that you can rely upon as you design your routines (see Module 4A).

Delivery plans are works in progress, and there is no such thing as a perfect plan. Your Delivery Unit should catalyze the production of operational, adaptable, working plans, with detailed descriptions and room for constant learning and improvement. You should never let the perfect be the enemy of the good, and plan writing should never become an excuse for delaying delivery. In any case, your Delivery Unit will continuously push to refine and revise these plans as necessary, long after delivery has begun.

REAL, OPERATIONAL PLANS

"When asked for a plan, [the bureaucracy's] traditional response is to write some thoughtful prose, and if it really wants to impress the recipient, to enclose the prose in a glossy cover. In short—to quote a colleague—[the bureaucracy] writes "essays decorated with the occasional number," the hope being that the recipients will be so impressed by the prose that, after reading it, they will leave you alone. This, of course, was not what we wanted. We wanted real, messy, practical plans, with folds and creases, scribbled notes in the margins and coffee stains." (*Instruction to Deliver,* 84)

This module will take you through the process of ensuring that your reform strategy and its constituent interventions are accompanied by a set of robust delivery plans that serve all three of these purposes.

ROLES OF SYSTEM LEADER AND DELIVERY LEADER

Your Delivery Unit should never write delivery plans disconnected from the system. To do so would defeat the purpose of energizing and empowering system actors to deliver results consistently and sustainably. Instead, your Delivery Unit's role is to guide the development of delivery plans by articulating the criteria for good plans and pushing system actors to develop plans that meet these criteria. Your system leader may need to approve these plans in some way but otherwise will not have a large role in the creation of the plans.

Process steps

The process steps below assume that your system is starting from scratch, with no existing plans in place. Depending on how your system developed its strategy, some delivery plans may be inherited, because the interventions (or the system activities that they affect) already have plans associated with them. In such cases, you may have less latitude to organize delivery plans or even to ask for new plans to be written, but you will still check and revise each plan (where necessary) to ensure that it is consistent with your criteria.

Step 1: Decide how to organize your delivery plans and who owns them
Step 2: Guide delivery plan owners in the development or refinement of their plans
Step 3: Test, challenge, and revise plans
Step 4: Create a master tracker for delivery plans

Step 1: Decide how to organize your delivery plans and who owns them

As your system strategy will likely include multiple interventions, your system will almost inevitably require more than one delivery plan. At the most basic level, delivery plans should cover every intervention. However, this may not be as simple as it sounds. What if an intervention affects multiple system activities? What if those activities are the responsibility of very different departments or even separate organizations?

To answer these questions, you will need to understand the *delivery plan organization* for your delivery effort. The idea of a delivery plan organization is taken from a concept at the heart of *program and project management:* any overall effort (a program) can and should be broken up into constituent pieces (projects). Each project will have an "owner" who is responsible for the outcomes of that project; the overall program will also have an owner who is responsible for progress across all projects. This idea is illustrated at its most basic level in Exhibit 3C.1.

This concept applies to your delivery effort. To review the work of Chapters 2 and 3, at this point, your system's aspiration has been broken down into one or more targets (e.g., increasing the number of effective teachers in a K–12 system). As part of the overall strategy for achieving

Exhibit 3C.1 Program and project management

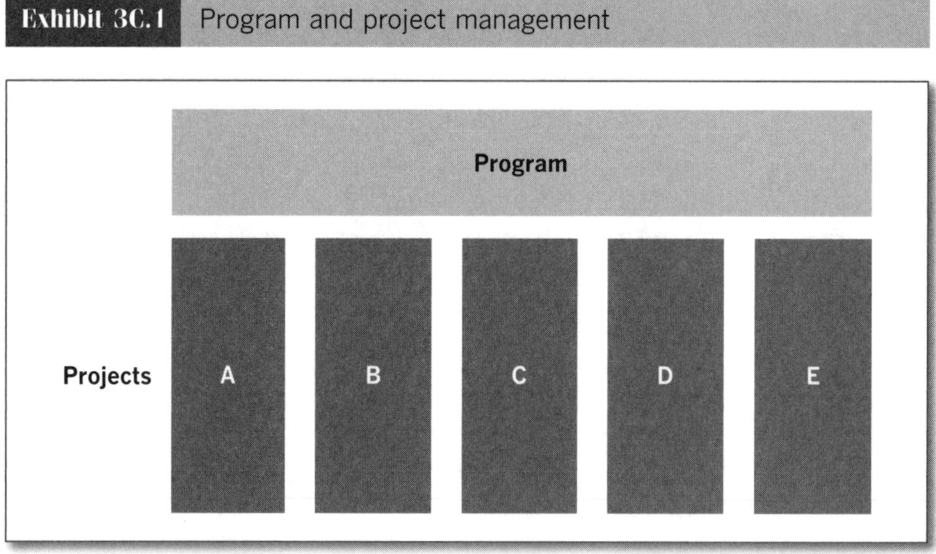

these targets, your system has selected one or more interventions (e.g., training principals to be better instructional leaders who increase teacher effectiveness), each of which is designed to help you achieve one or more of the targets in question. Each intervention is meant to achieve its assigned targets, either by changing existing system activities (e.g., a principal's day-to-day management, coaching, and development of the teacher workforce) or by creating new ones. And, each of these activities can be divided into subactivities at increasing levels of detail, until you have isolated the specific behaviors of individuals (e.g., a principal in a specific school doing a focus walk to provide feedback on teacher effectiveness).

As shown in Exhibit 3C.2, each of these levels of detail are related to one another in a similar fashion across the program and into projects, as shown in Exhibit 3C.1. The overall delivery effort (the Delivery Unit program) is overseen by the Delivery Unit and consists of one or more targets. These targets are broken down into interventions, which are broken down into activities, which are in turn broken down into subactivities, and so on.

This "map" of your delivery effort is your delivery plan organization. In high-performing organizations, delivery plans would be written at most or all of these levels. At the target level, a senior official at an SEA could be responsible for writing a plan for how the overall teacher effectiveness target will be achieved. At the activity level, the manager of teacher professional development might create a plan that details how his program will be improved. At the individual level, a specific principal might write a plan for how they will use training to improve teacher effectiveness in their school. Moreover, in high-performing organizations, the delivery plans at every level

Exhibit 3C.2 Delivery Unit program and project management

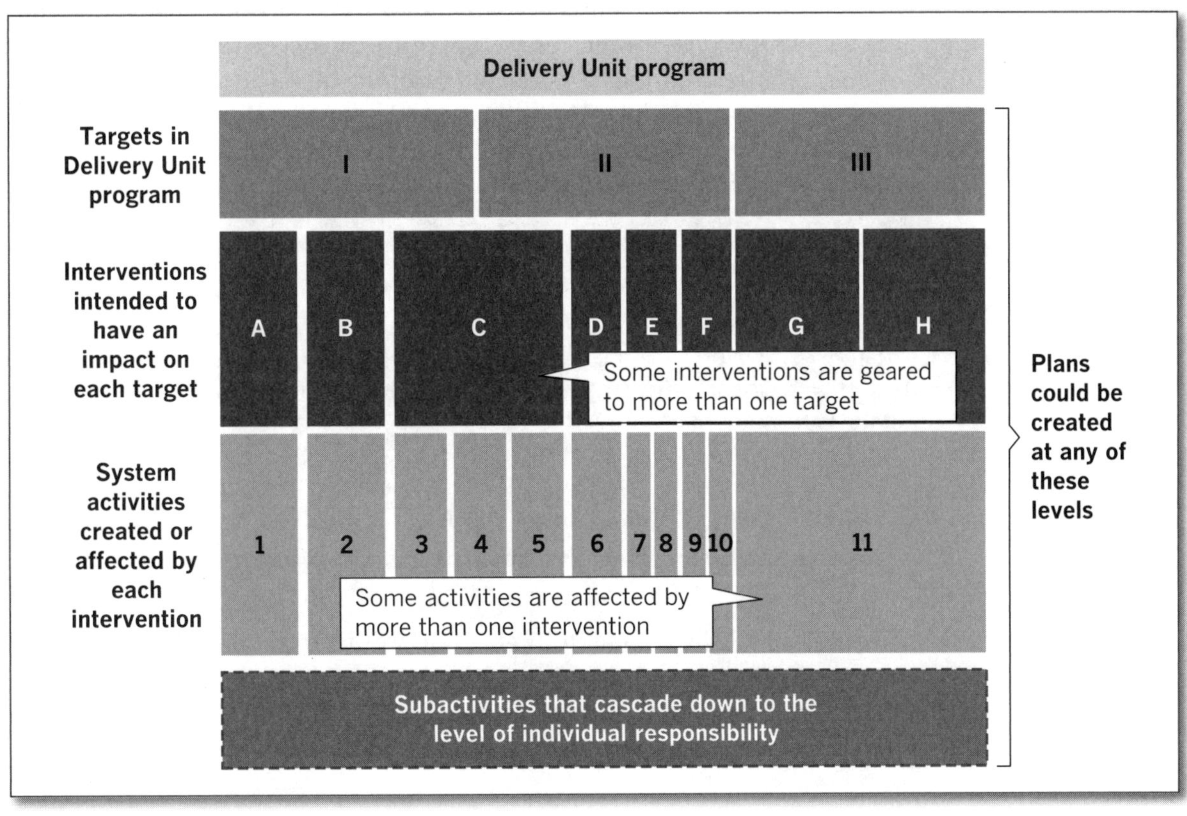

would be linked: Milestones for each plan would be consistent, and specific actions within one plan would not conflict with actions within another.

Your delivery plan organization will vary depending on the needs of your effort. Sometimes, the structure of your system will matter: If four targets are clearly the responsibility of one department, it might make sense to ask that department to write one plan for all four targets. On the other hand, if a single target spans multiple departments, a single plan for the target is appropriate. At other times, it will be important to account for local performance units: A higher education system, for example, may break down each of its targets to the campus level before further subdividing those targets into interventions and activities.

This begs a question that is immediately relevant to your Delivery Unit: At what level will your Unit be involved in actually reviewing (and eventually monitoring) plans? As Exhibit 3C.2 makes obvious, any decently sized delivery effort will present your Unit with the challenges of engaging at the right level of detail and avoiding the temptation to micromanage.

There is no exact answer to the question of monitoring by the Delivery Unit. You should be pragmatic about the scope of your Delivery Unit's overseeing of delivery plans, keeping a few principles in mind:

- **Manageability.** The number of plans should be manageable, based on the size of your Delivery Unit. The PMDU managed anywhere from 15 to 20 major priorities at a time.
- **Comprehensiveness.** Taken together, the plans should cover all of the aspects of your delivery effort.
- **Ownership.** At the level of detail where your Delivery Unit reviews and monitors plans, it should be possible to assign each plan to a single *delivery plan owner.* This will be crucial, as it will allow you to hold a single person accountable for the development of and progress against each plan. Moreover, it will give you a manageable set of individuals in your system in whom you can invest time building both capacity and strong, trust-based relationships (for more on capacity building, see Module 5A, Build system capacity all the time).

DELIVERY PLAN OWNERS IN THE PMDU

The PMDU monitored plans roughly at the level of the 15 to 20 priorities for which it was responsible:

"We asked [departments] to identify the single named official who was personally responsible for the delivery of each priority. 'This should be the person who spends most of his/her time on the priority and has sleepless nights, worrying about hitting the targets' . . . The idea was not just that these people could be held to account but that in addition we would organize a series of master classes in delivery for this select group. There would, in other words, be support as well as pressure." (*Instruction to Deliver,* 106)

Exhibits 3C.3, 3C.4, and 3C.5 give illustrative examples of how delivery plan organization might play out in practice. Exhibit 3C.3, Target focus, presents a situation similar to the one the PMDU faced: a large Delivery Unit

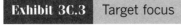

Exhibit 3C.3 Target focus

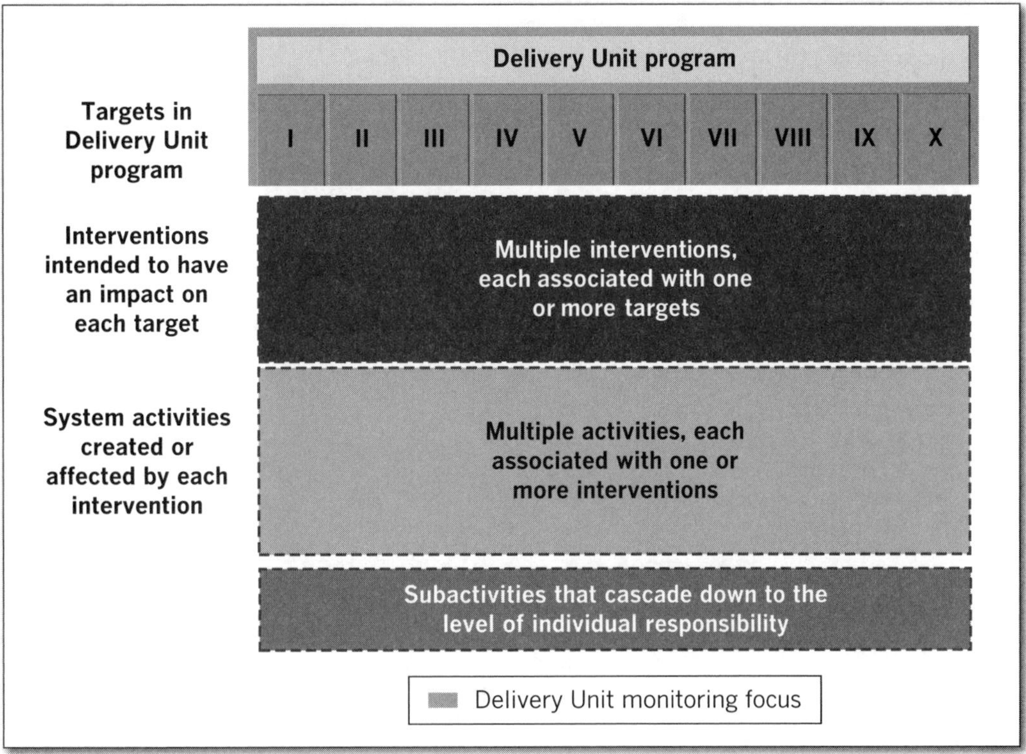

program consisting of 10 targets. In this case, the Delivery Unit has chosen to limit its monitoring to the target level and will ensure the appointment of a delivery plan owner and the writing of a delivery plan for each target.

In Exhibit 3C.4, Intervention focus, the Delivery Unit's program only has one target. The strategy to achieve this target consists of nine interventions. In this case, the Delivery Unit has chosen to monitor both the target and the interventions beneath it, such that delivery plan owners and delivery plans will be required at both levels.

Exhibit 3C.5, Performance unit focus, presents a common situation in higher education systems, where performance units (campuses) are large, few in number, and relatively autonomous, so much so that they will need to assume a distinct sense of ownership for a given target. In this case, the target has been broken down to the campus level first (for more on the negotiation of targets at the campus level, refer back to Module 3B, Set targets and trajectories). Interventions support these campus-level targets, but the Delivery Unit focuses on monitoring plans at the campus level and overall target level. In this case, each campus will have a delivery plan owner and a delivery plan.

In high-performing organizations, higher-level plans are broken down into plans at the activity and (eventually) the individual level, with all the parts linked in a cohesive manner. As Delivery Unit leader, you should advance this cohesive linking by encouraging your delivery plan owners to create delivery plan organizations and assign delivery plan owners within their own spheres of influence, so that the development of delivery plans

Exhibit 3C.4 Intervention focus

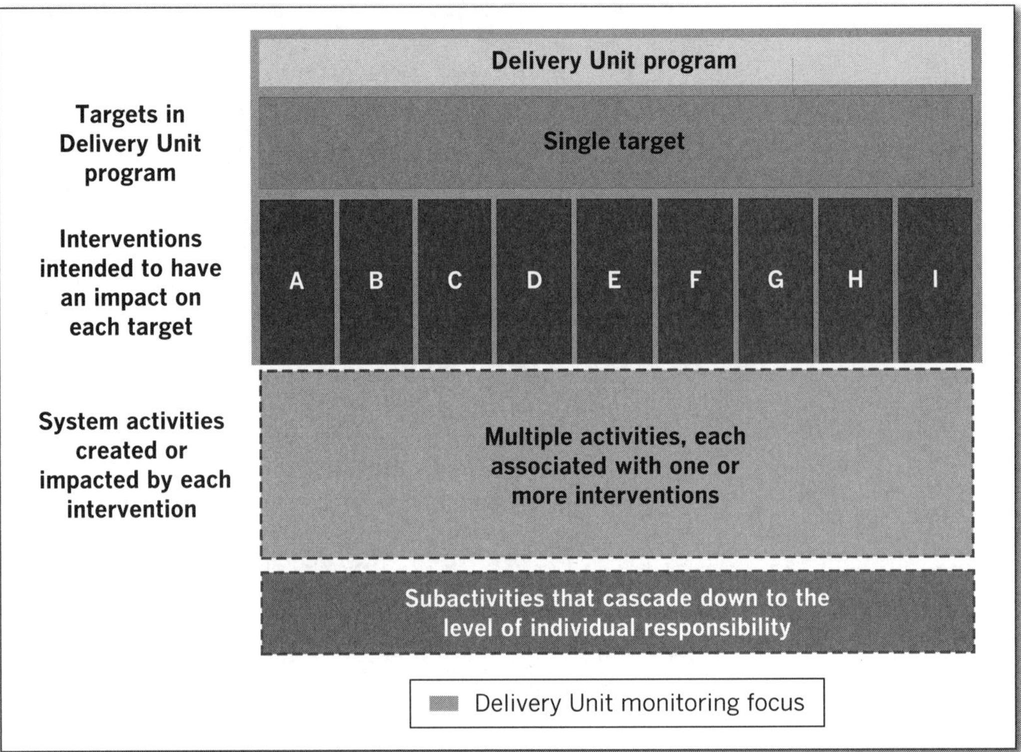

Exhibit 3C.5 Performance unit focus

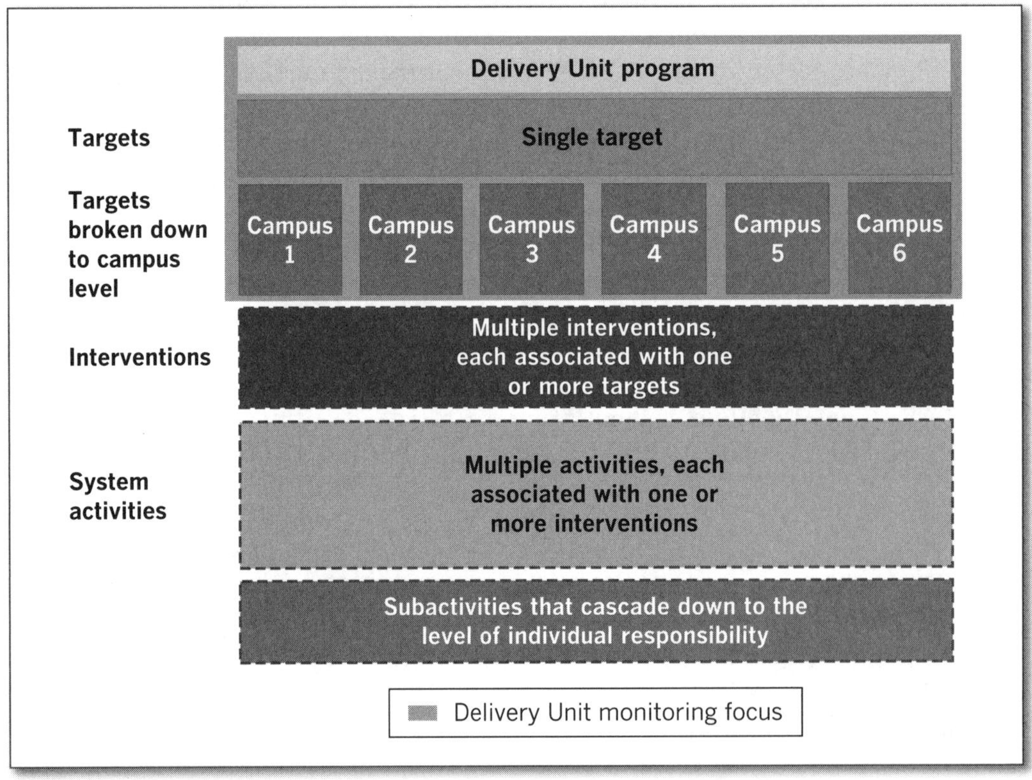

cascades all the way to the frontline. While you may encourage this practice, you will not directly review, oversee, or monitor these plans. The Delivery Unit would only need to concern itself with these plans if it found a barrier to delivery at this level.

CASE EXAMPLE

Delivery plan organization in Montgomery County, Maryland

At the Montgomery County Public Schools, officials at the district level monitored plans at the school level but gave schools considerable autonomy to develop and own their delivery plans

"Montgomery County Public Schools developed a common system for creating districtwide implementation plans and school-level plans that were consistent with the overall district goals. The consistent focus from the system level to the individual school level was raising performance for all students while accelerating the rate of improvement for the students who were farthest behind. Every school had the flexibility to create its own plans for differentiating its approach to meet its students' needs, but had to use the districtwide standards and planning process." (*Leading for Equity,* 96)

Step 2: Guide delivery plan owners in the development or refinement of their plans

Once you have determined which delivery plans your Unit will monitor—as well as the owners of those plans—you are ready to work with the delivery plan owners to write their first drafts. The guiding principle here is to empower delivery plan owners to take and maintain responsibility for their plans.

What are the criteria for a good plan? A good delivery plan will

- **Articulate its purpose.** What are you trying to do? How will you know if the delivery plan has been successful? How will things be different? How will the delivery plan help you to achieve your aspiration? What is the moral purpose?
- **Detail performance management.** What target metrics, leading indicators, indicators of unintended consequences, and/or **implementation indicators** should be tracked in monitoring this delivery plan? According to the delivery plan organization discussed above, every delivery plan will be associated with one or more target metrics (and their associated leading indicators), which you should observe for signs of the plan's impact. It may also be associated

AVOIDING PERFUNCTORY PLANNING IN THE PRIME MINISTER'S DELIVERY UNIT

In the U.K., the PMDU decided against offering a template for delivery plans, but instead it articulated the criteria for a good delivery plan and set a deadline for plans to be written:

"We decided firmly not to offer a template for a plan which departments could just fill in. That would have made their job too easy, too perfunctory, whereas we wanted them to engage with the harsh reality of getting something done. Helpfully, we could argue that by not offering a template we were responding to their plea that we should not micro-manage them." (*Instruction to Deliver,* 84)

with one or more indicators of unintended consequences, which you will also need to monitor. To track progress attributable only to the plan, you may also track plan-specific *implementation indicators.* An implementation indicator allows you to track progress against a plan.

- **Identify the relevant activities and delivery chains.** What **system activity** or activities will the plan change or introduce? What is the delivery chain (existing or to be created) for each of these activities? What action needs to be taken to strengthen the capacity, skills, and capabilities in each link of the delivery chain (district superintendents or school principals, for example)? The delivery chain analysis is at the center of any delivery plan. In order for a delivery plan owner to achieve results, she must demonstrate a thorough understanding of the delivery chains through which she will be working. For a reminder on how to conduct a delivery chain analysis, refer back to Module 2B.
- **Set a trajectory for implementation.** What is the overall timetable for implementation? What are the key milestones that you will use to track progress? What are the action steps that comprise each of these milestones, and what is the deadline for each? A *milestone* is a predicted event that demonstrates progress in implementing the plan. Milestones may or may not involve a target metric, leading indicator or implementation indicator. For example, for a plan to implement a literacy program, completion of the curriculum development would be a milestone. *Action steps* are the specific steps that must be taken in a delivery plan, with a timeline for each, toward achieving each milestone.
- **Assign leadership, management, and accountability.** Who owns the overall plan? Who owns each action step? Beyond specifying a delivery plan owner, each plan should assign action steps to specific people as a means of holding them accountable.
- **Incorporate benchmarking.** What benchmarks exist that relate to your plan, and what forums will you use to share best practice on an ongoing basis?
- **Describe the resources and Delivery Unit support required.** What resources are required for the plan's success, and if not currently available, how will they be obtained? What support is needed from the Delivery Unit?
- **Prepare to manage stakeholders and users.** Who are the relevant stakeholders, and how will you engage with and manage them effectively? How will the views of providers and users of service change over time?
- **Anticipate and prepare for risks.** What risks and constraints might throw the work off course, and how will they be managed?

Beyond providing plan owners with the above criteria for guidance, you should support them in the production of plans by providing examples of well-crafted plans from inside or outside your system.

At the same time, you should not delay implementation just because plans are still in development. In one K–12 system, some delivery plan owners had never created a plan before, so a great deal of investment was necessary to help owners create a functional plan. Had the Delivery Unit waited for a complete plan before beginning implementation, the delay would have been unacceptable. Instead, they chose to "build the plane while flying it." Exhibit 3C.6 shows an assessment of one K–12 program plan against the

Exhibit 3C.6 Strengths and weaknesses of a delivery plan for K–12 career and technical education

	Strengths	Weaknesses
Delivery chain, leadership, and accountability	• Identification of strong links (e.g., technical colleges) and weak links (e.g., communication with career and technical education teachers)	• Lists no next steps for strengthening weak links
Timetable, milestones, measuring progress	• Clear overall target: 4,200 new graduates by 2016 • Targets for leading indicators, such as program enrollment, enrollment in articulated credit courses	• No clear trajectory specified for data • Not clear all leading indicators are covered • Milestones and action steps do not take interdependencies into account
Resources and Delivery Unit support	• Specifies tangible actions that leadership can take to support (e.g., free them up from unnecessary tasks)	• Could be more specific (e.g., which tasks?)
Managing stakeholders	• Includes a comprehensive list of important stakeholders (e.g., SEA offices, State Board of Education, Career and Technical Education Advisory Committee)	• No approach or strategy specified for any of the stakeholders
Risks	• Includes a clear list of risks (e.g., tenuous position without legislative mandate, economic downturn)	• No approach or strategy specified to deal with any of these risks

SOURCE: Delivery plan from a K–12 SEA.

above criteria. As you will see, there are significant weaknesses—but the plan was good enough for implementation to begin.

Step 3: Test, challenge, and revise plans

Once you have received delivery plans, you will need to test their actual quality. Producing delivery plans is an iterative process, and your Unit should challenge and improve them constructively. As noted in the introduction to this module, the process of give and take in helping delivery plan owners to revise and improve their plans is at least as important as the plans themselves.

CASE EXAMPLE

Delivery planning as a means of discovery

In one state's K–12 system, the process of reviewing and giving feedback on plans helped the new Delivery Unit to understand what was currently going on in the system. The process further helped the delivery plan owners (program managers) to realize the potential for improvement in the way they managed system activities:

(Continued)

(Continued)

"While the resulting plans may not answer all the questions, plan writing is very reflective of what program managers actually do. Going through the process helps you understand the gap between what needs to be done and what's currently happening. In addition, it gives you an opportunity to help program managers see this gap as well. We worked with one program manager who felt powerless in her role, and was reluctant to seek changes to the status quo. By working through the planning process with her, we identified several opportunities for her to take on a more active management role, and we helped her initiate activities aimed at improving program outcomes rather than ensuring compliance." (EDI team member in a K–12 SEA)

CHALLENGE MEETINGS IN THE PMDU

"We asked each department to present to us during September on the progress it was making with planning for delivery. By then we had appointed a number of people—Delivery Unit associates—from outside the government with experience of delivery in both business and the public sector, and they joined us for these departmental presentations. We had careful pre-meetings to determine our line of questioning and then at the end of the meeting I summed up, offering what I thought the key messages were. If we had needed confirmation that departments were far from ready to deliver, these meetings provided it." (*Instruction to Deliver,* 102)

There are many different ways to facilitate this give and take. For many plans, your Delivery Unit staff may review them and provide feedback, either in written form or in a meeting with the delivery plan owner. If something more substantial is warranted, you may want to convene a challenge meeting. A challenge meeting is a structured problem-solving meeting that allows for a rigorous review of a delivery plan from multiple perspectives. More generally, you can use the challenge meeting process for several other aspects of your delivery effort (e.g., a subtarget set by a performance unit such as a campus). Some common characteristics of challenge meetings are

- The participation of experts (academics, individuals with experience in peer systems, individuals with relevant experience in the private sector, etc.), Delivery Unit staff, and the delivery plan owner;
- The presence of a limited number of individuals ("as few as possible but as many as necessary") and the exclusion of any potential participants who would prevent honest dialogue;
- Substantial preparation time, including a premeeting review of relevant information and drafting of questions (for the challenge team, without the participation of the delivery plan owner);
- An experienced chair who can quickly sum up and detail next steps; and
- A written record of the meeting and a summation of next steps, as well as follow-up that next steps were taken.

A sample process for a challenge meeting is given in Exhibit 3C.7.

Exhibit 3C.7 Sample process for a delivery plan challenge meeting

Body of the meeting

	Activities or questions to address
Prepare in advance of the meeting	• Determine participants (e.g., relevant external experts) • Have all participants review the plan in advance and prepare questions (this can be done in a premeeting, with everyone except the delivery plan owner)
Test the plan against criteria and for quality	• Does the plan address all of the criteria? Are all components of the plan credible? • Is the plan specific and comprehensive, by providing enough detail and accounting for everything relevant? Does it have a sufficient evidence base? Is it excessively complex? • Is it ambitious, by representing a change from "business as usual," but realistic in that those responsible for implementation have the necessary resources and capabilities?
Challenge the plan's logic and coherence	• Is the logic behind the plan sound or arbitrary? • Is the plan coherent overall? • Does it align with existing plans, goals, activities, etc.?
Challenge the rigor of the delivery plan owner and staff	• Does the delivery plan owner really know how to implement the plan? • Is the delivery plan owner really willing and ready to do it?
Compare the plan to relevant benchmarks	• How good is the plan relative to the best plan you received? • How good is it relative to the best external example of a plan that you have? (The Delivery Unit should have and be prepared to share examples.)
Determine next steps and follow-up	• The delivery leader should end the meeting by summing up next steps for the plan (e.g., the areas to be improved, questions to be answered, etc.) • The sum-up and next steps should be recorded and sent to all participants to ensure compliance • A designated individual should check that agreed actions were in fact taken

After you have challenged and revised delivery plans in your system, you are ready to begin implementing and managing them. While the revisions that emerge after a challenge meeting might not "perfect" the plans, this is not the objective; the challenge meetings will instead give you the critical insights and operational detail that you need to move forward.

Step 4: Create a master tracker for delivery plans

Your overall delivery program is at the top of your delivery plan organization. Your unit will want to devise a quick and easy way to track progress against each plan that it is monitoring. Plans that meet the criteria described in Step 2 above will have the following "trackable" elements:

- **Data** on projected progress on relevant target metrics, leading indicators, implementation indicators, or some combination of these;
- **Milestones**, as defined above; and
- **Support required from the Delivery Unit**, which should be arranged according to a timeline.

A sample master tracker is given in Exhibit 3C.8 for a set of delivery plans designed to improve high school teacher effectiveness in K–12 education.

Your master tracker will prove especially helpful as you begin to design **delivery routines** in the next module.

Exhibit 3C.8 Sample master tracker for delivery of high school teacher effectiveness

Delivery plans	Relevant elements	Time Q1	Q2	Q3	Q4
Teacher recruitment plan	Data		• 10% increase in applications (implementation indicator)	• 20% increase in accepted offers (implementation indicator)	• 5% increase in average teacher effectiveness (target metric)
	Milestone	• New awareness campaign launched	• New application and interview processes piloted		
	Support needed	• Delivery Unit benchmarking of teacher recruitment to best international practice		• Delivery Unit analysis and evaluation of piloted programs	
Teacher professional development plan	Data		• 50% of teachers observed in class by external evaluators (implementation indicator)	• 80% of teachers rate new PD program satisfactory or better (implementation indicator)	• 7% increase in average teacher effectiveness (target metric)
	Milestone	• Core team of external auditors identified and trained	• PD staff assigned to each school; new PD program piloted at all schools		
	Support needed	• Delivery Unit techniques for effective hiring, training, and professional development		• Delivery Unit audit of sample evaluation	

CASE EXAMPLE

A K–12 SEA's planning process from aspiration to implementation

Exhibit 3C.9 refers back to a hypothetical example first presented in Chapter 2. The example follows a K–12 SEA's path through the planning process from aspiration to implementation. For simplicity, the example follows a single target, performance pattern, driver, and system activity.

As presented in Chapter 2, this SEA identified its target metric, a particular performance pattern, a particular driver, and system activities that are related to that driver (Steps 1 through 5). In Step 6, the SEA identifies two interventions to improve the existing activity and one intervention to introduce a new activity. Two of these interventions (improving the quality of the program and expanding it) are combined into one delivery plan in order to rationalize the number of plans that the Delivery Unit will track. The SEA adds a new double-period program for CCR courses because it found that there were no activities currently addressing a crucial driver of the underperformance pattern: students who are multiple grade-levels behind.

In Step 7, the SEA builds its trajectory and sets its target for this target metric. The projected contributions to the trajectory of the first and third intervention are driven by research. The SEA projects the impact of the second intervention (spreading the program to more schools) using assumptions based on the data from the program's activity profile and the projected rate of program expansion. In total, the SEA projects that the three interventions will raise CCR graduation rates by 15% by 2017. After checking with stakeholders and schools to make sure it was realistic and ambitious enough, the SEA sets a stretch target: to raise graduation rates by 20% by 2017.

In Step 8, the SEA creates a plan for each intervention and chooses the metrics that it will use to track progress against this plan.

Again, this is a simplified example. In a real planning process, there will likely be more than one target and many more system activities and interventions to track.

In the final step, the SEA created a plan for each intervention. Exhibit 3C.8 shows sample metrics that are tracked in a plan for the first intervention.

(Continued)

Conclusion

By now, you have learned

- How to organize delivery plans and select delivery plan owners so that your Delivery Unit can monitor them effectively;
- The criteria for a good delivery plan;
- How to challenge and refine delivery plans by working through delivery plan owners; and
- How to set up a tracker that will monitor progress against delivery plans.

With this, you have completed the process of connecting your system's aspiration to the day-to-day steps that will allow you to achieve that aspiration. Now, it is time to begin implementation and drive performance. This is the subject of the next chapter.

(Continued)

Exhibit 3C.9 K–12 system going from aspiration to implementation: The delivery pyramid in practice

	Step	Aspect to determine	Example
Chapter 2	1	**Aspiration**	• State leads the nation in college and career-readiness
	2	**Target metric** and related leading indicators	• Target metric: College and career-ready (CCR) graduation rate • Leading indicator example: Algebra II course enrollment and passage rates
	3	**Performance pattern**	• CCR graduation rate in low-SES population is lower than the national average for low-SES students, and has been declining for each year that it has been measured
	4	**Drivers** of performance pattern	• Students are inadequately prepared to succeed in core CCR courses
	5	**System activities** that address driver	• Peer tutoring program that provides targeted help to students for core CCR courses

Chapter 3

6 Interventions that improve or add system activities

Identified changes to existing system activity

1. Improve quality of program
   - Select more effective teachers
   - Improve curriculum
2. Improve reach of program (offer at more schools)

Added additional system activities

3. Add double periods for students who are struggling in CCR courses

7 Trajectory of target metric, with accompanying **target**

① Created baseline

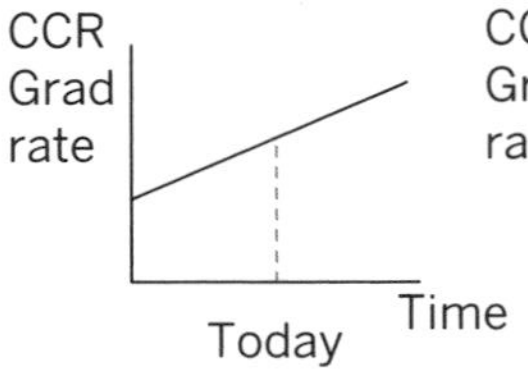

② Added impact of interventions

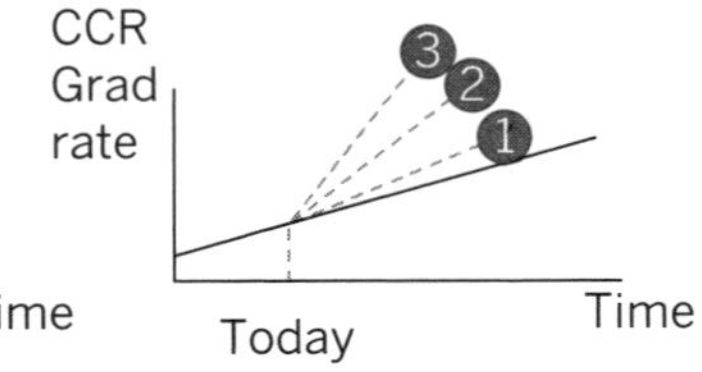

③ Set target

It is projected that the 3 interventions will raise CCR graduation rates by 15% over 5 years. After checking with stakeholders and schools to make sure it was realistic and ambitious enough, target is set: Raise graduation rates by 20% by 2017

8 Plans by intervention

Plan developed for ① Improve quality of program. Tracks:
- Target: CCR graduation rate
- Leading indicator: number of students enrolled in and passing core CCR courses
- Other milestone: number of schools using new curriculum

4

Drive Delivery

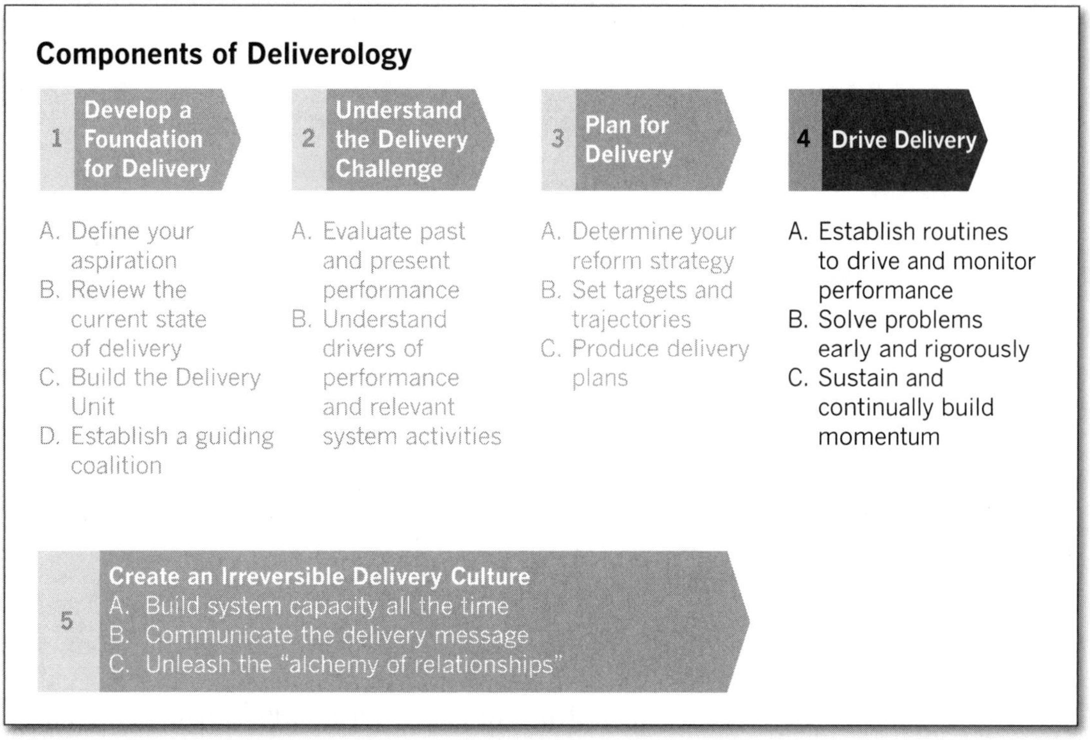

Components of Deliverology

1 Develop a Foundation for Delivery
A. Define your aspiration
B. Review the current state of delivery
C. Build the Delivery Unit
D. Establish a guiding coalition

2 Understand the Delivery Challenge
A. Evaluate past and present performance
B. Understand drivers of performance and relevant system activities

3 Plan for Delivery
A. Determine your reform strategy
B. Set targets and trajectories
C. Produce delivery plans

4 Drive Delivery
A. Establish routines to drive and monitor performance
B. Solve problems early and rigorously
C. Sustain and continually build momentum

5 Create an Irreversible Delivery Culture
A. Build system capacity all the time
B. Communicate the delivery message
C. Unleash the "alchemy of relationships"

Your **system's** strategy, targets, trajectories, and plans all represent commitments made by your system, which, if honored, should generate real results. Your **Delivery Unit's** role will be to track progress against these commitments, to identify challenges and change course where required, and above all to push your system to keep its promises.

In this chapter, you will be using the lessons you have learned and analyses and plans you have developed in the previous three chapters to drive delivery. This chapter will take you through the critical tools that are at the heart of a Delivery Unit's work: routines, problem-solving approaches, and tactics for pushing your system beyond its early wins. This chapter consists of three modules:

A. Establish routines to drive and monitor performance

B. Solve problems early and rigorously

C. Sustain and continually build momentum

Delivery at its core is not always exciting: As one journalist described it during the time of the PMDU, "There is no drama in delivery . . . only a long, grinding haul punctuated by public frustration with the pace of change."[1] But, completing this long haul is exactly what delivery is about.

4A. ESTABLISH ROUTINES TO DRIVE AND MONITOR PERFORMANCE

"Our biggest job was to keep the eye on the ball and keep the ball rolling. This is what routines allowed us to do."

—Claire O'Connor, former director of Los Angeles Mayor's Performance Management Unit

"If there was one contribution our team made to the delivery effort, it was establishing the routines. Routines are the core of delivery."

—USEDI team leader at a K–12 SEA

A family cannot be fairly judged on the basis of its photograph albums. Albums show birthdays, wedding anniversaries, and holidays. But, special occasions are not the real test of the quality of relationships in a family precisely because they are special. All of us know that it is the routine day-to-day interactions that shape a family—mealtimes, television viewing, getting ready for school, and coming home from work.

In a similar sense, the quality of a **delivery effort** is reflected not in specific events, but in a steady stream of implementation that slowly but surely leads to the attainment of the system's aspiration. For this reason, the most important contribution that your Delivery Unit can make to the delivery effort is in establishing and maintaining delivery routines: the regularly scheduled and structured opportunities for your system leader,

1. Matthew D'Ancona, *Sunday Telegraph*, 6 January 2002

delivery plan owners, and others to review performance, discuss major issues, and make decisions to drive delivery forward.

Routines are the engine of delivery. They follow the clock, with no excuses for delay. They can come in many forms, depending on information, frequency, audience, and format. But, the purpose of each is the same: to create a sense of urgency, to sustain focus and momentum, and to track progress. One of the main benefits of routines is their ability to focus the delivery effort despite the multitude of distractions that will plague any system.

THE IMPORTANCE OF ROUTINES

"Inevitably, [staff] attention would be drawn to things that were going wrong and the interventions this required us to make, but the danger came when any of us shifted from rightly paying attention to these interventions to wrongly thinking that they were the only way we had an impact. Often at staff meetings I would wrench people's attention back to the routines of **Deliverology**—the stocktakes, tracking the data against trajectory, writing Delivery Reports, keeping the focus. Just as historians and commentators can easily fall into the trap of focusing on the events, so can those in government. In fact, without the routine, events cannot be fully understood and, more importantly, results will never be delivered. From outside, government always looks chaotic, partly because it often is, and partly because only the events—in effect the breaks in routine—get reported. Part of the mission of the Delivery Unit was to establish, at least internally, the primacy of order over chaos." (*Instruction to Deliver,* 112)

In addition to distractions, there are a multitude of other barriers to successful reform, including:

- The cynicism resulting from the track record;
- The tendency to have pleasant little initiatives that tinker at the edges of a service but do not change the core business;
- The ever-present risk of watering down a proposal to gain consensus, with the result all too often that a roaring lion becomes a squeaking mouse;
- The risk that before a reform has really made a difference, the agenda shifts, attention is diverted elsewhere, and the service slips back into its preexisting state; and, most of all,
- The danger of underestimating the extraordinary deadweight force of institutional inertia.

Routines play a large part in overcoming these barriers by forcing the system to regularly check its progress on a consistent set of priorities.

ROLES OF SYSTEM LEADER AND DELIVERY LEADER

The role of your Delivery Unit is to encourage a smooth start to delivery, establish and maintain a set of official delivery routines, and ensure that routines are conducted in a manner that maximizes their success. System leaders, for their part, must take delivery routines seriously in order to lend credence to the delivery effort, supporting and engaging with each routine as their role in the routine requires.

PROCESS STEPS

Step 1: Start delivery
Step 2: Establish routines
Step 3: Create a master schedule of routines

Step 1: Start delivery

In one sense, establishing routines (Step 2) is the most effective way to begin delivery. After all, there is no better motivation to get things done than the knowledge that a check-in is already scheduled to occur one month from now. However, the routines by themselves will not ensure the most effective possible start. Making the right moves at the beginning can create early momentum that will be more easily sustained throughout the delivery effort (please see Module 4C for more on sustaining and building this momentum). Several principles should help guide the initial implementation of delivery plans, as indicated in Exhibit 4A.1.

The last principle in Exhibit 4A.1 is particularly important. The **implementation dip** is a period in which enthusiasm wanes shortly after the launch of a delivery effort. The excitement during the launch is quickly replaced by frustration, as people face the day-to-day challenges of the task at hand and do not yet see any fruits from their efforts. This slump in enthusiasm has the potential to drag down your entire delivery effort. One way to

Exhibit 4A.1 Guiding principles for a strong start to delivery

Understand that the perfect is the enemy of the good	• Attempts to "perfect" plans will be unnecessarily time-consuming • Encourage delivery plan owners to begin implementation as soon as possible
Engage your delivery system in the "launch"	• Consider building early momentum with an official delivery launch, to restate the moral purpose, communicate the delivery message, and set expectations
Capture and publicize quick wins	• Identify and communicate results that are more easily and quickly achieved to rally the effort and drive momentum • Note that "quick wins" need to be in the direction of the overall strategy and should never serve as distractors from your ultimate delivery goals
Plan-do-review, learn and replicate	• Even the best thought-out plans will require further refinement after they begin • Use delivery routines to ensure that your system creates and maintains a culture of reviewing progress, learning constantly, and adapting plans based on new insights
Prepare for resistance and the "implementation dip"	• Almost every exciting launch is followed by a dip in results as well as enthusiasm • Prepare your team for managing and persisting through any early slumps, controversies, or distractions • A mindset of persistence is necessary from the onset to ensure long-term commitment to the delivery plan.

minimize an implementation dip is to ensure that quick wins (early but demonstrable progress that people can see and feel) are sequenced into your strategy (see Module 3A). Another way to prepare for this dip is to understand and communicate that substantial change must come before results will be visible. As Exhibit 4A.2 demonstrates, better times are ahead; to get there, patience and persistence are required.

An exemplary approach to the management of current and future resistance was taken a few years ago by a new principal brought in to improve a troubled school in an urban neighborhood. This principal knew that there would be resistance to the changes that she was instituting, and she warned the district superintendent about this. She told the superintendent that if he reacted to these complaints or suggested alterations based on them, she would leave. The complaints did come, but the superintendent did not react. The complaints subsided after a few weeks, and results soon followed. This principal was able to predict the implementation dip, set expectations for stakeholders in order to help them ride it out, and achieve the changes she wanted as a result.

Exhibit 4A.2 The implementation dip

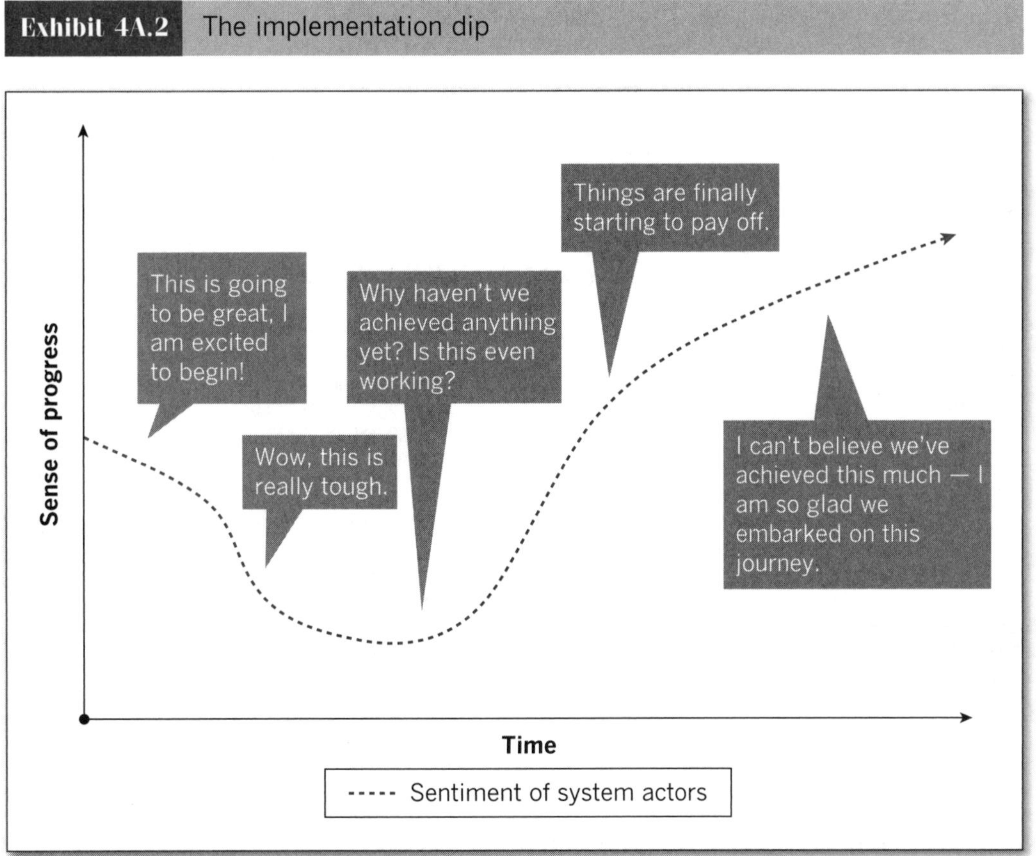

Step 2: Establish routines

At their core, routines work because they create deadlines, which in turn create a sense of urgency. Delivery plan owners are more likely to push hard to implement when faced with regular check-in meetings with the system leader. The following extended case example explains the approach to routines taken by the PMDU. It will be helpful to review this example before we explore more general principles for establishing your own routines. Your Delivery Unit can use similar tools and customize them to your own system.

CASE EXAMPLE

Routines in the Prime Minister's Delivery Unit

The PMDU developed three distinct, highly effective routines, which varied in the type and depth of the information they provide and in what ways and how frequently the information was communicated. The depth of each routine was inversely related to its frequency: Less information could be collected and analyzed for a more frequent routine, while less frequent routines could feature more in-depth information and analysis. For this reason, it was important for the PMDU to develop a mix of routines, ranging in frequency, depth of information, and means for communication. The three main routines used by the PMDU, as well as sample end products for each, are summarized in Exhibit 4A.3. A more detailed description of each follows.

Exhibit 4A.3 Routines in the PMDU

	Definition	Purpose	Frequency
Monthly notes	• Progress update briefing for the PM • Consists of a brief summary, followed by a short report	• Update the PM on progress against targets, key actions required, and warning signs of risks • Identify areas where PM needs to make decisions or recommendations • Raise visibility of PMDU by copying other stakeholders • Surface other issues that may impact Delivery Unit's agenda	• Monthly
Stocktakes	• Regular meeting of PM, leaders from relevant departments, and key officials	• Evaluate delivery of specific set of activities • Update the PM on progress • Enable the PM to hold individuals accountable • Provide focus, clarity, and a sense of urgency • Make decisions on key actions or new policies needed • Remove barriers to cross-departmental work • Celebrate success when milestones are met	• Quarterly
Delivery reports	• Comprehensive assessment of the status of all of the system's key priority areas • From delivery leader to PM	• Update PM on progress against priorities • Outline what success looks like for priorities over the next six months • Determine best path forward • Identify key actions that need to be taken • Surface areas of disagreement between the Delivery Unit and the frontline • Act as a reference document against which to chart progress	• Every six months

Monthly notes

Monthly notes were briefings sent to the prime minister (system leader), which updated him on relevant progress and issues for the system's **target metrics** (known as "priorities" in the PMDU). The PMDU prepared a monthly note for each of the four departments (each of which had multiple targets) on its agenda, which meant that the prime minister received a note an average of once per week. They were the most frequently occurring routine, and for this reason they covered less information than the others. The progress reported in monthly notes was sometimes at the leading indicator level, as data for the target metric were not always regularly available.

Each note consisted of a brief, succinct summary of progress, current and emerging delivery issues, and key actions required, followed by an appendix with any relevant supporting information. Data were presented in a standardized format. The purposes of the monthly notes were

- To update the prime minister on progress against targets;
- To update the prime minister on key actions required or key actions taken;
- To give the prime minister an early warning of risks;
- To raise issues beyond immediate performance that may affect the Delivery Unit's agenda;
- To ask the prime minister for decisions or recommendations, and enable him to comment on progress and make suggestions; and
- To reach key internal stakeholders beyond the prime minister (as copy recipients of the note) and serve as an important part of branding and visibility.

> "I urged my staff to prepare a note on each major department every four weeks, which would mean that Blair would get a note a week from us routinely and any other notes I did would be additional. To my surprise, the staff . . . argued that we should only send notes when we had something to say. In reply, I said that it was important to ensure our visibility at the vortex and that, if they were on top of their jobs, they would always have something to say . . . My task in editing [notes] was to delete management jargon . . . and to sharpen the messages to the PM [prime minister] . . . Since I thought Blair had enough to worry about, I also insisted that the notes told him what we planned to do about the problems we described. Often I then asked him to confirm that he was happy with the course of action. The simple, routine act of reporting progress to the PM consistently ensured the gentle pressure we required." (*Instruction to Deliver,* 120–121)

The PMDU would send these notes to the prime minister, with copies to the Cabinet Office ministers, the cabinet secretary, and other relevant staff in the prime minister's office. Each note could be read by the prime minister in no more than two or three minutes, ensuring good use of his precious time.

Monthly note guidelines are given in Exhibit 4A.4 and the PMDU's standard timeline for preparing the monthly note in Exhibit 4A.5.

Exhibit 4A.4 Monthly note components

Executive summary (cover page)	Supporting information (appendix)
1. Update on progress against trajectory 2. List of issues that are currently affecting progress 3. List of emerging issues that may impact delivery 4. Questions for the system leader or requests for recommendations 5. List of next steps to be taken by the relevant department, Delivery Unit, and/or system leader[1]	1. Recent performance data (any relevant target metrics, leading indicators, indicators of unintended consequences, implementation indicators, or milestones as appropriate) 2. More detailed description of issues affecting progress, with relevant data (when necessary) 3. More detailed description of emerging issues, with relevant data (when necessary) 4. Relevant context behind questions and requests for system leader 5. Relevant additional detail on next steps

1. Next steps will include previously planned actions as well as those actions that will be taken in light of progress against the trajectory and current/emerging delivery issues. Some next steps may be reliant on the answers/recommendations to be received in response to the questions and requests in Component 4.

(Continued)

(Continued)

Exhibit 4A.5 Monthly note timeline

Timing	At least a week before	A week before	3 days before	2 days before	Friday
Main processes	Prepare	Check data	Draft brief	Send to delivery leader	Submit
Description	• Get data, or draft note on performance, from department • Make sure delivery leader's office is aware of note timing	• Review data from departments • Go back to department with any queries	• Draft delivery leader's covering note • Agree on content for note with other team members	• Send appendices and draft covering note to delivery leader to clear the Wednesday before the note goes to system leader	• Compile and summarize notes from each department, drawing key takeaways and next steps • Note goes to system leader by EOD Friday
Owner	• Department head	• Department head	• Department head	• Department head	• Delivery leader

Stocktakes

Stocktakes were regular meetings to review and discuss performance for each priority area in depth. The PMDU organized a stocktake once every three months for each of the four departments on its agenda, which meant that a stocktake occurred an average of every 2 to 3 weeks. Participants included the prime minister (who chaired the meeting), Delivery Unit staff, and leaders from the relevant departments (including ministers and heads of departments). Each meeting focused on evaluating progress on the delivery of the key priorities.

A few features made stocktakes a distinctive practice. First, they relied heavily on the presentation of clear data. Trajectories were a key part of each stocktake discussion; meetings generally started with a data presentation—from the delivery leader or relevant department official—that examined actual performance versus **trajectory.** Second, they maintained a regular focus on a sustained set of priorities. Finally, having the prime minister personally there and holding the meeting in the Cabinet Room in No. 10 Downing Street ensured status and priority.

Overall, the purposes of stocktakes were

- To demonstrate the sustained priority the prime minister gave to the delivery agenda;
- To update the prime minister on progress;
- To enable the prime minister to hold individuals accountable for progress on targets;
- To provide focus, clarity, and a sense of urgency on issues affecting delivery;
- To discuss options and gain agreement on key actions needed;
- To remove barriers to the sharing of best practices and to support interdepartmental cooperation;
- To celebrate success when key milestones were met; and
- To identify new policy needs.

"To succeed, the Delivery Unit-organized stocktakes had to have certain key ingredients. The first was this focus on performance; the second was regularly focusing on the same handful of priorities; the third was the regular attendance of the Prime Minister himself and the relevant Secretary of State; and the fourth was ensuring that the data presented to the meeting was shared and accepted by everyone present. Each of these characteristics seems relatively straightforward, but the combination was revolutionary." (*Instruction to Deliver*, 92)

Key department officials and Delivery Unit staff were included, but attendance was limited. Preparation time was substantial, with premeetings to inform the prime minister of the review items, so that the questions in the meeting itself would be efficient, targeted, and thoughtful. A clear and succinct presentation of the key messages was crucial to stocktakes as well. The PMDU would spend hours going over a presentation, refining the communication to make sure that the data presented was both accurate and compelling. In addition, the same types of graphs were used in every stocktake so that, by the third stocktake, people would recognize what they were looking at. The typical cast list for a PMDU stocktake, and their roles and responsibilities, is given in Exhibit 4A.6.

Exhibit 4A.6 Roles and responsibilities for PMDU stocktakes

Prime minister	• Chairs the stocktake meeting • Holds department to account for delivery • Challenges progress • Approves policy
PMDU	• Head of PMDU represents the unit and in some cases presents the delivery update and delivers data presentation at the beginning of every stocktake • Other relevant staff attend and sometimes write the minutes • PMDU staff: - Secures slots in the prime minister's calendar - Identifies optimum timings of stocktakes - Manages relationships with prime minister's office and departments in preparation for stocktakes - Prepares the briefing (as part of joint brief with policy directorate) - Approves minutes and follow-up actions - Provides data and analysis to the persons preparing the update
Policy directorate	• Has significant influence and input into the agenda, agreeing the cast list and sending out invitations • Briefs the prime minister on any policy issues to be discussed at the stocktake (as part of joint brief with PMDU) • May provide prime minister with an oral briefing before the meeting • Clears and sends out minutes
Departments	• Secretary of state and relevant junior ministers will attend and in some cases present delivery updates • Permanent secretary and lead officials for areas to be discussed may also attend, and in some cases they may provide the delivery update

SOURCE: From *Instruction to Deliver*, by M. Barber, 2008, London: Methuen Publishing Ltd. Copyright by Michael Barber.

(Continued)

(Continued)

The PMDU's timeline for the preparation of a stocktake is shown in Exhibit 4A.7.

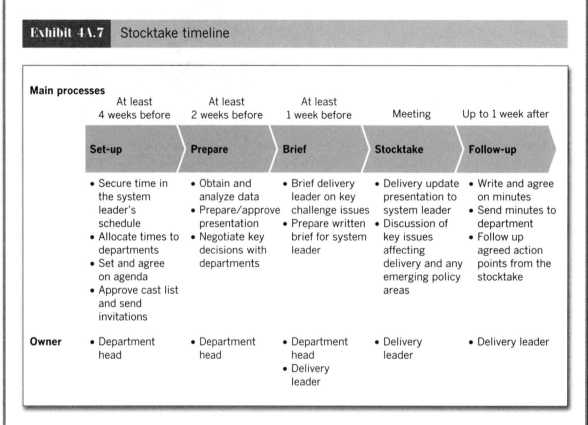

Exhibit 4A.7 Stocktake timeline

Main processes	At least 4 weeks before	At least 2 weeks before	At least 1 week before	Meeting	Up to 1 week after
	Set-up	**Prepare**	**Brief**	**Stocktake**	**Follow-up**
	• Secure time in the system leader's schedule • Allocate times to departments • Set and agree on agenda • Approve cast list and send invitations	• Obtain and analyze data • Prepare/approve presentation • Negotiate key decisions with departments	• Brief delivery leader on key challenge issues • Prepare written brief for system leader	• Delivery update presentation to system leader • Discussion of key issues affecting delivery and any emerging policy areas	• Write and agree on minutes • Send minutes to department • Follow up agreed action points from the stocktake
Owner	• Department head	• Department head	• Department head • Delivery leader	• Delivery leader	• Delivery leader

Delivery reports

Delivery reports were in-depth assessments provided to the prime minister on the status of all of the system's key priority areas. Delivery reports were the most comprehensive routine, and for this reason the PMDU undertook them the least frequently (every 6 months). As the most in-depth assessment of delivery, delivery reports generated numerous subroutines related to the collection, analysis, and communication of delivery information. The purposes of the delivery reports were

- To update the prime minister succinctly on progress against his priorities over the last six months;
- To lay out for the prime minister a vision of success for the priorities over the next six months and what key actions would be needed to realize them;
- To provide the prime minister an evidence-based prediction of the "likelihood of delivery" for each of the priorities;
- To enable comparison of progress across priorities;
- To drive a focused discussion around progress to date and the best way forward;
- To identify key actions that needed to be taken by relevant departments, with dates and named responsibilities, including major joint areas of work with the PMDU;
- To discover areas of disagreement between the PMDU and the relevant delivery plan owners;
- To form the basis of a joint action plan for next six months between the PMDU and relevant delivery plan owners; in effect, therefore, they ensured delivery plans were reviewed and strengthened in the light of evidence; and
- To act as a reference document against which to chart progress between delivery report cycles.

The main feature of a delivery report was an assessment of the likelihood of delivery for each of the system's priorities.

To understand and compare the underlying qualitative drivers of the likelihood of delivery, the PMDU developed the **assessment framework**, a tool for reviewing the likelihood of delivery for each priority by judging four categories:

- The degree of the delivery challenge (low, medium, high, or very high)
- The quality of planning, implementation, and performance management (traffic light at green, yellow-green, yellow-red, or red)
- The capacity to drive progress (traffic light at green, yellow-green, yellow-red, or red)
- The stage of delivery, from one (beginning) to four (advanced)

Each of those judgments was then combined with recent performance against the trajectory, as well as data on any other relevant leading indicators, to generate an overall traffic light judgment (green, yellow-green, yellow-red, or red) on the likelihood of delivery for the priority in question. For all four categories and the overall judgment, ratings were always given on a four-point scale in order to prevent a regression to the middle and to force a decision about whether a priority was more on or off track. Where necessary, the PMDU calculated judgments at a more granular level first (e.g., the intervention level) and aggregated these judgments to the priority level.

It is important to note that a traffic light judgment was not necessarily a judgment on whether a priority was being delivered well at the time of assessment. Rather, it was a judgment on the likelihood that the thing being evaluated would make its planned contribution to the achievement of the target. Thus, a responsible individual could be delivering well, but her priority area might still receive a red assessment if the likelihood of delivery was low for reasons outside her control (e.g., the challenge is very high, and the stage of delivery is advanced). In short, the purpose of the traffic light judgments was not to allocate blame but to drive action.

This innovative process allowed apparently unlike things (railway performance and health waiting times, for example) to be valuably compared, and enabled the PMDU to predict what would deliver in future and what would not, unless action was taken.

> "It needs to be emphasized, of course, that this was not pure science: it was a question of a small number of people making the best judgments they could with the limited information they had. The test, though, was not whether the . . . judgments were perfect—which they could never have been—but whether, when they saw light of day in the Prime Minister's or Chancellor's office, or even more tellingly in the various departments, they were accepted as being broadly right. More importantly still, the methodology underpinning the judgments would in time need to stand up to intense scrutiny." (*Instruction to Deliver,* 100)

The assessment framework and its overall architecture are given in Exhibits 4A.8 and 4A.9.

Exhibit 4A.10 shows a part of the detailed rubric used to arrive at these judgments, which includes questions to consider and examples of what "good" and "bad" look like for each set of questions. For the entire detailed rubric behind the assessment framework, please see Appendix A2.

Six weeks prior to the publication of a delivery report, the PMDU would formally ask departments to assess the priorities for which they were responsible against the assessment framework. The relevant Delivery Unit staff would then build on these assessments to arrive at an initial perspective on what the judgment for each priority should be.

The data for the traffic light judgments was then gathered and analyzed regularly by PMDU staff to prepare for the semiannual delivery report process. As one former PMDU staffer recalled,

(Continued)

(Continued)

Exhibit 4A.8 Template for assessment framework

Department: ____________ **Date of assessment:** ____________
PSA target: ____________ **Assessors:** ____________

Judgment	Rating	Rationale Summary
Degree of challenge	L/M/H/VH	
Quality of planning, implementation and performance management Understanding the challenge Governance, program, and project management Managing performance		
Capacity to drive progress Understanding and structure of the delivery chain Engaging the delivery chain Leadership and culture		
Stage of delivery	1/2/3/4	

Recent performance against trajectory and milestones

Likelihood of delivery

Key

Red	Highly problematic – requires urgent and decisive action
Yellow/Red	Problematic – requires substantial attention, some aspects need urgent attention
Yellow/Green	Mixed – aspects require substantial attention, some good
Green	Good – requires refinement and systematic implementation

Exhibit 4A.9 Overview of assessment framework criteria

Judgment area	Description
Degree of challenge	Scale of the task, obstacles to be overcome.
Quality of planning, implementation, and performance management	
1. Understanding the challenge	Clarity on what success looks like (what we're doing and why) and how much has to be changed to get there, taking account of historical performance.
2. Governance, program, and project management	A strategy that is translated into a usable implementation plan. Clear structures that support accountability for outcomes.
3. Managing performance	Fundamentals of monitoring and reporting performance (measures, trajectories). Proactive responses to reported performance.

Judgment area	Description
Capacity to drive progress	
	Highlighted and detailed in the next exhibit
1. Understanding and structuring the delivery chain	Understanding of the delivery chain; sophistication/comprehensiveness of key elements of the delivery chain, including incentives and prioritization.
2. Engaging the delivery chain	Winning hearts and minds: mechanisms for influencing; mechanisms for and response to feedback.
3. Leadership and culture	Extent to which the performance ethic of the department and delivery chain supports delivery: leadership, ambition, accountability, working across silos.
Stage of delivery	Current point on the scale between policy development and irreversible progress.

At any given point in time, each of us, if called upon to do so, could have given a judgment on the four areas of the assessment framework for the priority areas in our purview, simply on the basis of our day-to-day work there.

Four weeks prior to the publication of a delivery report, the PMDU staff conducted **moderation meetings** (also known as **calibration meetings**) in which they brought these initial judgments together to finalize them. The process for a moderation meeting worked like this: Delivery Unit leadership and the Delivery Unit staff responsible for each priority shared their initial judgments. Other staff would then question and challenge these judgments based on their own experiences and the judgments they had made, debating and discussing each priority until they arrived at a set of judgments that were consistent across priority areas. The moderation meetings ensured that all of the judgments and rankings were consistent, evidenced based, and defensible. They also aligned the staff behind the judgments and allowed participants to share and learn lessons on what makes delivery successful. They were a tremendous learning experience.

The summary output of these moderation meetings was a rank ordering of each priority area's likelihood of delivery, also known as a **league table.** League tables are essential tools for delivery routines. They make evidence about performance transparent, they focus minds on the priorities they encompass, and they make sure—in whatever system they are applied—that something is done about the individual units ranked on the table—whether they are schools, hospitals, police forces, or local authorities. A sample league table from the PMDU, which includes an overview of the overall judgments and the underlying assessment framework judgments, is given in Exhibit 4A.11.

The league table was always accompanied by a short, crisp report explaining the most crucial data on the target metric and leading indicators (where appropriate), an analysis of progress and its causes, and a proposed set of actions for the next six months, with a clear definition of how the PMDU would help. Exhibit 4A.12 gives an example of the types of issues that this report would highlight.

In addition to arriving at the traffic light judgments and rankings, the PMDU staff also contributed to the text of this report, each for the specific priority areas they covered. The report was compiled and edited centrally and delivered to the relevant government officials for discussion prior to its delivery to the prime minister. There were to be no surprises in delivery reports: Early distribution allowed recipients to discuss the report and air differences in judgments with those of the PMDU. The final decision on the judgments in the report remained firmly with the PMDU, however, and once made, the report was sent to the prime minister, his staff, and relevant officials at the Treasury and the Cabinet Office. Sometimes, the prime minister asked for the league table to be presented to the Cabinet both to keep them informed and to inspire further progress.

(Continued)

Exhibit 4A.10 Granular assessment framework criteria

Areas to consider	Example questions	Best case (Green) ⟷	Worst case (Red)	Rating	Rationale
1. Understanding and structure of the delivery chain					
Understanding the delivery chain	Has the structure of the delivery chain been identified? Are roles and responsibilities clear? Are the interests and influences of key stakeholders understood? Is there an appropriate strategy for tackling weaknesses in the chain?	Key people, stakeholders, and target customers have been mapped and cascaded. There is a strategy for strengthening the chain (where appropriate).	Functions of the delivery chain are opaque. Lack of clarity about who the main deliverers are.		
Prioritization	Are people throughout the delivery chain working to a ranked set of priorities? Are tough choices made at the strategic level sustained through the chain? Does the allocation of resources and activities reflect agreed priorities? Is there prioritization within the total portfolio of programs, as well as those relating specifically to the Public Service Agreement (PSA)? Is there an approach to ensure that ministerial priorities are aligned with agreed priorities?	Key deliverers and accountable leaders are focused on a ranked set of priorities, based on effective quantification and clear agreed criteria. Tough choices made. Priorities, and criteria for prioritization, are regularly reviewed.	People are working on numerous and conflicting "priorities," with no agreed ranking. Priorities are decided locally. There is no sense of expected impact or ease of implementation.		
Incentives	Are incentives in place, and do the forms of incentive (e.g. financial reward, freedoms vs. controls, recognition vs. shaming) reflect what matters to those to whom they apply? Do incentives apply according to the extent to which the PSA outcome is delivered? Do incentives act on key decision makers throughout the delivery chain? Do the incentives add up to a coherent whole, avoiding perverse incentives?	Incentives targeted using an analysis of who is important to delivery; leaders empowered to design local incentives. Strong incentives based on evidence of what motivates those to whom they apply. No perverse incentives operating.	Incentives that do not apply or are ineffective for important parts of delivery chain, or encourage the wrong behaviors/ outcomes. Incentives that are trivial or do not match what matters.		
Support	Is there transfer of best practice (vertically or laterally)? Are processes for evaluation/inspection understood and used? Is the current use and dissemination of incentives, training, and tools sufficient? Is there clear responsibility for challenging and supporting deliverers?	Good transfer of best practice. Delivery chain support mechanisms and challenge processes are understood and used. Effective evaluation and inspection is used to strengthen both capacity and accountability.	Department has no grasp on performance management mechanisms in the rest of the delivery chain. Limited knowledge of operational environment means that challenge and support levers are not used.		

(Continued)

Exhibit 4A.11 Sample league table with rankings for Public Service Agreement (PSA) priorities

July 2004

Dept		Assessment criteria				Overall judgment	
		Degree of challenge	Quality of planning, implementation, and performance management	Capacity to drive progress	Stage of delivery	Likelihood of delivery	Rank (out of 21)
A	PSA 1	L	G	G	3	G	= 1
B	PSA 2	L	G	YG	2	G	= 1
C	PSA 3	H	YG	YG	3	G	3
D	PSA 4	H	G	YG	3	YG	4
A	PSA 5	VH	G	YG	2	YG	5
B	PSA 6	H	YG	YG	3	YG	6
C	PSA 7	H	YG	YG	2	YG	= 7
D	PSA 8	H	YG	YG	3	YG	= 7
A	PSA 9	H	YG	YG	2	YG	= 7
B	PSA 10	VH	YG	YG	2	YG	= 10
C	PSA 11	VH	YG	YG	2	YG	= 10
D	PSA 12	H	YR	YG	3	YG	12
A	PSA 13	VH	YR	YG	2	YR	13
B	PSA 14	VH	YG	YR	2	YR	= 14
C	PSA 15	VH	YG	YR	2	YR	= 14
D	PSA 16	VH	YR	YR	2	YR	= 16
A	PSA 17	VH	YR	YR	2	YR	= 16
B	PSA 18	H	YG	YR	3	R	= 18
C	PSA 19	H	YG	YR	2	R	= 18
D	PSA 20	VH	YG	YR	3	R	20
A	PSA 21	VH	R	R	2	R	21

Key

Red — Highly problematic; requires urgent action

Yellow/Red — Problematic; requires action

Yellow/Green — Mixed; some good, some action required

Green — Good; requires only refinement

Degree of challenge:

L = low
M = medium
H = high
VH = very high

(Continued)

(Continued)

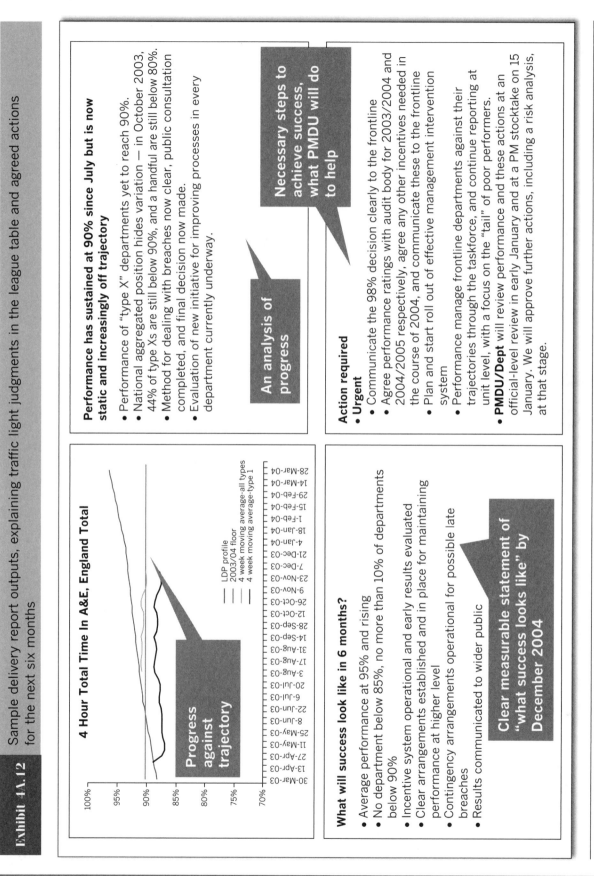

Exhibit 4A.12 Sample delivery report outputs, explaining traffic light judgments in the league table and agreed actions for the next six months

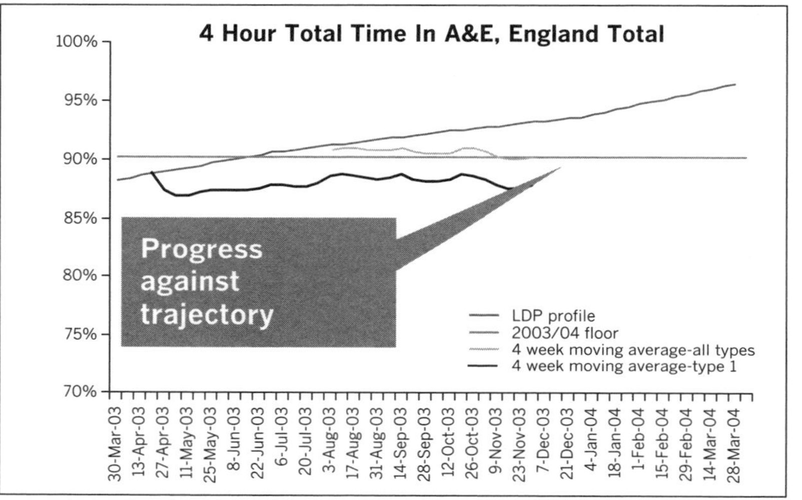

Performance has sustained at 90% since July but is now static and increasingly off trajectory

- Performance of "type X" departments yet to reach 90%.
- National aggregated position hides variation — in October 2003, 44% of type Xs are still below 90%, and a handful are still below 80%.
- Method for dealing with breaches now clear, public consultation completed, and final decision now made.
- Evaluation of new initiative for improving processes in every department currently underway.

An analysis of progress

Necessary steps to achieve success, what PMDU will do to help

What will success look like in 6 months?

- Average performance at 95% and rising
- No department below 85%, no more than 10% of departments below 90%
- Incentive system operational and early results evaluated
- Clear arrangements established and in place for maintaining performance at higher level
- Contingency arrangements operational for possible late breaches
- Results communicated to wider public

Clear measurable statement of "what success looks like" by December 2004

Action required

- **Urgent**
  - Communicate the 98% decision clearly to the frontline
  - Agree performance ratings with audit body for 2003/2004 and 2004/2005 respectively, agree any other incentives needed in the course of 2004, and communicate these to the frontline
  - Plan and start roll out of effective management intervention system
  - Performance manage frontline departments against their trajectories through the taskforce, and continue reporting at unit level, with a focus on the "tail" of poor performers.
- **PMDU/Dept** will review performance and these actions at an official-level review in early January and at a PM stocktake on 15 January. We will approve further actions, including a risk analysis, at that stage.

SOURCE: From *Instruction to Deliver,* by M. Barber, 2008, London: Methuen Publishing Ltd.

You should be able to build a set of routines for your delivery effort by basing them on the example of the PMDU. The routines must be tailored to the needs of your system. To build each routine, ask the following questions:

- What area is being reviewed? A target? A specific intervention? A plan? What specific information within that area is being reviewed? Where appropriate, you can design different routines to review performance in areas up and down the delivery pyramid.
- Who will receive and react to this information, and who will be accountable?
- What other stakeholders will be involved?
- What form will the routine take (e.g., document, meeting)?
- What deliverables will emerge from the routine (e.g., a set of next steps)? Who will be responsible for them? How sensitive are these deliverables?
- How frequently will this routine occur?

The answers to these questions depend on availability of data (and the frequency of this availability); preference of audience (most likely the system leader); the number and type of targets, interventions, and/or performance units being managed (and the number of delivery plan owners involved); and an overall assessment of what is most effective to keep leaders engaged and the effort moving forward. You should craft a combination of routines that maximizes the use of available data and holds the right combination of people to account often enough to yield results. It will be helpful to refer back to the **delivery plan organization** that you created in Module 3C to ensure that the routines reflect the intended focus areas for your Delivery Unit. In practice, this means that your routines should be designed to hold every delivery plan owner accountable in a meaningful way.

The deliverables from routines (for example, monthly notes, delivery reports, or next steps from either of these things) may or may not need to be confidential. The PMDU chose to make its delivery reports, league tables, and even its trajectories confidential, in order to allow for an honest assessment and discussion of the facts at hand without political pressure (some items, such as targets, were, of course, public).

Exhibit 4A.13 summarizes the PMDU's answers to the questions above for its three core routines.

ANNUAL REVIEWS ARE NOT ENOUGH

Many systems already have annual reviews in place and may question the need for more frequent check-ins. However, the lag between decision making and results is immense, especially in education. In general, from the time a decision is made, it can take two years to have actual impact. Moreover, systems simply do not know what they do not know: Action will often be necessary in the first three to six months of a reform effort in order to avoid disaster by the time the first annual review occurs. Having monthly, quarterly, and semiannual reviews were a key benefit of the PMDU's routines. These more frequent routines give the system capacity to identify problems earlier and to act faster and more efficiently, enabling it to achieve more.

Exhibit 4A.13 Example: The PMDU's formal routines each answered the critical questions in different ways

	Monthly notes	Quarterly stocktakes	Semiannual delivery reports
What is being reviewed?	• Performance and leading indicator data about a single target	• Performance and leading indicator data for a subset of targets • Critical areas for action	• Performance and leading indicator data for all targets • Judgments against all areas of assessment framework for all targets • Critical areas for action
Who is receiving information? Who is accountable?	• Prime minister receives • Relevant delivery priority leader (DPL) and PMDU accountable	• Prime minister receives • Relevant DPLs and elected ministers held accountable	• Prime minister receives • All DPLs held accountable
What other stakeholders will be involved?	• Key officials	• PM policy advisor • Permanent secretary • Relevant ministers • Junior minister	• PM policy advisor • Relevant minister • Relevant department officials
What form will the routine take?	• Brief covering note with data sent to PM • PM returns written comments or decisions	• Meeting between PM, relevant ministers, and key officials • Presentation and discussion of information	• League table assessing likelihood of delivery • Detailed synthesis of progress, critical actions, and next steps
What deliverables will emerge?	• Guidance and/or decisions from PM on direction to take	• Jointly agreed next steps	• Follow-up meetings • Key elements of the work program for the next six months
How frequently will the routine occur?	• Monthly per priority (every week)	• Quarterly per priority (every 2–3 weeks)	• Twice each year

You must also establish processes for collecting the information used in routines. The methods of collection will themselves become unofficial delivery routines that will contribute to driving delivery.

Those responsible for the information will determine the nature of these "unofficial" routines, but they will likely include some of the following mechanisms.

- **Ongoing relationships.** If your Delivery Unit staff are assigned to support different areas of your system, how will they stay in the loop as the "eyes and ears" of the unit? (For more on Delivery Unit organization, see Module 1C.)

- **Frontline meetings.** What interactions with the frontline are needed to gather and prepare the information for official routines?
- **Challenge meetings.** Would a challenge meeting with the Delivery Unit, as described in Module 3C, be useful for probing the information that will be used in routines?
- **Frontline observation.** To what extent will you observe "delivery in action" in the field to assess progress?
- **Data collection and analysis.** How will those responsible for the necessary information (target metrics, leading indicators, indicators of unintended consequences, implementation indicators, and milestones) collect and analyze it regularly?
- **Data sharing.** How will that data be shared in advance of routines and with whom?
- **Formal and informal interviews.** Is qualitative feedback necessary to inform routines? Through what "unofficial" routines will it be received?

Although your Delivery Unit will have varying levels of control over these types of routines, certain principles should guide your conduct of all delivery routines over which you have control. In particular, your Unit should understand the factors that could potentially undermine the effectiveness of your routines:

- Frequency and rigor of check-ins are too relaxed
- Check-ins become focused on crises that just occurred rather than a continued focus on core priorities
- Key individuals are unable to attend meetings
- Too many people, or an ill-conceived mix of people, are involved in the routine, such that its difficult to have honest, productive conversation
- Preparation for meetings becomes excessively bureaucratic
- Meetings are canceled either because something else is considered to be more important, or because from a superficial perspective, little seems to have changed since the previous check-in
- Discussions focus only on barriers to success instead of how to overcome them
- The time of the highest ranking participant (e.g., system leader) is not used well because the necessary preparation for meetings is not done properly
- Meetings are boring, complicated, or confusing
- Meetings are poorly chaired, with unclear objectives and no summing up
- Meetings do not finish on time, or time is poorly managed such that an agenda is not completed

You should also understand the principles that will help you to maximize the effectiveness of your routines, given in Exhibit 4A.14.

The following case example shows how the Ontario Department of Education developed and maintained routines to drive delivery forward.

Exhibit 4A.14 Guiding principles for effective routines

Useful content	• Present *clear and compelling* information • Use *evidence*, avoid opinion without evidence • *Gain alignment* on relevant data in advance • Prepare materials meticulously to ensure key messages are readily apparent • Determine in advance the *three messages* participants must remember • *Confront problems head on* and determine solutions
Efficient process	• *Be economical with time*; ensure meetings have a focused purpose and end early when possible • Vary style to ensure that routines are never boring or confusing • *Ask questions and listen*; be conscious of appropriate share of "air time" • *Follow up* after routines to maintain clarity and ambition in actions set out • *Avoid micromanagement*, additional bureaucracy, or unneeded work
Clear communication	• Remind participants of *moral purpose* of delivery to keep meaning in routines • Speak *plainly, truthfully,* and *calmly* • *Simplify the message* but do not oversimplify and distort facts • *Push the credit out* to the frontline • *Recognize* the hard work in preparing for routine and *thank* relevant actors

CASE EXAMPLE

Routines and education reform in Ontario, Canada

In 2003, the Ministry of Education in Ontario was charged with ambitious reforms in K–12 education: improving performance of elementary school students, increasing high school graduation rates, and reducing class size. Getting started meant bringing together the leadership team and posing the tough questions.

> "The very first thing I did was bring all of my senior managers together, looked at the big list of promises we had made, and asked, 'How are we going to do all this?' We did basic risk analysis on each promise to determine if we had the capacity to do these things. As we did the analysis, we started to figure out where we were in okay shape and where we weren't even at the starting line and needed reinforcements. For areas where we were in poor shape, we tagged these with red lights. We immediately established a routine where we went through anything identified as having 'red lights' and gradually planned and executed to put those back on track.
>
> "We had to have in place the mechanism to drive results . . . to turn those red lights into green lights. So, I instituted a routine whereby every quarter, we had retreats to look at the map of things we had to do. We assessed what was going well, what wasn't, and what we needed to do to get things on track. Then, every week, I would convene my senior management team and we would discuss where we were on each of these items. I specifically held lead individuals accountable for their items, though all of the important work was

done by teams. Wherever we had issues, we put together project teams to work on the issues. The project team would be responsible for developing the plans to fix the issues and communicate this regularly to the senior manager that was accountable. I also ensured that we met with external stakeholders and kept them in the loop, especially if they were directly or indirectly involved with the achievement of a specific goal or resolution of a particular issue.

"We met with the premier usually every six to eight weeks. The primary purpose of our meetings with him was to provide updates on the key goals. Both the premier and our current minister were really good at giving front end direction, responding to issues when we needed to, and letting people move on with the work (i.e., not too in the details and micromanaging) . . . which helped us tremendously in meeting goals and timelines that we set for ourselves."

—Ben Levin, Deputy Minister of Education,
Ministry of Education, Ontario, Canada

Exhibits 4A.15, 4A.16, and 4A.17 show how a K–12 SEA customized its monthly notes, stocktakes, and delivery reports to a single goal: achieving a graduation rate of 85% by the 2015 to 2016 school year.

Exhibit 4A.15 Sample delivery note for K–12 SEA

Overall assessment:

Update on progress	**Next steps**
• To reach an 85% graduation rate at our current cohort size, we would need 39,400 total graduates. Currently, we graduate approximately 29,400 students. Therefore, 10,000 additional graduates are needed. • Baseline growth and existing programs may reduce that gap by 5,350. We have evidence to suggest that this goal is possible. • This leaves a remaining gap of 4,650 graduates (see "trajectory" on following page).	• First stocktake will be held on March 15. • The Delivery Unit is working with program staff to write delivery plans for program goals. These are expected by August 18 and will build toward a full delivery plan for reaching the 85% goal. • The strategy unit is developing a strategy for closing the gap of 4,650 additional students. Specific ideas for accessing those students are being discussed. • A completion date for the overall delivery plan will be decided within two weeks.
Issues facing delivery	**Supporting data**
• A strategy for reaching the remaining 4,650 additional graduates has yet to be developed. • Programs are currently writing—but have not completed—detailed delivery plans for reaching the 4,650 students in their goals. • The quality of data supporting the trajectory is weak for most programs.	This graph shows our trajectory toward the 85% graduation rate goal based on our current programs. • This is a preliminary projection that will evolve and change over time as we track progress, test assumptions, and make decisions. • This is our best estimate of what our current programs can accomplish based on good implementation and the data we have available today.

SOURCE: K–12 SEA (disguised).

Exhibit 4A.16 Summary "storyline" of a stocktake meeting for a K–12 SEA—example

Where are we now?	• We have set a target of an 85% high school graduation rate by 2016. • We are off to a good start, as program managers now routinely refer to this target in conversation.
Challenges and Delivery Unit response	• We need to raise our grade-level promotion rate to 96% (from the current 92%) to achieve this graduation rate. • An assessment of current programs and their projected impact shows that we are off track: In 2014 we will fall 4,650 graduates short of our target. • In response, the Delivery Unit is supporting the development of a department wide plan to close this gap.
Actions to achieve the goal	• Coordination: Set specific targets for each school, and establish an accountability structure to oversee these targets. • Execution: Improve alliances with businesses, and improve service operations of the department with respect to schools. • Data: Expand the dropout data system to the entire state. • Strategy: Focus programming on high priority schools—the ones with the largest number of nongraduates.
Next steps	• What did we agree upon? • Who is responsible for each action? • When will it be done?

SOURCE: K–12 SEA (disguised).

When a K–12 SEA tracks only one target, a Delivery Unit's focus may be at the level of the individual interventions. Exhibit 4A.18 shows how a K–12 SEA might produce a league table of the various interventions that are a part of its delivery effort.

Step 3: Create a master schedule of routines

Because your routines will require significant time and effort to design and fulfill, they should be coordinated via a master schedule. This will help ensure that time is spent in the most effective way possible. A master schedule fosters understanding about how routines fit together, ensures that routines do not overlap or conflict with each other, and helps maintain systemwide coherence.

To generate the master schedule, simply align the key activities, timing, and frequency of each routine your system will engage in. An example of what a routine master schedule might look like is given in Exhibit 4A.19.

At first glance, this schedule may give the impression that routines take up too much of a system leader's valuable time. However, this depends on

Exhibit 4A.17 First delivery report for a K–12 SEA (one target only)—example

Legend

Red	Highly problematic – requires urgent and decisive action
Yellow/Red	Problematic – requires substantial attention, some aspects need urgent action
Yellow/Green	Mixed – aspects require substantial attention, some good
Green	Good – requires refinement and systematic implementation

Degree of challenge: VH (very high), H (high), M (medium), L (low)

Stage of delivery: 1 Policy development, 2 Implementation, 3 Embedding change, 4 Irreversible progress

Date of Assessment: 2/15/2007 **Description:** Increase the high school four-year cohort graduation rate to 85% by 2016

Judgment	Rating	Rationale summary
Degree of challenge	High	• While the challenge is a step change for the system, it has been achieved in several other states; we know exactly where we are starting from • Tight fiscal resources and time resources (i.e., many important personnel accountable for other delivery goals)
Quality of planning, implementation, and performance management	Y/G	• The target is specific, measurable, achievable, realistic, and time bound; we will have an 85% cohort graduation rate by 2015–2016 • Most programs aimed at this target currently have weak evidence of efficacy • Program plans have been developed; resources are being assembled to develop a strategic plan to achieve the 85% graduation rate • Annual milestones and lead indicators to monitor performance have been set • Risks to delivery have been identified; mitigation plans not developed
Capacity to drive progress	Y/R	• Delivery chain is still ambiguous, and there is no single point of accountability • Funding unpredictability over the long term makes rigorous planning difficult • Ability to influence the chain in districts and schools varies greatly—especially in the absence of funding and/or accountability measures to promote cooperation • The target does have several champions outside the SEA • State data is somewhat centralized, but accessing it can still be a challenge • Critical people in the delivery chain are overloaded
Stage of delivery	Policy development	• The delivery chain and strategic plans are being formed now

Recent performance
Graduation rate is 62% and increasing at a rate of 0.8 percentage points/year

Likelihood of delivery
Y/R

SOURCE: K–12 SEA (disguised).

Exhibit 4A.18 Rankings of priorities for a K-12 SEA—example league table

Target: an 80% college and career-ready graduation rate by 2017

Areas of concern

Program	Degree of challenge	Assessment criteria: Planning, performance management	Assessment criteria: Capacity to drive progress	Assessment criteria: Stage of delivery	Overall judgment: Likelihood of delivery	Overall judgment: Rank	Overall judgment: Justification
Midcareer math recruitment	Medium			1		1	Successful as expected in early stages of recruitment
Early college/high school	Medium			1		2	Well-received and some decrease in dropouts; need to benchmark rigor of programs
90% summer school enrollment	Low			2		3	Results as expected; some improvements needed in enforcement/performance management
Eighth-grade planning	High			2		4	Extremely effective where implemented; some need for additional counselor capacity
Literacy remediation	High			1		5	Results as expected in early stages of implementation, especially in English II scores
Ninth-grade readiness	Med-Low			2		6	Significant gains in student achievement in all classes by ninth-grade measures
Saturday Academy	Med-Low			3		7	Enrollment used as enrichment; needs to be communicated to intended beneficiaries
Extended time	Med-High			1		8	Insufficient teacher capacity; impact is only 25% increase in math scores
Early warning indicators	High			3		9	Dropout rate has not changed at all; needs further attention

how the time is used. If, in each routine, you succeed in planning and structuring every minute of the system leader's time for maximum effect, your Delivery Unit will serve as a multiplier of the system leader's time, helping him to accomplish much more than would be possible if the time were used for other purposes. Moreover, the time spent in routines will be far less than the time that would be spent managing the crises that would occur without these regular reviews.

In order to stay on top of, and drive progress on, the PM's top 15 to 20 domestic priorities, the PMDU routines required no more than one to two hours of his time a week at most. Yet across government, they were enough to create the optical illusion of constant prime ministerial focus. In short, they hugely amplified his impact.

Exhibit 4A.19 Master schedule for delivery routines—sample

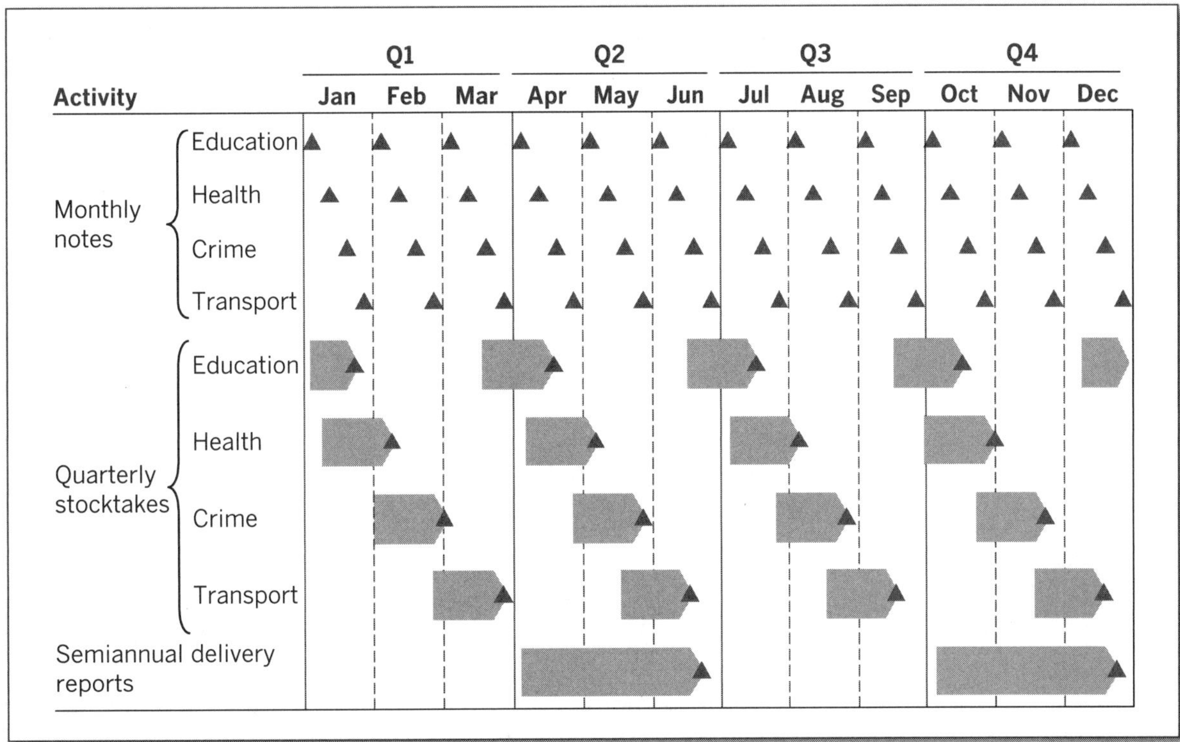

> "I saw one of my most important functions as securing sufficient time for stocktakes in the Prime Minister's [calendar]. I knew I was asking for a huge amount: four meetings of an hour in length every two months with, if possible, a pre-meeting in advance. This might not seem huge, but consider that in the first few months of the Delivery Unit's existence, Blair had meetings planned with seven European heads of state, two meetings of the European Council, a summit with the French, a visit from the Chinese Prime Minister and many other demands for his time for foreign policy issues . . . Blair's willingness to dedicate so much time to stocktakes—even when from within No. 10 there were countervailing pressures—is a measure of his commitment to delivery." (*Instruction to Deliver,* 92–93)

The routines pack a large amount of information that is rarely shared in any other type of meeting, information that is used as a basis for the direction of a system's delivery effort. The evidence of the PMDU suggests that, while much of the time government is dominated by crises and events, it is sustained, well-organized routines that deliver results.

Conclusion

By now, you have learned

- What routines are, and why they are important;
- The specific ways in which routines were put to use in the PMDU; and

- The questions you should ask and principles you should apply as you design your own routines.

By establishing routines, your system will drive delivery by ensuring focus and urgency, emphasizing performance, and identifying problems as they emerge. The next module will describe how to use routines for early problem identification and how to develop processes for addressing problems as they arise.

4B. SOLVE PROBLEMS EARLY AND RIGOROUSLY

"No problem can stand the assault of sustained thinking."

—Attributed to Voltaire

"Most people spend more time and energy going around problems than in trying to solve them."

—Henry Ford

All delivery efforts will inevitably encounter problems along the way. These problems test a system's ability to respond and become measures of the resilience of routines. The routines established in the previous module are crucial for identifying problems early, diagnosing them, and addressing them.

Your Unit's problem-solving approach has the added potential to affect your entire system positively. A systematic and efficient approach provides the opportunity not only to spread a culture of collaboration (rather than finger pointing) but also to promote the Delivery Unit as a thought partner rather than a bureaucratic body.

ROLES OF SYSTEM LEADER AND DELIVERY LEADER

Your Delivery Unit is responsible for identifying problems that may not be obvious or manageable at the frontline, for driving problem-solving routines in partnership with delivery plan owners, and for monitoring problem areas or adjusting plans and routines as necessary. By identifying and solving problems with rigor, you will ensure that your system maintains its focus on delivery no matter how significant those problems may be. System leaders participate in or react to this problem solving as appropriate; critically, they must sometimes make crucial decisions or put pressure on certain people in order to facilitate the implementation of solutions that you recommend.

PROCESS STEPS

Step 1: Identify problems early

Step 2: Classify, solve, and monitor problems according to their severity

Step 1: Identify problems early

To misquote an oft-used phrase, an ounce of prevention now is worth a pound of intervention in the future. The sooner you identify problems that must be addressed, the better. The first way to do this is to actively monitor routine information. The routines you established in Module 4A should produce a constant flow of information about your system's performance against its trajectory that will help you to identify emerging issues.

There are several types of patterns that you can look for in order to spot these problems:

- The performance units appear to have hit plateaus in performance
- The performance units show significantly less progress compared to previous evaluations
- The performance units show less progress compared to similar individuals or sets of units
- All (or a subset) of performance units exhibit wide, unexpected variations in performance
- Different data sources are not aligned, or external data sources conflict with the data your performance unit regularly monitors
- The indicators of unintended consequences that you are monitoring show signs of moving in the wrong direction

Another area to examine will be the qualitative information that your Delivery Unit observes and receives as part of the preparation for routines, along with the rapid feedback loops your Unit has established with the frontline. Even if your Delivery Unit's monitoring focus is at the target level, your individual staff will need to develop a perspective on the "likelihood of delivery" of the interventions (and underlying system activities) that have been put in place to deliver those targets. You and your staff should keep three tools in mind when reviewing qualitative information:

- The questions from the activity profile to help assess the quality and impact of system activities (see Module 2B)
- Delivery chain analysis (see Module 2B)
- The assessment framework, which can be adjusted to apply to system activities (see Module 4A)

In their day-to-day work, your Delivery Unit staff should use some combination of the following informal routines to gather the necessary information:

- Preparation meetings connected to the formal routines (e.g., the regular meetings that take place to prepare for a stocktake)
- Regular frontline observation
- Data collection and analysis routines
- Data sharing meetings
- Formal and informal interviews to assess the quality of progress

During the course of this regular information gathering, look for any of the following patterns as evidence that may indicate a larger problem:

- There is little confidence that system activities and/or interventions will have the planned impact

- Specific system activities are having little impact—or even a negative impact—on relevant performance data
- Specific activities are perceived as being improperly implemented
- Individuals along the delivery chains for system activities cite or exhibit a loss of alignment, focus, and/or momentum
- There is an increase in resistance above what normally occurs

Some problems may become apparent if you stay close to the **system actors** along the delivery chain who are critical to your delivery effort. While there will always be resistance to all or some aspects of delivery, the following patterns, if observed, may indicate a significant problem worth addressing:

- Confusion or misunderstanding of the delivery effort
- Influential individuals or groups with substantial opposition to the delivery effort and its agenda
- Widespread discontent with changes that have been or will be made
- Widespread discontent over things that have not or will not be changed
- Frequent unfavorable media coverage (or more frequent than usual!)

Your Unit should actively monitor the various channels through which these patterns can surface (e.g., relevant media coverage, open forums, community meetings). At the same time, you should not underestimate the role that informal feedback can play in identifying external problems. All participants within your delivery effort should utilize opportunities to discuss delivery with relevant individuals outside of your delivery effort as a means of identifying emerging threats to delivery that may not be immediately apparent to you. An example is how Margaret Thatcher was briefed for her meetings with Kenneth Baker on education policy in the late 1980s.

CASE EXAMPLE

Information from unusual places

When Margaret Thatcher was prime minister of the U.K., she did not depend only on her ministers to understand what was happening in the country she governed. An example from her interactions with Kenneth Baker, her secretary of state for education, is illustrative:

> "She had a note from his department, a note from her own Policy Unit in No. 10 and then sometimes . . . she would pull a note from her handbag with a flourish, make a telling point and say, "What do you think about that, Kenneth?" It turned out that some of this briefing came from her hairdresser in Lambeth, who had children in the local primary school and was appalled by what went on there. The key point is that Margaret Thatcher had independent sources of information, in contrast to so many Ministers who accept the reassuring accounts of their unruffled civil servants at face value." (*Instruction to Deliver*, 129)

The case example below describes how the Ministry of Education in Ontario identified problems as they emerged.

CASE EXAMPLE

Early problem identification in Ontario, Canada

In 2003, the Ministry of Education in Ontario was charged with ambitious reforms in K–12 education: improving performance of elementary school students, increasing high school graduation rates, and reducing class size. Those with responsibility for delivering these reforms placed a high priority on identifying problems early.

> "It was easy to flag problems because we had the leadership teams constantly tracking progress of the activities related to plans and goals. If there were any rising problem areas, they would get flagged and brought to senior management attention when the responsible team or manager felt something wasn't going to work. We would push them on this and try to understand the problems. Since we normally already had teams working on the plans and knew where problem areas were, we would attempt to be proactive and resolve any problems before they were brought to the senior management meetings. However, when the problem got to our level, we did our best to provide the support they needed to resolve the problem."
>
> —Ben Levin, Deputy Minister of Education, Ministry of Education, Ontario, Canada

Of course, problem identification is only the first part of the process. You must also decide what to do once problems are identified, which brings us to Step 2.

Step 2: Classify, solve, and monitor problems according to their severity

Given all of the different types of problems that may emerge, it can help to classify and understand each problem's severity in order to determine what is required to solve it.

CASE EXAMPLE

A triage system for government

In hospitals, triage processes exist for the explicit purpose of classifying the severity of cases and handling them with the appropriate resources. In the PMDU, the "levels of intensity" classification attempted to do something similar, categorizing problem areas by severity and calling for increasingly intense attention as problems got worse.

> "From the outset, it had been my intention to ensure that the Delivery Unit provided the Prime Minister with a means of responding systematically when there was a delivery failure, rather than relying on the ad hoc process of Blair's first term which I thought of—perhaps unkindly—as 'government by spasm' . . . I thought that if I could develop a system which not only categorized challenges, but also anticipated and managed them before they exploded, this would be a significant contribution to improving government. Out of these reflections . . . [we] developed the concept of 'levels of intensity.'" (*Instruction to Deliver,* 160)

The levels of intensity developed by the PMDU are described in Exhibit 4B.1.

(Continued)

Exhibit 4B.1 Four levels of intensity can be used to classify delivery problems

Classification	Approach	Characteristics of Problem	Potential Delivery Unit Actions
Level 1	"Timely nudge" from Delivery Unit	• Problem is causing delivery to be **somewhat** off track, and • Cause and solution are relatively clear	• Personally contact individual accountable for relevant aspect of delivery (e.g., phone call, e-mail) • Offer support, but ask individual to fix the problem • Follow up to ensure problem has been resolved • Continue routines as usual
Level 2	Standard problem solving	• Problem is **significantly** affecting delivery, or • Cause and solution are not obvious	• Designate Delivery Unit staff responsible for "co-owning" problem with relevant delivery plan owner • Conduct collaborative problem solving, potentially with challenge meetings, issue trees, and delivery chain analyses • Adapt normal routines to incorporate more frequent and/or deeper monitoring of problem area as needed
Level 3	Intensive problem-solving drive	• Problem is **severely** affecting delivery, or • Cause and solution are not clear, even after standard problem solving, or • Cause and solution have significant complexity	• Designate special problem-solving team (with Delivery Unit and frontline staff) • Loop in and receive input from delivery leader • Conduct "priority review" or similar method for deep problem solving • Adapt official routines to permanently incorporate monitoring of problem area; develop temporary new routines for reporting progress on problem (e.g., weekly)
Level 4	Crisis management	• Problem is **completely** impairing delivery, or • Cause and solution have extreme complexity, and • Problem is among the top one or two problems of the system	• Involve delivery leader full time in problem solving • Request active and frequent participation of system leader • Utilize your system's crisis management techniques (e.g., specialized teams with experts from outside system; rapid, deep reviews; PR blitz; etc.) • Develop new routines for monitoring problem (e.g., daily monitoring); incorporate problem insights into routines • Adapt delivery activities as needed to ensure prevention

(Continued)

How did the PMDU use these levels of intensity in practice? For each of the four departments with responsibility for delivery priorities, the PMDU would work with them to regularly review current delivery strategy and outcomes and identify the biggest risks to delivery. This could lead to the development of a joint action program between the PMDU and department and/or one of a number of more or less intense problem-solving tools. This process, summarized in Exhibit 4B.2 (along with some of the tools), describes the normal state of play for departments and priority areas in the first three levels of intensity.

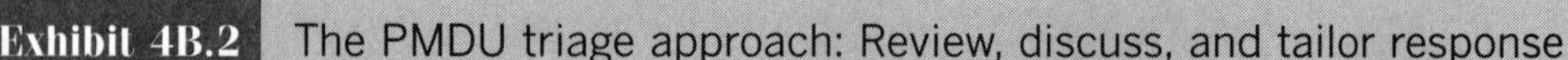

Exhibit 4B.2 The PMDU triage approach: Review, discuss, and tailor response

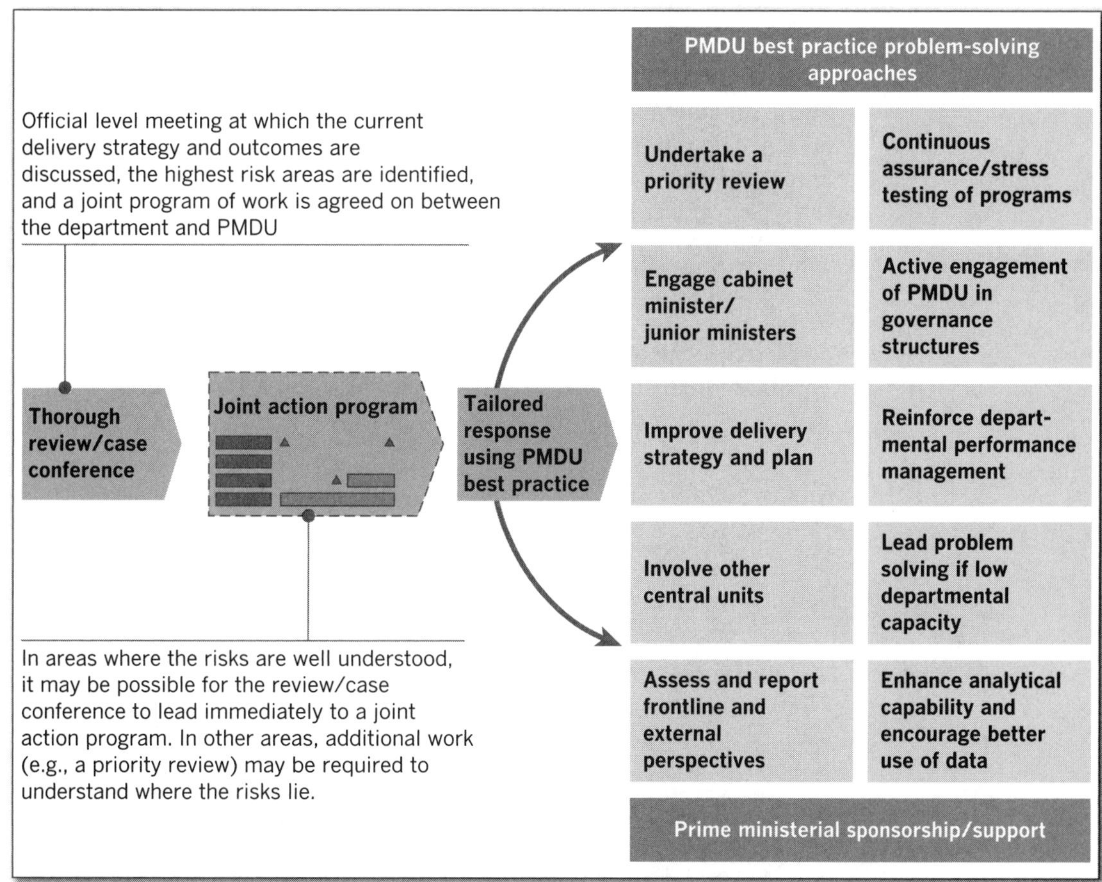

Sometimes, a problem was so dire and so urgent that it required an escalation to Level 4: crisis management. In the PMDU, this approach was first conceived by Tony Blair and David Blunkett to deal with street crime, a responsibility of the Home Office:

> "Out of the blue, Blair hit upon what he wanted: 'Why is it that when we have a real crisis . . . we get the job done? Perhaps we should call together COBRA [the Cabinet Office emergency committee] and deal with robbery through that mechanism.' With quiet enthusiasm, Blunkett said, 'I'd be up for that.' . . . We began to make plans for the first meeting of COBRA the following week. All Cabinet ministers or top officials with the slightest connection to street crime, along with top police people, were to be invited . . . Blair agreed to have the first meeting in the COBRA meeting room itself, in the bowels of the Cabinet Office. We felt this would symbolize clearly the crisis management approach Blair and Blunkett wanted to see . . . Home Office officials had not grasped how much their world had changed. Blair and Blunkett were talking about very regular meetings of COBRA . . . while the officials were talking about fortnightly meetings at most." (*Instruction to Deliver,* 148–150)

The PMDU approach provides a foundation for developing your own triage system. How can you customize the levels of intensity to your system? Some basic principles apply.

Use two criteria to establish levels of intensity: (1) the extent to which a problem is negatively affecting delivery, and (2) the extent to which the solution is clear. A problem that is having a moderate impact on delivery but has no clear solution could be as severe as a problem that is substantially affecting delivery but has an obvious solution. However clear the solution may be, the higher the impact of the problem on delivery, the more urgently the system should respond to it. Exhibit 4B.3 illustrates this idea. The principles for customizing levels of intensity to your system are given in the following bulleted list, including

- **Define your triage system clearly.** The system must be defined such that all participants in your delivery effort can understand it. This means communicating the above criteria and establishing clear and objective "rules" for
    - Classification in a level of intensity according to these criteria; and
    - Deciding which problem-solving approaches and corrective actions should be available and used at each level of intensity.
- **Get the information you need to properly classify problems.** If a problem is difficult to classify, approach it at a lower level of intensity and use problem-solving tools to learn more about it. You can then escalate to the proper level of intensity as appropriate.

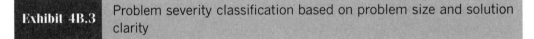

Exhibit 4B.3 Problem severity classification based on problem size and solution clarity

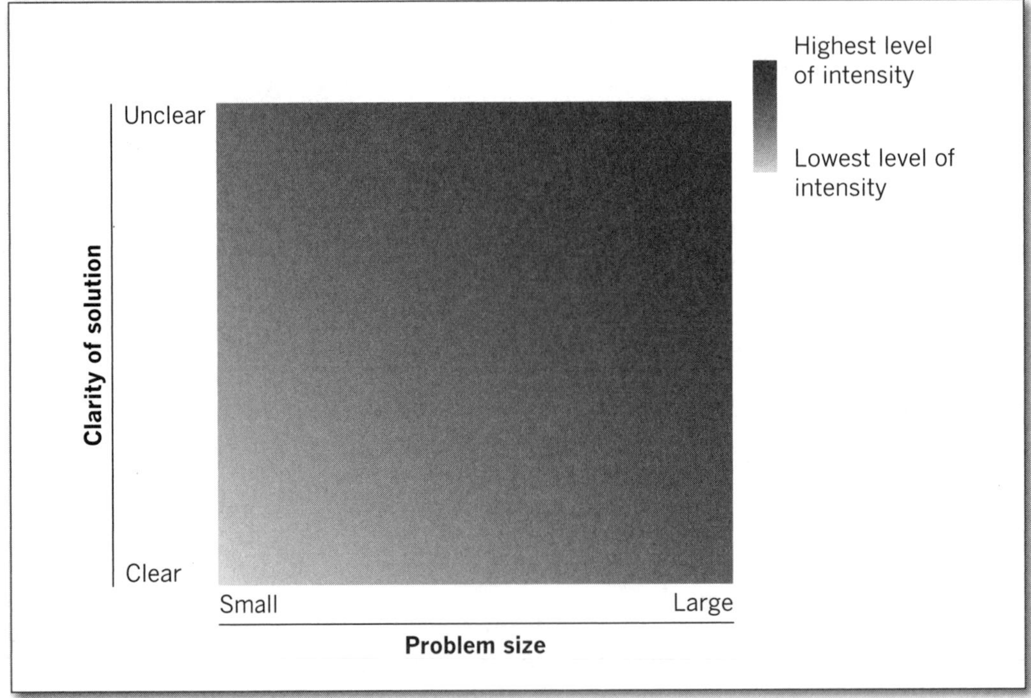

- **Beware of giving a problem the benefit of the doubt.** Do not be lax in your judgment of the intensity level of a problem or dismiss more complex issues lightly without an accurate assessment. If you are considering giving a department or official the benefit of the doubt, first ask yourself, why do you have a doubt in the first place?
- Position the Delivery Unit as a **problem-solving partner** to relevant delivery owners and frontline staff—never as a burdensome bureaucrat.

Even at lower levels like one and two, basic problem solving can decisively affect an outcome.

Problem-solving tools: A closer look

Several of the problem-solving tools you will employ, especially at lower levels of intensity, are common sense, intuitive measures (e.g., "personally contact individual accountable for relevant aspect of delivery"). For more complex problems, three tools in particular will be helpful for your Unit's problem solving.

- **A hypothesis tree.** Used to break a problem into all its possible components in order to identify the most likely cause, a hypothesis tree is a helpful tool for identifying solutions to problems that may seem puzzling at first. In order to develop a hypothesis tree, begin with the available facts, ask "why?" in a targeted fashion, and eliminate unlikely answers. For a more detailed description of this tool, see Module 2A.
- **Delivery chain analysis.** Use delivery chain analysis to analyze potential weaknesses in the relevant system activity or activities that may be contributing to the problem. In particular, the various system actors and relationships in your delivery chain provide a comprehensive framework that can help you identify potential areas where delivery may be going wrong. For a more detailed description of this tool, see Module 2B.
- **The priority review.** This is a tool for rapid problem diagnosis that was developed by the PMDU to understand priority areas (hence the name) in depth. Priority reviews utilize collaborative working teams, data analysis, and frontline observation through field work to help the PMDU quickly understand the nature of a problem and develop recommendations to solve it. For a more detailed description of the priority review methodology, see the following case example.

CASE EXAMPLE

A guide to priority reviews in the PMDU—and their application for you

What are priority reviews?

The PMDU established the priority review process as a way to develop its own capacity to rapidly review how effective implementation was, priority by priority. Most review processes in government were too slow (at least 6 months and often longer) to aid problem solving on the urgent timeline that was required. The PMDU wanted an approach that was much faster, and, since they did not plan to produce reports for publication, they did not need to dot every I and cross every T.

> "I decided we would design a process which took a month, made proposals which were 90 percent right, and then drove action." (*Instruction to Deliver,* 151)

(Continued)

(Continued)

What are priority reviews used for?

As the name suggests, the PMDU applies the priority review process to each priority (equivalent to a target, like graduation rates)—but the methodology can be used to evaluate any area of delivery, including system activities and interventions (e.g., a course redesign program to improve graduation rates). The outcome of a priority review is generally a short report to the system leader and relevant delivery plan owners with a summary of findings, agreed areas of action, and decisions to be made.

How does the PMDU decide when to do a priority review?

Because they are resource intensive and time intensive (up to 6 weeks and several staff are involved), priority reviews are reserved for areas where problems are particularly challenging (e.g., Level 3 or above) or "one-off" comprehensive assessments (in which the PMDU applies the process to every area systematically). They can also be used to provide reassurance that a priority area is on track as a target date approaches. Priority reviews do require some dedicated time from Delivery Unit staff, which means that they will be more difficult to do regularly for smaller Units. In such cases, you may consider adapting the process to suit your situation (e.g., less frequent or less intensive) or contracting with outside resources for additional support.

How does the PMDU conduct a priority review?

The PMDU conducts the priority review in conjunction with the relevant delivery plan owner of the problematic area of delivery. This team conducts the rapid diagnosis, examines and synthesizes findings, and reports them to the system leader for action.

> "For any given target, a joint review team of five or six people from the relevant department and the PMDU would be established. They would rapidly pull together all the data they could assemble on the issue and generate some hypotheses and answer the key questions—were we on track to deliver the target? If so, what were the risks? If not, what could be done to fix the problem? Armed with the background analysis and their hypotheses, the team would then go and see for themselves the reality on the ground. Often they would visit a place where progress was good and ask why, and a place where it was poor and ask the same question. They would ask everyone they met the same questions: is the target understood? What are the successes? What are the barriers? And what action is needed to strengthen delivery? Finally they would invite interviewees to identify their top three messages for the Prime Minister—an invitation few could resist. This way the team could test and refine their hypotheses. In effect, they checked every link in the Delivery Chain to see how it could be strengthened . . . Once the field work was done, a short, crisp report with some practical recommendations for action would go to the relevant Cabinet Minister and Permanent Secretary, and to the Prime Minister." (*Instruction to Deliver,* 151)

The main components of a priority review and a sample process for undertaking a priority review are given in the exhibits 4B.4 and 4B.5.

What makes priority reviews effective?

Though every system's priority review process may be slightly different, a few factors will ensure that your priority reviews are effective:

- A partnership between the review leaders and the sponsor organization
- A strong team approach with the right level of expertise and skill mix
- An external challenge to stress test strategies

Exhibit 4B.4 Conducting a priority review

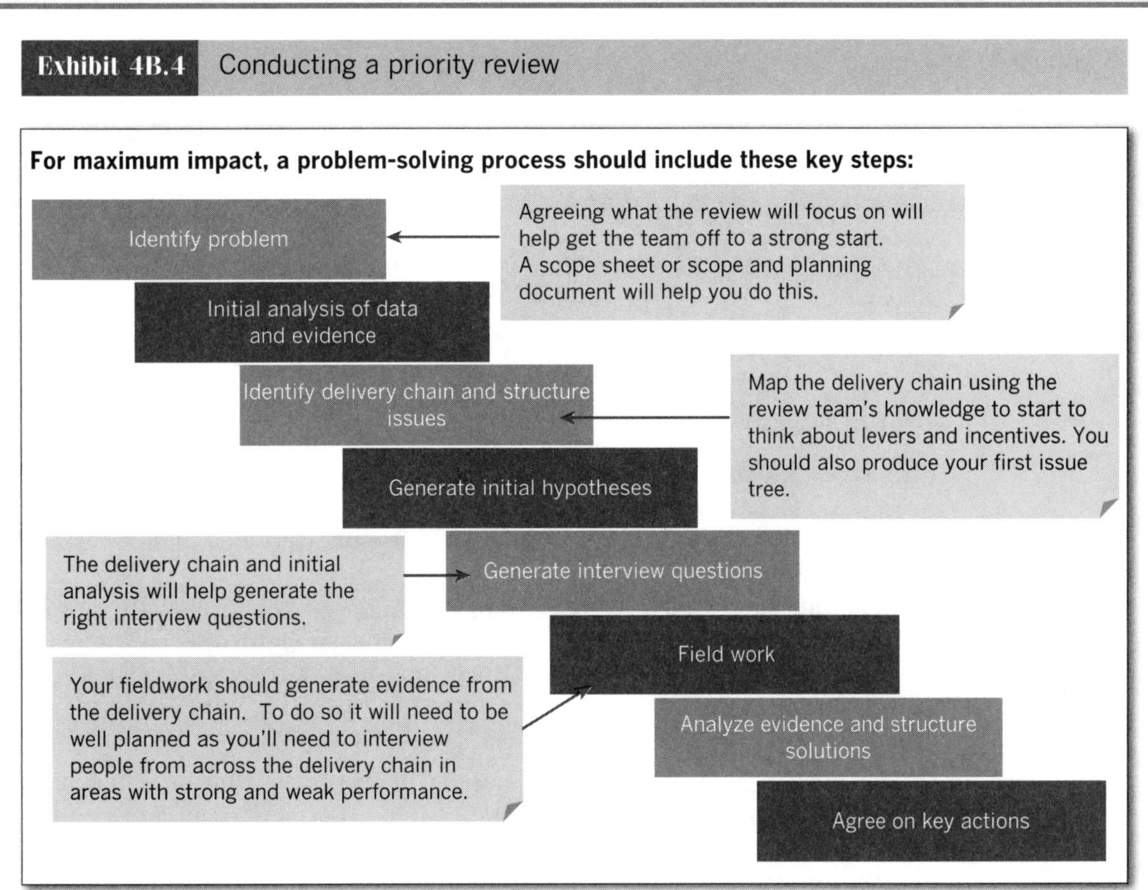
For maximum impact, a problem-solving process should include these key steps:
Identify problem
Agreeing what the review will focus on will help get the team off to a strong start. A scope sheet or scope and planning document will help you do this.
Initial analysis of data and evidence
Identify delivery chain and structure issues
Map the delivery chain using the review team's knowledge to start to think about levers and incentives. You should also produce your first issue tree.
Generate initial hypotheses
The delivery chain and initial analysis will help generate the right interview questions.
Generate interview questions
Field work
Your fieldwork should generate evidence from the delivery chain. To do so it will need to be well planned as you'll need to interview people from across the delivery chain in areas with strong and weak performance.
Analyze evidence and structure solutions
Agree on key actions

Exhibit 4B.5 Stages of a priority review

	Stage 1	Stage 2	Stage 3	Stage 4	Stage 5
	Set up	**Diagnose and plan**	**Field visits and interviews**	**Finalize recommendations and report**	**Implementation**
Possible timing	**Week 1**	**Weeks 2 and 3**	**Weeks 4 and 5**	**Weeks 6 to 8**	**Week 9 onwards**
Activities	• Preliminary meeting on scope and objectives • Review existing evaluations • Identify delivery chain and key issues • Approve detailed review objectives and timeline • Approve outline briefing pack with analysts	• Team workshop to review existing evidence • Refine key issues and develop initial hypotheses • Agree visits and interview lists • Prepare interview guides • Confirm arrangements for visits and interviews	• Complete fieldwork and interviews • Carry out additional analysis • Team meetings to test hypotheses and build initial storyline	• Team workshop to confirm findings and report structure • Close data gaps and draft report • Test and syndicate findings, recommendations and report • Present report and send to senior customers	• Recommendations implemented by department • Possible follow-up session with the review leaders to test implementation three to six months after report
Outputs	• Team in place • Objectives and scope • Briefing pack and project plan	• Initial hypotheses • Fieldwork program • Interview guides	• Interview notes • Outline findings and storyline	• Draft reports • Final report	• Action plan • Possible short follow-up report

SOURCE: ISOS partnership.

(Continued)

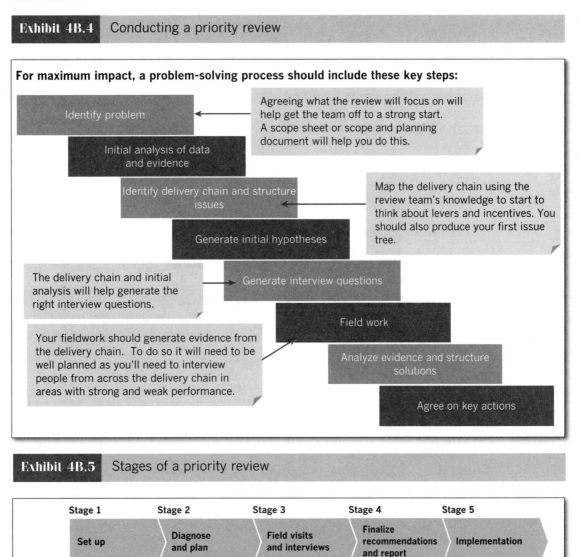

(Continued)

- A nonbureaucratic approach that is of minimum distraction from delivery
- A sharp, clear focus on the key delivery issues
- Urgency, real or generated
- Intensive fieldwork along the delivery chain, right out to the frontline
- A firm grounding in the evidence
- An end product that is a prioritized action plan for strengthening delivery
- Planned follow-up

Conclusion

By now, you have learned

- How routines and other information-gathering mechanisms will help you to identify problems early;
- The importance of developing a triage system to classify and solve these problems and some principles for designing such a system; and
- Some practical problem-solving approaches that your Delivery Unit should have in its tool kit.

No matter how grave or intractable the problems you face, it is important for your Unit to stay focused on its routines even as you devote resources to solving these problems. Your Unit's ability to stay focused on delivery will determine whether it can truly act as a Delivery Unit—or whether it will degenerate into a firefighting team. In the next module, we will discuss some more advanced techniques for maintaining this focus, so that you can sustain and build the kind of delivery momentum that will allow you to achieve visible, lasting impact.

■ 4C. SUSTAIN AND CONTINUALLY BUILD MOMENTUM

"The wire is high and the roar of the crowd may sound less friendly than before. But this is no time to wobble."

—Editorial about the PMDU's efforts after 2 years, *The Guardian,* July 31, 2003

Routines are the crucial and central tool that your Delivery Unit will use to drive success in your delivery effort. Done right, these routines will begin to show results quickly, as the increased attention they draw to certain system activities will spur a strong drive for results (also known as the "Hawthorne Effect"). However, it is crucial that you not declare victory prematurely. Even as the first positive results come in, the hard and grinding work of maintaining your trajectory is just beginning. It will be your Delivery Unit's job to see these early wins for what they are: fuel for momentum that can either be seized to take your system to the next level—or squandered in self-congratulation. This module provides a guide to some of the principles and tactics that your Unit can use to establish this early momentum, sustain it, and build it further.

ROLES OF SYSTEM LEADER AND DELIVERY LEADER

Your Delivery Unit's role is to be the source of persistence and constant improvement, identifying opportunities throughout the system to build on early successes to face the greater challenges down the road. In the face of new challenges, your Unit will have to force a consistent focus on targets and routines, manage the challenge of naysayers and cynics, constantly push to improve delivery, and celebrate success when appropriate. The system leader's role here is to back the Delivery Unit's work, using the power of her "bully pulpit" to reinforce the drive for continuous improvement.

RULES TO ESTABLISH, SUSTAIN, AND BUILD MOMENTUM

Rule 1: Persist through distractions
Rule 2: Persist through monotony
Rule 3: Manage those who resist change
Rule 4: Vigorously challenge the status quo
Rule 5: Celebrate successes

Rule 1: Persist through distractions

As important as delivery is, the delivery effort is only one of many things that a system leader must deal with. System leadership will inevitably be distracted by crises and external events. In times like these, it is especially crucial that your Delivery Unit be the one entity that is not blown off course. The case of the PMDU during the Iraq War describes how it persisted in the face of extraordinary distractions.

DELIVERY NEVER SLEEPS

"For me, the impact of the [Iraq] crisis was immediate. I had to maintain the drive for delivery while the Prime Minister's attention was elsewhere for an extended period. For my staff, this inevitably caused anxiety, but in the monthly staff meetings I stressed to them that this was precisely why we existed—to ensure delivery never sleeps. Even in the most difficult of circumstances, it was our job to sustain progress; it was a challenge to rise to, not a barrier to run into. I also took repeated opportunities in these monthly meetings to explain that our mission was not the Prime Minister's political future—that lay in the hands of others—rather it was to secure real improvements in the quality of services to citizens and to ensure that the vast sums of money being invested in the public services yielded a return to the taxpayer. To senior civil servants in Whitehall who saw in the Prime Minister's distraction a weakening of the drive for delivery, we issued a challenge: the Prime Minister has developed the view, we said, that when he stops paying attention, the drive for reform and delivery slows down; this is your chance to prove him wrong." (*Instruction to Deliver,* 176)

How can you apply the lessons from the PMDU to your delivery effort? The tactics will look different in each case, but some common principles apply.

- Avoid distractions from unexpected events or crises, and do not be driven by the headlines.
- In the face of external distractions, demonstrate continued commitment by maintaining your routines.
- When there is an internal delivery failure, resist the temptation to suspend or delay routines; instead, use your routines and the data they generate to solve problems systematically.
- Do not get caught up in temporary, public, or dissident pressure to focus on other issues, however pressing they may seem.
- When the system leader is preoccupied with external events or crises, it is your Unit's responsibility to drive delivery forward in her absence, limiting your demands on her time to the top-priority issues.

Rule 2: Persist through monotony

While distractions may threaten to derail delivery, so too may the sheer monotony of driving a delivery effort months—or even years—after an exciting beginning. As described above, one British political commentator wrote of the PMDU's efforts that "there is no drama in delivery . . . only a long, grinding haul punctuated by public frustration with the pace of change." In order to make it through these periods of monotony, it is critical for your Unit to maintain motivation and to focus always on the end game: the tangible results to be achieved.

Some principles for persistence through monotony:

- In everyday interactions, keep asking about progress on the delivery outcomes.
- Emphasize the importance of results for success, and see top priorities through until tangible, sustainable results are achieved.
- Communicate that recognition will come only from results, and use that as a motivation for driving delivery forward.
- Ensure focus on and implementation of the original priorities, no matter how strong the temptation or pressure to add to the list.
- Strategy is vital, but the details matter too; enjoy the minutiae, and know that they are what make the difference.
- Invest deeply in people—if they believe in you and enjoy working with you, they will be able to better persist through monotony.

RIDING THE TRANS-SIBERIAN RAILWAY

"I loved this journey—perhaps I am that kind of person—not because of the places on the way, but because of the steady roll of the train wheels along the track, because of the rhythm the train rattled out mile after mile after mile, across a thousand miles of frozen waste, because when the train arrived in Zima and every other place along the way, it was exactly on time (I checked), and because all the time, with a steady monotony, the landscape slipped away and slipped away. In short, there was a constant sense of steady progress." (*Instruction to Deliver*, 110)

CASE EXAMPLE

Maintaining Focus in the California State University (CSU) System

In 1998, Charles Reed, chancellor of the CSU system, identified minority recruitment as one of the key issues facing the CSU system and state of California. To address these challenges, Chancellor Reed established two primary goals:

- Increase preparation of high school students and parents for college admission and attendance; and
- Increase promotion of college attendance to underrepresented populations.

Through a laser-like focus on a prioritized set of goals, the CSU system was able to build and sustain momentum.

> "I think that one secret of the chancellor's success is his clear focus on a finite number of goals. He keeps a laser-like focus on these goals in working with the campus presidents, and will have the same topics on Executive Council agendas almost every meeting."
>
> —Gary Reichard, Executive Vice Chancellor, CSU System

Rule 3: Manage those who resist change

Another key aspect of sustaining momentum will be managing those who resist change, both system actors and external stakeholders—because their unwillingness to support your delivery effort could easily stall progress.

Every delivery effort will have its naysayers and skeptics—people who benefit from the status quo and/or are unwilling to make the necessary effort to bring about dramatic change. They may argue that the targets cannot be met, or they may offer empty rationalizations for why aspirations are unrealistic. Do not accept these excuses; instead, listen to them, take them off the table where you can, and reject them where necessary.

Some common excuses, and potential responses to them, are given in Exhibit 4C.1.

The following principles will help you to manage resistance to change:

- Do not fall for shallow arguments or rush to compromise at the first sign of resistance.
- Realize that resistance is often rooted in fear of personal accountability and change, and address those fears.
- Skepticism often collapses in the face of fact—use evidence from best-practice examples and from the delivery effort itself to disprove naysayers.
- Emphasize the risks of inaction with those who fear action is risky.
- Communicate the moral case for what you are doing.
- Tailor your overall communications to individuals' varying levels of resistance (for more on this, see Module 5B).

The following case example describes how resistance from teachers was managed during San Jose's extensive education reform by addressing teachers' fears of accountability.

Exhibit 4C.1 Battling excuses

Seven Common Excuses	Your Delivery Unit's Response
1. We're already doing these things.	1. The "how" is just as important as the "what"; we need not only to do these things, but to do them better.
2. The changes you're asking for will have unintended consequences.	2. We will have mechanisms for ensuring potential consequences aren't realized (e.g., monitoring indicators of unintended consequences).
3. The changes you're asking for are risky.	3. The risks of inaction are greater.
4. The changes are impossible to make.	4. The changes were chosen from fact-based analysis, and the Delivery Unit will help you make them—no matter how daunting they seem.
5. The target is wrong.	5. The target was chosen from evidence-based analysis and makes sense when viewed as part of the trajectory.
6. Delivery is just the flavor of the month.	6. Delivery is a long haul, and we will not stop until the targets are reached.
7. Delivery is just another layer of bureaucracy.	7. The Delivery Unit is here to make less work, not more; we will not ask you to do anything that you would not otherwise do in the pursuit of the targets we have set.

CASE EXAMPLE

Managing Resistance in San Jose

In the mid-1990s, San Jose Unified School District Superintendent Linda Murray set a bold goal that every student would graduate from high school college ready. She achieved not only higher standards but also higher achievement, with increases in graduation rates and in the percentage of students leaving high school college ready (for a chart of results, refer to the case example on San Jose in Module 1D).

Murray anchored the reform process in research with parents, students, teachers, and leaders from the community over a period of 18 months. Through focus groups, surveys, and town hall meetings, she learned that parents and students were very supportive of a challenging curriculum, while teachers were more skeptical. Listening to teachers helped Murray understand the root causes of skepticism. For example, part of their resistance stemmed from a fear that they would be held accountable for higher student achievement without being given necessary support. Teachers believed they needed high-quality professional development and support systems for students in order to be effective. This eventually led to a reform strategy that focused on rigorous graduation requirements, coupled with support for students and teachers. Says Murray, "Later, I asked [teachers], do you feel like you can go back to the way things were? And they said 'Absolutely not.' They believe kids can succeed, which is a real cultural shift."

Rule 4: Vigorously challenge the status quo

Building on successes will also be critical to your delivery effort's momentum. Even when your delivery effort is on track, your Unit should challenge the status quo by focusing and reprioritizing, demanding a shift from good to great, and emphasizing the need for urgency.

CASE EXAMPLE

Pushing the envelope

The PMDU began its work at the start of a five-year Parliament (equivalent to a presidential election cycle in the U.S.). In the third year of the PMDU's operation, service delivery outcomes had improved and disciplines of delivery were being established in government, but the PMDU realized that in order to ensure outcomes in years four and five, this third year would be a crucial year for delivery. This was because there would be less freedom of action in those later years: Year four would be spent winding down, and year five would be spent preparing for the next election. Therefore, the third year would be the government's last chance to make changes to set the course for the remainder of the Parliament. In a presentation to the cabinet that year, the PMDU leader made precisely this point in order to reinstill a sense of urgency. Exhibit 4C.2 is an excerpt from that presentation.

In order to capture the opportunity presented by this third year, the PMDU bucked the natural trend of bureaucratic organizations to expand their remits and instead narrowed its focus to the government's top priorities.

> "The case for refocusing firmly on the government's top priorities was strong. It was reinforced by the strong sense that progress would need to be accelerated if key targets were to be achieved. We agreed . . . to drop all the targets outside our core areas and refocused sharply on Blair's top priorities. In a note to him in early September, I argued for 'more ruthless prioritization, deeper collaboration (with departments) and more vigorous challenge' . . . Instead of steadily expanding our focus, we narrowed it. Instead of increasing our numbers, we limited them. Instead of seeking permanence, we set out to achieve the agenda we had been set in 2001 and let the future take care of itself." (*Instruction to Deliver,* 199–200)

Exhibit 4C.2 The Delivery Unit has already set the delivery agenda in year one and established delivery disciplines across Whitehall in year two. In year three, we will accelerate and intensify the drive for results

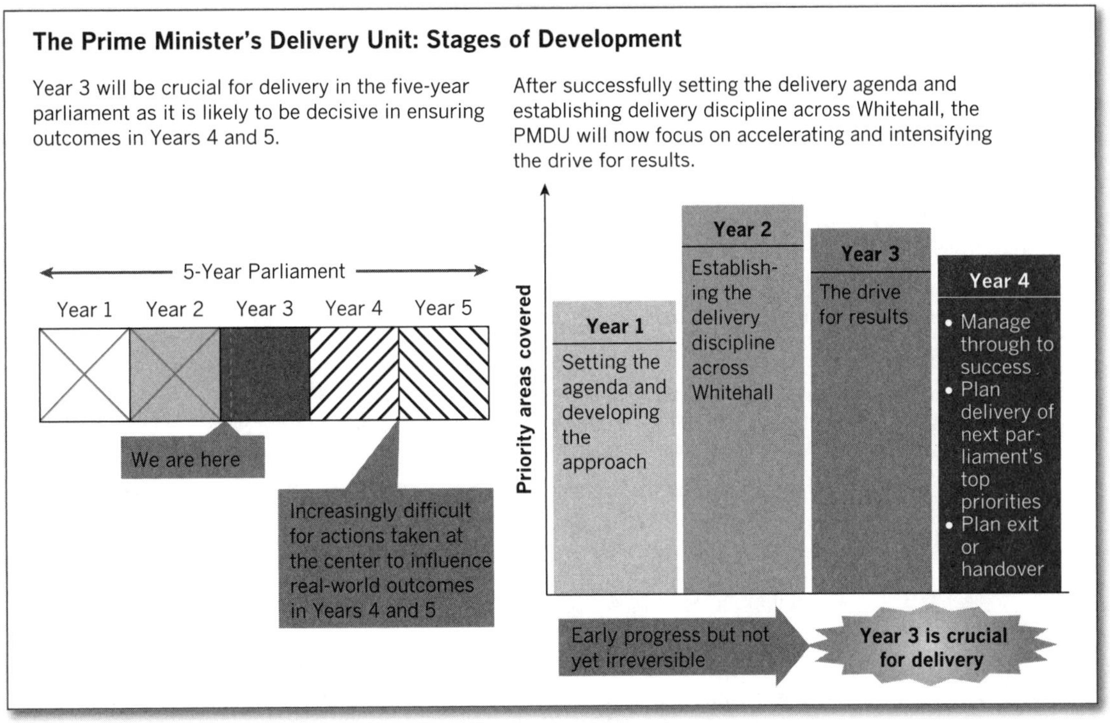

The Prime Minister's Delivery Unit: Stages of Development

Year 3 will be crucial for delivery in the five-year parliament as it is likely to be decisive in ensuring outcomes in Years 4 and 5.

After successfully setting the delivery agenda and establishing delivery discipline across Whitehall, the PMDU will now focus on accelerating and intensifying the drive for results.

5-Year Parliament
Year 1 Year 2 Year 3 Year 4 Year 5
We are here
Increasingly difficult for actions taken at the center to influence real-world outcomes in Years 4 and 5

Priority areas covered
Year 1: Setting the agenda and developing the approach
Year 2: Establishing the delivery discipline across Whitehall
Year 3: The drive for results
Year 4: • Manage through to success • Plan delivery of next parliament's top priorities • Plan exit or handover
Early progress but not yet irreversible
Year 3 is crucial for delivery

(Continued)

(Continued)

Exhibits 4C.3 and 4C.4, from the same presentation to the cabinet, explained the PMDU's narrowed focus and communicated to government officials how they could expect to work with the PMDU in the months to come.

Exhibit 4C.3 What we learned and why we needed to change our model

PMDU changes	Why we need to change
Ruthless prioritization	• Time is running out to influence delivery on targets by 2005—we need more impact. • In some cases, action programs to tackle delivery problems are still neither sufficient nor comprehensive.
More vigorous challenge	• We have not always challenged performance and progress in a way that led to enough change to affect prospects for delivery. • We need to engage ministers more to reinforce challenge. • We should make more use of customer perceptions and feedback to provide challenge. • Some of our core processes, like stocktakes and delivery reports, provide effective challenge—but we need to use them more flexibly. • Some of our most effective challenge has come from joint priority reviews—focusing on the frontline. • We need access to more staff who can provide credible extra expertise and challenge on program and performance management.
Stronger problem solving with deeper collaboration	• Some of our interventions have not led to enough change in key delivery systems. We have learned a lot about what works but need to apply and share that learning more effectively. • We sometimes failed to invest sufficiently in the follow-through of the findings of our assessments, priority reviews, and other problem solving. • We need to configure our resources to run an enlarged program of priority reviews.

Exhibit 4C.4 Working with PMDU in year 3—What will change?

PMDU changes	What the new model will be like
Ruthless prioritization	• Prioritize efforts on the prime minister's top priorities where PMDU can add most value • Organize around specific public service agreements (PSAs)—not departments • Develop alliances to attract new resources and levers • Introduce priority review style joint teams for more of our assessment, diagnosis, and problem solving • Exit lower priority PSAs and low impact non-PSA work
More vigorous challenge	• Challenge will come through the relationship and process, not just formal meetings • Sharper assessment of prospects for delivery by full application of the assessment framework

PMDU changes	What the new model will be like
	• Focus diagnosis on frontline and customer experiences to challenge strategy, progress, and reveal delivery problems • Flexible approach to formal meetings and introduce a new style of delivery reports designed to add maximum value • Integrate and align PMDU input and role within departmental program governance • More effective use of the prime minister's time and meetings
Stronger problem solving with deeper collaboration	• More resources focused on priority review style joint diagnosis and problem solving • Tailored approach for each area building on the lessons learned from previous activity • Follow-through the findings/actions generated by problem-solving interventions • Provide opportunities for junior ministers in frontline visits to stress test delivery • Manage the issues raised by the assessment framework through to a conclusion • Joint action program as a basis for transparent and accountable focus, agreement and support from PMDU—resulting from a dialogue and signed off in bilateral with PMDU leader

The following principles help you to challenge the status quo even when things are going well:

- Narrow your delivery focus, prioritizing even within your original set of priorities where necessary.
- Do not conflate "good" with "great"; instead, seek greatness.
- Instill a sense of urgency.
- Challenge cultural barriers and the belief that "we have already done all we can."

Rule 5: Celebrate successes

The final critical component of sustaining momentum will be the celebration of success. As noted above, it is important not to celebrate success too early. However, at the same time, celebration is an important means for recognizing the momentum that has been built and inspiring underperformers to make an extra effort. The guiding principles for celebrating success are as follows:

- Create "delivery heroes." Publicly recognize successes and those responsible for them, and hold them up as an example for others.
- Reward success with special processes and/or incentives.
- Celebrate in proportion to accomplishment: Not all victories are equal.

In the Boston Public School system, an official recognition program allowed the system to continually build momentum through the celebration of success.

CASE EXAMPLE

Celebrating Success in the Boston Public School System (BPS)

In 1996, BPS adopted "Focus On Children," a five-year education reform plan. The plan was designed to serve as a blueprint for improvement throughout the system. In 2001, BPS adopted Focus on Children II, which built on the successes of the first strategic plan and focused more specifically on maintaining high standards, accelerating the rate of improvement, holding schools accountable for results, developing leadership at the school level, focusing on family and community engagement, and cultivating external partnerships. In order to get the fuel they needed to build momentum, BPS recognized schools for their hard work.

> "In the beginning, we focused on improving literacy. We created a plan called the Effective Practice School plan—this helped call out the schools that were really making strides to improve their schools. We wanted to recognize them for their hard work and accomplishments, and this gave us the fuel we needed to show changes could happen."

—Tom Payzant, Former Superintendent, Boston Public Schools

Conclusion

By now, you have learned about the importance of momentum in delivery as well as some rules and guiding principles for establishing, building, and sustaining this momentum.

As one former PMDU staff member noted, a Delivery Unit is often the only organization that will press a system to "play to the final whistle." It is a role you will have to play. By applying these rules and guiding principles, you will ensure that your Unit drives delivery forward until your system achieves its targets.

With this, we complete our treatment of the tools and techniques of delivery. These last four chapters have laid out the steps that you and the system leader should take in order to start and manage a delivery effort. These tools and techniques will deliver results, but they will not make change irreversible by themselves. To do that, an important element must undergird your entire delivery effort from start to finish: a constant drive to create a **culture of delivery.** We turn to this subject in the next chapter.

5

Create an Irreversible Delivery Culture

"For organizational or systemic change, you actually have to motivate hordes of people to do something."

—Michael Fullan, *The Six Secrets of Change* (p. 63)

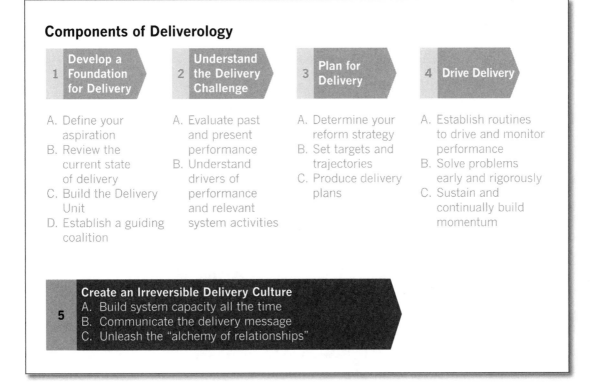

Components of Deliverology

1 Develop a Foundation for Delivery
- A. Define your aspiration
- B. Review the current state of delivery
- C. Build the Delivery Unit
- D. Establish a guiding coalition

2 Understand the Delivery Challenge
- A. Evaluate past and present performance
- B. Understand drivers of performance and relevant system activities

3 Plan for Delivery
- A. Determine your reform strategy
- B. Set targets and trajectories
- C. Produce delivery plans

4 Drive Delivery
- A. Establish routines to drive and monitor performance
- B. Solve problems early and rigorously
- C. Sustain and continually build momentum

5 **Create an Irreversible Delivery Culture**
- A. Build system capacity all the time
- B. Communicate the delivery message
- C. Unleash the "alchemy of relationships"

The previous four chapters have laid out the tools and tactics of delivery. While these tools and tactics are necessary elements of success, they will not be sufficient by themselves. Even if your system has a high-performing Delivery Unit that has guided system leaders through the process of diagnosis, planning, and monitoring of delivery, the question remains, how can a handful of people in a Delivery Unit make change stick in a bureaucracy of hundreds or even thousands? Put another way, how can you ensure that your delivery effort survives in the long term even if your Delivery Unit is disbanded and system leadership turns over?

The answer, in a word, is culture. The true success of delivery depends not only on excellent execution of the delivery activities in the previous four chapters, but also on the system's embodiment of the five key words of delivery: *ambition, focus, clarity, urgency,* and *irreversibility* (for more on this, please refer back to Module 1C).

In the first instance, it is your Delivery Unit's role to embody this culture. But to make change stick, your Delivery Unit will need to spread this culture throughout the system. As Exhibit 5 shows, this begins with system leaders and the **guiding coalition** that you helped build in Module 1D: the first and innermost circle of leadership for your delivery effort. Over time, your Delivery Unit must find ways to widen that circle to include mid-tier leaders, the frontline, and even users and the public.

What does this look like? It is a system in which everyone, from the system leader to your delivery plan owners to the teachers and students at the frontline, is empowered to take ownership of and responsibility for the aspirations of your delivery effort. It is a system in which you rely less and less on "hard" levers to force people to do things and depend instead on the excellence and capability of system actors who are as eager to hit the targets as

Exhibit 5 A system's concentric circles of leadership

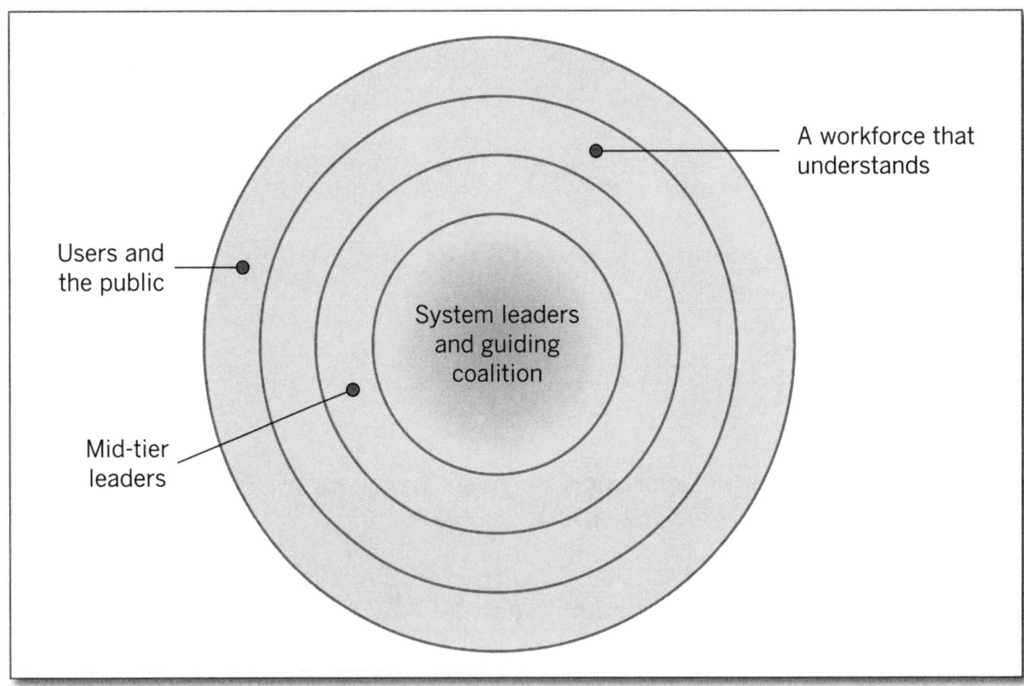

you are. Culture is transformative and it is essential. Without it, your Delivery Unit will be perennially swimming upstream, and your delivery effort will always feel like a revolution without enough revolutionaries.

This chapter lays out the core principles that will allow you to create and spread a culture of delivery throughout your system. In essence, spreading this culture requires that you build the right skills and mindsets, send the right messages, and develop the right relationships with system actors in a systematic and thoughtful way. The modules in the chapter are organized accordingly.

A. Build **system capacity** all the time

B. Communicate the **delivery message**

C. Unleash the **"alchemy of relationships"**

Unlike the other chapters in this field guide, this chapter is not chronological; it should be read neither as an afterthought nor as a last step in the delivery process. Rather, the principles in this chapter should be applied throughout your delivery effort, and they should underpin every **delivery activity** described in the previous four chapters, from delivery capacity reviews to trajectory setting to establishing routines.

The principles in this last chapter are the most difficult to master because there is no exact formula to get it right. However, they are the keys that can make the difference between achieving incremental improved outcomes and creating a systemwide transformation.[1]

5A. BUILD SYSTEM CAPACITY ALL THE TIME

"Once a district has a viable strategy, it faces two central capacity-building challenges. The first is delivering excellence when the scale is vast . . . the second is speed. The capacity of its people must be built at an accelerating pace over time to keep up with the momentum and expectations created by early wins."

—*Leading for Equity* (p. 73)

"Implementation is the study of learning (or failing to learn) in context."

—Michael Fullan,
The Six Secrets of Change (p. 89)

Most people who have engaged in any type of on-the-ground reform effort recognize that capacity is a crucial element of successful implementation. When change is demanded, even the most optimistic supporters might observe, "The leader is good," or "The reform is exactly what was called for," and then add, "But, there is no capacity to carry it out." The absence of capacity can mean the absence of delivery and often does—and not only for the "consumers" of what is delivered. System actors responsible for delivery must feel equipped to deliver before they can believe in their own ability to do so.

1. Please see the "Map of Delivery" in Module 1A.

For this reason, building capacity is crucial to any delivery effort. However, building capacity is a tremendously difficult task, as it involves more than just securing adequate time and resources. At every level of your system, you must ask and answer the question, what do people need to know and be able to do differently in order for delivery to succeed? How can capacity become collective in Michael Fullan's phrase, as well as individual? To make delivery truly irreversible, you must not only make sure that people have capacity initially but also continue to build capacity constantly.

Capacity is the potential for an organization—in this case, your system—to achieve its aspiration. It is constituted of four elements:

- **Structure.** Is the system structurally organized to do what needs to be done effectively?
- **Competencies.** Do system actors have the skills and abilities they need to do what is asked of them?
- **Motivation.** Do system actors, individually and collectively, have a "delivery mindset" as they approach the work they are being asked to do? (Recall the five key words that make up this mindset: *ambition, focus, clarity, urgency,* and *irreversibility.* For more on these words, please refer back to Module 1C.)
- **Resources.** Do system actors have the necessary time and/or funding to address the tasks at hand?

In order to understand where an organization's capacity is lacking, you must begin with the question, what exactly are we trying to do? At the highest level, the answer to this question is given as your system's aspiration, but that answer can be articulated such that it specifically addresses the various components of that aspiration: targets, interventions, delivery plans, and so on. For any of these, you can assess capacity with the following questions:

- What is the desired outcome?
- What is the process involved, and who are the system actors responsible for it? What will they have to do that is different from before?
- For those responsible, what will this new behavior require in terms of structure, resources, competencies, and motivation? How will we close the gap between the requirement and the current state?

In the context of delivery, capacity includes both **delivery capacity,** the potential to execute delivery activities successfully (e.g., how well a higher education system can define and track its targets), and **system capacity,** the potential to execute system activities successfully (e.g., how well it can implement a course redesign program).

In Module 1B, you reviewed your system's delivery capacity. Throughout your entire delivery effort, your Delivery Unit's role is to strengthen delivery capacity by implementing the delivery activities in this field guide, such as delivery chain analyses, routines, and priority reviews—in accordance with the needs identified in the delivery capacity review. In that regard, this entire field guide is a manual on building delivery capacity. This module will therefore focus on how your Delivery Unit plays a role in building system capacity.

ROLES OF SYSTEM LEADER AND DELIVERY LEADER

Your Delivery Unit's role is to ensure that system capacity is sufficient for the requirements of your delivery effort at multiple levels:

- The Delivery Unit. As delivery leader, your role is to develop the Delivery Unit's capacity directly.
- Delivery plan owners and others who interact directly with the Delivery Unit. You and your Delivery Unit staff play a direct role in building the capacity of the system actors with whom they work.
- Others in the system. You and your Delivery Unit staff play an indirect role in building the capacity of the rest of the system, ensuring that delivery plans include the requisite capacity building (for more on delivery plans, refer back to Module 3C).

Your Delivery Unit will help to identify and address specific gaps in capacity at all these levels using the capacity questions given above.

System leaders should allow resources to be dedicated to capacity building and, in some cases, can play an active and direct role in building the capacity of some system actors.

Principles for capacity building

Two key principles should permeate your capacity-building work:

- **Minimize blame and focus on improvement.** If people fear blame, there will be less transparency and less insight into the root causes of problems, which will inhibit capacity building. Instead, build a culture in which struggles or challenges are viewed as opportunities to learn and further improve delivery. It is important to communicate that people are being judged in order to strengthen performance and not for the sake of laying blame. In practice, a culture of no blame needs to exist alongside a culture of taking responsibility, so plain speaking and honesty will be crucial. As Michael Fullan (2008) explains in his book *The Six Secrets of Change,* "This doesn't mean that you avoid identifying things as effective or ineffective. Rather it means that you do not do so pejoratively" (p. 13).
- **Create a culture of continuous learning.** To truly sustain the capacity to implement change, all system actors responsible for delivery must be constantly going through the cycle of acting, reflecting, making adjustments, and trying again, each time refocusing their efforts on the actions that are found to be most effective. In this culture, all contributors to delivery are constantly increasing their effectiveness. As Michael Fullan (2008) put it, "Learning on the job, day after day, is the work" (p. 86). Exhibit 5A.1 gives an example of a basic process for encouraging continuous learning in your system.

Exhibit 5A.1 The cycle of continuous learning

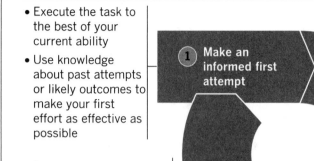

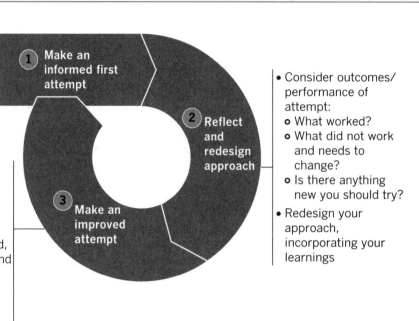

- Execute the task to the best of your current ability
- Use knowledge about past attempts or likely outcomes to make your first effort as effective as possible

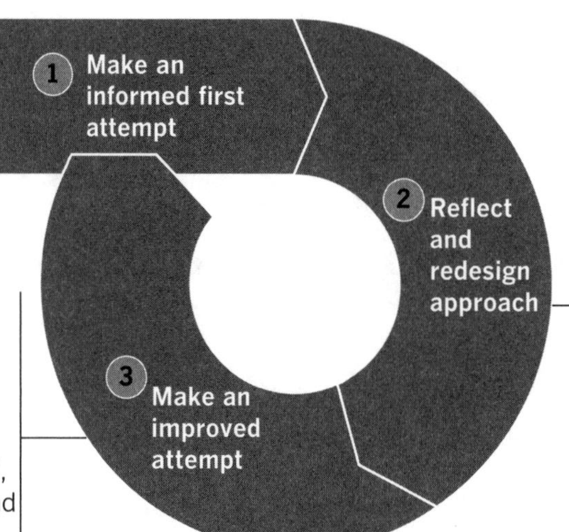

- Consider outcomes/performance of attempt:
  - What worked?
  - What did not work and needs to change?
  - Is there anything new you should try?
- Redesign your approach, incorporating your learnings

- Perform the task again, explicitly focusing on incorporating your learnings from the last attempt
- Emphasize what worked, leave out what failed, and add one or two new elements that your last attempt suggested might help

CASE EXAMPLE

Capacity-building principles in the PMDU

The two principles for capacity building were especially strong in the PMDU. With every interaction and process, the staff constantly reviewed progress, assessed what worked well and what could have been better, captured these learnings, and used them in future processes. Challenges were not setbacks but further opportunities for learning.

> "The key, when [we] turned out to be wrong, was to learn the lessons. Which assumptions turned out to be flawed? What changed that we hadn't anticipated? I used to quote the great conductor Benjamin Zander, who taught his musicians not to swear when they made a ghastly error, but to say to themselves, 'How fascinating!'" (*Instruction to Deliver,* 91)

These two principles are exemplified in the different tools and solutions that can be used to build capacity throughout your system.

Capacity-building tools

The tools outlined below are applicable at all levels of your system. They are organized according to the aspect of capacity for which they are designed (structure and resources or competencies and motivation). The case example below, from a school district in Maryland, shows how these tools can be combined in a comprehensive capacity-building effort. After the case, each tool is described in more detail, with additional case examples from the Maryland district and other systems.

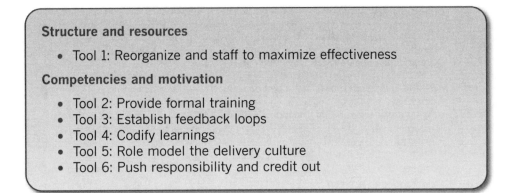

Structure and resources

- Tool 1: Reorganize and staff to maximize effectiveness

Competencies and motivation

- Tool 2: Provide formal training
- Tool 3: Establish feedback loops
- Tool 4: Codify learnings
- Tool 5: Role model the delivery culture
- Tool 6: Push responsibility and credit out

CASE EXAMPLE

A comprehensive approach to capacity building in Montgomery County, Maryland

In 1999, Jerry Weast became the superintendent of Montgomery County Public Schools (MCPS), with the mandate to dramatically improve performance, especially for students who had been historically underserved. In less than a decade, Weast led MCPS through a transformation resulting in a system committed to breaking links between race and class and academic achievement.

In 2000, MCPS launched the Professional Growth System for teachers, aimed at increasing classroom teaching skills via high expectations and a high degree of support. It included the creation of personal development plans, a peer review process, and a rigorous evaluation system. Over time, the district expanded these principles to build capacity for administrators and support service personnel. This investment in the overall system has exponentially improved results.

> "The Supporting Service Professional Growth System (SSPGS) addressed . . . more than 500 job classifications, with positions ranging from bus operators to mechanics to teacher assistants. Extending the PGS to noninstructional staff was an enormous step toward integrating important work that happens in the classrooms. In fact, the training and professional growth plans for supporting service employees have resulted in 235 staff members being promoted to supervisors and classroom teachers." (*Leading for Equity,* 86)

Exhibit 5A.2 shows how MCPS used all the tools outlined above in their capacity-building activities.

(Continued)

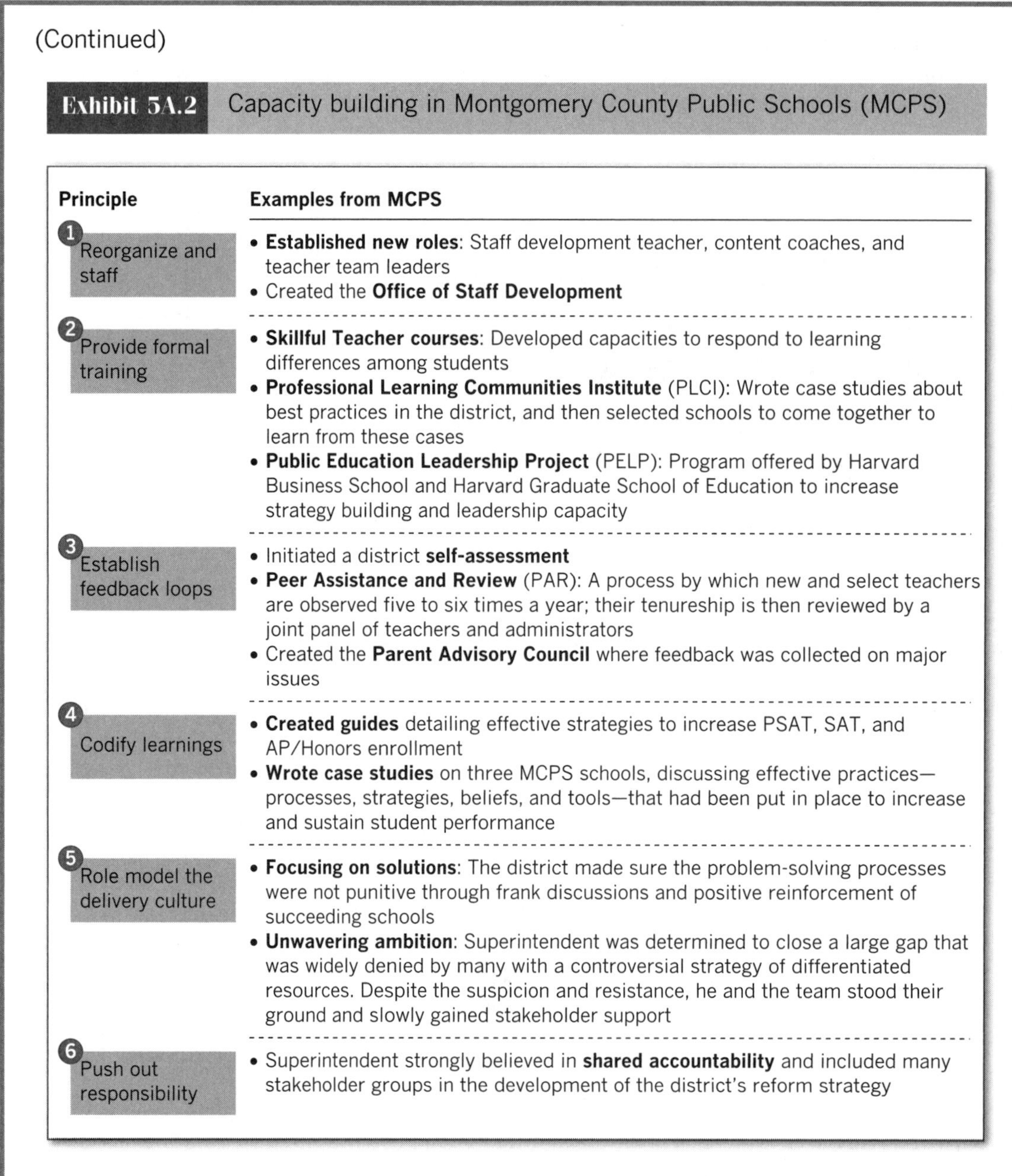

(Continued)

Exhibit 5A.2 Capacity building in Montgomery County Public Schools (MCPS)

Principle	Examples from MCPS
1 Reorganize and staff	• **Established new roles**: Staff development teacher, content coaches, and teacher team leaders • Created the **Office of Staff Development**
2 Provide formal training	• **Skillful Teacher courses**: Developed capacities to respond to learning differences among students • **Professional Learning Communities Institute** (PLCI): Wrote case studies about best practices in the district, and then selected schools to come together to learn from these cases • **Public Education Leadership Project** (PELP): Program offered by Harvard Business School and Harvard Graduate School of Education to increase strategy building and leadership capacity
3 Establish feedback loops	• Initiated a district **self-assessment** • **Peer Assistance and Review** (PAR): A process by which new and select teachers are observed five to six times a year; their tenureship is then reviewed by a joint panel of teachers and administrators • Created the **Parent Advisory Council** where feedback was collected on major issues
4 Codify learnings	• **Created guides** detailing effective strategies to increase PSAT, SAT, and AP/Honors enrollment • **Wrote case studies** on three MCPS schools, discussing effective practices—processes, strategies, beliefs, and tools—that had been put in place to increase and sustain student performance
5 Role model the delivery culture	• **Focusing on solutions**: The district made sure the problem-solving processes were not punitive through frank discussions and positive reinforcement of succeeding schools • **Unwavering ambition**: Superintendent was determined to close a large gap that was widely denied by many with a controversial strategy of differentiated resources. Despite the suspicion and resistance, he and the team stood their ground and slowly gained stakeholder support
6 Push out responsibility	• Superintendent strongly believed in **shared accountability** and included many stakeholder groups in the development of the district's reform strategy

Tool 1: Reorganize and staff to maximize effectiveness

If you find that your system or Delivery Unit is not structurally organized to do what needs to be done, then your role will be to reconfigure the organization in question to set it up for success in completing the task at hand. This can be accomplished by adding new staff, reorganizing existing staff, and/or eliminating existing staff.

To begin with, you will want to organize your Delivery Unit to provide the right level of support and challenge to the right system actors in your delivery effort. Sometimes, this may mean recruiting for talent that your system lacks (e.g., data capability). Sometimes, it will be a matter of strategic positioning. If, for example, financial aid reform is a crucial activity for a higher education system, and if the delivery chain for financial aid reform runs through a chief financial officer, you may select someone from his office to serve in your Delivery Unit. For more on organizing your Delivery Unit, please refer back to Module 1C.

At the system level, you will want to ensure that reporting lines and responsibilities are clear, roles are not duplicated or unfilled, and that each delivery plan owner has the necessary latitude to carry out her responsibilities. One important contribution your Delivery Unit can make is to identify capable system actors and recommend their placement in crucial positions. You can make this easier for your system by pushing for incentive programs that encourage and reward top talent for staying in these positions.

CASE EXAMPLE

The PMDU's role in personnel decisions

The PMDU took careful note of senior managers in the bureaucracy. Where necessary to the delivery effort, it acted to ensure that the right people were in the right places.

> "By far the biggest challenge in following up the Delivery Report was the Home Office. David Blunkett's political leadership had been immense and John Gieve as Permanent Secretary had steadily strengthened the organization, but beneath him management remained fragile and the mix of challenges—crime, drugs, bulging prisons, counter-terrorism, asylum, immigration—seemed to become more challenging with every passing week. I promised to do everything I could to support John Gieve and his colleagues in further strengthening his management team. Two appointments of senior people, given Permanent Secretary status, followed. It was an ad hoc solution, but provided John with some of the additional resilience he needed." (*Instruction to Deliver,* 174)

The following case examples demonstrate how successful education systems have used both staffing and reorganization to fill capacity needs. In Ontario, Canada, the system leader identified the gaps in a collaborative manner and designed the organization to fill these gaps. The leader of Maryland's Montgomery County schools ensured that there were ample incentives to attract the best talent.

CASE EXAMPLE

Building capacity by closing resource gaps in Ontario, Canada

In 2003, the Ministry of Education in Ontario was charged with ambitious reforms in K–12 education: improving performance of elementary-school students, increasing high-school graduation rates, and reducing class size. Before they could begin, they had to make sure that they had the necessary staff in place to drive delivery.

> "I had to change the organization and make required personnel changes to get things done. Personnel changes was a mix of filling vacancies and, in a very few cases, finding a new person for the job."
>
> —Ben Levin, Deputy Minister of Education,
> Ministry of Education, Ontario, Canada

CASE EXAMPLE

Reorganizing and rehiring in Montgomery County, Maryland

Montgomery County Public Schools (MCPS) Superintendent Jerry Weast used restructuring and hiring as key methods to increase capacity in the system. This was particularly evident in his transformation of teacher hiring.

> "The HR department streamlined its hiring process and implemented open contracts, year-round recruiting, and a 'grow your own talent' plan . . . MCPS began to aggressively seek out teacher candidates through formalized programs developed to source a candidate pipeline that more closely mirrored the demographics of the district's students and to recruit and retain teachers in high-need schools. The new processes, procedures, and relationships transformed the human resources function." (*Leading for Equity,* 77)

Moreover, when he discovered that the existing system of teacher professional development was insufficient, Weast reorganized it to better suit MCPS's needs.

> "Weast decided to restructure how training would be delivered. When he first arrived, responsibility for professional development was distributed throughout the system . . . offices did their own training . . . Frustrated with this fragmentation, Weast asked the associate superintendents to develop a reorganization plan that would bring all of the training under the responsibility of an Office of Organization Development. After convincing the county council members, Weast tripled the percentage of the budget that went to training from 1 to 3 percent, or approximately $50 million. Now, with a direct reporting relationship to the superintendent and considerable financial resources, the new Office of Staff Development had tremendous power within MCPS." (*Leading for Equity,* 79)

Tool 2: Provide formal training

As anyone who has ever worked in "professional development" will know, you will need to approach formal training very carefully. Training programs can be helpful; but, more often than not, they can become the subject of jokes on ineffectiveness. The sentiment is captured in the title of a paper by Peter Cole: "Professional Development: A Great Way to Avoid Change" (Cole, 2004). To avoid risk, it is important to ensure that training is of high quality, always has a direct application (preferably soon after the training session), and is provided by credible experts with experience in actually doing the work. System actors attending trainings should be able to reflect on, discuss, and apply the training in the context of their daily system activities.

In general, the training programs that you either design or provide should adhere to the adult learning principles given in Exhibit 5A.3.

Exhibit 5A.3 Adult learning principles

Adults learn . . .		Implications for training program design . . .
• When it matters to them	➧	• Build learning around activities that will make a difference to performance
• Through action and experience	➧	• Make participants responsible for doing and delivering in the workplace
• When they are at the edge of their "comfort zone"	➧	• Stretch people to do more than they think they can do
• From their peers	➧	• Enable a peer community to develop (e.g., via shared forums)
• With multiple learning interactions spread over time	➧	• Facilitate a mix of learning forums and interventions that reinforce learning while organization activities continue
• With immediate support	➧	• Support learners with coaching in the workplace
• When they understand why they succeeded or failed	➧	• Push learners to understand why successes and failures occur

SOURCE: McKinsey and Company.

You have already staffed the most capable people in your Delivery Unit, but even they may need training to further hone their abilities. In the PMDU, perceived needs drove professional development sessions, from "humility training" for a staff member who had behaved arrogantly to a conflict resolution session delivered by an expert in international peace and reconciliation.

Well-executed training programs have several benefits. First and most obviously, trainings help to build relevant skills. For example, in a K–12 system that was building a new Delivery Unit, the team recognized a need for skill building in basic leadership and management techniques for the new staff. To this end, they conducted a series of training sessions to ensure that the system had relevant skills to implement delivery: problem solving, work planning, meeting facilitation, process design, and communication through PowerPoint. The new Delivery Unit staff found these sessions helpful because they built skills that were vital to the unit's day-to-day work with the system.

Second, trainings can help change mindsets that are preventing the system from achieving its aspiration. For example, the PMDU held regular "delivery conferences" that helped spread the delivery mindset via inspirational dialogue. Though invitations were initially only extended to the most senior group of managers responsible for delivery, they soon grew to include teams as well, spreading the key tenets of delivery culture to 200 civil servants responsible for implementation of reform.

CASE EXAMPLE

Changing mindsets in Montgomery County, Maryland

Montgomery County Public Schools (MCPS) faced the challenge of changing beliefs that some children simply could not achieve, regardless of resources.

Its Skillful Teachers courses helped change this mindset, allowing them to see the link between improving teacher effectiveness and student achievement levels.

> "I think [Skillful Teacher] had a huge impact . . . just the whole theory about 'effort' and us switching to believe that you are not just smart because you were born smart. It just kind of brought it to [our consciousness], effort and hard work. You have to put in a lot of effort, and working hard makes you smarter."
>
> —Participating teacher
> (*Leading for Equity,* 80)

Finally, trainings can build capacity by "connecting peers with a purpose," (p. 41) as Michael Fullan (2008) puts it. As per the adult learning principles above, peer collaboration—the opportunity to share and discuss common challenges, successes, and failures in a safe setting—is a crucial tool for learning.

According to Fullan (2008), there are certain conditions for positive and purposeful peer interaction:

1. The larger values of the organization and those of individuals and groups must mesh.
2. Information and knowledge about effective practices should be openly and widely shared.
3. Monitoring mechanisms must be in place to detect and address ineffective actions while also identifying and consolidating effective practices. (Fullan, 2008, p. 45)

In the end, this constant learning from peers, close to the job itself, is the key to success.

CASE EXAMPLE

To establish peer learning mechanisms, the PMDU held special training and networking meetings for the most senior managers, attended by top business people and sometimes by the prime minister himself. This allowed participants to

- Feel a sense of collaboration about tackling a shared commitment;
- Role model delivery leadership for each other by setting priorities;
- Motivate each other via competition; and
- Learn from each other about how to handle functionally similar delivery challenges, even though their circumstances and organizations might differ.

> "We had begun a program to train the senior civil servants who were personally responsible for delivering Blair's top priorities. We introduced them to leading business people and arranged sessions in which they

explored each other's challenges as a way of jolting them out of their silos. Blair himself came to one of their events, answered questions and concluded by telling them that while they might worry that failing to deliver would affect their careers, he was certain that the risk to his career was greater." (*Instruction to Deliver,* 123)

The following are two case examples of peer networking in Canada. The York Region held a fair for this purpose while Ontario established a network with less formal interactions.

CASE EXAMPLE

The Annual Learning Fair in York Region, Canada

In recent years, York Region, just north of Toronto, has undertaken a massive effort to improve literacy across 181 schools (151 elementary and 30 high schools). Central to its success in student achievement has been extensive use of peer networking and continuous learning.

> "Each June, as part of our system wide strategy, York Region holds a 'learning fair' in which all 181 schools display and convey what they have accomplished over the previous year . . . this presentation is prepared and presented entirely by the school—that is, these are the ideas and words of the school leaders themselves . . . There is continuous, multifaceted data collection that is analyzed according to 'successes and challenges.' Successes are recognized; challenges are addressed. The whole approach is continuous and transparent to students, parents, teachers, and administrators alike . . . All schools in the system are learning from one another as they seek and implement effective literacy practices."
>
> —Michael Fullan (2008),
> *The Six Secrets of Change* (pp. 83–85)

CASE EXAMPLE

Peer Networks in Ontario, Canada

As part of a broad attempt to improve K–12 education, the Ontario secretariat of literacy and numeracy has invested heavily in "lateral capacity building." One example of this is peer mentoring opportunities where lagging school districts can learn from leading ones in a collaborative environment.

> "The secretariat has created a network of twenty-three school districts (five districts that are getting good new results and eighteen that are not moving forward) that work together for the improvement of all. All twenty-three district leaders voluntarily joined the network. In answer to those who object that organizations won't cooperate because of competition, we have found that time and again 'bad' competition (you fail, I win) is replaced by 'good' competition (how do we all get better, but I still want to improve as much as I can—friendly competition)."
>
> —Michael Fullan (2008),
> *The Six Secrets of Change* (p. 48)

Tool 3: Establish feedback loops

Feedback is the most effective way of maintaining a culture of continuous learning. This field guide is full of delivery activities that create constant feedback for the system (e.g., challenge meetings, routines). Through these activities, the Delivery Unit challenges system actors to constantly improve their delivery and move faster toward the aspiration.

Your Delivery Unit should also establish a norm of continuous and regular feedback on its own work. The PMDU considered this a defining characteristic of its distinct contribution to delivery: If they could not learn faster about delivery than everybody else, how would they drive delivery for everybody else?

To this end, the PMDU developed a rubric of four "key enablers" on which it scored itself regularly:

- World class tools and processes
- Excellent relationships
- Brilliant internal Delivery Unit systems
- Great people

Exhibit 5A.4 gives an example of a self-assessment framework that could be used to summarize these regular evaluations. The management team revisited performance on these four enablers every three months.

Exhibit 5A.4 PMDU's self-assessment framework

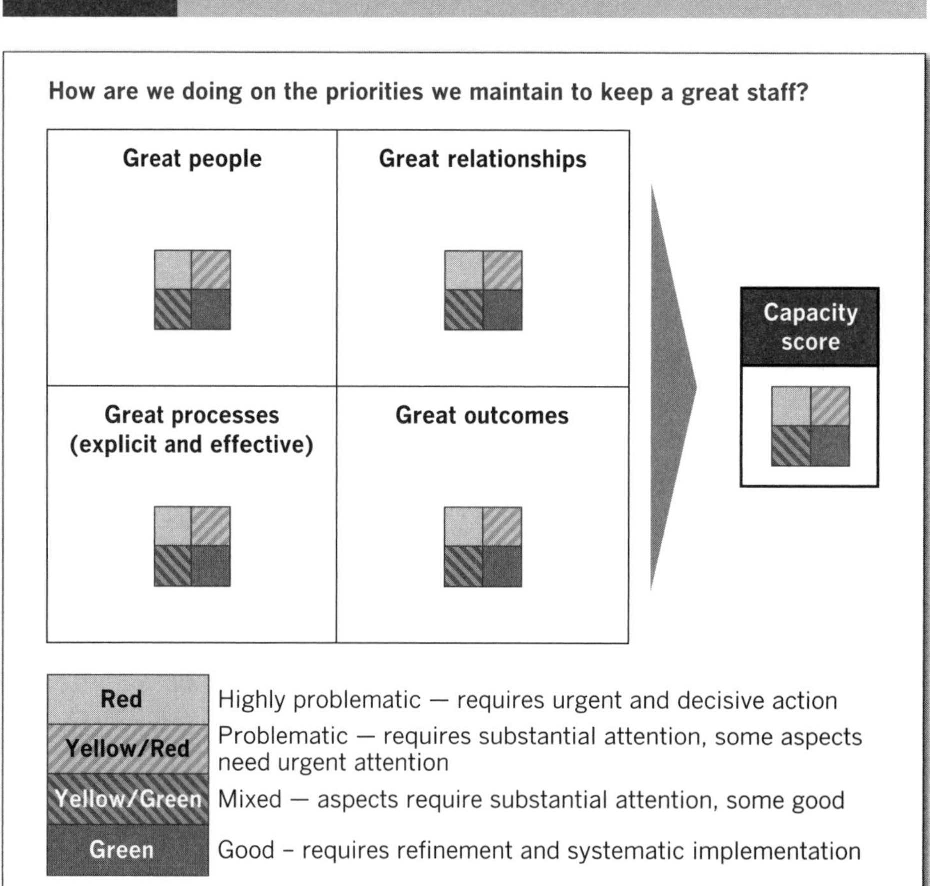

If they found themselves to be less than satisfactory in any category, they would return to the drawing board and seek to resolve any challenges that had arisen. In one instance, the PMDU found that the Department of Education had some concerns about interactions with PMDU staff. They realized that it was more difficult to foster a nonhierarchical, collaborative relationship with officials in this department because the PMDU leader had been the previous manager of some of those same officials. Through a series of discussions, the PMDU reassessed and adjusted the way the PMDU leader and staff interacted with the department. This strengthened relations with the department and ultimately allowed them to improve performance on their targets.

This regular review process was just one of many feedback loops that the PMDU established to assess its performance as an organization; other feedback loops ensured that the same care was taken in evaluating and developing the skills of individual staff members.

FEEDBACK CULTURE IN THE PMDU

"Staff began to expect feedback on how they had performed in, for example, a meeting with a department, and they wanted more than vague compliments. Regular 'knowledge-sharing' sessions were timetabled; each element of Deliverology—from stocktakes to Priority Reviews—was reviewed internally and the outcomes of the reviews debated and then applied . . . We also began to seek feedback systematically, from within and without, every six months . . . We arranged for external people to interview our key stakeholders in departments—Permanent Secretaries and top officials—and feed back to us what they thought about what we did and how we could improve it . . . The result was that we really did learn faster about delivery than anyone else." (*Instruction to Deliver,* 199)

As noted above, your Delivery Unit brings feedback loops to the broader system through several delivery activities—routines in particular. However, you may also explicitly encourage the independent development of internal feedback mechanisms at all levels of your system, so routines and other delivery activities do not catch system actors by surprise. For example, Montgomery County Public Schools initiated a district self-assessment in the fall of 2000, using the Malcolm Baldrige Education Criteria for Performance Excellence (*Leading for Equity,* 95). A Delivery Unit in a K–12 SEA solicited feedback after every training it gave to understand what portions were useful for its participants.

Tool 4: Codify learnings

The tools and frameworks that the PMDU brought into use were remarkable not because they were counter intuitive or different but because they made intuitive things explicit, allowing their teams to think together about them to solve some of the system's most challenging problems. Many of the PMDU tools and techniques explained in this field guide are examples of codification of the learnings from several delivery experiences: the assessment framework, the delivery chain analysis, and the trajectory methodology, for example. Indeed, this entire field guide is a codification in itself.

The PMDU is not the only example. Toyota, long considered best in class in operational excellence, is estimated to spend more time documenting its work methods and training its employees to apply them than any other company, by a factor of five (Fullan, 2008, p. 79).

In the same way that the Delivery Unit codifies many practices, so too should the system actors themselves. Encourage your delivery plan owners to make note of best practices and learnings from their various meetings and interactions. You can use peer networking events (see above) to share these codified learnings with others and further expand the capacity of your system. As the case example below demonstrates, in the Montgomery County Public Schools several ways to do this were found.

CASE EXAMPLE

Codification in Montgomery County, Maryland

Even as Montgomery County Public Schools (MCPS) Superintendent Jerry Weast initiated his reforms of the district, he made sure that crucial successes and learnings were captured and shared widely.

> "In August 2007, [MCPS] created a PSAT M-STAT Data Booklet detailing effective strategies to increase PSAT participation. Several months later, it did the same for SAT participation and honor/AP enrollment. The guides were then used to train school teams in a professional development session in February. It appeared the hard work was paying off . . . MCPS had the highest number of African American AP exam takers scoring well enough to earn college credit of any district in the nation save for New York City, which has nine times more African American students." (*Leading for Equity,* 125)

> "An internal team wrote case studies on three MCPS schools: Broad Acres, Ronald McNair, and Viers Mill Elementary. All three schools had experienced dramatic success with the new strategy, and the case studies discussed effective practices—processes, strategies, beliefs, and tools—that had been put in place to increase and sustain performance in each of these highly successful schools . . . Seeing results from schools within the same district with similar resources and student population was a powerful experience for school teams." (*Leading for Equity,* 87)

Tool 5: Role model the delivery culture

Your Delivery Unit will have ample opportunities to role model the delivery culture in everyday interactions with system actors, particularly delivery plan owners. You should make the most of these opportunities to demonstrate the mindset of delivery. For example, when the managers or their organizations struggle, you can help create a culture of plain speaking, problem solving, and learning by explicitly avoiding finger pointing and supporting them to solve the problem. And when managers succeed, you can ask them to reflect on the reasons for success and encourage them to build on this learning in future efforts. In this manner, you will be role modeling a culture of continuous learning, teaching system actors to reflect on past efforts to inform and improve future endeavors.

This type of role modeling is important within the Delivery Unit itself as well. It will be important for your staff to see your confidence and persistence in the face of challenge. They too will then be able to carry this theme through when they interact with delivery plan owners and other system actors. For more on how delivery culture is lived out in day-to-day relationships, please see Module 5C.

LEARNING IS THE WORK AT TOYOTA

Toyota exemplifies the importance of daily role modeling, by giving managers the responsibility of teaching on a daily basis through their work itself. In this way, it is able to constantly increase the capacity of its organization.

"Toyota 'gets' learning in context. Instead of workers leaving work to learn, learning is the job. Toyota's Job Instruction method is a top-notch training process because it is developed by using the job itself as the subject. The company selects and cultivates its leaders with one core purpose in mind: 'Toyota's philosophy is every team leader and manager is a teacher first.'" (Fullan, 2008, p. 87, referencing Liker & Meier, 2007, p. 283)

Tool 6: Push responsibility and credit out

Given the size of your staff, it will be mathematically impossible for your Delivery Unit to make change happen by itself. Pushing responsibility outward will encourage system actors not only to deliver change but to drive it as well. Pushing credit outward allows for a celebration of their success and motivation for future efforts. Only by empowering those around you will your Unit create reform that is transformational and sustainable.

At first, delivery plan owners may be acting largely in response to pressure from the Delivery Unit. Your Unit will initially play a role of facilitating processes, providing insight, managing regular performance reviews and problem solving, and making course corrections to the delivery effort as necessary. As delivery progresses, it will be to your advantage to push responsibility out to delivery plan owners and beyond, so each department or organization feels more and more responsibility for delivering on the targets, interventions, or system activities that they own.

One example of this theory in action in the PMDU was the evolution of the processes for two of its routines: **stocktakes** and **delivery reports.** For stocktakes, presentations were originally prepared and given by Delivery Unit staff. Over time, the PMDU devolved responsibility for some of these presentations to the departments, though always with the advice and support of the PMDU staff.

For delivery reports, the PMDU initially constructed its league table by relying entirely on PMDU staff judgments. After some time, they began asking departments to use the assessment framework to assess their own progress as a starting point. The PMDU continued to make the final judgment call, but the shift in responsibility was significant.

CASE EXAMPLE

Pushing out responsibility in Montgomery County, Maryland

For Montgomery County Public Schools (MCPS), PSAT scores were the key to the high school strategy, as they had become a gateway for qualified minority students to take Advanced Placement courses. This was one of several indicators that MCPS tracked at M-STAT, a stocktake-like process with community superintendents who oversaw individual clusters of schools.

At the first M-STAT meeting, Deputy Superintendent Frieda Lacey pressed the community superintendents about minority achievement on the PSAT: "What are you doing specifically for African American and Hispanic students at schools where the students are mostly white?" She asked them to bring back solutions to the next meeting. The result was a cascading of the M-STAT process and a pushing of responsibility out to the community superintendents:

> "Community superintendents worked with principals and one another to increase the participation of Hispanic and African American students in advanced courses and in the PSAT . . . Community superintendents adopted the M-STAT model with groups of their principals to discuss the PSAT issue. They struggled to make sure the process was safe and not punitive. As one principal noted: 'M-STAT also provided the forum for frank discussions and the opportunity for principals to hear about equitable practices that promote high expectations. The positive reinforcement and recognition that schools received from the executives and their peers through the process was unparalleled and was an additional catalyst for both school-wide, then district-wide change. It was catch us doing something great, not a gotcha.'" (*Leading for Equity,* 107)

By pushing responsibility out, Lacey empowered her community superintendents to create and role model a culture of delivery with their school clusters. As a result of this process alone, over half the district's high schools showed an increase in the number of minority students who were participating in the PSAT and in more rigorous upper-level classes. As a result of further interventions, results were substantial:

- By 2008, 88.1% of African American and 84.4% of Hispanic students took the PSAT, an increase of over 10% for both since the 2002 to 2003 school year; and
- By 2009, Over 60% of African American and Hispanic students were enrolled in at least one AP or honors class. (*Leading for Equity,* 108)

Conclusion

By now, you have learned

- What capacity building is and why it is important;
- Principles of capacity building; and
- Specific tools and techniques for building capacity (or causing it to be built) in your Delivery Unit and system.

Capacity building is not easy, but it is critical for sustaining delivery. The investment you make in developing capacity will multiply the impact and staying power of the change you are trying to implement. If you could give your entire system the right structure, resources, competencies, and motivation to deliver on its aspiration, your Delivery Unit would, in effect, be obsolete. This can be a lengthy process, though, and in the meantime, other tools are called for that can reach a broad audience quickly. This is the subject of the next module.

5B. COMMUNICATE THE DELIVERY MESSAGE

"Good communication is not just data transfer. You need to show people something that addresses their anxieties, that accepts their anger, that is credible in a very gut-level sense, and that evokes faith in the vision. Great leaders do this well almost effortlessly."

—John Kotter and Dan Cohen (2002), *The Heart of Change* (p. 84)

Communication is a second key element of creating a delivery culture, both within and beyond your Delivery Unit. The messages that your Unit and others send about your delivery effort can dramatically help or harm its cause. In addition to having the capacity to do the work, system actors need to understand the why of your delivery effort: Why is change important? What is its moral purpose? They must also understand your system's strategy, how it will be carried out, and, crucially, what it means for them. In addition, a good **communication plan** will engage them both analytically and emotionally to convey the necessary messages in a compelling way.

This module will explain how to identify the audiences who need to hear the delivery message and how to create a communication plan for reaching them.

In general, a communication plan must anchor on a *message*. There are two types of communication objects for your Delivery Unit to consider.

- **The Delivery Unit itself.** Though you will want to keep a relatively low profile, your Delivery Unit will not be able to operate completely unnoticed. You will need to communicate consistently about what the unit is, what it is there to do, and, perhaps most importantly, how its activities are different from business as usual. This communication should also reinforce the *brand* of your Delivery Unit. The most important audience for this type of communication will be the delivery plan owners who will have most direct day-to-day interactions with your Unit.
- **The delivery effort.** In this case, communication is about the specific content of your system's aspiration, its targets, its strategy, its interventions, and/or its plans. The audience for this type of communication can extend across the entire system, all the way to the users and public.

One important concept as part of the communication about the Delivery Unit is the brand of your Unit. A brand is a consistent message, idea, or experience associated with an entity. A positive brand helps people understand the entity and want to be a part of it.

Creating a successful brand for the Delivery Unit is critical for public sector reform because you must combat the preconceived notions people currently have about reform efforts in large public bureaucracies—that is, the impact will be minimal, but the process will be very burdensome. Changing this mindset will not be easy, but if you even begin to shift the way key actors think about their potential for impact, you will begin to see tremendous results. Part of exuding this brand will be through the constant and consistent messaging of your communication plan (as described later in the module). However, the majority of the brand image your Unit will generate will be from everyday interactions with those around you. For a deeper discussion on how to build your brand, please see Module 5C.

ROLES OF SYSTEM LEADER AND DELIVERY LEADER

As delivery leader, you are responsible for orchestrating all communications efforts that have to do with your Delivery Unit. For communications about the priorities overseen by your Unit, you will be communicating this to the system managers you work with. However, you will also work with your system leader and delivery plan owners to ensure that they create and execute communication strategies to the public according to the steps and principles outlined in this module. The system leader will bear a heavy share of responsibility for communication and will possibly have separate communications staff with whom you will need to work closely.

Process steps

The following process steps can be applied to any communication object. For the purposes of explanation, we will assume that the communication object is the delivery effort as a whole.

Step 1: Identify and understand stakeholders
Step 2: Develop the communication plan
Step 3: Monitor the communication plan

Step 1: Identify and understand stakeholders

Stakeholders are people who have a stake, or vested interest, in the process or outcome of your delivery effort. They are people whose support will matter in ensuring that change is successful. For a delivery effort, this would include every system actor in the relevant delivery chains, all the way to end users (e.g., students), who have an interest in the outcomes of your efforts and potential to help or hinder the process of change. It might also include external actors who have relevant interests and influence.

You can use the following questions to help you identify key stakeholders:

- Who has an influence on, or is influenced by, the delivery effort? This would include the system actors in the relevant delivery chains and the end users.
- Who is indirectly involved with the delivery effort? Are there parties inside or outside the system who could be influential or who are affected in some way? Interest groups such as teachers' unions fall into this category.

For each stakeholder group, your aim is to build support for your delivery effort. To do this, you must understand your stakeholders, which begins with understanding their viewpoint on the delivery effort. Every stakeholder group holds a different viewpoint in regards to your change effort.

Generally speaking, it is likely that these viewpoints will be normally distributed, as illustrated in Exhibit 5B.1.

In the example, a few stakeholders are out in front and are considered innovators. Little or no effort is needed to acquire their support; and in fact, they will often be the ones pushing you to be bolder in your efforts. Similarly, a few stakeholders on the opposite end of the spectrum will be extremely opposed to your effort. They are the "laggards," some of whom may never be convinced. Most stakeholders, however, will be somewhere in the middle.

Exhibit 5B.1 The changing distribution of stakeholders in a reform effort

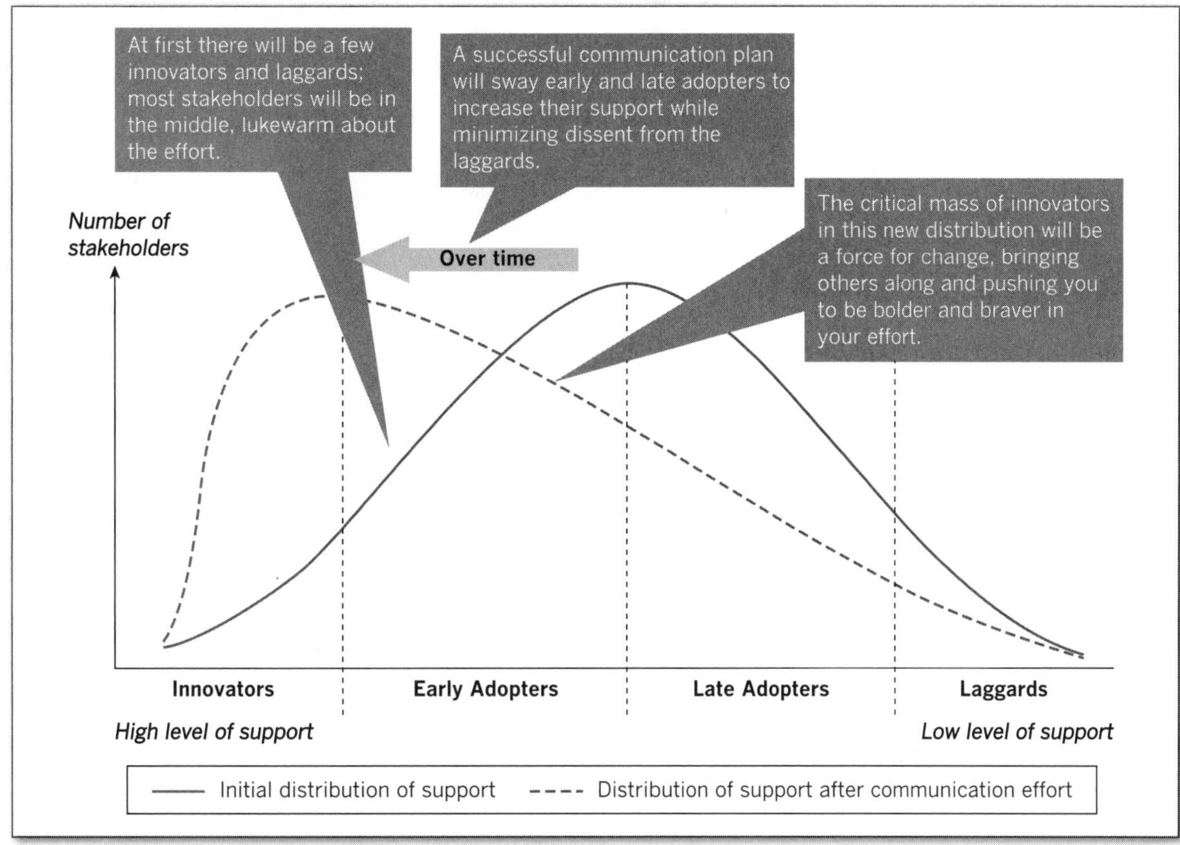

The goal of your communication plan will be to shape these stakeholders' views over time so that they become more supportive of your delivery effort. The **emotional trajectory** makes this goal explicit by charting their expected viewpoints (emotions) about your delivery effort over time. This emotional trajectory will differ from group to group, but it is a starting point for devising a comprehensive communication plan (see Exhibit 5B.2).

While the goal of your communication is to increase the support of all stakeholders, gaining the support of everyone can be difficult and sometimes impossible. Sometimes, minimizing or allowing quiet dissent is preferable to a loud and distracting debate. Therefore, it is important to know who the laggards are and to avoid being drawn into a high-profile conflict with any of them in your efforts to gain support or, if a conflict is unavoidable, to prepare well and see it through. At the same time, you should identify and reinforce your innovators, asking them to step up as champions of your delivery effort. They can play a crucial role in pushing you to achieve more and by being constructive critics of your efforts.

Exhibit 5B.2 An effective communication plan moves stakeholders along their emotional trajectory toward supporting your delivery effort over time

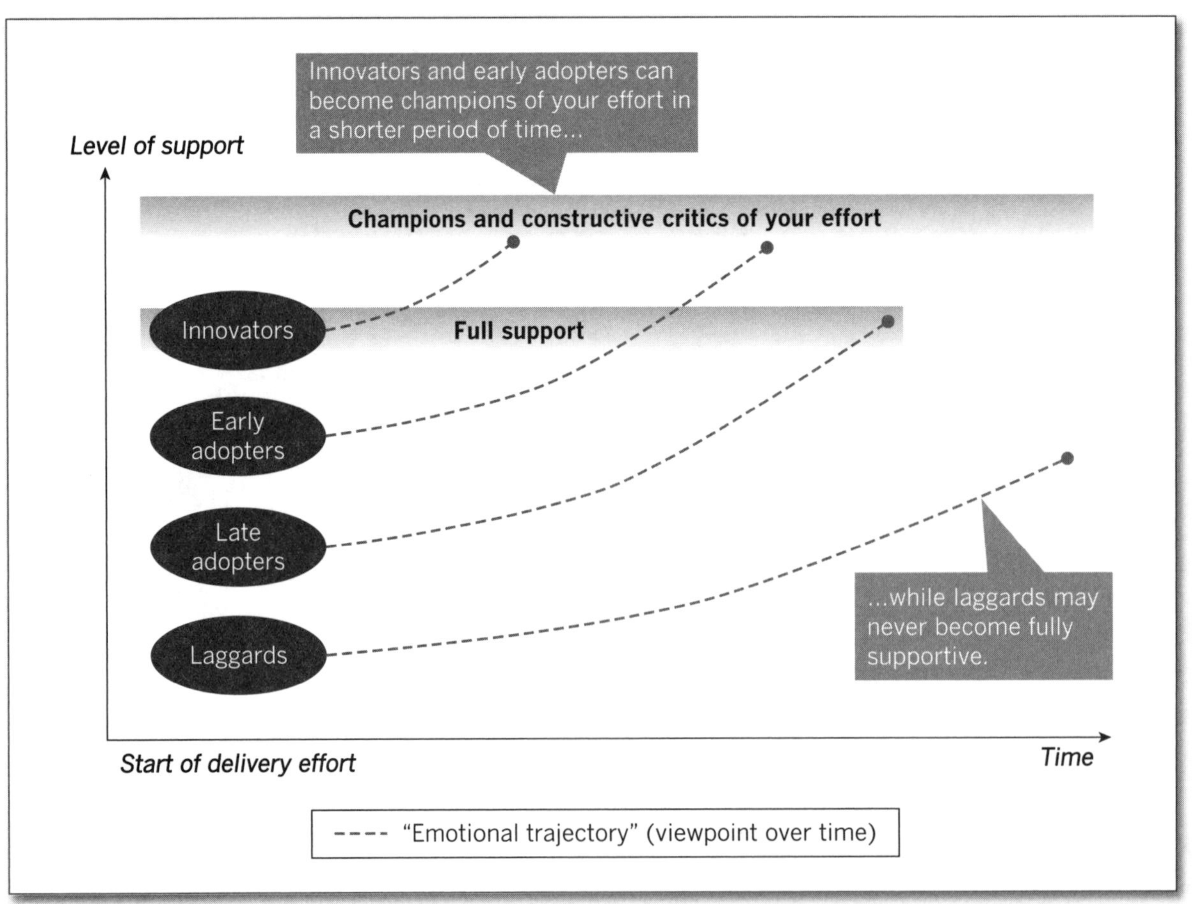

Exhibit 5B.3 PMDU: What the journey was like from different leaders' perspectives

	2001	2002	2003	2004	2005
Prime minister	I know what I want...but we're so far from achieving it.	We're not bold enough...all too incremental.	This is tough, and the civil service needs to change.	At last some results...what should the next phase be like?	Real progress... but why did all the drive have to come from my office?
Ministers	The prime minister's agenda is right...but the pressure from him is relentless.	I feel huge pressure from the public and opposition to communicate. How do I get this department to really deliver?	It's a real battle...and the public and media are never satisfied.	In the end, the PMDU and targets ensured we stayed focused.	Tough but worth it.
Top civil servants	The minister drives us hard...and the staff don't know what to do.	Is this just about the election result...or transforming Britain?	We seem to be antagonizing people at the frontline.	We need to develop our collective capabilities.	We're proud of our results...but the next phase will be harder.

Exhibits 5B.3 and 5B.4 give an ex-post view of the emotional trajectory of various stakeholders with respect to the PMDU and its agenda from 2001 to 2005. Note the shift in viewpoint at every level. Ideall y, your Delivery Unit should work with your system leader and others to create a prospective emotional trajectory that is similar. What would you want to be able to say about how stakeholder viewpoints shifted during the course of your delivery effort?

To understand what the emotional trajectory of your stakeholders might be, you need to understand their individual starting points. The following questions will guide you for each stakeholder:

- What is the stakeholder's *current position* toward your delivery effort? Are they a laggard, late adopter, early adopter, or innovator?
- What is the stakeholder's *relative power?* How much does their current position affect your delivery effort's success?
- Based on your answers to the first two questions, what is your *objective* for the stakeholder? Starting from their current position, where would you like to move them to? How will you know you have succeeded?

Your answers to these questions can be summarized per stakeholder in the mapping template given in Exhibit 5B.5.

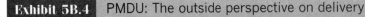

Exhibit 5B.4 PMDU: The outside perspective on delivery

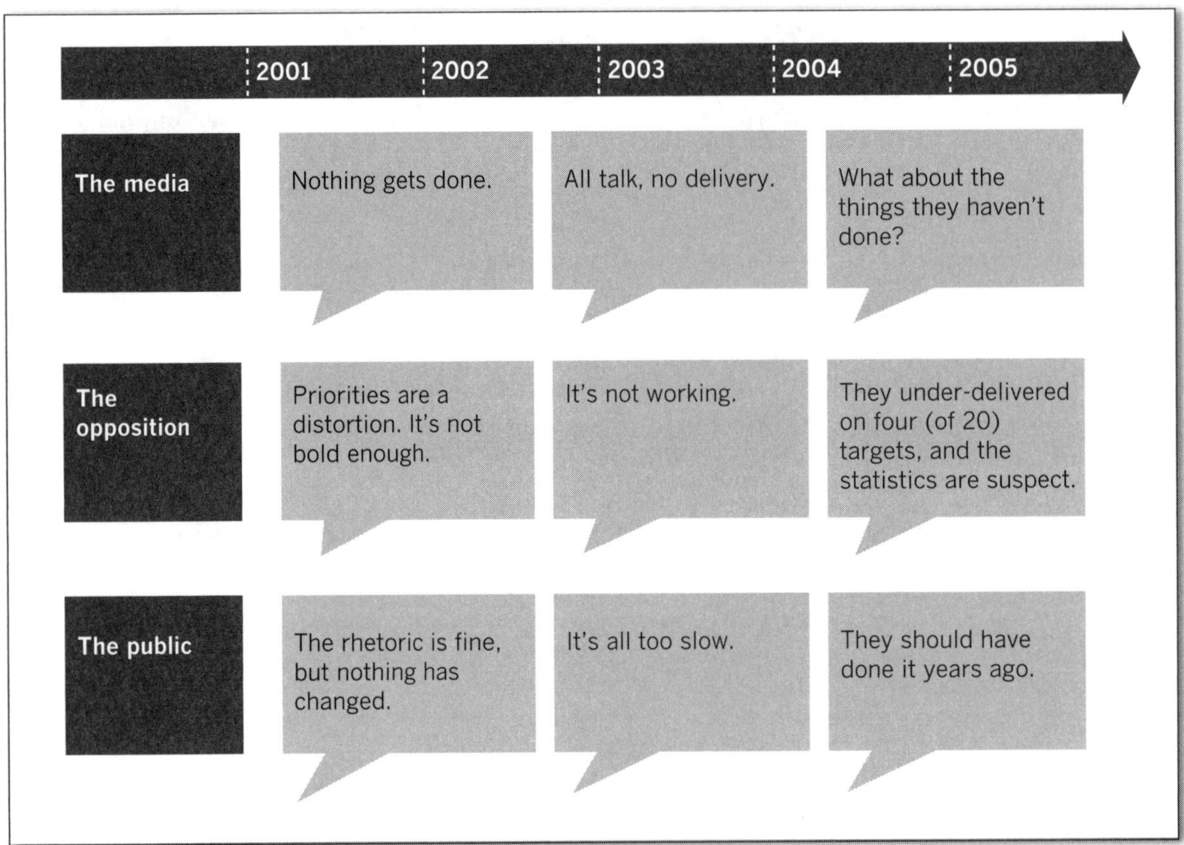

Exhibit 5B.5 Stakeholder mapping template

	Current position	Relative power	Objective
Stakeholder 1	•	•	•
Stakeholder 2	•	•	•
Stakeholder 3	•	•	•
Stakeholder 4	•	•	•
Stakeholder 5	•	•	•

In general, your objectives for each stakeholder will be determined by that stakeholder's current position and relative power. For example, your message should energize and mobilize early adopters and innovators. In particular, you should recruit powerful innovators to be champions of your delivery effort and additional communicators who reinforce your message. For laggards and late adopters, the response is a bit more complex. You may choose to ignore laggards and late adopters with little power, but you will need to think carefully and diplomatically about how to overcome or get around powerful laggards (or, in some cases, how you might bring them around).

Once you have identified and understood your stakeholders, you are ready to craft your communication plan.

Step 2: Develop the communication plan

A *communication plan* details your system's coordinated efforts to get the right messages to the right stakeholders at the right times, in order to ensure the necessary support for your delivery effort. An effective communication plan must state the following for each stakeholder over time:

- The message and its objective (e.g., give them confidence that our strategy will be successful),
- The frequency and/or timing of communication,
- The messengers, and
- The modes of communication (e.g., e-mail, speech, meeting, media).

There are four principles for the development and implementation of an effective communication plan:

A. Have a compelling message—the *what.*

B. Cater to different stakeholders—*to whom* and *when.*

C. Use the right messengers and media—*by whom* and *how.*

D. Communicate it consistently, constantly, and confidently.

The first three principles will help you to develop your communication plan; the last principle explains the most effective way to carry it out. The following sections will explore these principles in detail.

A. Have a compelling message. The core of your communication plan is your delivery message. A compelling message will (1) inform people about the *what* of your delivery effort, (2) adapt to changes in the effort over time, and (3) distinguish itself from the noise of regular communications that surround the system and the public.

The what of your message consists of answers to five questions:

- Why are we changing? (Where are we now? Why is that a problem?)
- Where are we going? (What is our aspiration? What do we hope to accomplish?)
- What will change? (How exactly do we plan to get there? What will be done differently?)
- Why choose this course? (Why is this the best way to get there?)
- What does this mean for you? (What will you have to do differently?)

A key part of an effective message is its moral purpose—the answer to the "why are we changing" question above. Not only should your stakeholders understand why you are undertaking a change but they should also feel inspired by the reason you give. Clarifying the moral purpose behind your aspiration will help secure deep and lasting buy-in from supporters, and it will give pause to the harshest of critics.

CASE EXAMPLE

Communicating the moral imperative in Montgomery County, Maryland

In 1999, Jerry Weast became the superintendent of Montgomery County Public Schools (MCPS), with the mandate to dramatically improve performance, especially for students who had been historically underserved. In less than a decade, Weast led MCPS through a transformation resulting in a system committed to breaking links between race and class and academic achievement.

A crucial but controversial component of Weast's strategy was to use resources equitably rather than equally: to invest more in schools that needed more rather than giving everyone the same amount. Communication of the moral purpose allowed Superintendent Jerry Weast to bring stakeholder groups together despite the fact that some stood to lose from the strategy.

> "Through endless outreach visits, town meetings, and presentations, Weast and his team were able to communicate a moral imperative that the community eventually recognized. In a feat that has been profoundly difficult in public education, Weast was able to convince enough people that resources should be distributed for equity because it was the right thing to do." (*Leading for Equity,* 26)

Once you have determined the what of your message, you must ensure that it will be heard. Your delivery message will be fighting for attention with a barrage of communications that is typical in most organizations and bureaucracies. Employees often receive many memos, numerous announcements, and countless reminders every day, not to mention a deluge of information from the media. Even before we consider channels of communication, how can you ensure that the content of your message is compelling enough to be heard through this din?

Make it clear and simple. Clarity—one of the five key concepts of delivery—is best achieved through simple, everyday language and brevity.

CLARITY AND SIMPLICITY IN PMDU PRESENTATIONS: A NOTE FROM THE PMDU LEADER

"Presentations to top officials and above all to Ministers and the [prime minister], especially at stocktakes, need to be really clear and simple. The presentation [on health] this week was a classic example. Paul and Tom produced an excellent presentation—but we went through it again and again stripping it down so that each slide made one point and had no clutter. This takes time, but it's well worth it." (*Instruction to Deliver,* 257)

Use metaphors. If a picture is worth a thousand words, a metaphor comes close, as it allows you to paint a picture using words. Metaphors capture the imagination and give listeners an image that they can hold onto.

For example, Maryland educator Jerry Weast used a metaphor to push for an ambitious aspiration in his school district. "Describing the state standards as baseball-sized, Weast declared that the new MCPS standards needed to be basketball-sized to ensure that students . . . were prepared for college and high-wage work" (*Leading for Equity,* 28).

METAPHORS: WHAT DOES EDUCATION HAVE IN COMMON WITH LEWIS AND CLARK?

"Lewis and Clark turned out to be right and accomplished their mission. There are three striking aspects of magnificent leadership in this story. First, Lewis and Clark used all their experience and expertise in reaching a judgment. Second, they were not swayed by an overwhelming majority who believed otherwise. Third, such was the confidence the party placed in them that they were still willing—cheerfully—to follow them (almost literally) to the ends of the earth. Education reformers sometimes face similar forks of decisive importance. The issue for any given reform, whether at school, district, state or national level, is when we reach those forks, do we have leaders of the stature of Lewis and Clark to choose the true Missouri and take us there?" (Barber, 2005, p. 16)

One word of caution: Do not get trapped in a metaphor. If your metaphor is pushed too far, is no longer relevant, forces a too-narrow interpretation of any aspect of delivery, or fails to respond to real changes in the facts on the ground, it will no longer serve your purposes. It may even start to undermine your ability to reach stakeholders, alienating them instead.

Be honest. As John Kotter and Dan Cohen (Kotter & Cohen, 2002) write, "By and large, people love honesty. It makes them feel safer. They often love honesty even when the message is not necessarily what they would most like to hear" (p. 95). The PMDU was exemplary in this regard. No matter what the results were, they always reported the plain facts. This gave them the reputation of being unbiased and fair, and it ultimately added to their credibility.

CASE EXAMPLE

Telling the truth in Montgomery County, Maryland

Montgomery County Public Schools (MCPS) Superintendent Jerry Weast used honesty and frankness to gain the trust of the school board and to force stakeholders to confront the real issue that MCPS faced.

> "During the [board] retreat, Weast presented the board with extensive data about the school system. He did not try to cover up any of the problems. A significant performance gap existed between white and Asian American students and their Hispanic and African American peers, and the current performance could not be sustained because of the dramatically changing demographics." (*Leading for Equity,* 64)

(Continued)

(Continued)

"In a speech in summer of 2005, he addressed stakeholders frankly at a leadership conference: 'I'm going to get right down into the race issue, and I'm going to talk about Hispanic and African American. And if it hurts, I'm sorry. I apologize respectfully, but I am going to talk about it. You need to talk about it.' Some members of his leadership team recalled that, at first, his forthright discussions . . . were often met with stunned silence by white business leaders and country power brokers unaccustomed to hearing another white man talk in those terms." (*Leading for Equity*, 122)

A **change story** is a useful tool for capturing and packaging the key elements of your message—particularly when a person in a leadership position is delivering that message. A good change story will provide a powerful narrative that gives answers to the five *what* questions articulated above.

Change stories are powerful because, unlike dreary announcements and bulletins, almost all audiences relate to them easily. Moreover, they are far more likely to be passed from person to person, multiplying their effect.

THE POWER OF A STORY

"Storytelling is one of the few human traits that are truly universal across culture and through all of known history. Anthropologists find evidence of folktales everywhere in ancient cultures, written in Sanskrit, Latin, Greek, Chinese, Egyptian and Sumerian. People in societies of all types weave narratives, from oral storytellers in hunter-gatherer tribes to the millions of writers churning out books, television shows and movies. However narrative is defined, people know it when they feel it. Whether fiction or nonfiction, a narrative engages its audience through psychological realism—recognizable emotions and believable interactions among characters . . . the best stories—those retold through generations and translated into other languages—do more than simply present a believable picture. These tales captivate their audience, whose emotions can be inextricably tied to those of the story's characters." (Hsu, 2008, para. 7)

In Exhibit 5B.6, you will find an example of a K–12 education system's change story as it embarked on its delivery effort. The focus of the change story is the new Delivery Unit and what it will do to drive progress.

B. Cater to different stakeholders. As mentioned earlier, for an effective communication plan, you will need to craft a version of your change story that meets each stakeholder's needs. Catering to different stakeholders means (1) framing your message to appeal to each stakeholder, (2) adapting your message to changing stakeholder views over time, and (3) determining the correct mode and frequency of communication for each stakeholder group. You can do this on the basis of the stakeholder map that you developed in the first step of this module.

One way of framing your message to appeal to every stakeholder group is to identify a common belief, and focus on that to bring your audience together. The speech at the bottom of page 199—a timeless classic from history—illustrates this perfectly.

Exhibit 5B.6 Change stories in education: What one SEA told its staff about the need for reform

1. Why are we changing?	• We are creating a world class education system for our students. • To get there, we need to reach ambitious goals. • But, we often work without a realistic understanding of whether we are on track to meet our goals, which means we miss opportunities to do more for students.
2. Where are we going?	• We need to improve our ability to deliver on our goals despite budget cuts. • To do this, we will adopt a delivery-oriented approach. • This means we will stay focused on the results that matter most to students, be ambitious in setting goals, urgent in achieving progress, clear about whether we are on track, and willing to identify and solve problems to make it more likely to reach our goals.
3. What will change?	• We are establishing a small, three-to-five person Delivery Unit that will analyze our delivery trajectories and plans. • As it gets started over the next several months, the Delivery Unit will focus just on our goal of an 85% high school graduation rate by 2016. It will work on other priorities later. • The unit is designed to support you and help us achieve this goal.
4. Why choose this course?	• Effective delivery can turn good policy and programs into excellent execution on strategy. • Delivery Units have helped other government organizations have greater impact by becoming delivery oriented.
5. What does this mean for you?	• You may be asked to develop more rigorous, actionable plans and to more frequently monitor your progress. • You will understand whether we are on track to meet our goals. • The Delivery Unit will provide you with support and challenge to make it more likely that we will reach our goals.

CASE EXAMPLE

Calling for unity: President Lincoln's second inaugural address, March 4, 1865

Given at a time when the nation was approaching the end of the Civil War, President Abraham Lincoln's second inaugural address repeatedly referred to the people's shared interests. The repetition of the words *all, we, both parties,* and *neither,* as well as the reference to praying to the same God, illustrate his efforts to bring unity to a deeply divided nation.

> "On the occasion corresponding to this four years ago, all thoughts were anxiously directed to an impending civil war. All dreaded it—all sought to avert it. While the inaugural address was being delivered from this place, devoted altogether to saving the Union without war, insurgent agents were in the city seeking to destroy it without war—seeking to dissolve the Union, and divide effects, by negotiation. Both parties deprecated war; but one of them would make war rather than let the nation survive; and the other would accept war rather than let it perish. And the war came.

(Continued)

(Continued)

"One eighth of the whole population were colored slaves, not distributed generally over the Union, but localized in the Southern part of it. These slaves constituted a peculiar and powerful interest. All knew that this interest was, somehow, the cause of the war . . . Neither party expected for the war, the magnitude, or the duration, which it has already attained. Neither anticipated that the cause of the conflict might cease with, or even before, the conflict should cease. Each looked for an easier triumph, and a result less fundamental and astounding. Both read the same Bible, and pray to the same God; and each invokes His aid against the other . . . The prayers of both could not be answered; that of neither has been answered fully . . .

"With malice toward none; with charity for all; with firmness in the right, as God gives us to see the right, let us strive on to finish the work we are in; to bind up the nation's wounds; to care for him who shall have borne the battle, and for his widow, and his orphan—to do all which may achieve and cherish a just and lasting peace, among ourselves, and with all nations." (Lincoln, 1865, para. 2–4)

In his first speech to Congress, President Barack Obama (2009b) similarly appealed to the patriotism of the young in exhorting them to stay in school, saying that dropping out is "not just quitting on yourself, you're quitting on your country" (para. 17).

Uniting stakeholders on the basis of shared interests is only one way to gain their support. Another is to cater to their specific interests. Depending on the stakeholder group you are addressing, you will want to emphasize different aspects of the same message. In K–12 education, for example, a general call for improved student achievement might need to be tailored to different audiences. For the business community, you might focus on the more qualified and talented labor pool that will result from improved performance. For parents who are skeptical, you might help them understand that their children's future is at stake and show them the evidence on what is required to have productive earning potential in the 21st century. For unions, you might need to offer an assurance that they will be full collaborators in building the strategy.

You must cater your message not only to the current views of multiple stakeholders but also to their views over time. To be truly effective, you should adapt your message for each stakeholder to the emotional trajectory that you predict as your delivery effort progresses. For this reason, your communication plan may tailor the message not only to different stakeholders but also to different stakeholders at different times. Exhibit 5B.7 shows how a K–12 education system in the United States planned their communication with different objectives in different periods. Communication would start with informing stakeholders, and then would engage them as they understood what delivery was, and finally would sustain their support once they were on board. The team then laid out the different activities via which communication would occur within these themes for two stakeholder

Exhibit 5B.7 A K–12 SEA developed a plan that described general activities based on communication objective and audience

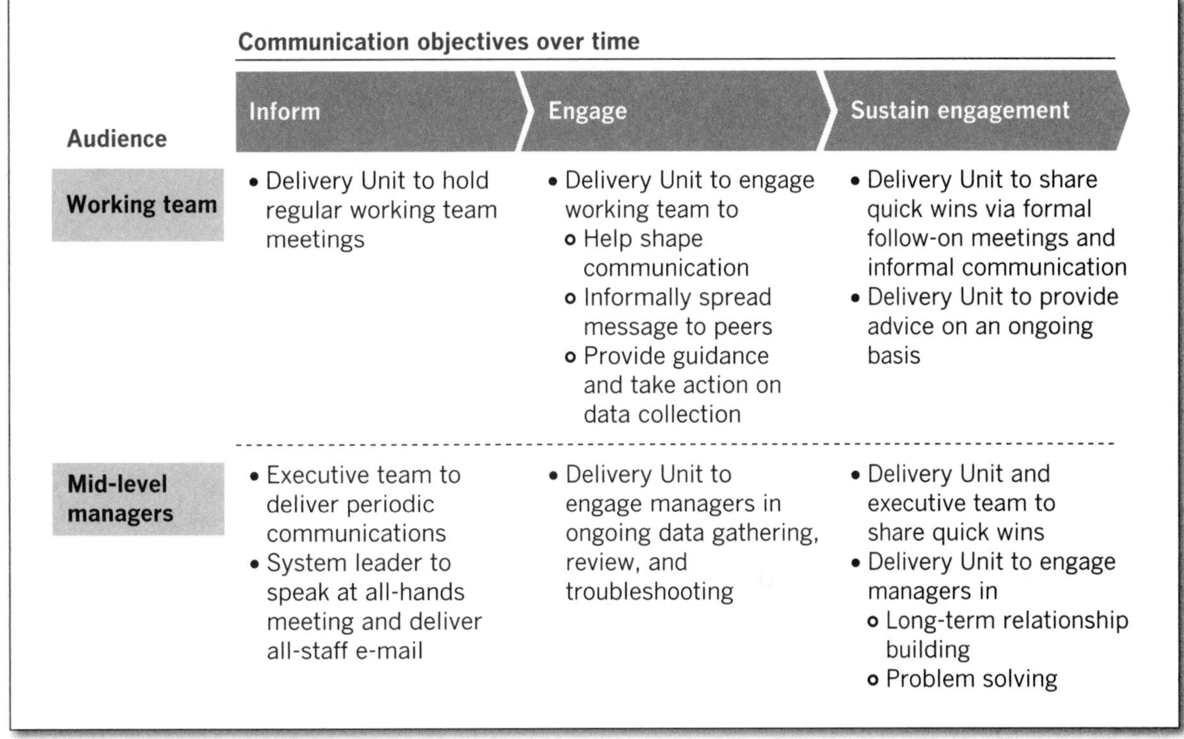

Communication objectives over time

Audience	Inform	Engage	Sustain engagement
Working team	• Delivery Unit to hold regular working team meetings	• Delivery Unit to engage working team to o Help shape communication o Informally spread message to peers o Provide guidance and take action on data collection	• Delivery Unit to share quick wins via formal follow-on meetings and informal communication • Delivery Unit to provide advice on an ongoing basis
Mid-level managers	• Executive team to deliver periodic communications • System leader to speak at all-hands meeting and deliver all-staff e-mail	• Delivery Unit to engage managers in ongoing data gathering, review, and troubleshooting	• Delivery Unit and executive team to share quick wins • Delivery Unit to engage managers in o Long-term relationship building o Problem solving

groups: their higher-level working team and the mid-level managers in the system (their delivery plan owners).

Finally, after determining the types of tailored messages that you will want to deliver to different stakeholders in different periods, you will need to plan the specific, individual communication events that you will need to have. *Communication events* are the building blocks of any communication plan; they are discrete instances in which a message of any kind is delivered, whether through a major speech to thousands or a face-to-face communication with a single stakeholder. Each communication event answers the following questions:

- Who is the audience? (Which stakeholders will you address?)
- What message will you send them?
- When, and with what frequency, will they be addressed?
- Who will deliver the message?
- How? (What media or channels will be used? Will communication be one way, or will the audience get to express its views?)

You should choose your communication events according to the plans you have developed for overall messaging to each stakeholder over time (see above). You may choose to start by deciding on the specific communication events that you want to take place over time, listing each type of communication and the stakeholders it will reach. Alternatively, you can start by planning around each of your stakeholders, identifying the communications necessary for each of them over time.

The last two questions for any communication event are the messenger and the specific medium of communication, which are the subject of the next section.

C. Use the right messengers and media. As you are designing the communication events in your communication plan, you need to ensure that the right messenger is assigned to each event to maximize impact on the target audiences. Each messenger, in turn, needs to communicate using a medium that makes sense for both messenger and audience: a speech, a phone call, a television appearance, a memo, a workshop, and so on. These choices should be made according to criteria that focus on the stakeholders in the audience: Who has the most credibility with them? How are they used to receiving messages? What medium of communication will resonate with them?

There are several main messengers that you can choose for each communication event: the system leader, yourself as delivery leader, guiding coalition members, and other major stakeholders (particularly the innovators you identified in Step 1). Some external third parties—those that have widespread credibility, such as community leaders—will be particularly influential if your audience is the public as a whole (and if you can get them to tell the story).

In many cases, the system leader or the delivery leader will be the key messengers. The main difference between the communications from these two sources is that the system leader will engage in both internal (to the system) and external (to the public) communications while you as delivery leader would engage mostly in internal communication with system actors.

The most publicly visible messenger is the system leader. Communications from the system leader are crucial because they reinforce the most important aspects of the original delivery message: the urgency of achieving the moral purpose and the confidence that you will deliver it. It is important for all audiences to hear from the system leader: The public will be assured of progress, the system will develop a sense of urgency and ownership, and the Delivery Unit will receive the backing it needs to push forward.

In Exhibit 5B.8, you will find several examples from the PMDU of how a system leader plays a pivotal role as messenger. In this case, the prime minister's public support of the PMDU and the delivery agenda as a whole went a long way toward ensuring its success.

As delivery leader, your communications are also very important. For many system actors, you will be the most frequent point of contact in matters related to the delivery effort.

While routines will be the most common and regular medium for your communication about the progress of the delivery effort, there are many other means by which your Delivery Unit might communicate where necessary. Exhibit 5B.9 shows a sampling of the different tools the PMDU used in its communication. Again, much of the communication is either about the delivery effort's progress or its importance.

Exhibit 5B.8 PMDU example: Communications from the system leader

System leader action	PMDU example
Visibly commits at founding of delivery	• **The prime minister sponsored the Delivery Unit and gave it visible symbolic importance:** When the Delivery Unit was first founded, the opening seminar "took place in the magnificent Pillared Room upstairs in No. 10." • **The prime minister made symbolic appearances:** Blair opened the seminar and expressed his commitment to its agenda, so that "the Delivery Unit had been anointed by the prime minister in the presence of its key stakeholders."
Continues to express commitment throughout	• **Blair's speeches reinforced commitment even after results start to show:** "There had been an awayday at Chequers, at which Blair reaffirmed his determination to drive through not just delivery of results, but serious structural reforms in health, schools and universities. There had been a sense that the DU had made a good start, but the real work of delivery had barely begun."
Appears to be "sharing the burden" with delivery team	• **Blair appeared shoulder to shoulder with the Delivery Unit:** When the PMDU leader presented the unit's progress at the annual press conference, "the crucial message was conveyed unscathed ... Blair himself was heavily involved in securing delivery and not even the momentous events on the international stage had deflected him."
Reassures in times of uncertainty	• **Blair wrote reassuring notes:** At a time of uncertainty, the Delivery Unit leader also persuaded "Blair himself to write notes asserting how important the Delivery Unit would continue to be."

SOURCE: From *Instruction to Deliver*, by M. Barber, 2008, London: Methuen Publishing Ltd. Copyright by Michael Barber.

Exhibit 5B.9 Toolkit for Delivery Unit communication

Tool	PMDU example
Speeches/ presentations	• **Stocktake presentations:** Highlighting both positive and negative performance, the PMDU fought to keep these presentations as crisp and effective as possible.
Conferences	• **Whitehall delivery conference:** This conference was a capacity-building mechanism, but it was also an important communication vehicle.
Meetings with key people	• **Regular meetings with the Cabinet:** The PMDU would meet with key stakeholders before routine check-ins to ensure they understood the main items that would be presented and to give them time to present relevant feedback during the actual meeting.
Notes/letters/ e-mails	• **Unusual notes from the PMDU leader:** "One way I sought from time to time to promote the Delivery Unit brand was to write the kind of letters around Whitehall that would be quite out of the ordinary."
Q&A/Murder boards	• **In-house rehearsal:** In preparation for a Q&A session with a parliamentary committee, the PMDU would arrange for internal debates with its staff to make sure it had solidified the message.

SOURCE: From *Instruction to Deliver*, by M. Barber, 2008, London: Methuen Publishing Ltd. Copyright by Michael Barber.

Members of your guiding coalition (see Module 1D) are also important messengers. As part of the guiding coalition, they should already have a deep understanding of your main message. For the most part, guiding coalition members do not communicate formally about the delivery effort, but their voices matter because of the number of informal opportunities that they will have to influence many groups.

Stakeholders also do not communicate formally about the delivery effort, but they are still critical people that will be communicating your message to narrower and more targeted audiences. With this group, your biggest challenge will be to ensure consistency in these informal communications. This requires that you regularly brief key stakeholders so that your talking points and message come easily to mind whenever a stakeholder is asked to comment on your delivery effort. If well informed, the innovators you identified above can be especially helpful.

One other note on guiding coalition members and stakeholders: Some of them, particularly delivery plan owners, will occasionally need to write more detailed communication plans for the parts of your delivery effort that they oversee. In cases like these, your Delivery Unit should support them to develop their own communication plans using the same steps outlined above.

At this point, you have determined all the major components to your plan: For each stakeholder, you have determined an objective, a message, its frequency and timing, its messenger, and its format. All these components can change over time, but they do not have to; variation by time depends on the level of detail you want to achieve and the variability of stakeholder views over time. Exhibit 5B.10 gives an example of a K–12 communications plan that incorporates all these components. Notice that for this particular plan, the objective for each stakeholder does not vary over time, but the specific messages, frequency, mode, and messenger do.

Whatever level of detail you use, you will need to evaluate your final plan to ensure that each stakeholder is receiving the right communication at the right times, such that the emotional trajectory you have set for that stakeholder is feasible. You will also want to make sure that your plan is aligned with your plans for capacity building (see Module 5A), such that people who need to do something differently will receive that message only when they are also receiving the support that they need.

COMMUNICATION AND CAPACITY BUILDING

Communication alone is not sufficient to garner strong support. People will believe they can achieve a goal when they know for a fact that they have the skills to do so. This requires capacity building: development of the structures, resources, competencies, and motivation necessary to accomplish the delivery tasks at hand. Your communication plan must therefore be coordinated with your capacity-building plan so that people who need to do something differently will receive a call to change only when the system is also providing them with the support that they need to make it. For more detail on capacity building, see Module 5A.

Exhibit 5B.10 Communications plan

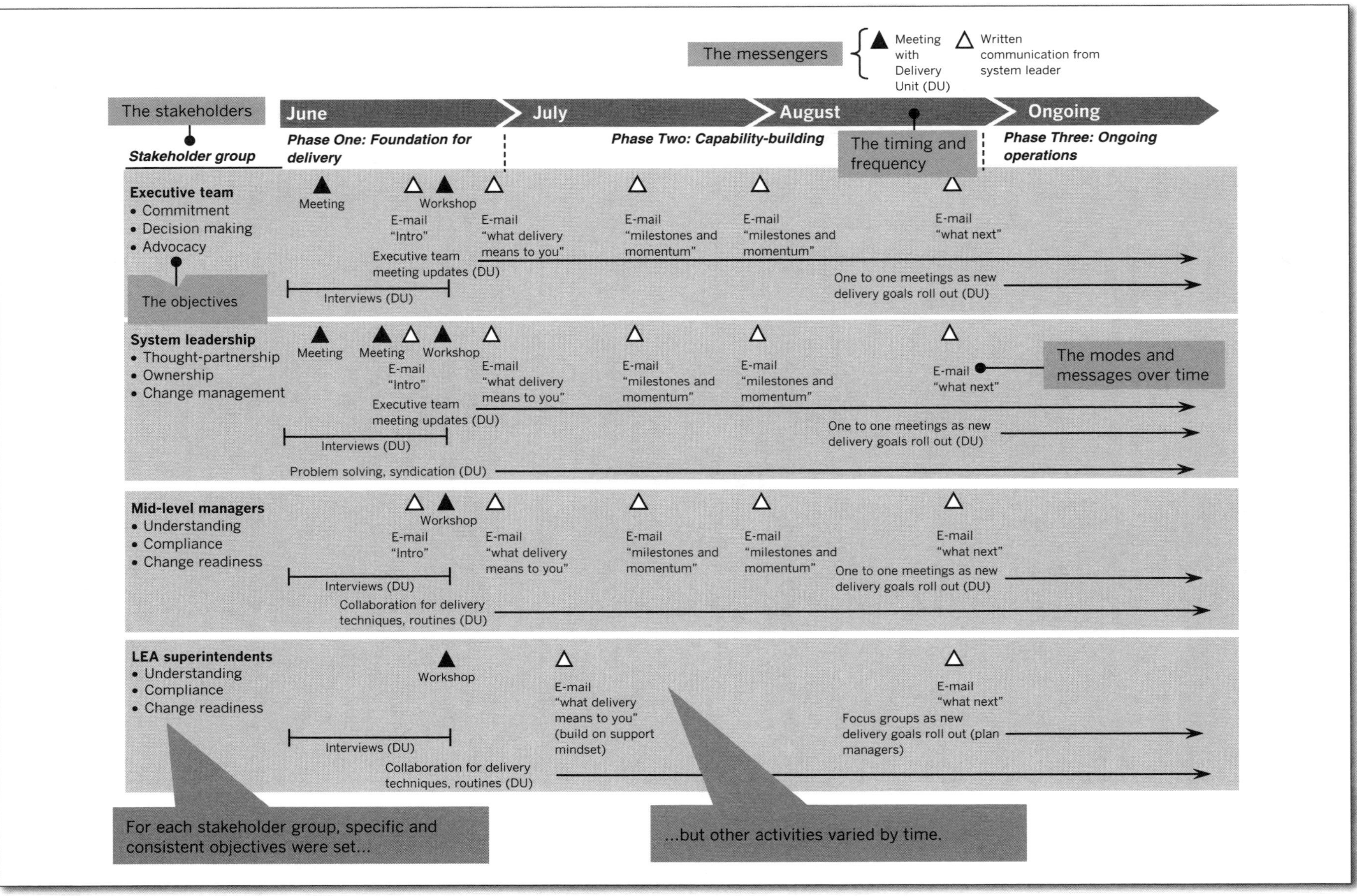

CASE EXAMPLE

Communication as a critical success factor: Increasing efficiency and effectiveness in the University System of Maryland

Beginning in 2002, the University System of Maryland (USM) faced a number of cost pressures, including accommodating 5,500 additional full-time-equivalent students, losing 500 filled positions in its state-supported budget, absorbing $75 million in increased costs annually, and, most significantly, losing 12.5% of its state funding. In response, USM created the Effectiveness and Efficiency (E&E) Initiative, which would eventually bring together senior leadership at different USM universities and the Board of Regents. Beginning in 2003, the E&E Working Group created, authorized, tracked, and managed a range of interventions to improve efficiency and reduce costs.

With such a sensitive set of issues, communication and stakeholder management would be just as critically important as the design of the interventions themselves. Brit Kirwan, USM's chancellor, describes the challenge:

> "We decided that we had to tackle the cynicism and skepticism that higher education could really manage any sort of cost-cutting effort—we were always seen as 'fat and happy.' The overall effort was one part education and one part culture. We needed to educate key stakeholders on what it was we were trying to accomplish with E&E, and begin attacking those mindsets and behaviors that would prevent success."

To address this challenge, the chancellor and Working Group undertook a comprehensive communications effort as they built and implemented their strategy:

- The first thing that the group did was to build internal support, starting with its own members.

> "The Board had appointed the initial E&E work group with a very strong group of independent-minded members who brought a lot of ideas, but they also highly respected the academic culture . . . They were willing to let ideas be generated and massaged—there was a back and forth, and give and take with the system leadership to develop an agenda that was bold, innovative, and built on the real expectation for results and a means of measuring progress. This committee built the initial ideas for the E&E effort."

- The group then widened the circle of leadership to include a crucial stakeholder group: university presidents. The first discussion took place at a group retreat with the chancellor and presidents.

> "I made clear to them that this had to get done, and this wasn't business as usual . . . The workgroup also communicated quite clearly to the presidents that we wanted to protect the quality of the institutions, and this message resonated with the presidents . . . There was a general consensus coming out of the retreat that this was an 'all hands on deck' effort, and everyone had a role to play and could make an impact."

- After the retreat, the working group built the policies and practices that would allow each initiative to be successful. As they did this, more stakeholders needed to be brought in to learn about the work and the results it was achieving.

"All of this had to be communicated to the Board and various communities . . . We had to sell these policies and get them endorsed . . . It was the rigor with which we went about doing this that made our communication effort successful, and, ultimately, got the buy-in we needed . . . I made regular reports to the Board to let them know where we were in the E&E process. The Board Chair and I also sent out regular messages to all faculty, staff, students, etc. about where we were. Through these various communications, people could see that things were actually happening and progress was being made."

- The working group also engaged the frontline.

"The primary way we did this was to engage them in Board meetings. This went over well—people recognized that we were able to generate more credibility with the state by being inclusive. If there was one thing that really stood out that demonstrated the effectiveness of our communication efforts, it was the consistency of the message and how widely understood it was. For a 25,000-person staff, there was a remarkable understanding of the value and importance of this agenda."

- Finally, the working group and presidents initiated a communication campaign to educate the public at large.

"I went on TV to talk about it. I spoke regularly with editorial boards. We wrote endlessly for national publications. I've recently started a national speaker's circuit to communicate our successes as well. It was an aggressive campaign to give the larger public a sense of what we had done."

The results came in multiple forms. First, large savings were realized, as Exhibit 5B.11 shows.

Second, USM gained a reputation as an efficient system—something that helped during budget negotiations.

"Our efforts to educate and shift mindsets and behaviors really paid off. E&E resonated with everyone beyond my wildest expectations. It gave us credibility with the state government. Now, there is a sense of trust and a pact between us that I don't think exists in most states. This partnership has transcended parties and two governors . . . In an unprecedented move and show of support, the state, despite the economic downturn, invested significantly in higher education. Over the past four years, there has been a 32% cumulative increase in state support—without raising undergrad tuition!"

The USM's story demonstrates the value of taking a communications-focused view throughout a delivery effort—from planning to implementation to monitoring and reporting performance.

(Continued)

(Continued)

Exhibit 5B.11 Total savings and new revenue realized by year (in millions of dollars)

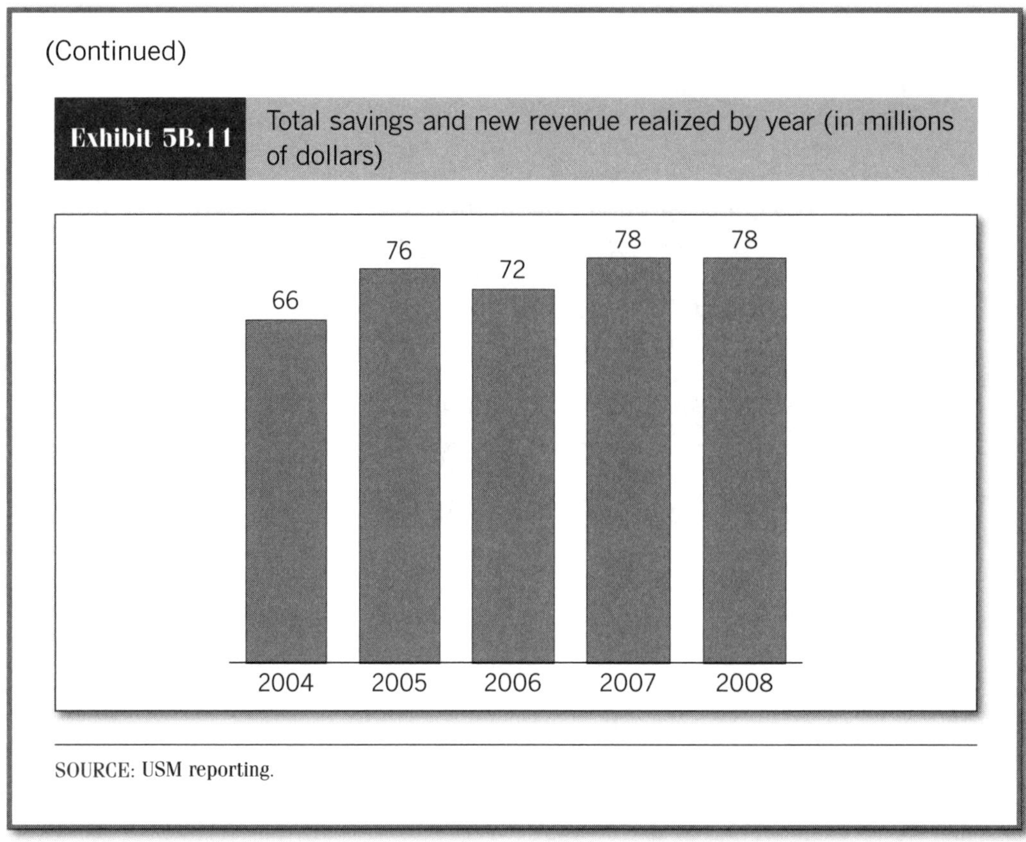

SOURCE: USM reporting.

D. Communicate constantly, consistently, and confidently. Once you have a communication plan, you can begin implementing it. Whatever the specifics of your plans for reaching different audiences, three principles apply to all communication events in your plan:

- You should communicate constantly, so the audience remembers the message;
- You should communicate consistently, so the message is reinforced by your other communications and behavior; and
- You should communicate confidently, so your audience will believe your message.

Communication is verbal, nonverbal, formal, and informal, and it happens in every interaction you have with any stakeholder—not just through words but actions as well. Therefore, you must ensure that your message remains constant and consistent through all of these interactions (for more on the importance of interactions, please see Module 5C).

"To convince the assembled company that the Delivery Unit really would do anything to help them deliver, I walked across two metres of broken glass in bare feet. A floor-level microphone conveyed audibly the crunching and splitting of the shards under my feet. I reached the far end without a single cut, received a sustained and rapturous round of applause and will no doubt be remembered in Whitehall for this moment of madness long after Deliverology is forgotten." (*Instruction to Deliver,* 202)

CASE EXAMPLE

Messaging in Montgomery County, Maryland

At the Montgomery County Public Schools (MCPS), consistency of message was extremely important. To gain the support of parents for a controversial strategy that entailed investing more resources in lower performing schools, Superintendent Jerry Weast had to tailor the message carefully and ensure its consistency, as it could easily be taken out of context and be made to sound unfair.

> "Critical to the success of MCPS' new strategy was the support of parents in the Green Zone [the schools that would receive fewer resources under the strategy]. The message that resources were being targeted in Red Zone schools had the potential to be misinterpreted and could sabotage MCPS's entire strategy. Weast and his team knew it was important not to become embroiled in a fight with parents that nobody would win. They had to stay above the fray and clearly communicate that the strategy made sense for everybody because all students would benefit. As Weast said, 'Staying on message was critical. And because there was a well-crafted communications plan, people were able to reiterate the message, and it wasn't just something that you read or saw. The message had been internalized so well that we had leaders in the community coming forward to support these efforts.'" (*Leading for Equity,* 66)

Confidence is also extremely important in delivering the message because for people to believe they should support a change in order to reach an aspiration, they must believe that the aspiration is truly achievable. At a minimum, that means that your audience must believe that you believe your own message!

This is especially important during the beginning of a delivery effort, when credibility may not yet be established. Public perceptions may plateau or even falter as the system adjusts to the new processes put in place through delivery. It is even more important at moments of crisis. Through these challenges, the system and delivery leaders should continue to reiterate and reassure all stakeholders that the aspiration will be achieved. Another timeless classic can illustrate the point.

CASE EXAMPLE

"We Shall Fight on the Beaches": Address to Parliament by Winston Churchill, June 4, 1940

Winston Churchill's most famous speech to Parliament during World War II, given in 1940 when the British were struggling against the threat of the Nazis, is a great example of the kind of confidence a system leader must project.

> "I have, myself, full confidence that if all do their duty, if nothing is neglected, and if the best arrangements are made, as they are being made, we shall prove ourselves once again able to defend our Island home, to ride out the storm of war, and to outlive the menace of tyranny,

(Continued)

(Continued)

if necessary for years, if necessary alone. At any rate, that is what we are going to try to do. That is the resolve of His Majesty's Government—every man of them. That is the will of Parliament and the nation . . . Even though large tracts of Europe and many old and famous States have fallen or may fall into the grip of the Gestapo and all the odious apparatus of Nazi rule, we shall not flag or fail. We shall go on to the end, we shall fight in France, we shall fight on the seas and oceans, we shall fight with growing confidence and growing strength in the air, we shall defend our Island, whatever the cost may be, we shall fight on the beaches, we shall fight on the landing grounds, we shall fight in the fields and in the streets, we shall fight in the hills; we shall never surrender, and even if, which I do not for a moment believe, this Island or a large part of it were subjugated and starving, then our Empire beyond the seas, armed and guarded by the British Fleet, would carry on the struggle, until, in God's good time, the New World, with all its power and might, steps forth to the rescue and the liberation of the old." (para. 22)

By following these principles, you will be able to create an effective communication plan. To ensure that it remains effective throughout the delivery effort, you should monitor your progress against this plan (just as you would for any delivery plan). As you might expect, the best way for a Delivery Unit to do this is through a routine in which you regularly revisit the status of each stakeholder and adjust the plan as issues arise. This brings us to our final step.

Step 3: Monitor the communication plan

How do you monitor the effectiveness of a communication plan? Unlike the targets and trajectories of Chapter 3, emotional trajectories can be more difficult to track. However, there are qualitative indicators that you can easily and reliably observe in order to determine whether stakeholders' views are changing. In *The Heart of Change Field Guide,* author Dan Cohen (2005) provides this list of indicators that will help you to know when stakeholders have come to support delivery:

- Stakeholders can concisely repeat the message in their own words
- Stakeholders can articulate what the effort means for their own unit or group
- There are discussions about the changes being made in routine management meetings, and in other formal and informal gatherings
- Discussions of the changes being made are found in everyday memos, presentations, and communications to staff and students
- People ask leaders an increasing number of questions about the delivery effort
- The "delivery language" becomes part of the language used throughout the organization

In PMDU, they used to say, "We'll know when people tell us, first, that it was easy and, second, that it was their idea."

These indicators will allow you to gauge whether your communication plan is working—and if it is not, to adjust course as necessary. This is why two-way communication is crucial. As much as you communicate about delivery, you also need to listen to everyone involved as they communicate about what is working, what is not working, and how delivery is affecting daily life. As the below case example demonstrates, this can have an impact not only on your communication plan but also on your strategy as a whole.

CASE EXAMPLE

From monologue to dialogue: Parent engagement in Montgomery County, Maryland

In Montgomery County Public Schools (MCPS, 2009), Superintendent Jerry Weast used two-way communication to inform the development of *Our Call to Action,* his system's reform strategy.

> "During the fall of 2000, Weast and his team conducted sixteen forums throughout the county, including four for multicultural communities, requiring interpreting services in Spanish, Chinese, Korean, Japanese, and Vietnamese. Parents were invited to be part of smaller working groups to discuss all aspects of school reform, including curriculum changes and budgeting decisions. Then Weast and his team . . . listened carefully and incorporated many of the suggestions into the strategy. Parents could see the result of their interaction with the district in the final version of *Our Call to Action.*" (*Leading for Equity,* 65)

As with delivery plans, not every communication plan is correct at the outset, but what is important is that you monitor communication plans and correct them if necessary. The following case example demonstrates how vital this flexibility can be.

CASE EXAMPLE

Correcting for undercommunication in U.K. education

In Tony Blair's first term, the soon to be PMDU leader drove a broadly successful reform of U.K. education, increasing levels of literacy and numeracy and significantly reducing school failure. However, this reform was not without its mistakes. Below, the PMDU leader explains how he discovered a flaw in his communication strategy and corrected it.

> "In that first bold, broadly successful phase of education reform between 1997 and 1999, in relation to the teaching profession, we made one of the classic errors listed by Harvard management guru John Kotter . . . namely 'undercommunicating the vision by a factor of 10 (or 100 or even 1000).' To be sure, we wrote what was widely recognized to be an ambitious White Paper and promoted it. We consulted widely in its formation too. We sent out thousands of pages of regulations and guidance on everything from the far-flung corners of school governance (unimportant) to the sequence of teaching phonics (vital).

(Continued)

(Continued)

In what was widely seen, remarkably, as an innovation, ministers, officials and I visited schools all the time. Less innovatively, ministers delivered speeches all the time. I did many myself. We couldn't be faulted for effort.

"Alongside these efforts to communicate directly with the school workforce, we also ran a largely successful media strategy aimed, of course, at parents and taxpayers rather than teachers. The message here was that performance in the education system wasn't good enough, failure would be tackled vigorously, poor schools would be closed . . . Parents and taxpayers heard and generally warmed to the message. Our error was a simple and obvious one—teachers read the *Daily Mail* or *The Guardian* and heard our message to parents loud and clear; they (understandably) didn't read the pages of guidance and White Papers we sent them, so they hardly understood our strategy. The result? They were confused and sometimes offended. It was hardly surprising, then, that when I visited schools the most common response was, 'You might think there's a strategy, Michael; we just think there's one damn thing after another . . . oh, and by the way, we don't like bureaucracy and league tables.'

"We understood this challenge soon enough and began to respond. We dramatically cut the amount of paper going into schools, but obviously this did not convey the vision in the way Kotter says you must. We realized that in order to do this we needed intermediaries. The government couldn't communicate directly with more than 400,000 teachers, so we focused on [principals]. [Elementary school principals] generally liked the literacy and numeracy events they attended; we introduced a spectacular annual conference from 1998 onwards, aimed at all the newly appointed [principals] in the country . . . We explained the vision and the strategy and debated them vigorously with the very engaged participants. Using interactive technology we asked them to tell us what the worst aspects of our approach were (teacher recruitment and bureaucracy, incidentally) and where we might go next with the strategy. These events were a great step forward, valued greatly by those who attended." (*Instruction to Deliver*, 369–370)

Conclusion

By now, you have learned

- How to identify and map the stakeholders who will be the audiences of your communication effort;
- The principles for designing effective communication plans;
- Basic rules for all communications: constancy, consistency, and confidence; and
- How to monitor progress against your communication plan.

Communication is challenging and it is important. Yet, it is often the part of the delivery effort that falls by the wayside, getting far less attention than it deserves. However, with an upfront investment in planning, you can send the right messages—about your Unit and your effort—to the people who need to hear them. A well-thought-out communication plan can not only clear the path of staunch dissenters but can also forge a path to your strongest supporters. Perhaps most importantly, it can bring more and more people into the fold, contributing to continuous widening of your delivery effort's circles of leadership.

5C. UNLEASH THE "ALCHEMY OF RELATIONSHIPS"

"The central Government . . . must entrust the execution of its will to agents, over whom it frequently has no control, and whom it cannot perpetually direct."

—Alexis de Tocqueville, *Democracy in America*

"The spirit of the Delivery Unit . . . was 'sharing [a] sense of purpose and creating the right relationships with departments. With the right relationships we could achieve almost anything (and often did), without it we could achieve nothing.'"

—PMDU staff member Simon Rea (*Instruction to Deliver,* 139)

Even if your capacity building and communication are superb, your delivery effort will struggle against powerful inertial forces. People will behave as people do, struggling to balance their interests against the interests of others, the known against the unknown, and hard work against what is easier. Moreover, bureaucracies will function as bureaucracies often do, piling too many tasks on individuals (especially the most capable) and sending conflicting mandates. To be successful, you will need a motivational force to ensure that people are focusing on the priorities of your delivery effort despite all of the factors that you cannot control.

This motivational force is the "alchemy of relationships"—specifically, the individual relationships developed and maintained by every staff member of your Delivery Unit. These relationships include every stakeholder with whom you and your staff interact, from the system leader and her staff to delivery plan owners to mid-level managers to the frontline.

More than anything else, the individual interactions of these stakeholders with your Delivery Unit will leave a powerful impression—for better or worse—about your work. Put another way, the relationships arising from these

CO-OPTING YOUR RIVALS

In American politics, there are several examples of relationship building with rivals as well as allies. President Abraham Lincoln famously achieved ambitious political goals by bringing key political rivals onto his "side," and including them in his cabinet. Most notably, Lincoln made his main rival, William Seward, secretary of state. President Barack Obama has chosen to follow a similar strategy of co-opting his Democratic rivals. First, he selected Senator Joe Biden as his running mate on his presidential ticket, and then, once elected, he appointed Senator Hillary Rodham Clinton, who had been his main rival for the nomination, secretary of state. Obama believed that this was the best way to consolidate his position and his party after a contentious primary campaign.

interactions will be a critical determinant of your ability to widen the circles of leadership of your delivery effort. For this reason, your Unit's success will stand or fall on the strength of these relationships.

This module describes the principles and techniques that all Delivery Unit staff members should use to build their relationships. They are applicable in every interaction detailed in this field guide, whether it is a workshop to design and build a trajectory, an interview in a delivery capacity review, a formal training session, or a stocktake with the system leader.

ROLES OF SYSTEM LEADER AND DELIVERY LEADER

Your role as delivery leader will be to build solid relationships with the stakeholders you interact with (likely, the system leader, his staff, and other senior leaders) and to ensure that your staff have the capability to do the same with their relationships. The role of any Delivery Unit staff member will likewise be to identify, cultivate, and maintain the relationships that will be necessary for the success of their work. The system leader can give you a boost in this regard by demonstrating his support and, where necessary, introducing you to those with whom you will be working.

Principles for unleashing the alchemy of relationships

The below principles describe the most important ways that you can build good relationships, escalating from your least contentious interactions (keeping people in the loop) to the most contentious (real and difficult conflict between your Delivery Unit and a stakeholder).

Principle 1: Keep people in touch and informed
Principle 2: Live out your values in every relationship
Principle 3: Identify the "win-win" in every relationship
Principle 4: Manage conflict actively

Principle 1: Keep people in touch and informed

As you might expect, the first thing that you need in order to build a relationship is an interaction or set of interactions. For many stakeholders, interactions will be a matter of course: Day-to-day interactions will happen by default, and your job will be to shape those interactions so that they improve the relationship and build the brand.

For other stakeholders, however, you will need to go out of your way to build relationships. For senior leaders, for example, relationship building can be a challenge because their time is limited and in demand.

Some stakeholders will not naturally be a part of your Unit's day-to-day orbit. Mid-level managers, frontline staff, and users of your system's services generally fall into this category. It may not be necessary to build relationships with all of these stakeholders, but depending on the nature of your delivery effort, some will be crucial.

It is very important to make conscious and consistent efforts to meet with the most relevant stakeholders and keep them informed. Routines are a great way of keeping many leaders in the loop.

Where necessary, you can also rely on regular update meetings, group events (such as retreats), or other creative means as a supplement or substitute for these routines.

FIGHTING FOR A LEADER'S TIME

"Around a Prime Minister, or indeed anyone really powerful, there is a vortex, and the nearer you get to the center of the vortex, the less space and time there is. The moment you step away, the space is filled, so no one notices you've gone . . . This is not a bad thing. It's how it has to be. In short, you have to develop a strategy for being noticed or you will get marginalized. There is nothing in between." (*Instruction to Deliver,* 55)

CASE EXAMPLE

Creating the necessary interactions

When a crucial stakeholder is not involved in one or more of the routines you have designed, you may need to think creatively about ways to engage with them. In the PMDU, the delivery leader recognized and addressed this need with Richard Wilson, the head of Britain's civil service:

> "Once in post, I had regular meetings with Richard. I made as few demands as possible on him, I shared with him some inside information from No. 10 which oiled the wheels, and I found his support, encouragement and goodwill genuinely helpful . . . I made a point of asking for his advice and listening carefully to it . . . Once we began to roll, the relationship was exactly as I wanted it—one of 'benign neglect' most of the time, but actively supportive where I needed it to be. In return I was more than happy for him to take credit for our success." (*Instruction to Deliver,* 62)

Sometimes, you will confront the challenge of engaging a stakeholder who does not have time. Such was the case for the PMDU and the busy staff of the prime minister. To solve this problem, the PMDU leader took advantage of his proximity to the place where they worked—No. 10 Downing Street—and perfected another technique whose name is drawn from the private sector: the "elevator pitch."

> "Though my staff were on the other side of Whitehall in those early days, I always spent some time each day in my little No. 10 office. Throughout my time as head of the Delivery Unit, I spent much of my day tramping around Whitehall and, even if it was sometimes a slightly longer way round, I used to pass through No. 10 on the off-chance of running into one of these characters. And since they were inevitably in a hurry, I would try to have one piece of positive news about Delivery Unit impact on the tip of my tongue so I could say it in a moment and then we'd both go about our business." (*Instruction to Deliver,* 53)

(Continued)

(Continued)

At other times, a stakeholder group will be crucial to the success of your reform effort but too numerous or dispersed for one-on-one relationship building. Montgomery County Public Schools Superintendent Jerry Weast faced this challenge with parents in his school district. He kept them informed by providing transparency on both the types of reforms he was instituting and their desired outcomes:

> "A district wide Parent Advisory Council was created, and . . . [the team] created television programs and videos for those parents who were not literate in their own language. Making information available—district strategy, standards, school success measures, student achievement across the board, and the achievement of their own children in particular—put parents in the driver's seat . . . Weast built on parents' engagement by inviting them to be a part of interventions and the implementation plans related to the strategy. This gave . . . Weast and his team the support they needed to implement their controversial strategy." (*Leading for Equity,* 66)

Principle 2: Live out your values in every relationship

Once you have a series of interactions on which to build relationships, what should those interactions look like? Fundamentally, the alchemy of relationships is the art of developing a positive rapport with stakeholders such that achieving your system's aspiration becomes more achievable. This applies both to those relationships you are actively striving to build (e.g., with your system leader) and to those relationships that are incidental to the effort (e.g., the receptionist at the department with which you work).

In the field of criminal justice, the "broken windows theory" states that systematic prevention of small crimes (e.g., acts of petty vandalism) can ultimately deter more serious crimes. Whatever one might feel about the plausibility of this theory, a similar concept does hold true in relationship building: A series of small positive interactions—a pleasant greeting, a patient encounter, a meeting that finishes early and does not inconvenience other staff—can have a large impact on the quality of relationships.

THE POWER OF RELATIONSHIPS

"Power is not a zero sum . . . Enhancing the crucial relationships at both political and official level . . . would generate additional power making it possible to enhance the quality, speed and impact with which reform is implemented. The alchemy of good relationships can, as the Delivery Unit showed, turn base metal into gold." (*Instruction to Deliver,* 342)

The collective impact of these interactions is similar to the concept referred to in the private sector as a *brand.* Though the term was adapted mainly to describe commercial efforts, the *concept* of a brand is a useful way to describe what you are trying to build. A brand is a consistent idea or experience associated with an entity—in this case, your Delivery Unit. A positive brand will help people to understand your Delivery Unit, to feel positive about your work, and to want to cooperate with you.

Creating a positive brand for your Delivery Unit will be important for your delivery effort, because you will need to overcome the preconceived notions that many people have about reform efforts in large public bureaucracies—essentially, that there will be a great deal of talk, very little impact, and a burdensome process. Changing this mindset will not be easy; but if you begin to shift the way that system actors think about the potential for impact, you will begin to see tremendous results.

Strictly speaking, your Unit will have a brand whether you like it or not; it will be a product of the relationships that you and your Unit build with others. But, if you are not deliberate about defining a brand and ensuring that it is reflected in each of these relationships, you run the risk of creating a negative brand that will harm your delivery effort.

Therefore, it is important to decide up front what you want your brand to be. What thoughts, feelings, and impressions do you want people to take away after every interaction with your Unit?

The following case example shows how the PMDU determined its brand early on and the results that followed. You may find a similar thought process useful for your Delivery Unit.

CASE EXAMPLE

Building the PMDU brand

In order to paint a picture of the types of relationships they sought to build, the PMDU staff created a "contract" that they shared with the civil servants who headed each of the departments that they worked with (Exhibit 5C.1).

Exhibit 5C.1 Guiding principles that defined PMDU's "brand"

Our working approach seeks to avoid	Our working approach emphasizes
• Micromanagement • Generating bureaucracy or unnecessary work • Getting in the way • Policy wheezes • Being driven by headlines • Short-termism • Opinion without evidence • Changing the goalposts	• Keeping the PM well informed about his key priorities • Consistent pursuit of those priorities • Data and evidence • Plain speaking • Early identification of problems • Imaginative problem solving • Application of best practice • Recognizing differences as well as similarities between departments • Urgency • Building capacity • Leaving responsibility and credit where they belong • The expectation of success

SOURCE: From *Instruction to Deliver,* p. 64, by M. Barber, 2008, London: Methuen Publishing Ltd. Copyright by Michael Barber.

(Continued)

(Continued)

The PMDU made a commitment to honor this contract in all of its activities and interactions with departments. Equally important, it made a commitment to stop any activity that was out of line with the contract. The PMDU thus created a name for itself that was in line with the image that they wanted to project.

> "[Departments] said they valued the Delivery Unit because it had clear priorities and would not be deflected from them, had excellent people, employed simple, clear, practical methodologies, worked on the basis of rigorous analysis and hard evidence, adopted a partnership approach to working, assisted in sharing best practice across departments, and provided a constant, sharp external challenge which helped them to do their jobs." (*Instruction to Deliver,* 217)

Moreover, when enough people shared this perception, it had a self-multiplying effect, something that the PMDU staff referred to as **resonance.**

> "The basic idea is that if you exceed expectations often enough and if you sometimes surprise and delight people, they start to mention it to each other, word gets back to the Prime Minister and you create a climate of success. As I put it in the leaving note to my staff: 'I've often conceptualized my job as managing the frontiers—making sure that in No. 10, the Treasury, the Cabinet Office and generally among the political classes we are trusted so that everyone in the Unit can get on with their job. As trust in and respect for the brand increases, each member of staff is quite literally able to add more value because departments are more receptive. . . . [After I have left, you] will need to invest in the brand all the time . . . Being associated with "can-do," "success" and "quality" will all be crucial.' Creating the climate provides the opportunity for staff to do their job well, and if they exploit this opportunity, the climate improves further . . . and so on. A harmonious progression—resonance." (*Instruction to Deliver,* 65)

Simply living by the values you espouse in your brand will go a long way toward building the right relationships. How well does the behavior of your staff reflect the elements of your Unit's brand? For each staff member, what do their day-to-day interactions with stakeholders look like? Are they professional and well prepared for meetings? Do they waste stakeholders' time or are they careful with it? The values implicit in your brand can be lived out in multiple ways that, when added together, make a significant impression.

The following case example demonstrates how the PMDU lived out the values in its brand.

CASE EXAMPLE

Living out values in the PMDU

PMDU staff found multiple ways to live out their values in the context of their day-to-day interactions. Here are a few lessons learned and examples of each.

First, *remember that the little things make the big things count.* Everything about the PMDU staff's interactions with stakeholders was deliberate, right down to scheduling:

> "Busy people hate meetings that overrun and love meetings that finish early, so I urged Delivery Unit staff to book, say, forty-five minutes but finish in thirty. In my one-to-one meetings with the [prime minister] I was usually allocated 30 minutes but I'd finish my business in twenty and only stay if he wanted to extend the conversation . . . Add up small things like this and you create a culture of action-orientation, people in a hurry to get things done, a Delivery Unit that contributes to delivery." (*Instruction to Deliver,* 65)

Second, *wield power with responsibility and humility.* As a Delivery Unit, you will often represent your system leader to other stakeholders—and this will often help you to get the access that you need. However, your Delivery Unit will need to make a crucial choice here: Will you spend this influence, throwing your weight around and bullying others into doing your bidding, or will you *invest* it to build relationships that empower those you work with to achieve results? The PMDU made the investment philosophy an article of faith:

> "As with all precious resources, you have to use prime ministerial influence carefully, wisely and sparingly. In the end, once the door is open or the phone answered, it's what you say and how you say it that counts . . . If you overplay your hand, you sound arrogant; if you make unreasonable demands, you weaken yourself for the next time; if you claim to speak for the Prime Minister on an issue but don't really, you risk ridicule; and if you are rude, aggressive or ill informed, you bring the Prime Minister himself into disrepute. Worse still, if you persistently do any or all of these things, in the rumor mill that is government the world over, the word soon gets back to the man himself. And if he loses confidence in you or your Unit, the game is up." (*Instruction to Deliver,* 53)

Third, *do not run away from the facts.* On several occasions, the PMDU had to confront stakeholders with evidence that would be unpleasant to them. Their objective for each such interaction was to get the message across while strengthening and improving the quality of the relationship. The evidence-based tools that they used—data analysis, logical structuring of issues, and the assessment framework, to name a few—helped them in these situations, giving them the necessary credibility to be taken seriously. In many cases, these tools brought a new level of depth to the conversation, as when an analysis of hospital waiting times revealed that although average waiting times had gone down according to trajectory, the data in a specific area (orthopedics) had remained static—a fact that would jeopardize achievement of the final target if left unaddressed.

(Continued)

(Continued)

A good relationship is not at odds with telling the truth, even when the truth is difficult. On the contrary, a willingness to challenge in a firm, evidence-based, and supportive way is crucial to building a relationship that is not just amiable but useful to those you work with.

> "Units in the past had considered their relationships on a linear spectrum with 'hard' at one end and 'soft' at the other. If you're hard you upset people, they thought, so on the whole they were soft. I thought this was a misunderstanding—senior people don't mind being challenged in a tough way as long as the challenge is based on evidence, made by people who know what they're talking about and expressed with due humility. In fact, this kind of conversation is worth giving up time for, whereas a 'soft' conversation with someone ignorant is a waste of time." (*Instruction to Deliver,* 64)

Fourth, *prepare for and reflect on every planned interaction.* The fashion in some units that oversaw performance was to rush from meeting to meeting, without the facts in hand or a thoughtful understanding of context. By contrast, the PMDU emphasized the importance of planning and preparing to be effective in meetings. In a meeting with a departmental official, it was a sign of respect and seriousness to know as much about the topic as the official in question. In a negotiation with a performance unit over targets, it was crucial to know their data as well as they did. And in any case, it was important to know what shift in attitude or opinion was desired on the part of the participants in the meeting and the strategy to achieve that shift.

This meant going beyond the use of the facts—speaking, as John Kotter and Dan Cohen (Kotter & Cohen, 2002) would advise, not only to the head but to the heart. How would the PMDU help others, not just to understand a new perspective, but to embrace and support it? What fears would have to be overcome? "We spent many hours in our office thinking through how to take someone through a particular story or piece of evidence," recalls one PMDU staff member. "We thought about how they would react and how we could bring them around to a different point of view."

- For the PMDU, this sometimes played itself out in broader strategic questions. For example, when the education figures were shown to be plateauing in 2004, this created a great deal of tension between the PMDU and the Department of Education. This prompted a broad rethink of the PMDU's overall set of relationships with Education and a strategy for strengthening those relationships overall.
- In other cases, the application was more specific, as when a PMDU staff member needed to tell officials at the Department of Education that a major program they had put into place to improve performance was not working. The staff member came to the meeting with a solid evidence base to make this case, but he also presented it in a way that was honest, clear, and constructive, demonstrating his understanding of the challenges they faced and providing ideas on how to overcome them. In the end, the information was so well received that the Department of Education invited the PMDU to train them on how to conduct short and rapid diagnostics (like priority reviews) to help them understand and confront these challenges on their own.

After these kinds of interactions, PMDU staff would reflect on how things had gone and think together about how to do even better next time. That self-reflection helped them to continually improve their relationship-building skills.

Fifth and finally, *remember that there is no "them"—there is only "us."* Throughout every PMDU interaction with others, there was a consistent attitude that "we are in this together"—a sentiment contrary to the blame cultures of many units that oversee performance. For the PMDU, the central approach was to arrive at a common understanding of challenges using the evidence, and then to empower others to achieve results.

This is particularly important when the evidence suggests that performance is low. "In cases like this," said one PMDU staff member,

> "the most important thing was to walk the person through the evidence and have them construct the solution. Then, if necessary, you would have to help them overcome any fears that might be associated with being honest about the data. If people worried that they could not tell a certain truth, our response would often be to ask, 'Well, what if you said it like this?'"

One example of this approach in action came when the PMDU had a particularly difficult set of data on emergency room wait times:

> "Rather than blaming the person who owned this target, we instead worked alongside him to help him present the results to the prime minister, along with a plan for how they were going to address the challenge. It was the proudest day of his life."

In this case, the PMDU took a potential scapegoat and instead turned him into a hero. Results subsequently turned around, and the person in question was promoted. In that oft-quoted phrase, usually attributed to President Truman, "A man may do an immense deal of good if he does not care who gets the credit for it."

Principle 3: Identify the "win-win" in every relationship

Keeping people informed and living your values will take you a long way toward building good relationships with stakeholders in your system. However, depending on the specific issue at hand and its impact on a given stakeholder, that stakeholder may occasionally want something that is at odds with what your Delivery Unit wants. At a most basic level, you may want to report on a department's performance, and they might feel threatened by this. More generally, the relationship your Delivery Unit desires may be costly for some stakeholders.

In such cases, we move beyond the style of interactions to the substance of them. In order to build meaningful relationships with your stakeholders, you must be able to answer a simple question for each stakeholder: What will the Delivery Unit do for me? The key is to create a *win-win situation*—one in which both parties gain something meaningful from their (sometimes costly) participation in the relationship.

To create a win-win situation, it is important to find common ground, going beyond superficial areas where your Delivery Unit and a stakeholder may disagree. Exhibit 5C.2 demonstrates how this might work in practice.

In most conflicts, what are most visible are the differences in positions—the most tangible and specific things over which two parties might disagree. Your Delivery Unit may want to change the program model a department head uses to manage teacher professional development, but that department head may want to continue doing things as she has in the past.

These differences in positions, however, ultimately arise from different underlying *interests* and *values.* At this deeper level, the potential for overlap and common ground is greater. For example, while both your Delivery Unit and the department head may disagree on how best to undertake teacher professional development, you may both agree on one value, that teachers are the most important driver of success in the classroom and that professional development must therefore help them to achieve results.

Moreover, you may discover that you and the other party have interests and values that differ *but do not conflict.* For example, while your Delivery Unit may have an underlying interest in changing the method of teacher professional development to one backed up by evidence, the department head may have a different interest in ensuring that any change to the program model does not result in a cut to funding. Both of these interests could potentially be satisfied by promising equivalent funding for a new program model.

Beneath these interests and values lie more human and basic *needs* and *fears,* and at this level, there might be even more common ground and more

Exhibit 5C.2 Identifying shared interests, values, needs, and fears is crucial to align parties when positions differ

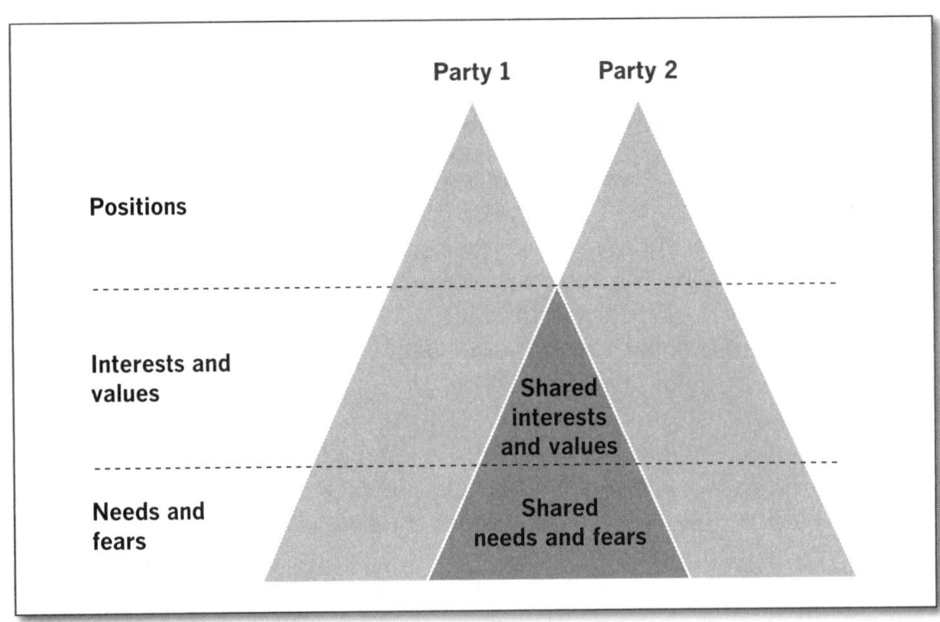

SOURCE: From Miall, H., Ramsbotham, O., Woodhouse, T. *Contemporary Conflict Resolution: The Prevention, Management, and Transformation of Deadly Conflicts.* Copyright © Hugh Miall, Oliver Ramsbotham, Tom Woodhouse. Published by Polity Press 1999 in association with Blackwell Publishing, Ltd.

areas of difference without conflict. For example, both your Delivery Unit and the department head likely need to feel that you are making a positive contribution, and you are both likely to fear wasting time on reforms that do nothing. Likewise, your Delivery Unit may need the department head's support while the department head may need a guarantee that the change will not threaten her job security. In some circumstances, both of these needs may be satisfied simultaneously.

These areas of shared and/or nonconflicting interests, values, needs, and fears are the building blocks for any win-win situation. Once you have identified them, creating a win-win situation for any given stakeholder is often more straightforward than you think.

- What are the current interests, values, and/or needs of the stakeholder?
- What are the fears of the stakeholder? What are the potential threats to the stakeholder posed by your delivery effort?
- What does your Delivery Unit need from the stakeholder?
- What is the win-win proposition? That is, what can your Delivery Unit offer the stakeholder that will give your Delivery Unit what it needs, allay any potential fears they have, and further their current interests, values, and/or needs?

Exhibit 5C.3 shows how the PMDU took the extra time to identify the win-win situation for each of its key relationships. The exhibit can also be used as a template for any situation in which you have to ask and answer questions about the stakeholders with whom your Delivery Unit will be working.

Exhibit 5C.3 "Win-win" relationships in the PMDU

	Current interests, values, and/or needs	**Fears (potential threats from PMDU)**	**PMDU's needs from stakeholder**	**Win-win proposition**
Prime minister	• Deliver his top priorities	• Shoddy work will reflect badly on him	• Access • Sustained focus • Backing and influence	• "Whatever you're doing, we're focused on your priorities."
Treasury	• Protect its framework for linking public service agreement targets with funding	• PMDU could become a means for departments to ask for more money	• Public support	• "We'll make sure the money you allocate delivers results." • "We assume that departments have all the money they need already."

(Continued)

Exhibit 5C.3 (Continued)

	Current interests, values, and/or needs	Fears (potential threats from PMDU)	PMDU's needs from stakeholder	Win-win proposition
Ministers in priority areas	• Achieve results and be recognized for them	• PMDU could disrupt their influence with the prime minister • PMDU performance reporting could harm them if made public	• Cooperation with delivery effort	• "We'll help you get your bureaucracy to deliver the government's priorities." • "Our work with you will never be a media story." • "If we achieve success together, you get the credit."
Top civil servants	• Protect their departments • Accomplish something at work	• PMDU could be irrelevant at best, an irritant at worst	• Cooperation with delivery effort	• "We'll sustain a focus on these priorities and help you solve your problems."

SOURCE: From *Instruction to Deliver,* by M. Barber, 2008, London: Methuen Publishing Ltd. Copyright by Michael Barber.

The following case example explores one of these stakeholder groups in detail: the cabinet-level ministers for the departments that were on the PMDU agenda.

CASE EXAMPLE

Relationship building with cabinet ministers

The targets that the PMDU oversaw were formally the responsibility of four departments: Health, Education, Transport, and the Home Office (crime-related targets). For this reason, the PMDU had an obvious need for good relationships with the cabinet ministers that headed these departments. All ministers would ultimately have a major influence on the level of access and cooperation that the PMDU would enjoy in working with their department.

The proposition for how the Delivery Unit could help these ministers was simple:

> "You and the Prime Minister are agreed about the priorities for your department during the course of [the next five years], and the entire government knows its success depends on them; the task of the Delivery Unit is to help you get your bureaucracy to deliver these priorities." (*Instruction to Deliver,* 59)

At the same time, the suspicions that these ministers might have had of this new agent of the prime minister were also obvious:

- For a cabinet minister, a direct relationship with the prime minister is central, and a Delivery Unit could potentially get in the way.
- A Delivery Unit could interfere with what a minister rightly sees as his mandate to run a department.
- The idea of a Delivery Unit checking on a minister's performance and reporting secretly back to the prime minister is insulting—if not frightening.

To allay these concerns, the Delivery Unit's win-win proposition had a second part:

> "While I do want access when required, I will never waste your precious time . . . I'll share with you what I share with the Prime Minister . . . and above all, if as a result of our collaboration a problem is solved or a success delivered, we, the PMDU, don't want any credit." (*Instruction to Deliver,* 59)

Finally, one last core concern of this stakeholder group helped to motivate the PMDU's overall operating model: the concern that potentially embarrassing information about a department would leak and become public as a result of the PMDU's work.

> "Nothing is more likely to upset a Minister than being caught on the hop by the media. By definition, the material the Delivery Unit generated for the Prime Minister was extremely sensitive since it commented unsparingly on departmental performance; it sought to provide explanations for underperformance and suggestions for solving problems. In effect, it was performing for the Prime Minister the internal performance management function of a large company. Many of the conclusions we reached were dynamite. So, from the outset, I was determined to avoid 'becoming the story' or even to do off-the-record briefings for journalists, except on the rare occasions when the No. 10 press office recommended it. This way, the Ministers' relationship with the media—always delicate—would not be upset by the PMDU. When the two leaks in four years did occur, it powerfully reinforced my gut caution." (*Instruction to Deliver,* 60)

Principle 4: Manage conflict actively

No matter how much effort you put into developing your key relationships, and no matter how good your win-win propositions are, any contentious change program will occasionally generate more intractable conflicts between your Delivery Unit and stakeholders. For this reason, the last important principle of relationship building is to be thoughtful, ethical, and deliberate about handling these challenging situations.

When conflict arises with a stakeholder, the first thing to consider is the stakeholder's perspective: What is the source of the conflict? In his book *The Heart of Change Field Guide,* Dan Cohen (2005) notes that people in conflict tend to have arguments that are based on both emotion (e.g., "I'm afraid of the change you're proposing") and logic (e.g., "I won't be able to change until someone teaches me how"). While you should always *acknowledge* the emotional arguments of a stakeholder directly and plainly, you should only *respond* to the logical arguments.

In K–12 education, for example, suppose that a state proposes the creation of new college and career-ready graduation requirements, with a default curriculum that students must pass in order to complete high school. Such a plan might encounter opposition from teachers who teach some of the subjects that are not emphasized by the new curriculum (e.g., vocational courses). An effective relationship manager's message to such a teacher might be as follows:

- **Acknowledge the emotional argument.** "I understand that you have fears about your own future if the courses you teach are de-emphasized. Moreover, I understand why you might be angry; I would not enjoy this if it were happening to me either."
- **Respond to the logical argument.** "You are right that this plan will sharply decrease the number of teachers that teach the subjects in which you specialize. I cannot bring those jobs back because there is too much evidence that the market no longer demands the skills taught in these subjects. Let's work together to figure out how we can compensate you for the difficulties that this shift will cause you, perhaps by preparing you to teach something different."

CASE EXAMPLE

Understanding conflicting perspectives: The Michigan Merit Curriculum

In 2006, in the face of a rapidly collapsing blue-collar economy, the Michigan State Department of Education passed a reform of its high school graduation requirements geared toward producing many more college- and career-ready graduates within the next decade. The Merit Curriculum, which mandated over 20 rigorous course requirements statewide for graduation, faced intense opposition and has continued to do so throughout the rocky process of implementation.

Much of the opposition has come from small but vocal contingents in traditionally blue-collar industries, such as mining, where parents and other members of the community insisted that not all students need the courses mandated by the curriculum. However, the reform's backers have resolutely stuck to their argument that these courses teach skills that will be required for future economic success.

On one visit to the mining region of Michigan's Upper Peninsula (UP), Superintendent Michael P. Flanagan faced a very unfriendly crowd. He recalls that one parent shouted at him, "Our kids are mud haulers, and they are always gonna be mud haulers! What do they need this for?" The parent's argument was partly emotional: the fear that the new requirements might be too difficult for his children or that success might take them out of the community if they decided to pursue a college education. At the same time, the parent made a legitimate logical argument: If, indeed, his children really did stay in mining, what use would the Merit Curriculum be to them? Flanagan acknowledged the man's fear. He then responded to the logical argument by questioning its premise. He asked the man to consider the possibility that the region might not always thrive economically on a "mud hauling" business alone. What skills would the man's children need then?

In actively seeking out and understanding the perspectives of stakeholders, you should also be forthright about your own. Conflicts will inevitably tempt you to find a resolution at all costs. While you may compromise on policies and practices, you should not compromise on your principles. Equally important, you must be honest and transparent when these principles put you in direct and unavoidable conflict with a stakeholder. In such cases, good relationship managers walk toward the conflict, name it, and explain their perspective.

Counterintuitively, this direct approach to dissent will often earn you the respect of those who disagree with you, while attempts to minimize conflicts that are real will likely have the opposite effect. Two examples below—one from the PMDU and one from the world of American politics—illustrate this point.

CASE EXAMPLE

Addressing conflicts in the PMDU

In keeping with its values, the PMDU shared the results of its first delivery report with all relevant stakeholders as it was sent to the prime minister. The judgments in the league table were hard hitting, and one top civil servant was particularly angry at the verdict that had been rendered on his department.

> "His basic objection was that I had sent the report to Blair before I had discussed it with him. The conversation became even more tense when I informed him of the league table and how we'd constructed it. 'Bloody hell,' he said. 'You've even traffic-lighted it.'" (*Instruction to Deliver,* 107)

In his response, the PMDU leader not only walked toward and addressed this conflict head-on, but gave a robust, forthright, and logical defense of the PMDU's ability to provide an objective perspective, which was a core operating principle from the start.

> "I said it was my job to inform the Prime Minister of the state of delivery. I also made a more telling point. Ever since there have been Prime Ministers, they have asked their closest advisors to comment on the performance of key Ministers and officials, and in reply the advisors had given their opinion. This was a closed process. What the Delivery Unit had developed was different. Yes, we had sent the report to the Prime Minister without consulting; importantly, though, our comments were evidence-based and we were sending them to the Permanent Secretaries, too, so our judgments on them were open. If they could provide evidence that our judgments were wrong, we would have to change them; if our judgments were right, surely the Prime Minister had a right to know. The case was unarguable." (*Instruction to Deliver,* 107)

CASE EXAMPLE

Courage of convictions

Sometimes, people will care as much about your integrity as they will about what you believe. In Fall 2002, as the U.S. Congress prepared to vote to authorize the war in Iraq, there was heated debate over the proposal. Barely more than a year after the events of 9/11, and with an election that November, the climate in Congress—particularly for members from swing states—was one of overwhelming pressure to vote yes.

(Continued)

(Continued)

Paul Wellstone, a U.S. Senator from Minnesota, felt this pressure in particular. He was in a close reelection battle against challenger Norm Coleman; polls had shown them running neck and neck for much of the summer. Moreover, some polls showed that up to 60% of Minnesota voters were in favor of the war—and Coleman had left no doubt that he would vote yes if he were in Wellstone's place.

Nevertheless, in October 2002 Wellstone became the only Democratic Senator facing reelection that year to vote against the war. His colleagues urged him to avoid the seeming "political suicide" of voting against the war. His response: "I would commit moral suicide if I voted for it."

When he returned to Minnesota after casting the vote, Wellstone found that voters—even those who disagreed with him—were "unbelievably respectful" when he explained his position. Perhaps more to the point, polls in October showed Wellstone taking a lead of nearly 10 points over Coleman, a reversal from a far less favorable showing in September.

We will never know if this change would have been decisive; days before the election, Wellstone was killed in a tragic plane crash. However, one thing seems clear: Despite public disagreement with his position, the voters seemed to give Wellstone credit for being honest and for standing up for what he believed in.

Exhibit 5C.4 Support for candidates in Minnesota U.S. Senate election, 2002

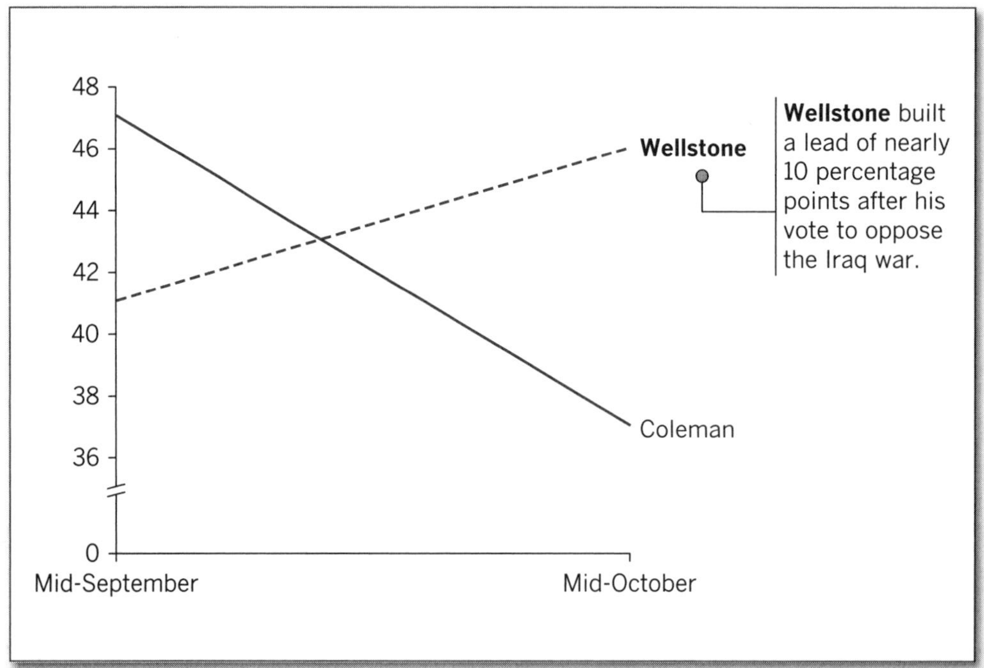

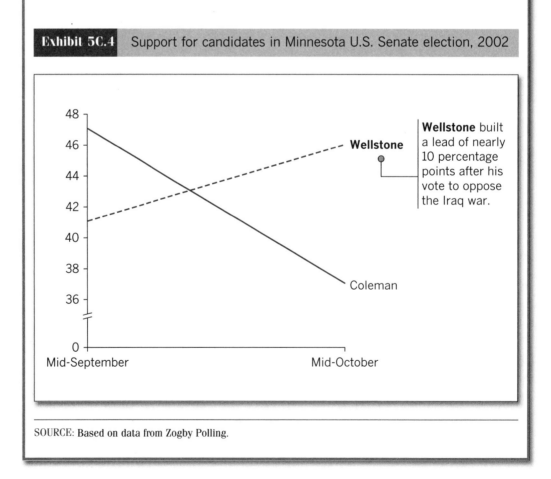

SOURCE: Based on data from Zogby Polling.

More generally, any conflict situation will present you with choices to make: (1) how much concern will you have for yourself, and (2) how much concern will you have for the other person? The balance struck will determine your behavior or approach in resolving the conflict, as demonstrated in Exhibit 5C.5.

Exhibit 5C.5 Approaches to conflict resolution

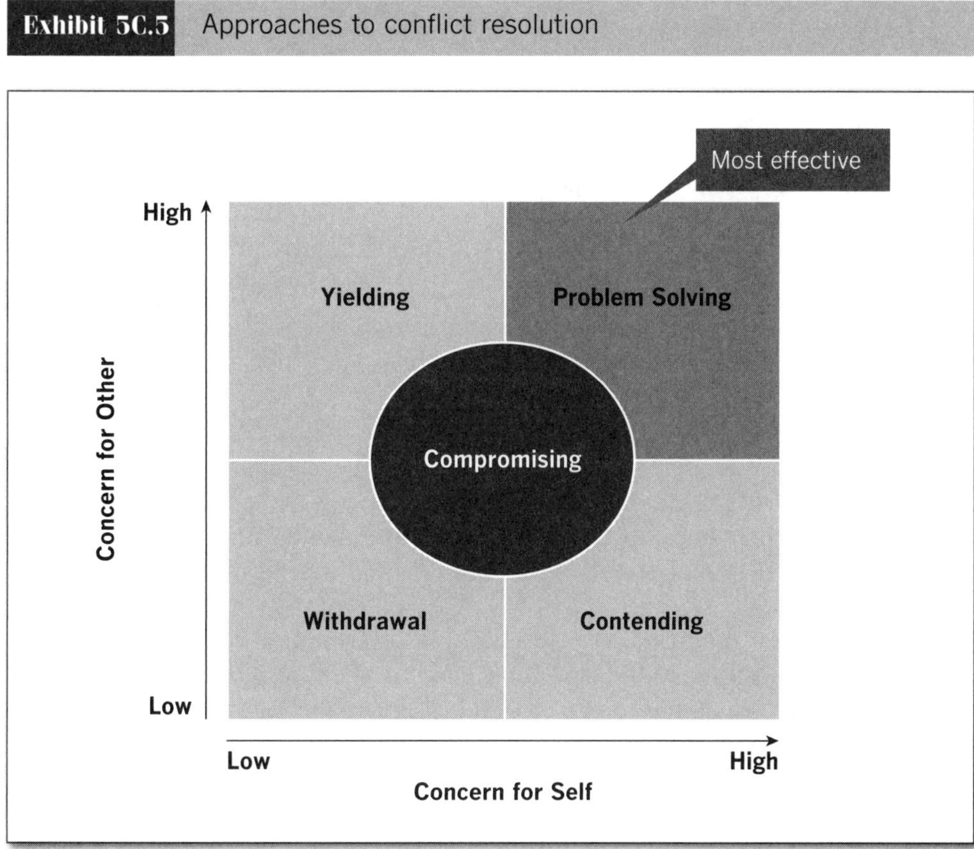

SOURCE: Created from several sources by Miall, et al. From Miall, H., Ramsbotham, O., Woodhouse, T. *Contemporary Conflict Resolution: The Prevention, Management, and Transformation of Deadly Conflicts.* Copyright © Hugh Miall, Oliver Ramsbotham, Tom Woodhouse. Published by Polity Press 1999 in association with Blackwell Publishing, Ltd.

The least effective approach is *contending,* in which you have a high concern for yourself and a low concern for others. It may also be the most common approach, as most people tend to view conflict as a zero-sum game in which one person can gain only at the expense of the other. Ultimately, however, this approach can escalate conflict and make a resolution even more remote.

Yielding and *withdrawal* both involve elimination of your concern for yourself—whether by giving in to the demands of the other person or refusing to engage in conflict. They are both methods of avoiding conflict and are essentially mistakes in the opposite direction, as they can never lead to a resolution that is satisfactory for both parties.

Finally, *problem solving* and *compromising* are the most productive ways of dealing with conflict because they balance the concern for self with the concern for others and seek a solution in which both parties have a say.

As with creating win-win situations, it will be important to search for common ground in the form of shared or nonconflicting interests, values, needs, and fears—and to use this common ground to generate options for resolving the conflict.

Conclusion

By now, you have learned

- Why relationship building is crucial to the success of your delivery effort;
- How to define and maintain a brand that will make your Delivery Unit effective; and
- Core principles for building relationships with stakeholders, including basic engagement, identifying the "win-win," and resolving conflicts.

Unlike many aspects of reform and management that can be handled by tools, techniques, and processes, relationships are much more of an art than a science. You can use the principles above to help you to consciously and consistently develop and use your relationships; but ultimately, it is your level of personal attention to each key relationship that will determine your success.

Remember, the principles described in this chapter do not apply only to those relationships that your Delivery Unit has with others. It is your responsibility to help others to unleash the "alchemy of relationships" among the people who are important to them (the ones who are a step—or more—removed from you and your staff). The circles of leadership that you wish to widen are all connected. If your key relationships are more successful because their key relationships are successful, then your delivery effort will multiply its potential impact several times over.

Frequently Asked Questions

As you begin your delivery effort and make use of this field guide, questions will arise, both for you and for those you work with, for which you will need a ready answer. The below list, organized by chapter and module, gives answers to some of the most common questions you will encounter.

1. Develop a Foundation for Delivery

1A. Define your aspiration

- **What if my system leader does not have complete control over the aspirations that are set?** Depending on the structure of the system, others (for example, legislatures) may have the authority to impose aspirations on the system. In cases such as these, your Delivery Unit can play a crucial role, breaking down the aspiration into specific targets and assessing whether existing strategies and resources will be sufficient to achieve the aspiration (for more on this, see Module 3B, Set goals and establish trajectories). If your system leader needs to negotiate an aspiration with someone else, she will be well served by this kind of information and analysis.
- **What is the difference between an aspiration and a target?** Practically speaking, an aspiration gets you as far as your target metric—your understanding of the thing you want to influence. Targets take aspirations one step further, defining how much you aspire to move the target metric and by when. For more on this, see Module 3B. In practice, an aspiration may implicitly contain a specific target (e.g., "a man on the moon within the next decade" is both an aspiration and a SMART target). However, if it is at all possible, specific target setting should wait until your Delivery Unit has a handle on the facts: the capacity of the system, the levers available to influence the target metric, and the extent to which those levers can be pulled. Needless to say, this is not always possible.

1B. Review the current state of delivery

- **Why does the delivery review focus on delivery activities and not system activities?** Delivery activities are the activities described in this field guide. They are your Delivery Unit's tools for understanding, assessing, improving, and sometimes adding new system activities in order to achieve your aspiration. While much of the rest of this field guide will describe how your Delivery Unit will assess and create improvements in system activities, you first need to understand the health of the delivery activities that will make this possible.

- **How should I think about delivery capacity after this first review?** As delivery leader, you should always be thinking about how to improve the quality of your delivery activities. The delivery capacity review rubric is a reference guide that you can use to constantly stay abreast (on an informal basis) of the current state of delivery in your system. You can also run the formal review process again as occasion may require. For more on the continuous improvement of your Delivery Unit, please see Module 5A.

1C. Build the Delivery Unit

- **What if my system does not have the resources or the commitment from system leadership to build a Delivery Unit like the one described here?** Every system's context will be slightly different; while the structure and size of the U.K. national government gave rise to the Delivery Unit design and organization explored in this module, an examination of different facts on the ground might lead others to different conclusions. Many features of Delivery Unit design and organization are flexible, but experience has shown that Delivery Units perform best when they adhere to the principles in this module. In particular, a Delivery Unit without full-time staff, access to the system leader, and independence from the line management hierarchy will find it much harder to carry out its mission. If your system leader cannot establish your Unit according to these fundamentals, it is worth asking whether he is truly committed to delivery as a top priority.
- **What do the "five key words" actually mean in practice?** The five words capture the attitude that underlies all of the delivery activities explored in Chapters 2, 3, and 4. Ambition, for example, is a key characteristic of the target-setting process described in Module 3B, Set targets and establish trajectories. However, ambition is imbued in many other activities, from the way your Delivery Unit will evaluate and challenge the quality of your system's delivery plans (Module 3C, Produce delivery plans) to the way it will review progress against your trajectory (Module 4A, Establish routines to drive and monitor performance) and solve problems that arise (Module 4B, Solve problems early and rigorously). The same is true for all of the key words; without them, the delivery activities described in this field guide are not really distinguishable from other activities that do not generate results. Chapter 5 provides an in-depth exploration of how your Delivery Unit can build a culture around those key words, starting with the unit itself and widening out to senior leaders, mid-level leaders, the frontline, and even users and the public.

1D. Establish a guiding coalition

- **How is a guiding coalition different from my system's leadership team?** Unlike your system's leadership team, the guiding coalition is not a formal management team. It is an informal group of people that draws its membership from diverse circles of influence. While a leadership team has the advantage of being formal and of concentrating influence in your system office, the guiding coalition will offer you a much broader reach—one that is often necessary in systems with complex or diffuse governance structures.

- **What should I do about people in my system who are staunchly opposed to our aspiration but too powerful to ignore?** Your first and best option is to find a group of 7 to 10 people who will be able to get the job done without this person's support. However, in some cases this person may hold an effective "veto" (real or figurative) over some crucial decisions that you will have to make. In such cases, a separate strategy of engagement may be appropriate. The person may not become a part of your guiding coalition right away (as this will risk poisoning the overall discussion), but the system leader might make a special effort to minimize the opposition through separate conversations. Over time, if conditions change, it may become appropriate to bring this person into the group.

2. Understand the Delivery Challenge

2A. Evaluate past and present performance

- **Do I really have to do all this analysis? Don't we already know what the major problems are?** Every system and every context is different. You may be in a situation in which you have known your greatest challenges for some time—and what is really necessary is the development of a strategy to address those challenges. However, the guidelines for analysis laid out in these modules are useful for a few reasons. First, they will help you to get under the surface of the data and pinpoint challenges at a more granular level. You may know the biggest performance challenges, but have you thought about the leading indicators that lie beneath these challenges? Second, they can serve to reassure you that you have correctly identified the biggest challenges. As long as you are relying on analysis that someone else has carried out (or—worse—conventional wisdom), it makes sense to flip through the pages of this module and make sure that the evidence is convincing. However, one sentiment behind this question is right: You should not spend a minute longer on performance analysis than you absolutely have to.
- **The methodologies for data analysis seem complicated. Where do I begin?** You should be pragmatic. The principles and examples given in this module are meant to give you ideas for how to conduct your analysis, but you will have to run those up against the realities of data availability in your system. Do not worry if you cannot do everything that the module suggests; instead, do what you can, and make a note of how you would like your system to improve its data capability in the future.
- **Why are indicators of unintended consequences important?** Because behavior that is measured will always drive out behavior that is not measured, a delivery effort will always put you at risk of driving out behavior that is desirable (e.g., preventing

dropouts) in the pursuit of the behavior measured by the target metric (e.g., increasing test scores). There are two ways to solve this problem. First, you could make the definition of your target metric so sophisticated that it accounts for potential perverse consequences (for example, including every dropout as a "zero" test score, which will bring the average way down). Second, you can include and measure the other metric as an indicator of unintended consequences (for example, tracking dropout rates separately and refusing to give schools credit if those rates are too high). In many cases, you will not be able to design the target metric to perfectly account for all other behavior that you will want to watch—so it will be important to identify and track indicators of unintended consequences instead.

2B. Understand drivers of performance and related system activities

- **This module focuses only on patterns of weak performance. What about the areas of strong performance that I identified?** It is true that the most important analysis from Module 2B is an understanding of where your system struggles the most. Areas of poor performance are where your system stands to make the most gains, and it is therefore appropriate to focus on them. However, areas of strong performance will help you to know where to look for best practices to share with your system; they are a strong indicator to use for internal benchmarking. At the point where you are looking for ideas for interventions, it would make a great deal of sense to disaggregate the data on areas of strong performance to identify places (schools, campuses, and districts) where you might search for promising practices.
- **The hypothesis tree seems obvious. Is it really necessary?** So much of delivery's power is in taking the intuitive and making it explicit. Like the delivery chain and many other tools, the hypothesis tree is helpful both because it forces some additional rigor in thinking and because it forces that thinking into the open where it can be debated and improved by multiple perspectives. Don't fall for the excuse that there is not enough time; you and your Delivery Unit can draw a solid hypothesis tree in a matter of a few hours or less.

3. Plan for Delivery

3A. Determine your reform strategy

- **Should a Delivery Unit ever really be involved in strategy?** It depends on your situation. As the module says, where the strategy is mature or some other unit or agency is responsible for it, your job may simply be to give feedback on it based on the principles in this module. This was the case with the PMDU. In some cases, however, your Delivery Unit will have to step up and give real strategic advice. There are also benefits to having an integrated strategy and delivery function. However, two caveats apply. First, make sure that your Delivery Unit is adequately resourced to perform a strategy function if that is what is expected. Second, do not let strategy distract you from delivery.

Most people tend to find strategy more interesting, and in a joint unit, you will always run the risk of emphasizing the "what" at the expense of the "how."

- **Part of the process is to consider removing some system activities. Will the Delivery Unit have time to do this?** Removing distracting activities is as important as adding or changing activities—sometimes more so. A frequent refrain in bureaucracies is that people—especially those who are most talented—are constantly overburdened, often with tasks that are particularly demoralizing because of their patent ineffectiveness. Anyone who is serious about delivery will pay just as much attention to not doing the wrong things as they will to doing the right things.

3B. Set targets and trajectories

- **A trajectory seems like little more than a guess. How can I really estimate the future?** First, a trajectory is much more than a guess. It is the best educated guess you can construct, given the data and information that you have. Even building a trajectory forces a robust and helpful debate about what the impact of each intervention will really be and which benchmarks are really feasible to hit. This is a vast improvement over a system in which targets are set in a vacuum, are never credible, and are always missed. That being said, you should never pretend that a trajectory is scientific. For this reason, the PMDU did not make data on trajectories public like the targets at their endpoints but instead used them as internal tools for learning. Indeed, a trajectory's value is in allowing for a comparison of the projection with the actual results that obtain. This allows for early warnings that a target may be missed; and in such cases, the analysis underlying a trajectory is a useful starting point for trying to change course and solve the problem.
- **What do I do if I am saddled with a target that I know—according to the evidence—is unattainable?** This should be a rare occurrence. Any Delivery Unit that has been in operation for an appreciable length of time should make a point of inserting itself into debates about target setting, doing the trajectory analysis that nobody else will, and helping to inform decision makers about what is feasible. However, no Delivery Unit can control the decisions made by leadership, and sometimes targets will be set that are contrary to the facts. In such cases, it is important for you to remember that you serve at the behest of those who have set the targets. Once a decision is made publicly, you cannot question it publicly. Rather, you must put your best foot forward to solve for the target that has been set, however impossible it may seem. You just might surprise yourself—or at least make progress in the right direction.

3C. Produce delivery plans

- **Is there an ideal way to organize my delivery plans?** This is an area where pragmatism reigns—more than in most of the modules in this field guide. This module gives you several options, ranging from a target-level focus to a focus on individual performance units.

Choose what works best for you, and mix and match as appropriate. The most important thing is that your Delivery Unit holds the right set of people accountable for the results of your delivery effort, and they internalize and apply the principles of delivery planning. Your Delivery Unit is too small to "force" a certain kind of planning from the top down. Instead, your best option is to articulate criteria for good delivery plans and to meet delivery plan owners, working with them to gain mutual clarity about what it will take to successfully execute every part of your delivery effort.

4. Drive Delivery

4A. Establish routines to drive and monitor performance

- **There simply is not enough data to report to the system leader on a monthly basis, let alone a weekly one. What do I do if the only data available comes out annually?** The PMDU staff used to make the same objection to the PMDU leader. His response to them was that, if they were on top of their jobs, they would always have something important to say to the prime minister about performance. The bias of literally everyone else in your system will be toward talking about performance less frequently. Your Delivery Unit has to be the one voice calling for accountability—not next year, when it is too late to change course, but next month or even next week, when something can still be done. The absence of weekly or monthly data should not be a reason to shy away from more frequent conversations; rather, it should be an impetus to improving your system's capacity to identify and track the right leading indicators. In the meantime, qualitative information—gleaned from your everyday interactions with the system—should always be available.
- **What if my system leader does not take his responsibility seriously at review meetings?** One of the central functions of routines is to amplify the overseeing and influence of the system leader. This, however, requires that the system leader engage in these routines in specific and focused ways: reading the necessary materials, knowing his facts, and being tough where necessary. If you have a system leader who seems disengaged, your first task should be to ensure that your routines are using his time well. Are the presentations crisp, clear, and relevant? Is your staff well prepared? Are routines designed to produce results and decisions? Even so, you need to take account of the personality of the system leader and adapt the routines as appropriate. Ask what kind of information does he like? What are his working patterns? Tell him that delivery will suffer otherwise. If this does not work, then there may be something fundamentally lacking in either the skill or the will of your system leader . . . but remember, in the end, delivery matters to the citizens—so never give up!

4B. Solve problems early and rigorously

- **My Unit is too small to conduct a priority review. Should I not do them?** Priority reviews can be more or less detailed, depending on the resources your system has available. If your Delivery

Unit consists only of one or two people, you might consider a process that still takes a month but only uses a fraction of a person's time. You can make up the difference by scaling back some of the priority review activities and relying more heavily on the joint team members from the system. You can also bring in outside support: The PMDU, for example, had a contract with a consulting firm to provide extra people when demand was high.

4C. Sustain and continually build momentum

- **If a target metric is off trajectory or a target is missed, what should I say when I encounter the "excuse" that promised resources were not provided?** This is always difficult territory. Absence of the necessary resources is the most commonly used excuse for not delivering, but often it is not the real reason. Even so, if your system has broken a promise that it has made—especially a promise that was linked to the target, as would have been the case with a Public Service Agreement (PSA) in the U.K.—then it is reasonable for a delivery plan owner or other accountable official to ask whether the target promise can still be kept. In the first instance, you should make sure that the missing resources do indeed explain the low performance, either because they were written to some kind of performance contract linking them with the target or because the cut clearly had an effect.

5. Create an Irreversible Delivery Culture

5A. Build system capacity all the time

- **Should my Delivery Unit really expect to build capacity for the entire system?** Your Delivery Unit's work can never substitute for a comprehensive capacity-building program (which is the subject of numerous other books!). Your Unit is too small to provide the right kind of development to hundreds or even thousands of people, and in any case, capacity building will not be the primary expertise of your Delivery Unit. However, this module exists because your Delivery Unit should build capacity to the extent that it can. This means taking direct responsibility for the capacity of the unit itself, doing direct capacity building with those who work most closely with the unit, and using your substantial influence to ensure that the right kinds of capacity-building programs—run by other people—are included in delivery planning. Your Delivery Unit might not be able to change the capacity of your entire system, but it can punch far above its weight.

5B. Communicate the delivery message

- **How do I decide when I should make performance data and information public?** This is another difficult and tricky issue, and often one taken up by the system leadership. On the one hand, public targets are a way of tying one's self to the mast, of making a commitment that is more difficult to break. On the other hand, some performance data—particularly the more frequently measured trajectories—could create a culture in which the fear of failure is so intense that accountable officials dare not be ambitious or honest about progress. However, in some ways, this debate misses the point. Whether or not to publish performance data is a matter of choice. What is important is that targets are set, that performance data is tracked, and that both are taken seriously. One other thing is certain: Once you have decided what information is public and what information is not, guard the non-public information zealously. It is a serious breach of trust to allow sensitive information to leak when you have promised that it will be kept in confidence.

- **What do I do when the public seems dead set against the delivery effort?** Public perceptions of your work will only be as good as your efforts to educate the public. The burden of argument will always be higher on the person advocating for change, as the status quo has numerous beneficiaries who will vociferously defend it. It is for this reason that communication is so important: Your job is to help your system leader make the argument for change and to persuade a skeptical public to listen, learn, and alter their viewpoints accordingly (the case of Jerry Weast in Montgomery County Public Schools is an excellent example of this). If you get to the point where the public is extraordinarily well educated about what you are trying to do and still disagrees, then the democratic imperative might suggest that a different course is warranted. Of course, few if any systems ever reach this point, and the vast majority of failed communication efforts are matters of poor communication rather than outright disagreement. Trust that if your goal is good, your strategy is good, and your communications are good, the merit of your argument will prevail.

5C. Unleash the "alchemy of relationships"

- **There is a relationship I simply cannot crack, but I also cannot avoid this person. What do I do?** Most of this module discusses relationship building that is incidental to interactions that have an explicit purpose—advancing your delivery effort. If a crucial person is very hostile toward your delivery effort, then it might make sense to try to build a relationship for its own sake. Arrange for interactions without an agenda. Get to know the other person on a basis other than the fact that you are colleagues. It is much more difficult to oppose a person that has been humanized by meaningful interaction without a solid logical argument. Moreover, the fruits of such interaction may "grease the wheels" in areas of substantive disagreement where the other person is on the fence. An example illustrates this point. The US Supreme Court is often regarded as one of the most collegial bodies in government. Though there are undoubtedly many reasons for this, one contributing factor is the Supreme Court lunchroom, where an unwritten rule prevails: no conversations about work. The justices of the Supreme Court may disagree, but they can still work together. At a minimum, you should strive to build this kind of relationship with even the most vehement partisans against you.

Glossary

Action step: A specific step that must be taken, with a timeline, toward achieving a milestone in a delivery plan. (See also: **delivery plan, milestone.**)

Actors: Please see **system actor.**

Alchemy of relationships: The art of developing a rapport with all stakeholders around you such that achieving your system's aspiration becomes easier. This applies both to those relationships you are actively striving to build (e.g., with your system leader) and to those relationships that are incidental to the effort (e.g., the receptionist at the department with which you work). (See also: **stakeholder.**)

Aspiration: A system's answer to three questions:

- What do we care about?
- What are we going to do about it?
- How will we measure it?

An aspiration is not necessarily a specific and time-bound target. However, an aspiration should lend itself to measurement by one or more target metrics. (See also: **target, target metric.**)

Assessment framework: A tool used by the PMDU for reviewing the likelihood of delivery for each priority by judging four categories:

- The degree of the delivery challenge (low, medium, high, or very high);
- The quality of planning, implementation, and performance management (traffic light);
- The capacity to drive progress (traffic light); and
- The stage of delivery, from 1 (beginning) to 4 (advanced).

Baseline: A future projection of your target metric if no interventions were to occur, taking into account the historic performance and predicted movement of any other major external factors that would affect the target metric. (See also: **target metric, trajectory.**)

Brand: A consistent idea or experience associated with an entity—in this case, your Delivery Unit. A positive brand will help people to understand your Delivery Unit, to feel positive about your work, and to want to cooperate with you.

Calculated Bounce: A projected leap from today's level of performance to a level that is inspirationally ambitious: It signals a transformation in performance and a substantial change from business as usual. A calculated bounce often takes the form of a public commitment.

Calibration meeting: See **moderation meeting**.

Capacity: The potential for an organization to achieve its aspiration. In the context of delivery, it consists of both delivery capacity and system capacity. It is composed of four elements:

- Structure: Is the system structurally organized to do what needs to be done effectively?
- Resources: Do system actors have the necessary time and/or funding to address the tasks at hand?
- Competencies: Do system actors have the skills and abilities they need to do what is asked of them?
- Motivation: Do system actors have a "delivery mindset" as they approach the work they are being asked to do?

(See also: **aspiration**, **delivery capacity**, **system capacity.**)

Challenge meeting: A structured problem-solving meeting that allows for a rigorous review of a delivery plan from multiple perspectives. More generally, you can use the challenge meeting process for several other aspects of your delivery effort (e.g., a subtarget set by a performance unit, such as a campus).

Change story: A tool for capturing and packaging the key elements of a communication message—particularly when a person in a leadership position is delivering that message. A change story provides a powerful narrative that describes our current situation, our aspiration, why we must change to meet that aspiration, and how, through ups and downs, we will achieve it.

Communication event: The building block of any communication plan; a communication event is a discrete instance in which a message of any kind is delivered, whether through a major speech to thousands or a face-to-face communication with a single stakeholder. A communication event is defined by the answers to five questions, which conform to an overall messaging plan for each stakeholder over time:

- Who is the audience? (What stakeholders will you address?)
- What message will you send them?
- When, and with what frequency?
- Who will deliver the message?
- How? (What media/channels will be used? Will communication be one way, or will the audience get to express its views?)

(See also: **communication plan**, **stakeholder.**)

Communication object: In a communication plan, a communication object is the thing about which you are communicating. There are two types of communication objects for your Delivery Unit to consider: The Delivery Unit itself and the delivery effort or parts thereof. (See also: **communication plan.**)

Communication plan: A plan that details your system's coordinated efforts to get the right messages to the right stakeholders at the right times in order to ensure the necessary support for your delivery effort. An effective communication plan must state the following for each stakeholder over time:

- The message and its objective (e.g., give them confidence that our strategy will be successful);
- The frequency and/or timing of communication;
- The messengers; and
- The modes of communication (e.g., e-mail, speech, meeting).

(See also: **stakeholder.**)

Comparative benchmarking: A set of tools used to analyze and compare your system's performance historically, internally, externally, internationally, and functionally.

Concentric circles of leadership: Layers of people and organizations that are involved with your delivery effort, starting from the system leaders and guiding coalition in the center and extending out to users and the public in the last (and widest) circle. In order to make change irreversible, a Delivery Unit must strive to widen these circles of leadership, such that everyone feels ownership of the delivery effort's aspirations. (See also: **aspiration, guiding coalition.**)

Culture of delivery: Summarized in five words: ambition, focus, clarity, urgency, and irreversibility. A culture of delivery encompasses a desire and drive for continuous learning, minimizing blame, and focusing on improvement.

Deliverology: A systematic process for driving progress and delivering results in government and the public sector.

Delivery activity: A specific activity described in this field guide, usually undertaken by your Delivery Unit and system leadership team, that helps to make delivery happen. Examples of delivery activities include analyzing system performance against the aspiration and running routines to monitor progress. It should not be confused with a system activity. (See also: **system activity.**)

Delivery capacity: A system's potential to successfully execute delivery activities. It can be measured according to the kinds of delivery activities a system is undertaking and how effective they are in improving the impact of the system's activities. It should not be confused with system capacity. (See also: **delivery activity, system capacity.**)

Delivery capacity review: A process that the system leadership team or Delivery Unit can undertake, using the delivery capacity review rubric, for the purpose of assessing the existence and strength of a system's delivery activities, based on each of five stages of delivery. (See also: **delivery activity, delivery capacity review rubric.**)

Delivery capacity review rubric: A detailed questionnaire that is used for conducting a delivery capacity review. (See also: **delivery capacity review.**)

Delivery chain: The set of system actors (people or organizations), and the relationships between them, through which a given system activity will be implemented. A delivery chain has one question at its core: Starting from the policy intent of a leader in your system and ending with the frontline behaviors and practices that this policy is designed to influence, how—and through whom—does a system activity actually happen? (See also: **delivery chain analysis, system activity, system actor.**)

Delivery chain analysis: The process by which you map and understand the delivery chain for a system activity (See also: **delivery chain, system activity.**)

Delivery challenge: The nature and size of the barriers that your system faces to delivery of your aspiration, and what your system is currently doing about them.

Delivery effort: The process undertaken (usually by a Delivery Unit) to go through the steps in the field guide, from setting an aspiration to delivering on it.

Delivery leader: Person who heads the delivery effort and is dedicated to it on a full-time (or nearly full-time) basis. The delivery leader also heads the Delivery Unit (if there is one), reports directly to the system leader, and has access to the system leader and the system's top team. The delivery leader is the person who has "sleepless nights" worrying about whether the system is delivering on the aspirations it has set. (See also: **aspiration, delivery effort, Delivery Unit, system leader.**)

Delivery plan organization: The means by which delivery plans are written to cover all relevant interventions in a reform strategy, depending on the complexity of the Delivery Unit and sophistication of the system. The idea of a delivery plan organization is taken from a concept at the heart of program and project management: Any overall effort (a program) can and should be broken up into constituent pieces (projects). (See also: **delivery plan, intervention, strategy.**)

Delivery plan: The guiding tool that system actors responsible for interventions or system activities will use to carry them out. (See also: **intervention, system activity, system actor.**)

Delivery plan owner: A single person accountable for developing and making progress against a delivery plan. (See also: **delivery plan.**)

Delivery pyramid: A map that summarizes the key concepts involved in going from aspiration to implementation, including their relationships with one another. (See also: **aspiration.**)

Delivery reports: An in-depth assessment that the PMDU provided to the prime minister on the status of all of the system's key priority areas every six months.

Delivery routines: Regularly scheduled and structured opportunities for your system leader, delivery plan owners, and others to review performance, discuss major issues, and make decisions to drive delivery forward. (See also: **delivery plan owner, system leader.**)

Delivery Unit: The person or group of people who are responsible for driving the achievement of the system aspiration, no matter what. (See also: **aspiration.**)

Dimension of comparison: A means of grouping performance data in order to better understand and compare performance amongst individuals and performance units. There are broadly three dimensions of comparison: on the individual level, grouping by similar characteristics, and grouping by performance bands. (See also: **performance unit.**)

Driver: A root cause of one or more performance patterns. (See also: **performance pattern.**)

Emotional trajectory: The way in which stakeholders' viewpoints change (or are expected to change) throughout the course of a delivery effort. The goal of your communication plan will be to move stakeholders along an emotional trajectory so that their viewpoints become more and more supportive of the delivery effort. (See also: **communication plan, stakeholder, trajectory.**)

External peer comparison: A type of comparative benchmarking that compares a system's performance (or the performance of its performance units) against systems or performance units from different states. (See also: **comparative benchmarking.**)

Functional comparison: A type of comparative benchmarking that looks for best practices in organizations, which, while they may be dissimilar to your system, perform a function that is vital to your system (e.g., human resources). This type of comparative benchmarking is unlikely to contribute to your understanding of performance (as it does not rely on data), but it comes into play when you are generating ideas for how to improve your system's performance. (See also: **comparative benchmarking.**)

Guiding coalition: The group of people that enables the pursuit of your system's aspirations by (1) removing bureaucratic barriers to change, (2) using their influence to support your Delivery Unit's work at crucial moments, and (3) giving you counsel and guidance in your efforts. (See also: **aspiration.**)

Historical comparison: A type of comparative benchmarking that compares performance today with performance in the past. (See also: **comparative benchmarking.**)

Hypothesis tree: A tool that allows for a comprehensive identification of potential drivers of a given performance pattern via a series of why questions, which can then be narrowed down and tested to determine the most important drivers. (See also: **driver, performance pattern.**)

Implementation dip: A period in which enthusiasm wanes shortly after the launch of a delivery effort. The excitement and positivism during the launch is quickly replaced by frustration as people face the day-to-day challenges of the task at hand and do not yet see any fruits from their efforts. (See also: **delivery effort.**)

Implementation indicator: An indicator, usually specific to a delivery plan, that allows you to track some aspect of that plan's progress. For example, if a government's target is to reduce crime (the target metric), and one of its interventions is to hire and place additional police officers in troubled areas, some implementation indicators might include the number of police officers hired (quantity) and the satisfaction of neighborhood residents with the new hires (quality). (See also: **delivery plan, intervention, target, target metric.**)

Indicator of unintended consequences: A metric that measures the unintended (possibly negative) consequences of pursuing your aspiration, particularly when that pursuit is centered on a specific target metric. These metrics are important to monitor in order to ensure that the delivery effort does not have unintended consequences. A system's aim should be to improve performance on the target metric while minimizing or avoiding unintended consequences. (See also: **aspiration, target metric.**)

Internal peer comparison: A type of comparative benchmarking that compares performance units (or groups of them) within your system. (See also: **comparative benchmarking.**)

International comparison: A type of comparative benchmarking that compares a system's performance (or the performance of its performance units) against systems or performance units from different countries. (See also: **comparative benchmarking.**)

Intervention: A change to one or more system activities that is designed to help your system achieve its aspiration. Interventions can take two forms:

- Changes to current system activities (including improvements to activities, expansions of effective activities, and removal or replacement of ineffective activities); and
- Creation of new system activities to address unmet needs.

(See also: **aspiration, system activity.**)

Joint action team: A team consisting of a person from the Delivery Unit, a relevant system actor, and (possibly) an external third party. Joint action teams are created to investigate or lead a certain area of priority for delivery or to conduct a delivery capacity review. (See also: **delivery capacity review, system actor.**)

Joint team: Please see **joint action team.**

Leading indicator: A metric that helps to predict the future performance on a target metric. (See also: **target metric.**)

League table: A rank ordering of the likelihood of delivery of the various items being assessed in a delivery report (usually targets or interventions). In the PMDU, this rank ordering relied on the criteria in the assessment framework. (See also: **assessment framework, delivery report.**)

Level of analysis: The level of your system at which you choose to examine performance. This can range from the most granular individual level (students and teachers) to performance units for which data can be averaged and/or aggregated, such as schools, campuses, districts, and even whole systems. (See also: **performance unit.**)

Milestone: A predicted event that demonstrates progress in implementing a delivery plan. Milestones may or may not involve a target metric, leading indicator, or implementation indicator. For example, for a plan to implement a literacy program, completion of the curriculum development would be a milestone. (See also: **delivery plan, target metric, leading indicator, implementation indicator.**)

Model of implementation: A component of a theory of change that describes the relationship between the source of change (leaders) and the implementers of change (the frontline). Examples of models of implementation are command and control, devolution and transparency, and quasi-markets. (See also: **theory of change.**)

Moderation meeting: A process used by the PMDU to calibrate and finalize judgments of the likelihood of delivery of each priority area on the PMDU agenda. These judgments relied on the PMDU's assessment framework. Moderation meetings and helped the PMDU to publish the league tables that were a part of its semiannual delivery reports. (See also: **assessment framework, delivery report, league table.**)

Monthly note: A PMDU briefing sent to the system leader to update him or her on relevant progress and issues for the system's target metrics and other relevant performance data. (See also: **target metric.**)

Performance gap: The difference, as measured by the target metric, between the target and the level of performance you have today. (See also: **target, target metric.**)

Performance pattern: A theme or trend in a system's performance on a particular metric with respect to a particular benchmark that is consistent and recurring across levels of analysis and dimensions of comparison. (See also: **comparative benchmarking, dimension of comparison, level of analysis.**)

Performance unit: a grouping of individuals (e.g., classroom, school, district, campus, system) for which performance data can be averaged or aggregated. These averages can be used as levels of analysis to compare past and present performance. (See also: **level of analysis.**)

Priority review: An in-depth, comprehensive review of the state of delivery that the PMDU conducted in areas where challenging problems had been identified.

Reform strategy: Please see **strategy.**

Resonance: A positive "buzz" surrounding your Delivery Unit and delivery effort. It results from many distinct but positive interactions that create a brand for your work that is self-reinforcing. (See also: **brand, delivery effort.**)

Stakeholder: A person or group of people who have a stake, or vested interest, in the process or outcome of your delivery effort. (See also: **delivery effort.**)

Stocktake: A PMDU-facilitated meeting between the system leader (Tony Blair) and relevant department officials that occurred every three months in each priority area, featuring in-depth discussions of the PMDU's main priorities.

Strategy: A coherent set of interventions that combine to maximize impact on your target metrics. The interventions in a strategy are chosen and arranged according to four principles:

- Each intervention is consistent with your theory of change, which lends your strategy its internal coherence;
- Each intervention is powerful on its own, proven or promising in its potential impact on your target metrics;
- The interventions in a strategy are integrated, building on each other such that the effect of the whole is greater than the sum of the parts; and
- The interventions in a strategy are sequenced, taking into account their interdependencies with each other, your resources over time, and the constant need to build momentum and sustain energy.

(See also: **intervention**, **target metric**, **theory of change.**)

System: The entity that is providing public services, setting an aspiration, and attempting to deliver the aspiration. Examples: State Education Agency, higher education system, city government. (See also: **aspiration.**)

System activity: An activity undertaken by one or more system actors to achieve the system's aspiration. This is the "real work" of any system. It can consist of day-to-day work, such as classroom teaching, or specific programs, such as outreach for students of low income to help improve freshman year retention rates in college. It should not be confused with a delivery activity. (See also: **aspiration, delivery activity, system actor.**)

System actor: A person or organization in your system that holds direct responsibility for implementation of one or more system activities. (See also: **system activity.**)

System capacity: The potential for system actors to execute system activities successfully. It should not be confused with delivery capacity. (See also: **delivery capacity, system activity, system actor.**)

System leader: The person who leads a system. In K–12 education, it is the chief state school officer (CSSO), while in higher education, it is the system CEO. (See also: **system.**)

System map: A diagram of the set of major system actors, their roles, and their relationships to one another. Unlike a delivery chain, a system map is a broad overview of the major players in a system and is not anchored on a specific system activity. (See also: **delivery chain, system activity, system actor.**)

System user: A person who is the ultimate beneficiary of a system's services. For example, students are the users of an education system, and the public at large is the user of a health care system. (See also: **system.**)

Target: A commitment by your system to achieve a specific level of performance on a target metric by a defined point in time. Targets should be SMART: specific, measurable, ambitious, realistic, and time bound. (See also: **target metric.**)

Target metric: A metric that a system uses to measure the achievement of one or more of its aspirations. Target metrics represent the actual outcomes desired by a system. (See also: **aspiration, target.**)

Theory of change: A succinct articulation of your system's belief about the best way to achieve your system's aspiration. A theory of change is the organizing force of a system's strategy. It is expressed as a set of interrelated themes that focus your system's efforts on those things that are most likely to affect your target metric. These themes can be content areas that your system will focus on, models of implementation, or a combination of the two. (See also: **aspiration, strategy, target metric.**)

Trajectory: An evidence-based projection of a metric's path over time from its current level to the level suggested by the target. It is your best estimate of the levels of performance your system will achieve en route to achieving its overall target. (See also: **target.**)

Appendix A1 Delivery Capacity Review Rubric

This rubric is a tool to assist in understanding the current state of each component of delivery from an organizational perspective. Ideally, this rubric should be completed by the team to help identify the areas where the system has strengths in delivery capacity and the areas in which it has to improve.

To complete: Please read the questions to consider and the indicators of weak and strong delivery for each aspect of delivery (e.g., 1A. Define your aspiration.) Based on the above, please rate your system and state a rationale for why you selected a particular rating for each aspect of delivery.

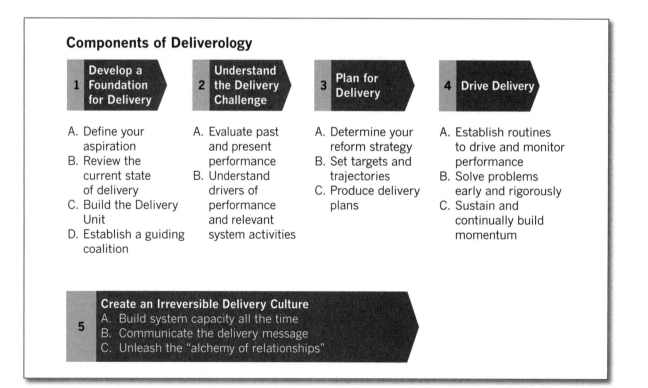

Components of Deliverology

1 Develop a Foundation for Delivery

A. Define your aspiration
B. Review the current state of delivery
C. Build the Delivery Unit
D. Establish a guiding coalition

2 Understand the Delivery Challenge

A. Evaluate past and present performance
B. Understand drivers of performance and relevant system activities

3 Plan for Delivery

A. Determine your reform strategy
B. Set targets and trajectories
C. Produce delivery plans

4 Drive Delivery

A. Establish routines to drive and monitor performance
B. Solve problems early and rigorously
C. Sustain and continually build momentum

5 Create an Irreversible Delivery Culture

A. Build system capacity all the time
B. Communicate the delivery message
C. Unleash the "alchemy of relationships"

1. Develop a Foundation for Delivery

Areas to consider	Example questions	Best case (Green) ⟺	Worst case (Red)	Rating	Rationale
1A. Define your aspiration Does the system have a clearly articulated and shared aspiration?	• Does the system currently have an aspiration? What do the system officials consider as the "aspiration"? Does the answer differ across different system officials? • Does the aspiration define what the system cares about, what they will do about it, and how they will measure success? • Is the aspiration shared? Do system leaders agree with this aspiration? • Is the aspiration sufficiently focused? Are system actors energized by this aspiration? • Do aspirations align with external influences (e.g., mission statement, laws, etc)? • Can the aspiration be calculated and summarized in one or more metrics using data that is or will be readily available?	• System has an overarching aspiration or set of aspirations that are focused, prioritized, clearly understood, and agreed upon by system leaders and system officials. • The aspiration is sufficiently ambitious: if achieved, there will be a substantial impact on the things the system cares about. • The aspiration takes into account external influences. • The aspiration can be measured by a defined metric that is or will be readily available.	• There is no clearly defined aspiration—system actors cannot definitively state a consistent aspiration. • There are too many aspirations or aspirations are not focused. • System has not articulated what it cares about, what they will do about it, and how they will measure success. • System leaders and actors do not all agree on the aspirations. • Aspiration lacks ambition—little progress is required to achieve it. • The aspiration does not align with external influences. • There are no metrics to measure aspiration or metrics identified are impossible to quantify.		
1B. Review the current state of delivery Is the system aware of its existing capacity to drive progress against aspirations?	• Does your system reflect on its ability to deliver on its aspirations? • Does system leadership have a good understanding of the system's landscape and levers of influence? • Do you know the general strengths and weaknesses of your system's delivery activities? Can you identify areas where your system does well and areas where it does not do well?	• Leaders have a clear understanding of the people and organizations, relationships, and leverage necessary to get things done in their system. • System has a thorough understanding of its delivery activities and is aware of its limitations. • System allows this understanding to influence its decisions and resource allocation.	• Leaders exhibit a poor understanding of the system or do not incorporate that understanding into their decision making. • System is not aware of its strengths and weaknesses in delivery activities.		

(Continued)

(Continued)

Areas to consider	Example questions	Best case (Green)	Worst case (Red)	Rating	Rationale
1C. Build the Delivery Unit Is there a designated group with the focus, tools, and skill set needed to drive delivery?	• Who in your system is responsible for ensuring the delivery of the aspiration? How large is this team? • Do they have the tools and skill set needed to drive delivery and achieve the aspiration? • Do they have access to the people/data they need? Are their roles and models of interaction with the system clearly defined? • Does the organization ensure continuity, objectivity, multiple perspectives, and sufficient skills to meet department needs? • Does the team promote a culture of delivery?	• Delivery is led by a strong leader with personal commitment to driving progress. • There is clear accountability for driving progress against the aspiration. • The individual accountable for delivery reports directly to the system head, and the team has access to people/data it needs to conduct delivery activities. • The team's size and organization is created to fit the system's needs and ensures continuity of relationships with system, objectivity, and multiple perspectives. • The team embodies, is known for, and spreads a culture of delivery.	• There is no clear person or group of people who are responsible for delivery. • Those responsible for delivery operate in silos, with little or no access to the people/data they need to drive/monitor progress. • Roles and interaction models are not clearly defined and understood by system officials or delivery team. • The team's size and organization does not fit the system's need. • The team does not embody a culture of delivery.		
1D. Establish a guiding coalition Does the system actively manage the stakeholders who will be influential in driving progress against our aspirations?	• Does the leadership have a group of stakeholders in key positions that are committed to the success of the aspiration? • Does this group have diverse spheres of influence throughout the system? • Does the group have a balanced combination of leadership, management, position power, expertise, and credibility? • What is the potential of the members of this group to work together to build collective agreement and commitment to the aspiration and delivery strategy? • Does the system leader continually work at maintaining the coalition?	• At least 7–10 change leaders share a consistent understanding of the aspiration, the strategy, how it is to be implemented, and what will define success. • The group of change leaders is consciously expanded to form a cadre of leaders throughout the system. • The skills, credibility, and spheres of influence are balanced in this group. • The group is consulted on a consistent basis, and relationships are nurtured. • The group's members work well and efficiently together, and they enable progress of the effort in their respective spheres of influence.	• There is no deliberately identified leadership group. • The leadership group represents a limited and/or irrelevant range of stakeholders. • The leadership group is not aligned on the aspiration. • The leadership group has a poor understanding of other stakeholders, and fails to expand the coalition to critical mass (e.g., support only comes from management). • This leadership group is rarely called upon for advice and suggestions, and there is little effort in maintaining contact with members.		

2. Understand the Delivery Challenge

Areas to consider	Example questions	Best case (Green)	Worst case (Red)	Rating	Rationale
2A. Evaluate past and present performance Has the system been using a data-driven, fact-based approach to evaluating performance?	• How easy or difficult is it to access historical and real-time data on performance of the system against its aspiration? • Is this data relevant to the aspiration, clear, detailed, robust, accepted, and accurate? • Does your system have a set of leading indicators to better predict performance against its main outcome metrics? • How well are trends and patterns that arise in the data identified and understood? Are they benchmarked against history within your system and with other systems? • Does the system identify and track indicators of unintended consequences?	• Data systems provide readily accessible historical, longitudinal, and real-time accurate data on main outcome metric, leading indicators, and indicators of unintended consequences. • Data is available at the individual level and can be grouped, analyzed, and compared across subgroups and performance units (e.g., schools, campuses). • Trends and patterns are identified in the data through rigorous analysis, and performance is benchmarked against history within your system and across other systems. • Performance comparisons are used to identify areas contributing most to poor performance of the target metric.	• Only historical data is available (big lags) or data is not available by relevant "slices." • Data is difficult to access or is not useful for decision making. • System relies only on target metrics for performance data, despite the relatively long lag time. • Little or no identification of trends and patterns in data. • Little or no use of data benchmarking to evaluate performance. • Data cannot uncover largest contributors to poor performance against its main outcome metrics. • System does not identify or track indicators of unintended consequences.		
2B. Understand drivers of performance and related system activities Does the system understand the efficacy of individual activities underway that support the aspiration?	• Do you know why you are not doing as well as you think you could be doing? • Have you come to this conclusion via a systematic and rigorous assessment (e.g., a hypothesis tree)? • Is there a clear understanding of the largest contributors to underperformance? • Have you accurately and comprehensively identified and profiled system activities that address these contributors to underperformance? • Do these activity profiles include a description, assessment of efficacy, resources required, and a delivery chain analysis?	• System has a thorough understanding of the root causes of the performance challenges it faces. • System has comprehensively identified and analyzed its activities that impact these root causes. • This analysis includes the current impact of each activity, the resources required, and a delivery chain analysis that exposes strengths and weaknesses in implementation.	• No systematic assessment of performance and identification of root causes of underperformance. • There are no hypotheses about root causes of underperformance, or the hypotheses that exist are not focused or prioritized. • System does not have a clear understanding of what it is doing, if anything, to address underperformance. • Minimal research into expected efficacy of activities and their connection to aspiration.		

3. Plan for Delivery

Areas to consider	Example questions	Best case (Green) ⟷	Worst case (Red)	Rating	Rationale
3A. Determine your reform strategy Does the system take a cohesive approach to its interventions and try and maximize synergies and understand inter-dependencies?	• Does your system have a theory of change that articulates how it believes it will achieve its aspiration? • Does your system have a reform strategy with a coherent set of interventions that are consistent with the theory of change? • Are the interventions powerful on their own, with proven or promising efficacy to improve performance against the aspiration? • Are the interventions integrated, having a combined effect that is more powerful than their individual effects would otherwise have been? • Are the interventions sequenced to balance resources required, impact, and interdependencies over time?	• System has a well-defined theory of change that tells a coherent and compelling story about how the system achieved its aspiration. • Different possible interventions are analyzed in terms of expected impact, cost, feasibility, scale, rigor, and requirements for skill and participation along the delivery chains; this analysis informs the choice and sequencing of interventions. • Chosen combination of interventions represents a coherent strategy, is aligned with the theory of change, and is complementary and mutually reinforcing.	• System lacks a well-defined theory of change. • Combination of interventions lacks coherence. Little or no benefit arises from implementing all the interventions as part of a single strategy. • Little analysis of different combinations of interventions or interdependencies between them. • Interventions themselves have little evidence that they have large impact on performance against the aspiration.		
3B. Set targets and trajectories Has the aspiration been translated to concrete targets and cascaded down to the relevant level?	• Are there clear system targets to measure progress against the aspiration? • Are the targets SMART (specific, measurable, ambitious, realistic, time limited)? • Has the system developed baseline trajectories of performance based on historical data and projection of external factors?	• A set of targets exist that are SMART. • Robust baseline trajectory created that takes into account past progress, causes of peaks and troughs, and seasonality considerations. • Interim benchmarks between the current date and the date of the target (trajectory) are set for each target.	• Targets do not exist or are not SMART. • There is no baseline or overall trajectory, neither a measurable end goal nor numerical markers of progress along the way. • Trajectories created do not take into account a baseline understanding of what would		

Areas to consider	Example questions	Best case (Green)	Worst case (Red)	Rating	Rationale
Have realistic trajectories been created that link projected impact with evidence?	• Has the system developed trajectories of performance? • Are these trajectories based on accurate assessment of expected impact from planned interventions? • Are the trajectories based on an accurate understanding of relevant internal and external benchmarks? • Do targets and trajectories extend beyond the system level to performance units (districts, campuses, schools)? How well accepted are these subtargets and trajectories?	• Targets and trajectories demonstrate a thorough understanding of the impact of the strategy's interventions and/or benchmarks within and across systems. • Subtargets are set for individual campuses/districts/schools, and are well-understood and accepted at every level. • Together, these sub-targets add up to the overall system targets.	happen if no interventions were implemented, based on historical data and projection of external factors. • Trajectories created do not take into account all interventions and/or are not based on analysis of benchmarks. • Subtargets for individual campuses/districts/schools not set or well-accepted by system and campuses.		
3C. Produce delivery plans Does the system use meaningful plans against which to track performance?	• Is there a clearly defined organization of delivery plans based on the needs and characteristics of the system and its targets? • Do these plans link to subplans that reach all the way to front-line individuals? • Has the system prioritized which plans the Delivery Unit will monitor based on manageability and comprehensiveness? • Do plans track relevant performance metrics, leading indicators, and implementation indicators for each intervention?	• Plans are organized to fit the needs of the system and the planned strategy. • Delivery team monitors a manageable but comprehensive set of plans at the right level. • Organization of plans indicates an awareness of the crosscutting work and for the need for coordination across multiple departments where necessary. • Plans are coherent; frontline individual plans are connected to system-level plans.	• There are far too many plans for the Delivery Unit to manage, or the plans combined do not cover all planned interventions. • Little or no connection between plans at different levels of the system. • Plans do not include specific system activities, resources required to implement interventions, stakeholder management or capacity building activities, nor risk management.		

(Continued)

(Continued)

Areas to consider	Example questions	Best case (Green)	Worst case (Red)	Rating	Rationale
	• Do the plans set their own trajectories for implementation, including milestones of progress and action steps with clear owners? • Are plans detailed enough to drive accountability, management of stakeholders, and allocation of resources? • Do plans identify and address gaps in capacity and changes required in system activities?	• Every plan has a specific owner who will be accountable for results. • Plans identify a sequence for implementing interventions to improve performance and overcome both capacity and implementation barriers, detailing milestones, timelines, and action steps.	• Plans have multiple or unclear owners. • Ownership of plans is determined by "default" (e.g., existing organization structure) rather than being logically thought through. • Plans do not include timetables with specific milestones, action steps, and owners for each step.		
	• Are plans concrete enough to identify milestones and risks but flexible enough that they are expected to change over time? • Has the system created processes to review, challenge, and revise?	• Plans specify the relevant delivery chains and allocate responsibility and resources along them. • Plans take into account stakeholder and risk management. • Plans are implemented as soon as they are actionable but are continually improved once implementation begins.	• System allows the plan development process to delay implementation. • There is no process to refine plans once implementation has begun.		

4. Drive Delivery

Areas to consider	Example questions	Best case (Green)	Worst case (Red)	Rating	Rationale
4A. Establish routines to drive and monitor performance Is there a regular, fact-based, results-driven cycle of updates?	• How do you track progress against your aspiration (measure against plan, or trajectories)? • What kind of information is regularly tracked (outcome vs. implementation)? • How (and how frequently) is that information reported to decision makers? Is the information reported clear, concise, and easy to understand? • Are there clearly defined criteria used to understand progress and quality of implementation?	• Target metrics, leading indicators, and other relevant data (quantitative and qualitative) are identified, monitored against trajectories, and reported centrally, including progress on delivery plan milestones. • Routines reinforce accountability but also serve as learning opportunities.	• Little or no data is regularly tracked, and the delivery plan is rarely if ever referenced. • System leaders do not hold system or campus staff accountable for outcome data. • Conversations about performance are tense, reinforcing a blame culture.		
	• What is the focus of these discussions? (Qualitative/Quantitative? Is the focus on discussion on solving the problem or assigning blame?) • What are the outcomes of these discussions? Are there documented action steps with follow-up discussions and check-ins? • Is there a master schedule of routines?	• System has instituted a set of performance monitoring routines that differ in frequency, level of detail, and audience, but which together provide system leader with a clear and frequent (e.g., monthly) picture of performance. • Close-to-real-time data is readily available to inform routines. • Information in routines is presented clearly and precisely. • Clearly defined criteria for judging progress and quality of implementation allow for identification of areas where delivery is off track before key milestones are missed. • Routines drive the actions/follow-ups necessary to get back on track or stay on track. • Routines are tracked on a master schedule.	• Analysis is superficial (e.g., does not identify implications of data), cumbersome (i.e., takes too long and requires too many resources), or poorly presented (i.e., hard to understand key takeaways, not prioritized). • Criteria that clearly indicate levels of progress and quality of implementation are not well defined. • Data and reports are not produced frequently enough to drive action. • Results data not compared against trajectories. • There are no systematic updates on delivery progress to the system leader, or updates take place annually. • Routines to review performance result in no action or insufficient action. • There is no master schedule of routines.		

(Continued)

(Continued)

Areas to consider	Example questions	Best case (Green)	Worst case (Red)	Rating	Rationale
4B. Solve problems early and rigorously Are there mechanisms to ensure problems are identified and raised early and solved in order of priority?	• Does analysis uncover key issues, anticipate problems, and prioritize them for resolution? • When problems arise, are they brought to the attention of leadership quickly enough? • Are resources deployed based on the severity of each problem? Are priority reviews used for very severe problems if resources are available? • Are solutions and/or learnings from problem solving captured and shared throughout the system?	• A variety of methods are used to identify problems early. • There is a clear "triage" system to categorize severity of issues as well as the resources needed based on severity. • Problem solving is comprehensive and rigorous, using several problem-solving tools to ensure that issues are resolved quickly and thoroughly. • Solutions are integrated into plans. • Best practice is identified and shared throughout system. • Priority reviews are used efficiently and effectively to understand areas of high priority if resources are available.	• Problems are logged but not prioritized and acted upon in a systematic way (i.e., system solves problems by firefighting). • The system is ineffective at identifying problems early before they become crises. • Reviews of implementation efforts are long and cumbersome or do not identify weaknesses and suggestions for improvement. • Analysis of problems is superficial (e.g., benefit of the doubt frequently granted).		
4C. Sustain and continually build momentum How does the system maintain dedication to the approach through adversity and celebrate success?	• How stable (unwavering) are aspirations and targets? • What efforts does the leadership make in ensuring that staff persists in achieving goals despite distractions and monotony? • What does the system do to manage those who resist change? • Does the system vigorously challenge the status quo? • How does the system celebrate successes?	• The reform message has been internalized along the chain: "We should have done this years ago." • Those accountable for delivery ensure that leaders stick to and see through the agendas they have defined, allowing for adjustments based only on the facts on the ground. • Priorities remain, even through crises, and routines are consistently carried out. • The system strives for greatness and continues to refocus and reprioritize relative to the aspiration as progress unfolds.	• Priorities shift frequently. • Leaders do not demonstrate a commitment to any agenda and are likely to change their emphasis with political winds. • Change is sustained only as long as leaders are focused on it. • The system focuses on fighting fires rather than the delivery effort during crises. • The system does not celebrate successes.		

5. Create a Culture of Delivery

Areas to consider	Example questions	Best case (Green)	Worst case (Red)	Rating	Rationale
5A. Build system capacity all the time Is building capacity to deliver a priority for the leadership and an ongoing endeavor?	• What efforts are underway to build capacity (structure, resources, competencies, and motivation) to support system goals? Are they built into plans? • What actions are taken to make change irreversible? • Are frontline leaders developing skills needed for delivery at a sufficient pace to implement the changes? • Is this capacity being built throughout the system?	• Delivery and system capacity required is analyzed, and gaps are identified. • Management makes ensuring these skills are present a top priority, integrating capacity building in plans. • Action is taken to quickly develop capacity using a variety of methods such as hiring, reorganizing, formal training, and feedback loops. • Learnings are codified, responsibility is pushed outward, and leadership role models a can-do attitude of delivery culture.	• Little or no analysis of the delivery and system capacity required and there are no perceived current gaps in capacity. • Eliminating gaps in skills is not a management priority and is not integrated into plans. • Core delivery skills not integrated into performance assessment. • Delivery skills are not spread throughout the system—no pushing responsibility out. • There is little to no use of formal training, feedback loops, or codification of learnings. • No plans are in place to reinforce and lock in the culture of delivery.		
5B. Communicate the delivery message Does the system regularly communicate about the delivery effort and associated priorities?	• Are there communication strategies to highlight your delivery efforts? • Is communication both about the Delivery Unit itself and about the delivery effort? • Have the right stakeholders for communication efforts been identified?	• Communication is two way. • There is a clear communication plan that details the message and the objective, the modes of communication, the frequency or timing of communication, and the messengers. • The system provides consistent, clear communications, with prioritization of key messages. • Audiences understand both what will be accomplished and how the goal will be accomplished.	• Communication is not two way. • Communications from the system are poorly planned and often fail to highlight the central priority and message. • Messages are inconsistent or conflicting across the system or do not indicate strategies and action steps. • Limited set of stakeholders identified; stakeholder views are not clearly articulated.		

(Continued)

(Continued)

Areas to consider	Example questions	Best case (Green)	Worst case (Red)	Rating	Rationale
	• Do communications have a compelling message, cater to different stakeholders, use the right messengers, and communicate consistently, constantly, and confidently?	• The system has identified a broad and complete set of stakeholders that have influence throughout the delivery effort. • Tailored communications target both internal and external stakeholders with messages that are consistent yet relevant to each group. • The communication plan is monitored and adjusted as necessary.	• Communications are not targeted to different stakeholder groups or reach only a subset of stakeholders. • The communications plan is not monitored or adjusted throughout the effort.		
5C. Unleash the "alchemy of relationships" Are relationships that are central to success cultivated and maintained?	• Is there a culture of building relationships throughout the delivery team? • How are relationships built and sustained? • Are relationships set up to be win-win for all involved? • Is conflict managed proactively?	• Delivery team members create and maintain effective relationships with all people that they interact with, establishing win-win situations and staying true to their core values. • Conflict is managed with a fact-based discussion that acknowledges the emotional arguments of others but does not compromise on core principles. • The delivery effort is regarded as positive and beneficial; people not only are willing to help the effort but want to help it.	• Relationships between delivery team members and system officials are strained, unproductive, or dissatisfying to those involved. • Conflict is unexpected and contentious. • Interactions are purely transactional and have no sense of values. • There is no positive brand image or resonance associated with the delivery effort.		

Appendix A2 Assessment Framework Used by the Prime Minister's Delivery Unit

Assessment framework—guidance for departments

What is the framework for?

(1) The assessment framework is designed to provide a structure to help you to judge the likelihood of delivering your Public Service Agreement (PSA) targets. It will also be used by the Prime Minister's Delivery Unit (PMDU) and the Treasury to develop assessments of your prospects for delivery. It is used in our internal moderation process to ensure that we are consistent in how we make judgments.

(2) The main reason for agreeing upon the assessment with you is so that jointly we can identify the areas where you can take action to improve the prospects for delivery.

Your self-assessment

We will be asking departments to assess their likelihood of delivering each PSA using

Your joint action leader will be able to provide further support to you in using the framework

- We have provided an overview of the architecture of the framework and further explanation of each judgment in the framework on the pages that follow.
- The framework breaks down each judgment into "areas to consider" accompanied by some example questions to prompt your thinking.
- As every PSA target is different, these questions are intended as a guide rather than a strict checklist.
- **They are not designed to be a checklist or tick box, where every issue has to be addressed.** You should judge which are the most relevant for your target and consider whether there are any other questions worth asking.

Recent performance

Recent performance is defined as progress against trajectories over the previous 6 months. Recent

(Continued)

(Continued)

the high-level summary sheet. The assessment requires four judgments:

- Degree of challenge
- Quality of planning, implementation, and performance management
- Capacity to drive progress
- Stage of delivery

We are only expecting three or four bullet points as the rationale for each judgment.

performance is a factor that we take into account throughout our assessment.

Delivery chain

Much of the assessment framework relates to the delivery chain as a whole (e.g., capacity to drive progress). This starts with, and includes, the government department, and departments will need to bear the whole chain in mind when completing self-assessments.

Likelihood of delivery

Department: ____________ **Date of assessment:** ____________

PSA target: ____________ **Assessors:** ____________

Judgment	Rating	Rationale Summary
Degree of challenge	L/M/H/VH	
Quality of planning, implementation, and performance management Understanding the challenge Governance, program, and project management Managing performance		
Capacity to drive progress Understanding and structure of the delivery chain Engaging the delivery chain Leadership and culture		
Stage of delivery	1/2/3/4	

Recent performance against trajectory and milestones

Likelihood of delivery

Key

Red	Highly problematic — requires urgent and decisive action
Yellow/Red	Problematic — requires substantial attention, some aspects need urgent attention
Yellow/Green	Mixed — aspects require substantial attention, some good
Green	Good — requires refinement and systematic implementation

Architecture of assessment framework

Judgment area	What are we looking for?
Degree of challenge	Scale of the task, obstacles to be overcome
Quality of planning, implementation, and performance management	
1. Understanding the challenge	Clarity on what success looks like (what we are doing and why) and how much has to be changed to get there, taking account of historical performance.
2. Governance, program, and progress management	A strategy that is translated into a usable implementation plan. Clear structures that support accountability for outcomes.
3. Managing performance	Fundamentals of monitoring and reporting performance (measures, trajectories). Proactive responses to reported performance.
Capacity to drive progress	
1. Understanding and structuring the delivery chain	Understanding of the delivery chain; sophistication/comprehensiveness of key elements of the delivery chain, including incentives and prioritization.
2. Engaging the delivery chain	Winning hearts and minds: mechanisms for influencing and mechanisms for and response to feedback.
3. Leadership and culture	Extent to which the performance ethic of the department and delivery chain supports delivery: leadership, ambition, accountability, and working across silos.
Stage of delivery	Current point on the scale between policy development and irreversible progress.

Degree of challenge

Areas to consider	Example questions	Best case (L) ⟷	Worst case (VH)	Rating	Rationale
Historic performance	Is a demanding step change or reversal in performance required? How close is the date for achieving the target? Has recent performance been on track?	Continuation of trend could achieve target/relatively small change required over long timescales	A major reversal in performance trend is needed within short timescales	L M H VH	
Constraints	Are there any constraints that make the target particularly difficult to achieve (e.g., timescales, resources, technical, political)? Is the public/customer supportive or resistant to the policy?	No constraints, or only a few constraints, that can be worked around; public/customer generally supportive	Major constraints exist that will be difficult to work around and that will significantly affect the ability to deliver	L M H VH	
Organizational change	Is any major organizational change required along the delivery chain (including the department) to achieve delivery (e.g., cultural, behavioral, structural)?	No major organizational change required	Major organizational change required with significant barriers to success	L M H VH	
Delivery chain	How complex is the delivery chain? What mix of departmental, other public body, private sector, or other agency action will be needed?	Relatively uncomplicated/manageable delivery chain	Wide ranging and multiorganizational delivery chain and very difficult to manage	L M H VH	
Interdependencies	How dependent is this target on the delivery of other targets or change programs? Or on cross-departmental working? How manageable are these interdependencies?	Interdependencies are well understood and manageable	Several major and critical interdependencies; a number of departments and/or agencies must work together to achieve	L M H VH	
Additional risks	What additional risks are associated with meeting this target? How great an impact could they have? How manageable are the risks?	Generally low risk with any higher risks easily manageable	Many high-impact risks that are difficult to manage	L M H VH	

Quality of planning, implementation, and performance management

Areas to consider	Example questions	Best case (Green) ⟷	Worst case (Red)	Rating	Rationale
1. Understanding the challenge					
Understanding the desired outcome and target	Is the overall vision clear? Is the target SMART, and does it match the policy objective? Is there a sound understanding of the degree of challenge based on historical performance? Is the challenge understood in terms of changing perceptions as well as meeting the target?	SMART, challenging, outcome-focused target that reflects underlying real-world improvement sought. Understanding of degree of change required. Analysis of historic data including impacts of past activities/external influences.	Target is not outcome focused. Significant ambiguity/evidence that target and policy are in conflict. Lack of appreciation of urgency and scale of change required. Analysis has not taken into account historical performance.		
Understanding causation and "what works"	Have performance drivers been understood? Are effective levers identified? Is there quantified analysis of the expected impact of policies/action (level of impact and timing)? Has evidence of what works been identified and used? Are missing levers identified, and gaps in knowledge being addressed?	Sound analysis of drivers/levers. Full quantified trajectory by policy/activity based on credible model of causality. Systematic reference to evaluations, studies, and analyses of what works.	Drivers and levers unclear/no evidence base. Lack of recognition that new levers need to be found. No analysis of previous experience or evidence about what has had most impact or of contributions of actions to success measure.		
Customer and public perceptions	Is the public/customer supportive or resistant to the policy? Are the drivers of customer and public satisfaction known? Do key players in the delivery chain understand their role in improving public perceptions? Is there an effective strategy for improving public perceptions?	Alignment of public/customer perception with actual performance is understood. Where the gap is challenging, there is a plan for improving public perceptions, with ownership by key deliverers.	No clear picture of public/customer perception of performance, and a limited strategy for tackling it, or low priority given to addressing public/customer perceptions		

(Continued)

(Continued)

Areas to consider	Example questions	Best case (Green)	Worst case (Red)	Rating	Rationale
2. Governance, program, and project management					
Business strategy	Is there clarity about what success looks like at milestone points? Have the desired outcomes and activities been prioritized—where necessary, have tough choices been made? Is there a clear blueprint that defines success in terms of the changed business processes, people, tools, information, and measures?	Leaders throughout the delivery chain are clear about which are the priority activities and what the benefits of the PSA outcomes are. They refer to shared definitions of success, which are translated into tangible outcomes.	Activities are planned without a common understanding of what they will deliver and/or why those outcomes are important. No prioritization of activities. Success is not defined or is defined in terms of vision statements, which are not translated into meaningful outcomes.		
Implementation planning, milestones	Has the strategy been turned into a rationalized plan? Is the plan fit for purpose? Have the right actions been identified to implement the strategy? Have meaningful milestones been set at sufficiently frequent intervals to focus progress assessment? Have all the options for acceleration been considered?	An ambitious and credible plan is being used, and it identifies resources, the right activities, and milestones. Plan is clearly related to the business strategy, and is being systematically monitored.	No plan, or inadequate plan, which does not identify or is unrealistic about required resources and activities. Infrequently monitored and/or insufficiently challenging.		
Maximizing the impact of programs	Have the benefits of projects and change programs been articulated? Is there a regular review of the outputs of projects and their contribution to desired outcomes? Is action being taken where further benefits can be gained? Is there a communication strategy?	Change programs are reviewed early, and continual review of actions establishes which are contributing to PSA outcomes. Action is taken quickly to maximize impact. There is an effective communication strategy.	Program/project managers are not able to articulate the benefits of actions/interventions. Infrequent review of outputs, and no action is taken to get full value. No communication strategy.		

Areas to consider	Example questions	Best case (Green) ⟷	Worst case (Red)	Rating	Rationale
Risk management	Are the major risks to delivery and risks of implementation understood? How effective is the management of risk—ownership, measurement and monitoring, and mitigation?	Operational and contingency risks are identified and have responsible owners; mitigations are identified, and contingency plans are in place (where appropriate).	Definition of risk too narrowly focused, and key risks to implementation are overlooked. No ownership of major risks, and inadequate process for monitoring risk.		
Governance and program management structures	Is there a senior responsible owner (SRO) and/or board focused on managing risks, resolving issues, tracking milestones and benefits, and monitoring performance? Are specific individuals accountable for outcomes and benefits? If more than one change program underpins delivery, is there a governance tier in place where the full picture is reviewed? Is it clear what the relationship should be between departmental and ministerial governance arrangements?	SRO and/or board members are clearly accountable for outcomes and actively tackle poor performance. They take difficult decisions where necessary. Collectively able to look above the detail at the strategic picture. Performance is reviewed alongside action plans.	SROs/boards are not clearly accountable for outcomes; boards act as discussion forums with little decision making. Risks overlooked and/or difficult decisions avoided or delegated. Performance is reviewed separately from action planning.		
3. Managing performance					
Measures (or indicators)	Have effective measures of assessing progress toward the target been identified? Are proxy measures or lead indicators that are being used suitable? Will measures quickly show whether actions are working? Are there measures in place to track customer satisfaction and public perceptions of performance?	Good measures selected that will enable monitoring at frequent enough intervals and drive the right behaviors. Public perceptions of performance are also measured and tracked.	No measures or proxy indicators identified, or measures identified with timelag too great to inform delivery, or they distort priorities/drive the wrong behaviors.		

(Continued)

(Continued)

Areas to consider	Example questions	Best case (Green)	Worst case (Red)	Rating	Rationale
Trajectories	Are there trajectories showing the expected outturn at each intermediate point between the baseline and the target year? If tracking the target measure is not sufficient to assess progress, are adequate proxy or lead indicators with trajectories monitored?	Each measure has a well-considered trajectory clearly linked to key activities and milestones and sound progress tracking processes.	No trajectories or trajectories not based on any analysis.		
Reporting performance	Is the content and analysis of performance information appropriate? Is it reviewed frequently enough to drive swift action? Is there sufficient data on local and regional performance and on contribution by category (e.g. segment group)?	Systems efficient and reviewed regularly. Good quality performance reports being used by senior managers to drive timely action.	Poor quality performance reporting means problems are not identified or tackled urgently. No/inadequate analysis of local/regional performance.		
Acting on performance information	Where problems arise, is remedial action taken promptly? Is the support and/or intervention sufficient/appropriate? Are there dialogs about performance all the way down the chain?	Appropriate support or intervention at the right time. Discussions about performance take place at many tiers of the organization.	Support or intervention is too little, too late. No dialogue follows from circulation of performance information.		
Evaluating actions	Are appropriate evaluations undertaken to understand whether the actions are having the intended effect? Does this happen at all tiers of the organization, including the frontline?	Well-designed evaluations provide clear assessment of what is working. Frontline participates in evaluation. Good use of inspection data.	Little evaluation taking place or planned, or it is conducted only by the center/top of the organization.		

Capacity to drive progress

Areas to consider	Example questions	Best case (Green)	Worst case (Red)	Rating	Rationale
1. Understanding and structure of the delivery chain					
Understanding the delivery chain	Has the structure of the delivery chain been identified? Are roles and responsibilities clear? Are the interests and influences of key stakeholders understood? Is there an appropriate strategy for tackling weaknesses in the chain?	Key people, stakeholders, and target customers have been mapped and cascaded. There is a strategy for strengthening the chain (where appropriate).	Functions of the delivery chain are opaque. Lack of clarity about who the main deliverers are.		
Prioritization	Are people throughout the delivery chain working to a ranked set of priorities? Are tough choices made at the strategic level sustained through the chain? Does the allocation of resources and activities reflect agreed priorities? Is there prioritization within the total portfolio of programs, as well as those relating specifically to the PSA? Is there an approach to ensure that ministerial priorities are aligned with agreed priorities?	Key deliverers and accountable leaders are focused on a ranked set of priorities, based on effective quantification and clear, agreed upon criteria. Tough choices are made. Priorities, and criteria for prioritization, are regularly reviewed.	People are working on numerous and conflicting priorities, with no agreed ranking. Priorities are decided locally. There is no sense of expected impact or ease of implementation.		
Incentives	Are incentives in place, and do the forms of incentive (e.g., financial reward, freedoms vs. controls, recognition vs. shaming) reflect what matters to those to whom they apply? Do incentives apply according to the extent to which the PSA outcome is delivered? Do	Incentives targeted using an analysis of who is important to delivery; leaders empowered to design local incentives. Strong incentives based on evidence of what motivates those to	Incentives that do not apply or are ineffective for important parts of the delivery chain, or they encourage the wrong behaviors/outcomes.		

(Continued)

(Continued)

Areas to consider	Example questions	Best case (Green)	Worst case (Red)	Rating	Rationale
	incentives act on key decision makers throughout the delivery chain? Do the incentives add up to a coherent whole, avoiding perverse incentives?	whom they apply. No perverse incentives operating.	Incentives that are trivial or do not match what matters.		
Support	Is there transfer of best practice (vertically or laterally)? Are processes for evaluation/ inspection understood and used? Is the current use and dissemination of incentives, training, and tools sufficient? Is there clear responsibility for challenging and supporting deliverers?	Good transfer of best practice. Delivery chain support mechanisms and challenge processes are understood and used. Effective evaluation and inspection is used to strengthen both capacity and accountability.	Department has no grasp on performance management mechanisms in the rest of the delivery chain. Limited knowledge of operational environment means that challenge and support levers are not used.		
2. Engaging the delivery chain Shaping direction	Do departmental leaders actively enable people throughout the delivery chain to contribute to policy development? Are staff involved in monitoring progress through program governance?	There are clear channels through which people are actively engaged in policy development. Governance structures include all relevant people from the delivery chain.	Policy development is top down, and there is no visibility of progress monitoring process by key people in delivery chain.		
Influencing the chain	Does the department have influence with the accountable people in the rest of the delivery chain? Are departmental leaders able to engage the chain without giving up "non-negotiables"? Does the department have processes to strengthen areas of weakness (in itself and the rest of the delivery chain)? Do relevant parts of the center provide adequate challenge to strengthen accountability throughout the chain?	Departmental leaders are able to influence key elements in the delivery chain, leading to change in people, tools, processes, or culture within their own department and the rest of the chain. Deliverers throughout the chain are supported by constructive challenge from the center.	Departmental leaders have no influence, or do not use it, over the rest of the delivery chain. Tendency to give in on key areas of policy/process in order to get buy-in. Areas of weakness are left unchallenged. Challenge from the center is inadequate or fails to strengthen accountability.		

Areas to consider	Example questions	Best case (Green)	Worst case (Red)	Rating	Rationale
Communication and engagement	Is there a communications strategy and a strategy for staff engagement? Are the right communications channels being used for stakeholder and staff communication? Along the chain, are staff being focused on understanding what they are trying to achieve and why? Is there a mechanism for regular feedback on key delivery issues? Do staff act as advocates of the service?	Department can demonstrate that the right communication channels are being used. Key people in the chain own delivery messages and cascade clarity on contribution of targets to delivery. Department listens to these people and acts on feedback.	No clarity on who the key stakeholders are. Conflicting messages pervade the delivery chain, and large sections are not covered by the communications strategy. Department is not receiving, or ignoring, feedback.		
3. Leadership and culture					
Leadership	Do leaders at all levels dedicate a significant part of their time to driving delivery? Do they actively engage partners and stakeholders and lead the delivery agenda? Are leaders' personal development plans linked to leadership assessments? Are key risks (e.g., effective leaders moving on) managed actively?	Leaders at all levels set clear expectations and own targets and delivery plan. Staff know that they will be regularly challenged on performance. Leaders are committed to developing leadership capacity in themselves and in the wider organization.	Leaders pay lip service to delivery and lack determination or understanding of what is needed. Focused on problems, not solutions. Conflicting agendas at different levels; leaders in the delivery chain are isolated.		
Ambition	Are people ambitious to improve—do they believe it can be done? Are people given room to deliver and innovate? Is success celebrated?	Ambitious, results seen as important. Obstacles overcome, belief in ability to deliver. People are trusted to deliver and rewarded for success.	Lack of faith in ability to make progress; focused on obstacles rather than finding ways round them. No rewards for or celebration of success.		

(Continued)

(Continued)

Areas to consider	Example questions	Best case (Green) ⟷	Worst case (Red)	Rating	Rationale
Accountability	Are people held accountable throughout the delivery chain? Do key deliverers have clear roles and responsibilities? Do the most senior officials use all of the powers that they have to make as much change as they can? Are they able to prioritize delivering targets? Are people accountable for outcomes and influencing others as well as for activities and contributions from resources under their personal control?	All the key people in the delivery chain have clear responsibilities and have power to make changes. Key deliverers see themselves as accountable for influencing others and for outcomes/progress toward delivery targets.	Single named official has nominal responsibility (but no ownership), with multiple objectives, no tradition of power to make changes, and an expectation of moving on quickly. Focus of accountability is on processes and activities rather than outcomes.		
Integrated working	Is there a culture throughout the delivery chain of seeking evidence, learning from analysis, and acting on data? Is there a shared understanding of frontline data? Is there good integration of analysis with the delivery team? Are there strong links between policy, analysis, and communications teams? Is there a common sense of purpose down the delivery chain?	Sufficient analytical skills and experience available; good integration of analysis with delivery team. Good local analysis influences local delivery agents and is shared throughout the delivery chain. Communication, analysis, and policy teams are integrated (real or virtual).	No (or inadequate) analysts; complacency about lack of evidence/understanding. No evidence of local analysis, or local analysis is seriously deficient or unused. No evidence of planning to test assumptions or get useful learning from experience. Minimal interaction between policy, analysis, and communications teams.		
Delivery skills	Do the people and teams (in the department and the local agencies in the delivery chain) have the necessary skills? Are people clear about what delivery skills are required for key roles? Are the right people being given the right jobs? Is sufficient priority being given to filling gaps? Is there a clear process for identifying skills gaps (e.g., a skills audit), and are there training and development programs in place to deliver the skills needed? Are delivery skills rewarded?	Teams critical to driving delivery exhibit full range of "core" delivery skills. The right people with the right skills are given the right jobs. Senior managers are aware of and take immediate action to fill delivery skills gaps. High priority placed on developing core delivery skills. Promotion opportunities closely linked to the development of core delivery skills.	None or few of the core delivery skills present within teams critical to driving delivery. Wrong people with the wrong skills in the wrong jobs. No process in place for assessing skills means that delivery skills gaps are not being identified. Promotion opportunities not linked to delivery skills.		

Stages of delivery

Possible stages	Description
Stage 1. Policy development	At this stage policy is still being written, and the major steps toward implementation have not yet commenced.
Stage 2. Implementation	The key policies are in place, and early implementation is beginning. Pilots are under way. Systematic communication of objectives is under way.
Stage 3. Embedding change	Implementation is now affecting the entire audience. The emphasis is now on strengthening and deepening the impact of policies. The objectives of policies are well understood down the delivery chain. Approaches to implementation are being refined in response to experience. Regional variations in quality of implementation are being addressed.
Stage 4. Irreversible progress	Implementation is now complete, and progress would continue without central government attention.

References

American Cancer Society. (n.d.). *Who we are.* Retrieved October 19, 2010, from http://www.cancer.org/AboutUs/WhoWeAre/index

Associated Students. (2009) *California's Higher Education Governance and California State University.* Fullerton, CA: California State University, Fullerton.

Barber, M. (2005, February 10). *Journeys of discovery: The search for success by design.* Keynote speech given at the Annual Conference of the National Center on Education and the Economy, Orlando, FL.

Barber, M. (2007). *Three paradigms of public-sector reform.* McKinsey & Company. Retrieved July 3, 2010, from http://www.mckinsey.com/clientservice/publicsector/pdf/TG_three_paradigms.pdf

Barber, M. (2008). *Instruction to deliver: Fighting to transform Britain's public services.* London: Methuen.

Barber, M., & Mourshed, M. (2007). *How the world's best performing school systems come out on top.* McKinsey & Company. Retrieved July 3, 2010, from http://www.mckinsey.com/App_Media/Reports/SSO/Worlds_School_Systems_Final.pdf

Blair, T. (2010). *A journey.* London: Hutchinson.

Bogdanor, V. (2007, August 11). Target practice. *Financial Times.* Retrieved July 4, 2010, from http://www.ft.com/cms/s/0/72d81f96–47a2–11dc-9096–0000779fd2ac.html

Brewer, D. J., & Smith, J. (2007). *Evaluating the "crazy quilt": Educational governance in California.* Palo Alto, CA: Stanford University, Institute for Research on Education Policy & Practice.

Childress, S. M., Doyle, D. P., & Thomas, D. A. (2009). *Leading for equity: The pursuit of excellence in the Montgomery County Schools.* Cambridge, MA: Harvard Education Press.

Churchill, W. (1940, June 4). *We shall fight on the beaches.* Speech given to the House of Commons. Retrieved July 10, 2010, from http://www.winstonchurchill.org/learn/speeches/speeches-of-winston-churchill/128-we-shall-fight-on-the-beaches

Cohen, D. (2005). *The heart of change field guide.* Boston: Harvard Business School Press.

Cole, P. (2004). *Professional development: A great way to avoid change.* East Melbourne, Australia: Incorporated Association of Registered Teachers of Victoria. Retrieved July 10, 2010, from http://local37.teachers.ab.ca/SiteCollectionDocuments/Local37/2009–2010/Notices%20and%20registration%20forms/Rpt%20-%20Joint%20PD%20Framework%20Attachment%20X.pdf

The Education Trust. (2009, June). *Identifying action plan priorities: Leading indicators and sample interventions.* Washington, DC: Author.

Fullan, M. (2008). *The six secrets of change: What the best leaders do to help their organizations survive and thrive.* San Francisco: Jossey-Bass.

Hsu, J. (2008, August–September). The secrets of storytelling: Why we love a good yarn. *Scientific American Mind.* Retrieved July 15, 2010, from http://www.scientificamerican.com/article.cfm?id=the-secrets-of-storytelling

Kotter, J. P. (1996). *Leading change.* Boston: Harvard Business School Press.

Kotter, J. P., & Cohen, D. (2002). *The heart of change: Real-life stories of how people change their organizations.* Boston: Harvard Business School Press.

Lincoln, A. (1865, March 4). Second inaugural address. *Bartleby.com.* Retrieved July 2, 2010, from http://www.bartleby.com/124/pres32.html

Miall, H., Ramsbotham, O., & Woodhouse, T. (1999). *Contemporary conflict resolution: The prevention, management, and transformation of deadly conflicts.* Cambridge, UK: Polity Press.

Montgomery County Public Schools. (2009, June). *Our call to action: Pursuit of excellence: The strategic plan for Montgomery County Public Schools.* Rockville, MD: Office of Communications and Family Outreach for the Office of the Chief Operating Officer. Retrieved July 10, 2010, from http://www.montgomeryschoolsmd.org/about/strategicplan/strategicplan.pdf

National Commission on Excellence in Education. (1983, April). A nation at risk: The imperative for educational reform. Washington, DC: Author. Retrieved June 16, 2010, from http://www2.ed.gov/pubs/NatAtRisk/index.html

Obama, B. (2009a, February 24). *Address to joint session of congress.* Retrieved July 3, 2010, from http://www.whitehouse.gov/the_press_office/remarks-of-president-barack-obama-address-to-joint-session-of-congress/

Obama, B. (2009b, September 8). *Prepared remarks of President Obama: Back to school event.* Retrieved July 10, 2010, from http://www.whitehouse.gov/MediaResources/PreparedSchoolRemarks/

Ohio Department of Education. (n.d.). *Interactive local report card.* Columbus, OH: Author. Retrieved July 11, 2010, from http://ilrc.ode.state.oh.us/

Sammons, P., Nuttall, D., Cuttance, P., & Thomas, S. (1995). Continuity of school effects: A longitudinal analysis of primary and secondary school effects on GCSE performance. *School Effectiveness and School Improvement, 6,* 285–307.

Sammons, P., Thomas, S., & Mortimore, P. (1997). *Forging links: Effective schools and effective departments.* London: SAGE Publications Ltd.

Index